DISCARD
MIAMI-DADE COM. COLLEGE
NORTH CAMPUS LIBRARY

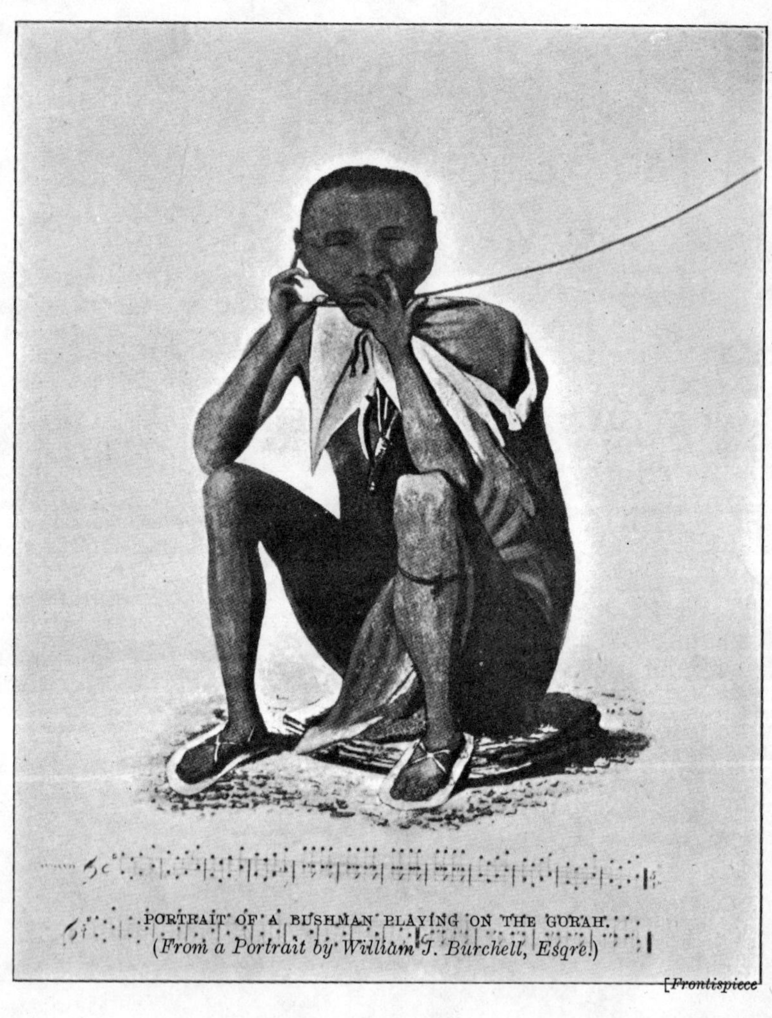

PORTRAIT OF A BUSHMAN PLAYING ON THE GORAH.
(*From a Portrait by William J. Burchell, Esqre.*)

THE YELLOW AND DARK-SKINNED PEOPLE OF AFRICA SOUTH OF THE ZAMBESI

A DESCRIPTION OF THE BUSHMEN, THE HOTTENTOTS, AND
PARTICULARLY THE BANTU, WITH FIFTEEN PLATES
AND NUMEROUS FOLKLORE TALES OF THESE
DIFFERENT PEOPLE

BY

GEORGE McCALL THEAL, Litt.D., LL.D.

NEGRO UNIVERSITIES PRESS
NEW YORK

Originally published in 1910
by Swan Sonnenschein & Co., Ltd., London

Reprinted 1969 by
Negro Universities Press
A DIVISION OF GREENWOOD PUBLISHING CORP.
NEW YORK

SBN 8371-1557-4

PRINTED IN UNITED STATES OF AMERICA

PREFACE.

THE difficulties that I laboured under in getting out my *History of South Africa* were so great that I was compelled to insert chapters on ethnography and memoranda on the same subject in different volumes, instead of bringing all together to be read and studied as one whole. For this some of my critics have been severe upon me, though none of them realised the disadvantages of such a mode of publication more than I did myself. There are many men interested in the uncivilised people of South Africa who have neither time nor inclination to pore over the history of the European colonists, and to compel them to read eight or nine volumes in order to extract the information that might have appeared in one would have been unpardonable if it could have been avoided. But I cannot upbraid myself with want of honesty or want of skill in this matter: it was sheer necessity that compelled me to act as I did, or not to publish at all. In my history, however, there is a great deal of ethnographical matter that cannot be separated from the other text without causing the information there given to be defective, and that is therefore in its proper place.

Now at last I am able to collect the scattered chapters, memoranda, folklore, etc. together and to arrange them in proper order, and while doing this I have added so much to them as to make this practically a new book. ‑I trust it will be found of use by ethnologists, as no pains have been spared to make its contents as accurate as human work is capable of.

GEO. M. THEAL.

WNYBERG, SOUTH AFRICA,
June, 1910.

CONTENTS.

CHAPTER I.

THE BUSHMEN OR ABORIGINES OF SOUTH AFRICA.

CHAPTER II.

THE BUSHMEN (*continued*).

CHAPTER III.

The Hottentots or Khoikhoi.

CHAPTER IV.

The Hottentots or Khoikhoi (*continued*).

CHAPTER V.

The Dark-skinned People termed by Europeans Bantu.

CHAPTER VI.

INFORMATION GIVEN BY MOHAMEDAN WRITERS.

CHAPTER VII.

SETTLEMENT OF BANTU TRIBES SOUTH OF THE ZAMBESI AND KUNENE RIVERS.

CHAPTER VIII.

General Description, Form of Government, and Religion of the Bantu.

CHAPTER IX.

Superstitions and Customs of the Bantu.

CHAPTER X.

DESCRIPTION OF THE BANTU (*continued*).

CHAPTER XI.

DESCRIPTION OF THE BANTU (*continued*).

CHAPTER XII.

SPECIMENS OF BANTU FOLKLORE.

CHAPTER XIII.

SPECIMENS OF BANTU FOLKLORE (*continued*).

CHAPTER XIV.

RAPID INCREASE OF THE BANTU IN NUMBER.

CHAPTER XV.

The Mystery of South Africa.

LIST OF ILLUSTRATIONS.

            List of Illustrations.

ETHNOGRAPHY OF SOUTH AFRICA

CHAPTER I.

The earliest inhabitants of South Africa, termed by
Europeans Bushmen, by Hottentots Sana, by Bantu
of the eastern coast Abatwa, of the western
coast Ovatwa, of the interior Baroa.

In the present condition of geological knowledge it is impossible
to determine whether South Africa has been the home of human
beings for as long a time as Europe, but it is certain that men
have roamed over its surface from an exceedingly remote period.
The ancient shell mounds along the coast are usually regarded
as furnishing one proof of this fact. The first of these that was
examined carefully was a heap formerly to be seen in a cave at
Mossel Bay, but one much larger was discovered a few years ago
on the left bank of a tributary of the Buffalo river at East
London. Its discovery was due to the opening of a way to
a quarry, for it had the semblance of a natural mound, being
covered with a deep layer of vegetable soil, in which trees were
growing ; and this appearance it had presented as far back as
could be traced. Upon examination—which was very thorough,
as over thirty-two thousand cubic metres of it were removed to
fill a lagoon—it was found to consist of a mass 45·72 metres or
one hundred and fifty feet long and 12·19 metres or forty feet
deep, composed of oyster, mussel, and other shells, mixed with
bones of animals of various kinds, ashes, and pieces of coarse
pottery. No stone implements were obtained in it, but stones
showing the action of fire were common.

This mass of shells must have been collected by a small community, for a large number of people could not have existed at the
same time upon the food obtainable within walking distance. It

must have been abandoned several hundred years, to allow time for dust to be blown over it, and plants to grow and decay, until at length vegetable mould half a metre in depth was formed, sufficient to support large shrubs and trees. Some pestilence may have destroyed the whole of the people who obtained subsistence there, or they may have been attacked and killed by men of their own race who lived by hunting wild animals, or they may have existed until the arrival of Hottentot immigrants some time about the year 1400 of our era, when they would certainly have been exterminated. The cause of the abandonment is thus conjectural, and all that can be asserted concerning it is that it cannot have been more recently than A.D. 1400, and may have been many centuries earlier. Of the length of time required for the collection of such a vast mass of shells no estimate whatever can be made.

This and other heaps of refuse along the South African coast, however, may have had their origin at a time not very remote, for those who have examined them carefully have found no apparent change in the physical features of the country since the earliest deposit was made. The shore was then where it is to-day, though the rocks along it may have undergone some slight change from the action of winds and waves. Much older are various stone implements shaped by human hands, which have been found in situations where they must have lain undisturbed for an incalculable length of time. They have been picked up, for instance, in gravel washed by a stream into a recess when its bed of hard rock was more than twelve metres higher than it is at present; in a stratum of clay that once was the muddy bottom of a pond, but is now the crown of a hill, and where they must have been deposited before the commencement of the wearing down of the ravine that separates the hill from a long slope beyond it; and at great depths in æolian rock, where bones of animals and shells are also found.*

* See the paper on *The Antiquity of Man in South Africa*, by George R. Mackay, Esqre., in the pamphlet No. 2 of *Belangrijke Historische Dokumenten*, published by me in Capetown in 1896. See also the numerous proofs given by Mr. G. W. Stow in his volume on *The Native Races of South Africa*, edited by me, and published in London in 1905.

None of the arrowheads, spearheads, scrapers, knives, or choppers for cracking bones found in these ancient deposits were ground or polished, as chipping comprised all the labour that was bestowed upon them. They were the products of the skill of man in the lowest stage of his existence. Workshops where they were manufactured have been discovered in various places, and to some of these the raw material, or unchipped stone, must have been brought from a considerable distance. The artisans may have lived there permanently, or, what is more probable, some superstition may have been connected with the localities. At these factories a quantity of stone from which flakes have been struck, some raw material, a very few finished articles, and a great many broken ones usually lie wholly or partially hidden by drift sand or mould, and it is generally by accident that they are discovered.

The most ancient implements were almost as skilfully made as those in use for similar purposes by the people termed by us Bushmen when Europeans first visited the country, but during the long period that must have elapsed the inventive faculty of man had not been entirely idle. One implement at least, and that one requiring more skill, time, and patience to prepare it than were needed in forming any of the others, had been brought into general use. The spherical perforated stone, which is not found in any of the oldest deposits, shows a considerable advance in art upon the chipped lancehead of the early river gravel washings. Still, progress, though thus measurable, was exceedingly slow during the countless centuries that had passed away. In the earliest stages of man's development three principal causes must have operated in forcing him to think : hunger, disease, and war. These were the elementary factors of civilisation. In favourable localities in other parts of the world commerce, as a powerful factor, came at a later period, but in South Africa that stage was not easily arrived at.

This is apparent if the physical condition of the country be considered. The land rises from the ocean level in terraces or steps, until a vast interior plain is reached. Deep gorges have been worn by the action of water, in some places internal forces have caused elevations, in other places depressions, and everywhere along the margins of the terraces distortions may be seen. There are no navigable rivers, and the coast is bold and unbroken. The steep fronts of the terraces, which from the lower side appear to be mountain ranges, and the absence of running water in dry seasons over large surfaces, tended likewise to prevent intercourse between the different parts of the country. The rude people of each section were left to themselves, without that stimulus to improvement which contact with strangers gives. There was very little necessity to exert the mind to provide clothing or habitations, for the climate is mild, and even on the elevated interior plain, though the nights in winter are sharp and cold, snow never lies long on the ground. Like the wild animals, man on occasions of severe weather could find some temporary shelter. In this respect a savage is far more callous than a civilised man.

Hunger must have forced him to think, to plan the destruction of game, to search for edible plants, and to reject those that were noxious ; but after becoming acquainted with the flora in his locality and with the use of poison in the chase, that factor would lose much of its potency. The cultivation of the ground or the domestication of animals could no more enter the mind of a savage in the early palæolithic stage than into that of a child learning to walk. Disease would compel him to think, but only in an exceedingly slight degree when compared with a modern European, for his ailments were few and were in general attributed to witchcraft. War, whether against his fellows or the powerful carnivora, would be a more important factor in obliging him to exercise his mind, and to it was probably due the gradual though tardy improvement in his weapons by the selection of harder stone and by fashioning them more carefully. But slow indeed was the progress in cultivation from the hunter who used the roughly formed spearhead of shale found in the æolian conglomerate to the Bushman who shot his bone-tipped arrow at an antelope at the beginning of the nineteenth century.

Where the race of savages who occupied this country so long, the race now termed the Bushmen, had its origin cannot be stated, but it is highly probable that its early home was in some part of Central Asia, and that when it was compelled to migrate by increase in number or by pressure of more powerful people, one section moved gradually into Europe, another section proceeded to the south-east, and still another found its way into Africa. What is known of the palæolithic pygmies in Europe tends to strengthen this view. Their weapons are the same in form and size, so much so that if a handful of Bushman arrowheads and scrapers were thrown into a heap of similar implements say in the museum at Brussels, they could not be separated again except by some one with a thorough knowledge of the composition of the rocks from which they were taken. The engravings of animals on ivory and slate found in Europe are of exactly the same class as the engravings on stone found in Africa. Very recently, near Pau in the south-west of France, some caves were discovered blocked up with earth, as they must have been for ages. On opening them, paintings of animals were seen on the walls, corresponding in style and degree of art with those on rock shelters everywhere from the Zambesi to the Cape of Good Hope.* This, therefore, can be said with certainty, that the people who left those records of their existence behind them were either real Bushmen, or were at the same stage of advancement as the Bushmen of South Africa.

Dr. Bleek has pointed out that these people show affinities with some tribes in Australia, and Mr. Stow has shown that some of their characteristics are those of the Mongolian race. There are also people living in South-Eastern Asia, such as some of the inhabitants of the Philippine islands, the Andamanese, and the Semang in the Malay peninsula, who are so like the Bushmen, that it is almost certain they are of the same stock. The type must have been fixed in the common primeval home of them all in some far remote time, and the changes in each that have since taken place have been so small that the close relationship may still be seen. Mentally especially is this the case. Their power of thought in most respects is not greater than that of a European

---

* Dr. Peringuey, director of the South African museum in Capetown, who is a native of that part of France, very kindly gave me this information, and showed me copies of the pictures and accounts of their discovery, with reports of the leading French anthropological society upon them.

child six or seven years of age, and they have all the credulity of such a child. It must have been the same with the palæolithic pygmies in Europe.

The points of resemblance between the Bushmen and the Semang are so numerous that they can hardly be accidental.* The average height of Semang men is 1491 millimetres, of Bushmen of South Africa 1444 millimetres, and of pygmies of Central Africa 1400 to 1450 millimetres. The average horizontal cephalic index of the Semang is 78·9 (of their women 81·1), but this index is variable. This hardly differs from that of Bushmen. The cranial capacity of the Semang is 1348 cubic centimetres, which is greater than that of Bushmen, but still very low.

The noses of the Semang are remarkably broad and flat, and the root is depressed ; the chin is feebly developed. The cheek bones are broad, the ears are small, and very few of the men have any beard.

They are nomads, use rock shelters or screens of leaves for habitations, coil themselves up to sleep on a heap of leaves without a pillow, make baskets and mats, eat anything and everything edible, produce fire by the friction of two pieces of wood, and cook their food in the most primitive manner. Their implements, made of stone, are not ground or polished.

Their marriage rites are of the slightest kind, they bury their dead entire, there is no trace of an actual cult among them, they make traps, pitfalls, and snares to catch game, their only domestic animal is the dog, they have no words for any numeral higher than three or four, and yet they are decorative artists. On ornaments for the heads of their women and on their quivers they trace geometrical patterns, outlines of animals, and figures believed to be charms.

Every assertion in these paragraphs applies to the Bushmen, and though there are some characteristics mentioned in addition to these, which are not applicable to those people, they are such as might have easily arisen from their different environments.

* The characteristics of the Semang are taken from *The Pagan Races of the Malay Peninsula*, by Walter William Skeat, M.A., and Charles Otto Blagden, M.A., published at London in 1906.

For instance, the skin of the Semang is of a dark copper colour, or chocolate brown to shiny black.   The skin of the Bushmen is yellowish brown, darker or lighter according to the locality frequented by them.   In every case the colour of the skin seems to denote that it was acquired for a purpose of the greatest utility.

The Semang, living in forest gloom, required a very dark skin in order to conceal themselves.   Their remote ancestors may have been of quite another tint.   The Bushmen on the arid plains and bare mountain sides of South Africa were of the colour that was most advantageous to them, for they were invisible at a short distance, so closely did the tint of their skin resemble that of th dried-up soil.   Even their scantily covered scalps were of advan- tage to them in this respect.   After rains when high grass sprang up, through which they could creep covered with a few tufts, or in a bushy country where they could adopt disguises, their colour would be a matter of little importance, but on the great plains of South Africa it meant a very great deal, for it enabled them, by keeping to leeward and making use of anthills or boulders or shrubs, to stalk their prey until within distance of their arrows.

Is it not reasonable to suppose that the same guiding mind which coloured so many of the lower animals in accordance with their environment should have exerted its beneficent power in aid of savage man in the same way?   In the far distant time when the ancestors of the Bushmen made their first appearance in South Africa, they may not have been of the same colour as they were when Europeans first saw them.   In the early years of the nineteenth century the traveller Burchell observed that the Bushmen north of the Orange were differently coloured from those south of that river, though each section had the tint best suited to its surroundings.   Many others have noticed this peculiarity since Burchell wrote, though no such accurate records were made as could be desired.   This cannot be accidental.   Of course when clothing came to be worn by primitive man such changes were useless and consequently ceased to take place.

If it must be considered doubtful whether the palæolithic dwarfs of ancient Europe and the negritos of South-Eastern Asia are of identically the same stock as the Bushmen, there can be no question that at least the greater portion of the African continent was once occupied exclusively by these people. In the gloomy forest west of the Albert Nyanza they are found by European travellers of the present day, and the descriptions of them given by Schweinfurth, Junker, Stanley, Casati, Von Wissmann, and many others could be applied with perfect accuracy to the Bushmen of the southern extremity of the continent. They could not have migrated to that locality through a country inhabited by stalwart negroes, by whom they were always regarded as noxious animals, and as such destroyed, nor could the section of their race south of the Zambesi have moved down through Bantu tribes. They must have occupied the country alone, maybe for countless generations, before stronger invaders destroyed or absorbed all of their kindred except the puny remnant that was forced into the depths of the forest where they could not be pursued. Just so, at a later date, they were exterminated or absorbed all the way down to the Zambesi, except possibly a very few who may have made their escape across that river.

Of their existence far north in the continent there is ample proof, but only after other races had settled along the Mediterranean shore and peopled the valley of the Nile as far up as Abyssinia. There are references to them in the earliest histories that were written, though the dates were modern compared with the memorials of their existence that their stone implements supply in the southern part of the continent. The first of these in order of time shows us a long-established kingdom of Egypt, with a people far advanced in civilisation, and a form of hieroglyphic writing in extensive use. Nubia too had then a settled population. Many inscriptions in hieroglyphic characters have been translated into English,* and among them is more than one record of expeditions being sent southward to obtain pygmies to amuse the king by dancing before him.

---

* See *Egypt in the Neolithic and Archaic Periods*, continued as *A History of Egypt from the End of the Neolithic Period to the Death of Cleopatra VII*, B.C. 30. By E. A. Wallis Budge, M.A., Litt.D., Keeper of the Egyptian and Assyrian Antiquities in the British Museum. Eight crown octavo volumes, published at London in 1902.

Thus one official in the time of the fifth dynasty has placed his services on record. He states among other notable occurrences that he was sent to the land of ghosts to bring back a pygmy for the purpose indicated, and that he went by the way of Nubia to Punt, where he managed to secure one. How realistic this appears to South Africans who can remember the habits of the people living on the inland plateau in the middle of the nineteenth century. One of the commonest ways of many a farmer there to amuse his guests and himself was to get one of his Bushman herdsmen to dance or caper before them, with a promise of a big glass of brandy or a long piece of roll tobacco if he did it well. On being told to dance springbok, he would bound into the air again and again with as much ease apparently as one of those animals, without quivering his body or seemingly bending his limbs. Then he would be told to dance baboon, when at once every joint in his body was in motion. The agility of the little imp, the elasticity of his limbs, the wonderful contortions that he was capable of displaying, gave as much delight to the South African farmer as a similar performance by another individual of the same race gave to Pharaoh, lord of Egypt, so many thousand years ago.

The historian Herodotus,* writing about 440 before Christ, mentions the pygmies, but in his time they were no longer to be found in the valley of the Nile below Senaar, nor had they been seen there probably for a very long period. Evidently more stalwart people had occupied the valley, and the little hunters had either been exterminated or compelled to retire from the field. They were reported to be south of the desert, and though Herodotus never saw one, he obtained information that enabled him to give a most graphic description of them. He described them as troglodytes, that is dwellers in caves or caverns, as eating serpents, lizards, and other reptiles, as being the fleetest

---

* See *History of Herodotus : a new English version, edited with copious notes and appendices, illustrating the History and Geography of Herodotus, from the most recent sources of information.* By George Rawlinson, M.A., Canon of Canterbury and Camden Professor of Ancient History in the University of Oxford. Four thick royal octavo volumes, published at London in 1880.

of foot of any people he had ever heard of, and whose language was like the squeaking of bats. It would be hardly possible to express in fewer words a description of the Bushman race.

But that is not all he related of the pygmies. He had been informed that five young Nasamonians, actuated by a spirit of inquiry and adventure, had set out on a journey of exploration from the coast of the country now called Tripoli, and having travelled first to the south and then to the west through the inhabited parts and the desert, reached a territory where they were made prisoners by men of small stature. These conducted them through extensive marshes to the bank of a great river flowing from west to east, in which were crocodiles. All the people they saw were pygmies, black in colour, addicted to magic, and speaking a language unintelligible to the Nasamonians. How the travellers escaped we are not told, but they succeeded in retracing their steps, and reached their homes again in safety. Probably the river which was the terminus of their journey was the Niger, a stream which baffled the curiosity of Europeans down to 1830, when it was traced to its mouth by the brothers Richard and John Lander. Herodotus believed it to be the upper course of the Nile, which he thought must flow for a great distance from west to east, as otherwise he could not account for the great volume of water in it.

In 1849 the traveller Barth on his way southward from Tripoli discovered many ancient engravings on rocks in a valley near Murzuk in Fezzan, approximate latitude 26° north, longitude 14° east of Greenwich. He has given copies of three of these, though they cannot be regarded as absolutely correct, as two are from sketches and the other from memory only. But they are unmistakably of exactly the same class as Bushman engravings, the oxen represented being fairly well outlined, but without feet, as in South Africa, and the men having the heads of animals. Barth noticed that there were no engravings of camels, beasts of burden unknown there until long after the introduction of the ox, from which it may be assumed that these engravings were made at a time when the country was partly occupied by pastoral hamitic tribes, but before the arrival of Arabs. The outlines of the figures were cut very deep into the rock.*

In Southern Algeria many engravings of animals on rocks have recently been discovered by Mr. G. B. Flamand, of the geological survey department, among others some of an extinct buffalo, whose bones are found in that region. These and some others must be of very great age. Mr. F. Foureau found similar engravings on the faces of masses of granite in the Sahara, all of a style and degree of art exactly corresponding to those in South Africa, and all made by punching holes or lines with sharp pieces of stone.†

It is therefore as certain as anything resting on circumstantial evidence can be that the whole continent of Africa was at some exceedingly remote period occupied solely by people of the Bush-man race. Then at some time, which cannot be ascertained, but must have been many thousands of years ago, a stronger and better equipped race entered the north-eastern extremity of the land, and gradually spread along the Mediterranean coast and up the valley of the Nile, exterminating the earlier inhabitants, or possibly taking the young females and killing all the others. This went on until the country as far south as the great desert was filled with the people now usually termed hamites, who were a little darker in colour than modern Europeans, and who had long black hair. The purest descendants of these people at the present day are believed to be the Guanches in the Canary islands and the Basques in Spain, the Copts in Egypt and the Berbers all over the north-west having a larger mixture of alien blood in their veins.

* See *Travels and Discoveries in North and Central Africa : being a Journal of an Expedition undertaken under the Auspices of Her Britannic Majesty's Government in the years* 1849 *to* 1855. By Henry Barth, Ph.D., D.C.L. Five demi octavo volumes, published at London in 1857 and 1858. The account of the discovery is given in chapter *ix*, volume *i*, and the pictures are on pages 197, 200, and 201.

† See the paper on *Rock Engravings of Animals and the Human Figure, the Work of South African Aborigines, and their relation to similar ones found in Northern Africa,* by Dr. L. Peringuey, in the *Transactions of the South African Philosophical Society* for 1906.

After this, how long after there are no means of ascertaining, negroes came into the continent, in all probability by the way of the straits of Bab-el-Mandeb, and spread out south of the desert and along the Atlantic coast. Wherever they went the Bushmen disappeared, the girls being absorbed, and all the others being destroyed.

Then other races invaded the continent, Arabs, various tribes of more distant Asiatics, among whom were the progenitors of the modern Bantu, some of whom settled in the north-east, and others pushed their way southward. All were deadly foes of the Bushmen, sparing only the young females, and so it came to pass that by the year 1500 of our era there were none of the ancient inhabitants left north of the Zambesi, except the few wretched little bands that had managed to take refuge in places so difficult of access that they could exist there almost undisturbed.

A question now arises whether there were any people whatever in Africa before the Bushmen, meaning by the word people beings able to communicate ideas to each other by means of vocal sounds, acquainted with the use of fire, and having sufficient knowledge to make rough implements of stone. This question cannot be satisfactorily answered. The Bushmen in their folklore speak of an older race, but that cannot be accepted as evidence. No tradition can have passed down the enormous length of time that they certainly occupied the country, and it is difficult to conceive of beings entitled to be termed human existing in a more degraded condition than some of them.*

Pieces of hard stone, fashioned by human hands, and until

* The traveller Andrew A. Anderson, in his *Twenty-five Years in a Waggon in South Africa*, describes some savages that he met in the Kalahari as lower in the scale even than ordinary Bushmen, and he was of opinion that they belonged to an older race. But all Bushmen were not exactly alike, a great deal depending upon the circumstances in which they lived, and the degraded beings seen by him, scarcely human in appearance and mode of existence, probably bore the same relation to the more favoured specimens of the race that the wretched Bakalahari bear to the Bakwena among the Bantu of the interior. It must be added, however, that there is a tradition among the people of a Bantu tribe in the Transvaal that when their ancestors arrived on the banks of the Limpopo eight generations ago they found some savages there who were unacquainted with the use of fire and were without other weapons than natural stones and sticks.

recently believed to be spearheads, but much too large and heavy for use in that manner by Bushmen, have been found in various places, and gave rise to a supposition that a race of savages of very large stature might once have occupied the country. But among these so-called spearheads are some of such enormous size that no giant could have used them, and it is evident they were merely material from which arrowheads could be easily struck off as needed, or implements in course of construction, lost or thrown away for some reason or other.*

There are some of considerable size, though not too large to be handled easily, showing signs of having been used. It is highly probable that these were employed for digging game pits before the drilled weight and stick came into use. The huge pachyderms could only be captured by means of pits, for the stone-headed lance or arrow, until poison was discovered, could have had no effect upon them. To excavate a pit in the hard ground or clay a heavy sharpened instrument was needed, and these stones seem fairly well adapted for that purpose, though they were not so effective as the weighted digging stick, which was an implement of a more recent date.

The heaviest may have been the property of unusually stalwart men, for there were individuals among the Bushmen larger and stronger than others, just as in every race elsewhere, though probably none exceeded 152 centimetres or five feet in height. Europeans living for only two or three generations in the Sneeuw-bergen attain a greater size than in other parts of the Cape Colony, and it may have been the case with the savages that in some localities they were larger than in others. Unfortunately, there are no means of ascertaining now whether that was so, or not.

Still there is one reason for doubting whether there were not waves of human life thrown out from the primeval home before

---

* In the South African museum in Capetown a fine collection of these stones is to be seen, well arranged by the director, Dr. Peringuey. There is also a very excellent collection of engravings on stone,—including casts where it was not possible to cut out the originals,—among which is a zebra beautifully executed. Casts of Bushmen and mixed breeds of various more modern races tend to make this museum of vastly greater utility for purposes of study than it was in former years.

the Bushmen, and if so, whether one of these races did not penetrate into Africa. That reason is their language, which contains a verb of such wonderful power that it must be a very long way removed from primitive speech. Beyond this, there seems to be no reason to believe that the Bushmen were not the first inhabitants of the country, and consequently its true aborigines.

It is probable indeed that they reached the extremity of the continent in a series of waves, and there may have been a long interval of time between the first and the last of these. It may have been that one advancing horde drove its predecessors to the margin of the ocean, and by occupying the hunting grounds forced the fugitives to live mainly upon the produce of the shore. But this is uncertain, and to carry conjecture further would be worse than useless, for it would more than likely be incorrect.

If one of the ancient palæolithic cave dwellers of Europe could make his appearance there again in flesh and blood, what an interest would be taken in him ! He would be regarded as being able to throw a flood of light upon the early existence of man, and from all sides students and members of scientific societies would gather round him to learn all that he could teach. In point of fact he could tell them nothing, even if they could understand his speech. He could not explain the dim religious thoughts, or rather apprehensions of fear from something vague outside himself, that passed through his brain, nor give reliable information of any kind upon the past of his race, where they came from, or when or how they had their origin. His conversation would be limited to narratives of the game he had killed, or the girl he had won by sending an arrow through a rival's heart as he lay sleeping, or how his brother had been bewitched by an enemy and had died, or how somebody had been turned into a wild animal and was still spell-bound and only to be seen in his proper form by those whose eyes had been cleansed by charms.

Only in the evening, when he was surfeited with the flesh of some large animal he had slain, and when weary of the dance he reclined by the fire and admired the patterns made with ochre and soot and grease on his otherwise naked body, he would tell some story of insects or birds or beasts that he had heard from his mother when he was a child, and though he did not know this, had really been as it were stereotyped long centuries before, and was even in those ancient days told in almost identically the same words by people living far away towards the morning dawn and others as far away towards the setting sun. The students and savants would listen, and wonder how a full-grown man, though a pygmy, with a fairly well shaped head but for the great prognathism of the jaws, could delight in such absurd stories and really believe in the truth of many of them. They would soon realise that he could tell them nothing of what they wanted to know, that though he was not an idiot, his reasoning power and his credulity were those of a little child. They would observe that his passions were those of an adult, that his physical strength was great, that he could distinguish objects clearly at a distance that they could only see with a good field-glass, that he could outrun with ease the fleetest of their athletes, and yet that his thoughts were no more lofty than those of the dullest peasant's infant boy.

But the palæolithic savage restored to life, though he could *tell* nothing of importance concerning the history or origin or religion of his race, would still be an object of exceeding interest. He could be studied as a workman engaged in the manufacture of timepieces studies the mechanism of a clock, and a very great deal relating to the history of man could be learned in this manner from him. He could not explain the structure of his language, but his words, or the uncouth sounds that issued from his throat and teeth and lips which correspond to words among civilised men, could be taken down and analysed, their meaning could be gradually gathered, the grammatical form in which they were put together to represent ideas could be solved, and a link in the chain of language from its origin to that of the most cultured individual of the present day would be obtained. For this painted savage, disgusting in his habits, almost hideous in his appearance, represented a stage of human existence through which our own ancestors must at one time have passed. That time may have been exceedingly remote, but we cannot get rid of the fact that this repulsive being, who ate and enjoyed the taste of carrion, and who never cleansed even the intestine of an animal before he devoured it, was a blood relative of our own, and that we ought to take greater interest in him than in any animal of the brute creation.

The Europeans who settled in South Africa after the middle of the seventeenth century had the palæolithic man, just as he roamed over Europe in times long preceding the dawn of history, living in flesh and blood before their eyes. They were indeed far more familiar with his presence than they desired to be, for he was not at all a respectable neighbour. He belonged to an unimprovable race, incapable of adopting the habits of other people much higher in culture than itself, though, as now known, it could amalgamate with those only slightly in advance. Before the arrival of the Hottentots and Bantu in parts of South Africa, it was not in contact with any other branches of the human species, and hence it remained at its own low level, the level of palæolithic man in Europe, without making much advance of any kind during the long long time it occupied the secluded extremity of the continent. When the Europeans arrived therefore, an opportunity was afforded of becoming intimately acquainted with the condition and language of one of the lowest, if not the very lowest, of all the races on the face of the earth, and of making the information gained known to the civilised part of mankind.

That opportunity was not taken advantage of. The white settlers were entirely occupied with making a living, and regarded the Bushmen simply as robbers, just as the Hottentots and Bantu did. Then down to our own times the savage wanderers were generally considered to be outcast Hottentots, even Dr. Bleek himself when he began his researches believing that they had separated from a common ancestral stock only a few centuries back. There were exceptions to this statement, notably Dr. Henry Lichtenstein,* but they were few in number. Further,

---

* "Equally untrue is the assertion that the nation of the Bosjesmans is composed of fugitive slaves and Hottentots. They are, and ever have been, a distinct people, having their own peculiar language, and their own peculiar customs, if the terms *language* and *customs* can be applied to people upon the very lowest step in the order of civilisation, as the Bosjesmans may certainly be esteemed : one might almost call this extraordinary race without customs

there were no men of sufficient education and inclination wealthy enough to afford the time requisite to conduct the necessary researches. When at length, under the auspices of the late Sir Bartle Frere, a philosophical association came into existence, its pecuniary resources were too limited to render any aid, and it was obliged to confine its attention to other subjects. These are the reasons why long and close research regarding the inner life of the Bushmen was not commenced until the nineteenth century was far advanced.

Scattered about in the early records of the Cape Colony there are many references to the Bushmen besides those relating to war with them, and though these are of considerable value, none of them give all the particulars that a student would like to know. Thus in the journal of Commander Simon van der Stel's expedition to Namaqualand in 1685 it is related that on a certain occasion five Bushmen were met, to whom a sheep was presented, which they killed and ate, rejecting nothing but the gall and four little pieces from the thighs. Beyond stating that they gave as a reason for not eating these little pieces that it was their custom to reject them, no information is given, or probably was obtained, concerning the matter. Recent research by Dr. Bleek and Miss Lloyd fills in this gap, however. The wild people believed that animals and men could change their forms, and that these particular pieces remained part of the human body.

Many travellers and missionaries have also given accounts of the habits and mode of life of the Bushmen, but none of them remained in contact with the savages long enough to learn their language or penetrate into their innermost minds.

The reverend J. J. Kicherer, a missionary of the London Society, was the first to attempt to establish a station purely for the benefit of Bushmen. With a party of assistants, including

and without language. No Hottentot understands a word of the Bosjesman language ; and the nation was hated by all others on account of its habits of plunder and disregard of the rights of property, long before the Europeans settled in South Africa."—*Travels in Southern Africa in the Years* 1803, 1804, 1805, *and* 1806, by Henry Lichtenstein. Translated from the original German by Anne Plumptre. Two quarto volumes, published at London in 1812 and 1815. The above is found on page 116 of the first volume.

a half-breed Hottentot and his wife, who were born in the territory near the southern bank of the Orange river, and who spoke both the Dutch and the Bushman languages, so that they were useful as interpreters, on the 6th of July 1799 he took up his residence at a place which he named Blijde Vooruitzigt, or Joyful Prospect, on the bank of the Zak river. Being provided with a good stock of tobacco and a considerable number of oxen and sheep, presented to the mission by religious farmers, he was able to induce a large party of the wild people to listen to his teaching, and they remained with him as long as his stores lasted. In 1800, after he had been with them several months, he wrote of them as follows : *

"Although they are not idolaters, the doctrine of a Supreme Being was to them entirely unknown. . . . Their manner of living is very horrible. Their dwelling and resting place is between the rocks, where they dig a round den of about three feet deep, in which they lie, with their whole family. This den is sometimes covered with a few reeds, to shelter them from the wind and rain, which, however, seldom answers the design, as they are generally soaked through by the first shower. They mostly lie down and sleep, except when hunger greatly torments them ; then they go a-hunting ; but they live many days without any food. When they find no wild beast, then they make shift with a sort of small wild onions and wild potatoes, which the women seek, but never the men. They are content to eat snakes and mice.

"Their language is so very difficult to learn that no one can spell or write the same. It consists mostly of a clicking with the tongue.

"They are total strangers to domestic happiness. The men have several wives, but conjugal affection is little known. They take no great care of their children, and never correct them except in a fit of rage, when they almost kill them by severe usage. In a quarrel between father and mother, or the several wives of a husband, the defeated party wreaks his or her revenge on the child of the conqueror, which in general loses its life. Tame Hottentots

---

* *Transactions of the Missionary Society* quoted in *The History of the London Missionary Society*, 1795–1895, by Richard Lovett, M.A. Two demi octavo volumes, published at London in 1899.

seldom destroy their offspring, except in a fit of passion ; but the Bushmen will kill their children without remorse on various occasions, as when they are ill-shaped, when they are in want of food, when the father of a child has forsaken its mother, or when obliged to flee from the farmers or others ; in which case they will strangle them, smother them, cast them away in the desert, or bury them alive.

"The Bushmen frequently forsake their aged relations when removing from place to place for the sake of hunting. In this case they leave the old person with a piece of meat, and an ostrich egg-shell full of water : as soon as this little stock is exhausted, the poor deserted creature must perish by hunger, or become the prey of wild beasts. Many of these wild Hottentots live by plunder and murder, and are guilty of the most horrid and atrocious actions."

Dr. Henry Lichtenstein was the first to attempt to gather a number of words used by them and to place them against words with the same meanings used by Korana Hottentots, thus showing the great difference between the two languages. His information was obtained in 1804 and 1805 from Bushmen living on the great plain south of the Orange river, and he had a competent interpreter and was himself well qualified for the work. But he used no symbols except figures to denote the clicks, and did not distinguish the differences between several of these sounds. No attempt was made by him to ascertain the mode of structure of the sentences, and therefore his list of words is of little or no use to a philologist. His general remarks upon the language are :

"Among all the Hottentot dialects, none is so rough and wild, and differs so much from the rest, as that of the Bosjesmans, so that it is scarcely understood by any of the other tribes. It is, in the first place, much poorer in sounds : many sounds, which may be expressed by our letters, in the Gonaqua, the Coran (*i.e.* the Korana), and the Namaqua languages, are either totally wanting among them, or very rarely occur. Pure vowels are seldom to be heard ; but the cluck and the diphthongs are much more frequent. The cluck, in particular, seems the most completely at home among them : scarcely a word occurs without it. The gurgling in the throat

is much deeper, and hence ensue the most disagreeable nasal tones.
The speech ends with a sort of singing sound, which dies away by
degrees, and is often some seconds before it wholly ceases."

The reverend Thomas Arbousset, of the French mission in
Basutoland, has also given a vocabulary,* seven pages in length,
but unfortunately he confused Hottentots with Bushmen, and
his list contains many words adopted even from Sesuto. It was
prepared about the year 1837. In his vocabulary he did not
attempt to introduce any symbols whatever to represent the
clicks, so that to the philological student it is valueless. His
remarks upon the language, as he heard it spoken, are, however,
to the point. He says :

"Their language is harsh, broken, full of monosyllables, which
are uttered with strong aspirations from the chest, and a guttural
articulation as disagreeable as it is difficult. . . . It is not without
reason that it has been said of them that they cluck like turkeys. . . .
The clucks are especially found at the recurrence of a letter which
is of a harsh guttural pronunciation. . . . As this horrible aspira-
tion recurs incessantly in the mouth of the Bushmen, one is inclined
to say that they bark rather than speak."

In 1862 the late Dr. W. H. I. Bleek, a man of great learning,
patience, and industry, was appointed custodian of the Grey
Library in Capetown. In that capacity he had much to do,
but he found time out of office hours to carry on the philological
studies for which he had been specially trained, and in which
pursuit he was an enthusiast, though his judgment was clear
and even cold. At first his only opportunity of acquiring any
knowledge of the Bushman language was by visiting Robben
Island and picking up words and short phrases from prisoners
there, but after a time the government allowed him to take to his
home two decrepit men of that race whose terms of imprisonment
had nearly expired, and when they were liberated two others were

* *Narrative of an Exploratory Tour to the North-East of the Colony of the
Cape of Good Hope*, by the revs. T. Arbousset and F. Daumas. Translated
from the original French, and published in a foolscap octavo volume in London
in 1852.

obtained in the same manner. These induced some of their relations to join them, and presently a whole Bushman family was living on his ground. From time to time as one party left another arrived, so that the material to work with was always abundant.

To his surprise Dr. Bleek soon found that he was in contact; not with degraded Hottentots or even with people closely allied to Hottentots, but with representatives of an actually primitive race. From that moment he devoted his attention almost entirely to the study of the habits, folklore, and particularly the language of the Bushmen, for their race in South Africa in its purity was almost extinct, and he realised that in a very few years such researches would be no longer possible. In this study he was warmly assisted by his sister-in-law, Miss L. C. Lloyd; who was fortunate in possessing a very sharp ear, and who was soon able to distinguish the different clicks, smacking of the lips, and guttural sounds that form so large a portion of Bushman speech.

A mass of material was collected, but was not ready for publication when, to the great loss of students throughout the world, the death of Dr. Bleek on the 17th of August 1875 put an end to his devoted and most useful labour. His *Comparative Grammar of South African Languages* is, and must always remain, a standard work, though it too was left incomplete and contains very little upon the Bushman tongue.

Miss Lloyd was then engaged to take charge of the Grey Library until a competent successor to Dr. Bleek could be obtained; and she resolved to continue the Bushman researches out of office hours and gather as much material as she could, before arranging for publication. In all South Africa there was no one so well qualified for the task as she. Not a few European children on farms had in earlier times learned to utter the strange sounds which constitute Bushman speech, and could converse freely with the savages, but none of these had ever been able to commit their knowledge to writing and it had died with them. Miss Lloyd was acquainted with two dialects, was accustomed to take down the sentences as they came from the lips of the speakers and was therefore familiar with the various symbols used to represent the different sounds, and had the great advantage of having been trained to the work by so able a teacher as her deceased brother-in-law.

In addition to what was in manuscript at the time of Dr. Bleek's death, she collected materials upon the mythology, legends, fables, poetry, history, customs, and superstitions of the Bushmen, in two dialects, and then proceeded to Europe with her papers with a view of obtaining competent philological assistance in preparing the work of her brother-in-law and herself for the press. Some of it she had already translated into English. But most unfortunately her health broke down so completely that it was only as a confirmed invalid that she was able to write a little, and so the result of the labour of her brother-in-law and herself remained unavailable for the use of others until 1910, when one volume of Bushman text with English translations appeared. This is a volume of great interest, for the language of the Bushmen is already almost entirely lost, and it would not be possible now to collect the material used in it. The few individuals of the race that remain south of the Zambesi and the Kunene have either adopted the language of their neighbours, as those in Central Africa seem to have done, or they have been compelled to use so many foreign words and phrases that the idiom is too corrupt to be of any scientific value as far as the vocabulary goes. A knowledge of the mode of putting words together to express ideas, or the grammatical structure, is of even greater importance than a knowledge of the words themselves used singly, and it would be with very great difficulty that this could be obtained now from individuals still living, but it can be acquired with ease from Miss Lloyd's book.

To show how cautiously Dr. Bleek proceeded in his researches into the Bushman language, and how he at length came to realise that he was dealing with the speech of a race either identical with or at the same stage of culture as palæolithic man in Europe, some extracts from his writings are given here. In 1857, after he had been about two years in South Africa, he wrote as follows in an article in the *Cape Monthly Magazine :*

" It is curious to notice that the Bushman tongue apparently agrees most, of all the Hottentot dialects, with that of the Cape, and next to it, with that of the Koranas, the latter being, in many respects, the connecting link between the Cape dialect and that of the Namaquas, in which the fullest and most original form of the Hottentot language has been preserved. But we must not forget here, that what materials for a knowledge of the Bushman tongue are at hand are as yet limited to vocabularies of one dialect, namely that of the district of the Winterveld, from the vicinity of Colesberg and Burghersdorp. Other Bushman dialects may be widely different, nor is it impossible that many so-called Bushmen are of quite different origin. However this may be, these Bushmen from the Winterveld have decidedly been distinct from the Hottentots, as a nation, for many centuries ; for their language presents more than dialectical differences from that of the Hottentots. There are, indeed, many Bushman words similar to those in use among the Hottentots, and in the general features of their structure both languages agree together. But the grammatical forms which my vocabularies of the Bushman tongue contain are peculiar, and also the construction of sentences appears to be different from that of the Hottentot language."

Before 1869 a great stride forward was made, for in *The Cape and its People,* published in that year, an article appeared from Dr. Bleek's pen dealing with the Bushman language from a scientific point of view. He wrote :

" The additional information which I have been able to collect (unsatisfactory as it is in extent) has impressed upon my mind this truth, that the Bushmen have been separate from their neighbours, the Hottentots, for at least many thousands of years. . . The task of taking down as exactly as possible the sounds of this language was, of course, a great difficulty, for as many as six different clicks, formed either by the tongue or the lips, can at the least be distinguished here. When endeavouring to give the right mark for each click, I have no doubt frequently erred, as my ear is not very acute nor accustomed to distinguish these sounds ; but as the clicks and other different sounds are not contained in the grammatical portions of the words, my observations on the structure of the language are not affected by this deficiency.

" To show that the Bushman language, as far as we are acquainted with it, is entirely different from the other tongues of South Africa, we will briefly glance at the structure of them all. The South African languages, with the exception of the Bushman, all belong to one of two families. One of these great families of language is that called the Bantu, which contains Kaffir, Setshuana, etc. The other family—that of sex-denoting languages—is represented in South Africa by one member only, the Hottentot, the dialects of which do not differ essentially from each other.

" The Hottentot and Bantu languages have one very essential feature of their structure in common. In both, as a rule, each noun originally consists of two portions, one of which we will call the stem, and the other the representative element. The latter is a part of the noun which is also used to represent the whole noun, and in this manner either appears as a pronoun, or combines with other parts of speech, which are thereby referred to the noun. For example . . .

" These examples are sufficient to show the peculiar structure of the Zulu language, in which the nouns are divided into thirteen classes, by being formed with thirteen distinct prefixes, which are also used to represent their respective nouns. The structure of all South African languages, excepting Hottentot and Bushman, is essentially the same as that of Kaffir and Zulu, with regard to the concord and the classification of the nouns. The Hottentot language also possesses the same method of representing a whole noun by one of its parts ; but in Hottentot the representative portion is not at the beginning of the noun (as prefix), but at the end (as suffix).

" There are in this manner eight different representative elements in Hottentot, as there are thirteen in Kaffir, and sixteen in some of the languages akin to Kaffir. . . . We have not been able to discover any trace in Bushman of such a system of representation of the nouns ; and we cannot but conclude that it does not exist in this language. This may be explained in two different ways. Either the Bushman language never possessed the faculty of thus representing a noun by one of its parts, or, at least, had not a regular set of representative elements or pronouns, and has not developed a classification of the nouns dependent upon their forms of concord. If so (and there is no certain proof against such an assumption), the Bushman would belong to a very low order of language,—a stage in which no true pronouns (*i.e.* representatives of the nouns) were developed. But it may also be that Bushman, like many other languages descended from those in which the nouns were originally divided on the basis of this system of representing a noun by one of its parts, has lost this characteristic entirely. . . . It may have descended from a language possessing a rich system of concords based upon the representation of each noun by one of its parts. Such a system may have dwindled away (a process of which we have so many examples), and all traces of its existence may thus have disappeared. This is possible, but *primâ facie* not so probable as the reverse proposition, that the Bushman language belongs to a lower stage of development, in which neither true pronouns, nor grammatical classes (or genders) of nouns, had any existence.

"The only instances which I have met with of anything like forms of concord in Bushman are the adjectives *small* and *large*, which, in this language, have different forms for the singular and plural respectively. Thus |*eri* is the singular of the adjective indicating small, and |*ĕn* the plural ; ‡*uiya* is the singular of the word for large, and ‡*uita* the plural ; ||kuken e !oai gan |eri *one veldschoen is small*, ||ku||ku e !u gan |ĕn *the two veldschoens are small*, ||kuka gan ||u ‡uiya *the veldschoen is large*, ||ku||ku e !u gan ||u ‡uita *the two veldschoens are large*, ‡nūî yan ‡uiya *the seacow is large*, ‡nūî e ‡oaya yan ||u ‡uita *the many seacows are large*. . . . We should lay more stress upon this grammatical peculiarity, and conclude that we could discern in it the remnant of a former system of concords, if it were not that, as yet, it has only been observed in the sentences taken down from the mouth of one informant, who was not a pure Bushman. Yet it is difficult to see how he could have introduced this grammatical feature into the language, as the Hottentot construction is by no means identical in this instance.*

"Many nouns in Bushman vary in their terminations according to their position or use. Thus veldschoen may be ||kuki, ||kuka, or ||kuken. Our knowledge of the language is not yet sufficiently advanced to enable us to discern the exact value of these endings ; but it does not appear that they have anything to do with the concord, or even clearly with the distinction of singular and plural. . . .

* At a later date Dr. Bleek ascertained that not these only, but other adjectives referring to size, as short, long, etc., have in the plural a form different from the singular. All other adjectives have the same form in both numbers.

As the Bushman nouns do not appear to possess any representative parts, the singular and plural cannot, of course, be distinguished by the mutual correspondence of such parts. The mode in which singular and plural are distinguished from each other in the Bushman language is far more primitive, viz. by reduplication of the first portion of each noun. Thus |nũm is *beard*, and |nũ|nũm *beards*, ‖nũ *ear*, ‖nũ‖nũntu *ears*, ‖nõa *foot*, ‖nõa‖nõa *feet*, tũ *mouth*, tũtũ *mouths*, ‖kun *wing*, ‖ko‖kun *wings*, ku *arm*, kukun *arms*, ‡koa *leg*, ‡koa‡koaken *legs*. In some of the latter nouns it appears as if the ending n, or en, or ken were, besides the reduplication, a distinguishing mark of the plural; but as this ending sometimes certainly also occurs in the singular, it would be rash to consider it as the indicator of the plural. The reduplication, on the contrary, has as yet only been observed in the plural of nouns. This particular employment of the process of reduplication for the purpose of forming plurals is, as far as I am aware, peculiar to the Bushman language. . . .

"Next to the plural, the feature as yet most clearly perceived with regard to Bushman nouns is the formation of the genitive. . . . In Bushman the genitive particle is suffixed to the noun, but as there is no sort of concord by which the noun in the genitive can be referred by a representative element to the noun which it defines, the noun in the genitive can only precede the other noun. The suffixed genitive particle is perfectly different in Bushman and Hottentot, the Bushman particle being ka, ga, ya, or a ; *e.g.* ‖kã is *lion*, and ‖kã ga ãn *lion's flesh*, sa ga ãn *eland's flesh*, ‖kã ga !nu *lion's foot*, *i.e.* lion's traces. This Bushman genitive particle may, like the corresponding one in Hottentot, be also totally omitted. In fact, the cases of such omission appear to be more frequent than those in which the genitive particle is employed, *e.g.* ‖kã ‡kui *lion tail*, koro ‡kui *jackal tail*, toï ‡kui *ostrich tail*. The difference in the form of the suffixed genitive particle in Hottentot and Bushman is as significant as the difference in the use of the prefixed genitive particles *of* in English and *de* in French. Although the former is identical in meaning with the French particle, the difference in its form shows at what a distance English grammar stands, genealogically speaking, from that of the Romance languages.

"One other point of great and conclusive dissimilarity between Bushman and other South African languages is discernible in the forms of the so-called personal pronouns. They are, as far as we

know them, n *I*, a *thou*, ha *he, she, it,* i *we,* u *you*.   Of the numerals,
the second, !ku or !ú, at least offers no resemblance either to the
same numeral in the Bantu languages, or in Hottentot ; and beyond
two every higher number is ‡oaya *many*, although the Bushman
may indicate with his fingers to some extent the exact number, *e.g.*
‡oaya, showing four fingers, *i.e.* as many as four, will indicate four,
and ‡oaya, showing seven fingers, seven.

"In this deficiency of higher numerals the Bushman race
appears to be even more primitive than the Australian tribes, which
generally have distinct names for the numerals as far as three or
four. But the exceedingly ancient character of the Bushman
language appears to be in no way better indicated than by their
very curious phonetic system. It is customary to class Hottentot
and Bushman together under the category of clicking languages ;
and, to a certain extent, this is correct. But in the frequency of
these strange sounds, in the number of their varieties, and in the
range of organs which are employed in their pronunciation, the
Bushman tongue by far exceeds the Hottentot language. In
Bushman, clicks are not merely produced by the tongue, but also
by the lips. There can be no question that among the sounds of
human language clicks are those which it requires the greatest
effort to produce. The study of the history of language shows us
that the further the speech of a people develops, the more it throws
off such sounds as impede the pronunciation or render it more
difficult. Those languages, therefore, in which the sounds are
easiest of utterance are the farthest removed from the primitive
phonetic systems of human speech, whilst those which abound in
uncouth and almost unpronounceable sounds must be presumed to
have better retained their ancient phonetic features."

As late as 1873 Dr. Bleek intimated in an article in the *Cape
Monthly Magazine* that he had not even then completely acquired
all the information that he needed. His words were: "the present
attempt thoroughly to master the Bushman language has been
dictated by purely scientific motives." And in classifying the
languages of South Africa, he said :

"Three kinds of native languages are spoken within the borders
of this colony :—1, Kaffir, belonging to the great family of prefix-
pronominal languages, which fill almost the whole of South Africa,

and extend to the north-west at least as far as Sierra Leone ; 2, Hottentot, the only known South African member of the very extensive sex-denoting family which has spread itself over North Africa, Europe, and a great part of Asia ; 3, Bushman, relationship unknown as yet, presenting outward features of the so-called genderless (or, as Max Müller calls it, Turanian) class, if related to Hottentot, so exceedingly metamorphosed as to be more different from it than English is from Latin ; yet very primitive in its uncouth sounds and in certain structural features, while many others are evidently the result of processes of contraction, and of strong grammatical and phonetical changes, the explanation of which leads us back far into the former history of this original language.''

It might be thought that human organs of sound would be incapable of producing a greater variety of clicks and guttural aspirations than those used by Bushmen in ordinary conversation, but it was not so. They put language into the mouths of various animals, and in doing so gave to each variety of beast and bird a peculiar click, or lisp, or grunt, or hiss, or bleat, usually an imitation of the natural sound produced by it, which they introduced in every word. No adult European could ever hope to imitate these sounds, and Dr. Bleek's widow informed the writer that her husband abandoned the attempt in despair. They were not needed, however, for an analytical study of the language, and therefore nothing was lost through not being able to imitate them. To the ordinary clicks a European ear soon becomes accustomed, and they are not then unpleasant, as men find who are long in contact with the Xosas or the Namaqua Hottentots, who, however, use them far more sparingly than did the Bushmen ; but the deep guttural sounds proceeding from the throats of the pygmy savages remained always very disagreeable. A Bushman on a hillside calling to another at a distance, for instance, might be said to croak rather than to speak.

A remarkable circumstance in connection with the Bushman language is its possession of a verb of such wonderful power, conjugated by means of particles, that any action that can be expressed in English can be expressed with equal precision in it. In the infancy of language it is evident that the verb became more highly developed than the other parts of speech, as it was more necessary to meet the wants of the people. Stand, run, eat, stood, ran, ate, for instance, would be more useful words for a savage to know than the names or qualities of the objects around him.

The roots of many Bushman words are apparently poly-syllabic, thus marking a great difference from Hottentot, all of whose roots are monosyllabic. But it is possible that upon very close analysis some of those polysyllables might prove to be really composites.

In counting, besides the method of showing the fingers described by Dr. Bleek, some Bushmen used the expression two two for four, two two one for five, two two two for six, and so on up to ten, beyond which none of them could proceed. The dialects differed from each other as widely as German from English, if not much more so, and it is possible that in some of those now extinct the means for expressing numbers may have been more perfect than in those that are known, in none of which has any word for a numeral higher than three been discovered. They could, however, easily make their friends acquainted with the exact number say of five elands over a ridge by describing them as two lying down, one looking towards the water, and two looking towards a particular hill.

The principal cause of the Bushmen who still survive having lost the use of their ancestral tongue was the extreme facility with which they learned other languages. In this respect their minds were like those of children, who acquire a foreign tongue, when brought into contact with those who speak it, far more readily than their parents do. A young Bushman on a farm in the interior of the Cape Colony in the early years of the nineteenth century, after four or five months' residence, could usually speak Dutch quite fluently. But this acquirement of a new language did not affect his way of thinking or his conduct in any high degree : he remained as he was before, a savage.

Note 1.—Mr. E. J. Dunn, an accomplished geologist, during many years of search in South Africa made a very large collection of stone implements, which he was good enough to allow me to inspect on several occasions. I was unable to detect any difference between the most ancient of these implements and the magnificent exhibits of chipped stones which I saw afterwards in the museums of London and Brussels, but of course I was unable to compare them side by side. Mr. Dunn's collection included when I saw it arrowheads, knives, axes, spearheads, hammers, flakes with systematically serrated edges to be used as saws, scrapers, notched scrapers, borers, grooved stones, mullers, rubbers, perforated stones, cores, and chips. He was convinced that they were all of Bushman manufacture, and that some of them had lain undisturbed since the beginning, or nearly the beginning, of the present geological period, but he had found none in the later tertiary deposits. Most of the tiny perforated stones found by him were irregular in shape, but he could not ascertain to what use they had been put, though an old Bushwoman showed him how they were drilled, as well as how to attach a stone head to an arrow. A very interesting paper on *The Stone Implements of South Africa*, by Mr. Dunn, is to be found in the *Transactions of the South African Philosophical Society during* 1880.

Note 2.—Two short papers entitled *Stone Implements in South Africa*, with a sheet of illustrations, by Sir Langham Dale, Superintendent General of Education in the Cape Colony, were published in the *Cape Monthly Magazine* of October and December 1870.

Note 3.—A short paper entitled *Notes in connection with Stone Implements from Natal*, by John Sanderson, Esqre., of Durban, Natal, is to be found in the *Journal of the Anthropological Institute* for August 1878.

Note 4.—A lengthy paper on *The Stone Age of South Africa* was read by W. D. Gooch, Esqre., C.E., M.A.I., before the Anthropological Institute on the 11th of January 1881, and is published in Volume XI of the *Journal*. It is illustrated with numerous plates.

Note 5.—A very interesting volume on *The Stone Implements of South Africa, with* 258 *Illustrations*, by J. P. Johnson, crown quarto, 53 pages, was published in London in 1907.

Note 6.—As regards the cradle of the Bushman race, the eminent French anthropologist A. de Quatrefages in his work on the *Pygmies* places that locality in Southern Asia, and gives very strong reasons for doing so. From that locality he maintains that the negritos spread eastward through the different peninsulas and archipelagoes to Japan, and westward into Africa by the strait of Bab-el-Mandeb and the gulf of Aden. He deals chiefly with the pygmy people of the east, but devotes fifty pages to the Hottentots and Bushmen. Other anthropologists, however, hardly less eminent than M. de Quatrefages, have assigned different localities as the cradle of this race.

BUSHMAN DIGGING STICK.

CHAPTER II.

THE BUSHMEN (*continued*).

THE Bushmen occupied the whole of South Africa, except the district bordering on the Indian ocean between the Zambesi and Sabi rivers, until a century or two * before the discovery of the Cape of Good Hope by Europeans, when they were deprived of a considerable portion of it by the people known to us as Hottentots and Bantu, who came down from the north. Being better armed and disciplined than the aboriginal savages, the invaders had little difficulty in exterminating them or driving them into the barren parts.

The variations between the three classes of human beings occupying the country after that event were very marked. In order to bring them clearly before the reader they are given here in consecutive paragraphs, though this chapter deals particularly with the primitive inhabitants only.

Bushmen : frame dwarfish,† colour yellowish brown, face triangular or fox-like in outline, eyes small and deeply sunk, root of nose low, and the whole organ extremely broad, jaws very protuberant; but upper part of face almost vertical, head dotted over with little knots of twisted wiry hair not much larger than peppercorns, in general no beard whatever, ears without lobes,

* The time cannot be given more closely than this. That it could not have been longer than a very few centuries will be shown in the chapters upon the Hottentots and the Bantu.

† Occasionally among the Masarwa in the Betshuana country individuals over one hundred and sixty-seven centimetres or five feet and a half are found, but these are mixed breeds. They show Bantu blood in their darker colour as well as in their general form and size. On account of their habits they are termed Bushmen by Europeans, but their descent from mixed parentage is known to themselves and to their pure Betshuana neighbours.

chest particularly well developed, stomach protuberant, back exceedingly hollow, limbs slender, hands and feet diminutive, skin looser than that of other races, so that in times of scarcity or old age it was not only deeply wrinkled, but often formed folds ; weapons chiefly bow and poisoned arrow ; pursuits those of a hunter ; government none but parental and leadership in war or the chase ; habitations caverns, rock shelters, holes scooped in the ground, or mats spread over slight frames made of branches of trees ; only domestic animal the dog ; demeanour that of perfect independence ; language abounding in clicks and in deep guttural sounds.

Hottentots : frame slight but sometimes tall, better formed than Bushmen, but back hollow, head scantily covered with little tufts of short crisped hair, occasional marks of beard, cheeks hollow, nose flat, eyes far apart and often to appearance set obliquely, hands and feet small, colour yellow to olive ; weapons assagai, knobkerie, bow and arrow, shield ; pursuits pastoral and to a very limited extent metallurgic ; government feeble ; habitations slender frames of wood covered with reed mats ; domestic animals ox, sheep, and dog ; demeanour inconstant, marked by levity ; language abounding in clicks, but less so than that of the Bushmen, and without the croaking sounds of the wild people.

Bantu : great variety of form, feature, and colour in the various tribes, but, generally speaking, frame of those on the coast robust and as well formed as that of Europeans, of those in the interior somewhat weaker, head covered closely with crispy hair, frequently bearded, cheeks full, nose usually flat but occasionally prominent, hands and feet large, colour chocolate brown to deep black ; weapons assagai, knobkerie, shield, and among the northern and interior tribes battle-axe and bow and arrow ; pursuits agricultural, pastoral, and metallurgic ; government firmly constituted, with perfect system of laws ; habitations strong framework of wood covered with thatch ; domestic animals ox, goat, sheep, dog, barnyard poultry ; demeanour ceremonious, grave, respectful to superiors in rank ; language musical ; words abounding in vowels and inflected to produce harmony in sound.

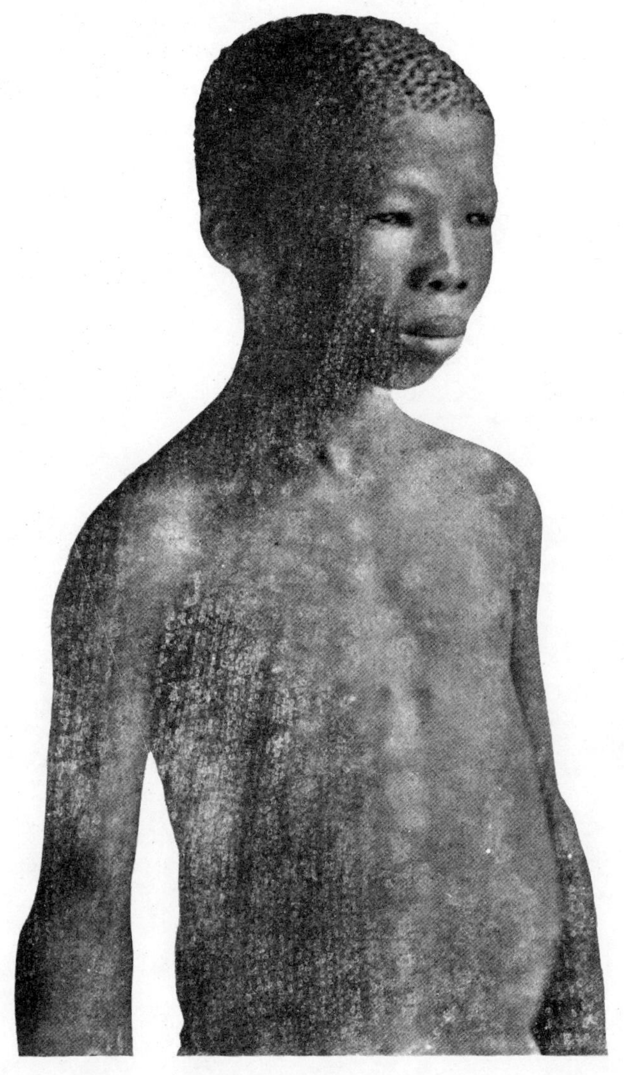

PHOTOGRAPH OF A BUSHMAN GIRL.

[*To face p.* 32.

The skull measurements show great differences in the three classes, though the number—especially of Hottentot skulls—carefully examined by competent men is as yet too small for an average to be laid down with absolute precision.

What is termed the horizontal cephalic index, that is the proportion of the breadth of a skull to its length, is given by Professor Sir William Flower, conservator of the museum of the Royal College of Surgeons of England, from thirteen Bantu specimens as 73 to 100. The highest in this series is 76·8, and the lowest 68·4. Dr. Gustaf Fritsch, from thirteen specimens, gives the average as 72 to 100. The highest in this series is 78, and the lowest 64·3. M. Paul Broca, the French authority, gives the average of his measurements as 72. Thus the Bantu are dolichocephali, that is people whose skulls average in breadth less than three-fourths of their length. The average horizontal cephalic index of white people is 78·7.

Of Hottentots, only four that are certainly genuine specimens are given in Professor Flower's volume. The average horizontal cephalic index of these is 72·7, the highest being 75, and the lowest 70·3. Dr. Fritsch had also only four skulls which were certainly those of Hottentots. The average horizontal cephalic index of these he found to be 72·6, the highest being 77, and the lowest 65·9. M. Broca gives this index from his measurements as 72. The Hottentots are thus certainly true dolichocephali. But even in those that are regarded as pure Hottentot there may have been a mixture of Bushman blood, from causes that will be explained in the next chapter, so that the skull measurements are not altogether to be depended upon. This, however, would have raised the average, not lowered it.

Of genuine Bushman skulls, Professor Flower gives the measurements of five. The average horizontal cephalic index is 76·6, the highest being 78·4, and the lowest 75·7. The late Dr. George Rolleston, professor of anatomy in the University of Oxford, in an appendix to Oates' *Matabeleland*, gives the measurements of six Bushman skulls in the museum of the university. The average horizontal cephalic index was 75·7, the highest being 81, and the lowest 70. Dr. Fritsch measured five Bushman skulls,

and found the average horizontal cephalic index 74·2, the highest
being 78·5, and the lowest 69·5. M. Broca found the average
of his measurements as low as 72, but it is doubtful whether
his specimens were not Hottentot skulls. It would appear that
the Bushmen are on the border line separating the dolicho-
cephalic from the mesaticephalic races, the breadth of skulls of
the latter averaging between three-fourths and four-fifths of the
length.

The cranial capacity, or size of the brain of each, is given by
Professor Flower as : Bantu 1485, Hottentot 1407, and Bushman
1288 cubic centimetres. The average brain of a European is
1497 cubic centimetres in size. Dr. Rolleston found the average
cranial capacity of his six Bushman specimens as low as 1195
cubic centimetres, and all other recorded measurements place
these people among the extreme microcephalic or small-skulled
races. The Hottentots in this classification are mesocephali, a
name applied to races whose average cranial capacity is between
1350 and 1450 cubic centimetres, and the Bantu, like Europeans,
are megacephali or large-skulled.

The alveolar index, index of prognathism, or the slope of a
line from the top of the forehead to the point in the upper jaw
between the insertion of the front teeth, is an important characteristic. According to the angle which this line makes with the
horizontal plane of the skull, races are classified as orthognathous,
mesognathous, or prognathous. In this classification the Bushman comes nearest the European, his face above the upper jaw
being much more vertical than that of either of the others.
Between the Hottentots and the Bantu there is scarcely any
difference.*

A marked feature of the Bushman skull is the smallness of
the lower jaw and the want of prominence of the chin. In this
respect he is among the least advanced of all races. The lower
jaw of the Hottentot is much better formed, but is not by any

* Measurements of Bushman, Hottentot, and Bantu crania of high
scientific value are given by Mr. Frank C. Shrubsall in a paper forty-four
pages in length, entitled *Notes on some Bushman Crania and Bones from the
South African Museum, Capetown,* published in London in 1907 in Volume V
of the *Annals of the South African Museum.*

means as massive as that of a member of the Bantu family or a European.   The skulls of the three classes of people described also differ from each other and from those of Europeans in many particulars which are only intelligible to professional anatomists. The subject can be studied in special works, and it is not necessary therefore to enter more deeply into it here.*

The pygmy hunters, who were the primitive inhabitants of South Africa, received from the first European colonists the name of Bushmen, on account of their preference for places abounding in bushes or shrubs, where they had a wonderful faculty of concealing themselves, partly owing to the colour of their skins being almost the same as that of the soil.

After the advent of the Hottentots and Bantu the Bushmen lost the ground that the invaders chose to occupy, but they managed to keep possession for a long time of the mountains and even the lower country between the widely separated kraals of the recent immigrants.   Constant war was carried on against them, but they fought with the utmost determination, and could not be expelled as long as a dozen men in any locality remained capable of making resistance.   They never thought of submitting and becoming the slaves of the invaders, but like the lions and leopards whose habits they knew so well, when brought to bay they did all the harm they could to their opponents, and died breathing defiance.   The struggle was not over when Europeans arrived on the scene, and the Bushmen at that time still held sole possession of almost the entire interior plain from the Limpopo river southward to the second range of mountains from the sea,

---

* It is perhaps presumptuous for one who knows nothing of anatomy to venture to make observations upon skull measurements, but it strikes me forcibly that in some particulars at least the form of the cranium might be slightly changed by the food ordinarily consumed by the people. Take, for instance, the Bushmen living for numberless generations on the seacoast of South Africa, and consuming food easily masticated, the muscles that move the lower jaw would not be so powerful as those of people of the same race living upon tough flesh and hard roots. This might in time cause modifications, though maybe very slight, in the bones of the skull. The teeth of the Bushmen did not become loose and fall out, as with us, but they wore down with age, until in extreme cases they were almost level with the jaw.

of the larger portion of the Kalahari desert and the land bordering on it, and of many parts of the first two steps upwards from the ocean, west, south, and east.

Though regarded and spoken of by the Hottentots and the Bantu as wild animals of a noxious kind that should be exterminated, in one particular this opinion was not acted upon. Bushman girls when captured were generally kept as concubines by the destroyers of their families, and thus a mixture of blood was gradually taking place. Hottentot and Bantu women on the other hand would have looked with horror upon intimacy between Bushmen and themselves.

A cave with its opening protected by a few branches of trees, or the centre of a small circle of bushes over which mats or skins of wild animals were stretched, was the best dwelling that they aspired to possess. Failing either of these, they scooped a hole in the ground, placed a few stones round it or bent a few sticks over it, and spread a mat or skin above to serve as a roof. A little grass at the bottom of the hole formed a bed, and though it was not much larger than the nest of an ostrich, an individual by bending the body into a curve could lie down in it. Each person, male or female, except young children, in such circumstances thus required a separate reposing place.

The ordinary food of these people consisted of roots, berries, wild plants, grass seed, locusts, larvæ of ants—now commonly called Bushman rice by European colonists,—honey, gum, fish, reptiles, birds, and mammalia of all kinds. Those who lived on the sea shore gathered oysters, mussels, cockles, and salt water fish for their subsistence. They did not know how to make any kind of boat or raft that could be used on the water, but gathered all the small fish left in pools among rocks when the tide was low. No chance of plundering the intruding tribes of domestic cattle was allowed to escape them. They were capable of remaining a long time without food,* and could then devour immense

---

* Dr. Alfred Hillier, who has made a special study of these people, is of opinion that this is at least partly due to the great quantity of adipose matter stored up in their protuberant buttocks, which is most observable when they have abundance of food.

quantities of meat without any ill effects. They were careless of the future, and were happy if the wants of the moment were supplied. Thus, when a large animal was killed, no trouble was taken to preserve a portion of its flesh, but the time was spent in alternate gorging, sleeping, and dancing, until not a particle of carrion was left. When a drove of domestic cattle was stolen, several were slaughtered at once and their carcases shared with birds of prey, while if their recapture was considered possible, every animal was hamstrung or killed.

Such wanton destruction, more than any other circumstance, caused the wild people to be detested by the Hottentots and the Bantu, as well as by the European colonists at a later date. From their point of view, however, they regarded any injury they could inflict upon members of other races as justifiable. Those races were intruders into the land that had been solely possessed by their ancestors from the earliest times, the game, which was their cattle, was killed without scruple by the invaders of their domains, their fountains and streams were appropriated without their consent, only the deserts were left to them ; why then should they not retaliate, and do as much harm as they possibly could to those who had done such grievous wrong to them ?

In some parts of the country the Bushmen made long walls by piling up stones, for the purpose of capturing game. These walls were constructed in the form of the sides of an isosceles triangle, with a narrow open space at the apex. Just beyond this was a deep pit carefully covered over, into which the animals that were driven forward fell without chance of escape. The construction of these walls required much labour, but the hunters were not deficient in energy when the capture of game was the end in view, and the embankments were probably only gradually lengthened and increased in height as the utility of the device became more apparent. They made pits for entrapping the elephant and the hippopotamus at the approaches to rivers, and poisoned pools of water, so that any animal which drank perished. Those who lived in the vicinity of streams containing fish used long baskets shaped like scoop nets made of reeds for the purpose of capturing the smaller kinds, and speared the huge barbels and yellow fish with harpoons of bone.

Honey was obtained in many localities in large quantities. The bees frequently make their hives in crevices in the faces of precipices, but it was a very lofty precipice that a Bushman would not scale or be lowered down from above to secure the spoil. A peg driven into a crack in the rock or any little projecting ledge gave him a foothold, and no baboon would venture where he feared to go. The comb was used for food, but most of the honey was fermented and consumed as an intoxicant. The Bushmen were inveterate smokers of dacha or wild hemp, a plant widely distributed in South Africa, and which possesses great intoxicating properties.

Their principal weapons were bows and arrows, but when hard pressed by an enemy and in the chase they used anything that came to hand, stones for throwing, sticks, darts, stone-headed spears, or anything else that could be improvised. The bows were nothing more than pieces of saplings or branches of trees scraped down a little and strung with a cord formed by twisting together the sinews of animals. It was thus almost useless in wet weather, as the cord when damp was liable to relax, so at such times the Bushmen never went abroad. The arrows were made of reeds, pointed generally with bone, but sometimes with chipped stone flakes. The arrowhead and the lashing by which it was secured to the reed were coated with a deadly poison, so that the slightest wound caused death. The arrows were carried in a quiver usually made of the bark of a species of euphorbia, which is still called by Europeans in South Africa the kokerboom or quiver tree. They were formidable chiefly on account of the poison, as they could not be projected with accuracy to a distance of over fifty metres, and from their frailty had in general little penetrating power. The most expert Bushmen were able to discharge arrows in very rapid succession and at short distances with a fairly accurate aim.

They—or at least some of them—were acquainted with antidotes to the poisons which they used, but were very careful not to inflict wounds upon themselves or even to allow the deadly substance to come in contact with any part of their bodies. The poisons were obtained from snakes, some kinds of caterpillars, and different shrubs.

With the flora in his neighbourhood the Bushman was much better acquainted than Europeans who are not botanists in general are. He knew the qualities of every plant, could at once select those that were edible and reject those that were noxious, and could even make use of those with medicinal properties in case of illness. In this branch of knowledge he had been educated by his mother, when as a little child he went with her daily to seek for food.

The Bushmen used stone flakes for various purposes, but took no trouble to polish them or give them a neat appearance. Many implements were commonly made of horn or bone. There was a stone implement, however, upon which a large amount of care and labour was bestowed in general use among these people when Europeans first became acquainted with them, though it was unknown in very remote times. It was a little spherical boulder, from nine to fourteen centimetres or $3\frac{1}{2}$ to $5\frac{1}{2}$ inches in diameter, such as may be picked up in abundance in many parts of the country, through the centre of which the Bushman drilled a hole large enough to receive a digging-stick, to which it gave weight. With the tools at his disposal, this must have required much time and patience, so that in his eyes a stone when drilled undoubtedly had a very high value. On it he depended for food in seasons of drought, when all the game had fled from his part of the country. Drilled stones of smaller size have occasionally been found in places once the favourite abodes of Bushmen, but from which those savages have long since disappeared. None not large enough to give weight to a digging-stick have been seen in use by any European who has put his observations on record, but from Bushman paintings it is known that moderately sized ones were employed as heads of fighting sticks, and it is conjectured that the very small ones were intended as amulets.

It is not safe, however, for a European to make any surmise regarding the use of a stone implement which he has never seen used, because he cannot analyse the working of the mind of a savage. Flat circular stones with a hole drilled through the centre have been found in different parts of the country, but until quite recently no one could conceive any use that could be made of them. They were not adapted for digging-sticks, as they were not more than three or four centimetres in thickness, and the surface was too large for such a purpose. What could they have been designed for ?

Not long ago a farmer was digging a pit in his ground near Kimberley, and at some depth below the surface he came across some ostrich eggshells. Still deeper he found a flat stone firmly fixed on the surface of a stratum of rock or very hard ground, and on examination the stone was seen to have a hole in it, which was carefully plugged. When the plug was removed, a little stream of water flowed out, which explained the whole matter. The Bushmen who occupied that part of the country until the beginning of the nineteenth century had desired to conceal the water, in order either to preserve it for themselves alone, or to compel the game to resort to poisoned pools, and therefore had closed the eye of the spring in such a manner that neither animals nor men, except themselves, could have access to it. A European would never have imagined that a stone of this kind was intended for such a purpose, if he had found it by accident somewhere else.*

Mr. Stow mentions various implements of stone which were manufactured by Bushmen with much labour and skill, but these were only produced after their contact with other races, and were confined to small localities. None of them surpassed the common spherical weight as a work of labour or art.

There is no record of a European having ever seen a Bushman manufacturing other stone implements than knives and arrow-heads, and no one except Mr. Stow appears to have made inquiry into the matter until it was impossible to derive any information from the people themselves. Even he commenced his investigations at least half a century too late to gain full knowledge of the

---

* For this information I am indebted to Miss Wilman, the talented lady who is in charge of the museum at Kimberley, and who takes the keenest interest in researches of this nature.

matter. But as the various crude unpolished implements found in all parts of South Africa were in use by the Bushmen when white men first came in contact with those savages, there can be no doubt that they fashioned them.

In many other parts of the world perforated stones are plentiful, but most of them differ in some respects from those drilled by the Bushmen, which were all of one type. In the Antiquarian Museum at Edinburgh there is a very fine collection of such stones found in Scotland. There are small ones evidently used in comparatively recent times as weights for nets and in spinning, there are enormously large ones also of not very ancient manufacture, and there are many of the usual size of the Bushman implement. Some are elegantly ornamented, showing the use of tools of metal. Others have holes the same size throughout, leading to a similar conclusion. Those that have holes narrowing from both sides towards the centre, like all the Bushman stones, are usually flat at top and bottom, not globular in form. The Bushman for some unknown reason preferred an approximate sphere, thus any observant eye with a series of each in view would at once detect that they were made by different classes of workmen.

People in a low condition of society do not use clothing for purposes of modesty, but to protect themselves against inclement weather. And as the Bushmen were hardly affected by any degree of either heat or cold that is experienced in South Africa, whether on the plains in midsummer or on the mountains in midwinter, the raiment of the males was usually scanty, and in the chase was thrown entirely aside. At the best it consisted merely of the skin of an animal wrapped round the person. Adult females wore a little apron, and fastened a skin over their shoulders. Both sexes used belts, which in times of scarcity they tightened to assuage the pangs of hunger, and on festive occasions they rubbed their bodies with grease and coloured clays or soot, sometimes powdered with aromatic plants such as buchu, which made them even more ugly than they were by nature.

When the men expected to meet an enemy, they fastened their arrows in an erect position round their heads, in order to appear as formidable as possible. But they never exposed themselves unnecessarily to danger, and tried always to attack from an ambush or a place that would give them the advantage of striking the first blow before their adversaries were aware of their presence. A poisoned arrow, shot from a little scrub in which a Bushman was lying concealed, often ended the career of an unwary Hottentot traveller.

This habit caused them to be feared by Hottentots and Bantu alike. There is an excellent representation of the feeling of the Bantu towards the primitive people, given by a Zulu to the reverend Canon Callaway, and published by him in his *Nursery Tales, Traditions, and Histories of the Zulus.* It reads as follows :

"The Dreadfulness of the Abatwa.

"They are dreaded by men ; they are not dreadful for the greatness of their bodies, nor for appearing to be men ; no, there is no appearance of manliness ; and greatness there is none ; they are little things, which go under the grass. And a man goes looking in front of him, thinking, 'If there come a man or a wild beast, I shall see.' And, forsooth, an Umutwa is there under the grass ; and the man feels when he is already pierced by an arrow ; he looks, but does not see the man who shot it. It is this, then, that takes away the strength ; for they will die without seeing the man with whom they will fight. On that account, then, the country of the Abatwa is dreadful ; for men do not see the man with whom they are going to fight. The Abatwa are fleas, which are unseen whence they come ; yet they teaze a man ; they rule over him, they exalt themselves over him, until he is unable to sleep, being unable to lie down, and unable to quiet his heart ; for the flea is small ; the hand of a man is large ; it is necessary that it should lay hold of something which can be felt. Just so are the Abatwa ; their strength is like that of the fleas, which have the mastery in the night, and the Abatwa have the mastery through high grass, for it conceals them ; they are not seen. That then is the power with which the Abatwa conquer men, concealment, they laying wait for men ; they see them for their part, but they are not seen.

"The bow with which they shoot beast or man does not kill by itself alone ; it kills because the point of their arrow is smeared with poison, in order that as soon as it enters, it may cause much blood to flow ; blood runs from the whole body, and the man dies forthwith. But that poison of theirs, many kinds of it are known to hunters of the elephant. That then is the dreadfulness of the Abatwa, on account of which they are dreaded."

The Bushmen wore few ornaments, not because they were careless about decorating their persons, but because it was difficult to obtain anything for the purpose. They were without metals of any kind, and in the vast interior, as they knew nothing of commerce, they could not obtain sea-shells. The best they could aspire to was to cut little circular disks of tortoise and ostrich egg-shell, drill holes in them, and string them on thongs. It requires some reflection to realise the amount of patient labour expended upon a single ornament of this kind, manufactured with stone and bone implements. In other cases they made grooves round the teeth of animals, and then strung a number together. These ornaments were worn on the forehead, and round the neck, arms, waist, and legs. Sometimes a cord of sinew was passed through the nose and ostrich egg-shell disks were strung on each side, which then hung over the cheeks.

A consideration of how much value such a simple implement as a tinder-box would have had to these people may aid in enabling a European to comprehend the life that they led. They knew how to obtain fire by twirling a piece of wood round rapidly in the socket of another piece, but the preparation of the apparatus took much time, and a considerable amount of labour was needed to produce a flame. Under these circumstances it was a task of the women to preserve a fire when once made, and as they moved their habitations to a large animal when it was killed, instead of trying to carry the meat away, this was often a difficult matter. Sometimes it necessitated carrying a burning stick for four or five hours, or, when it was nearly consumed, kindling a fire for the sole purpose of getting another brand to go on with. No small amount of labour would therefore have been saved by the possession of a flint and a piece of steel.

These wild people lived in little communities, often consisting of only a few families. It was impossible for a large number, such as would constitute an important tribe, to gain a subsistence solely from the chase and the natural products of the earth in any part of South Africa at any time, and more especially after the Hottentots and the Bantu had taken possession of the choicest sections. When a Bushman tribe is spoken of therefore, the term implies only a puny horde never exceeding two or three hundred souls at most. Such a band claimed the right to a fairly well defined tract of country, and any aggression beyond its borders would naturally be resented by the occupants of the next section. If a mountain intervened, the probabilities would be that the dialects of the language spoken on the different sides would vary so greatly as to prevent intercourse, had there been no other cause to keep each little band within its own bounds. Mr. Stow ascertained that these groups called themselves by the names of the animals that were depicted on the walls of their principal caves or engraved on the rocks at their principal residences, thus one band would be the people of the ostrich, another the people of the python, another the people of the eland, and so on.

The early Dutch colonists observed that they were amazingly prolific, a circumstance that is not surprising if one reflects that they were much less subject to disease than Europeans, and that every woman without exception bore children. Their numbers must therefore in remote times have been kept down by war or violence among themselves, just as they were kept down by constant strife in the territory bordering on that occupied by the Hottentots and Bantu after the intrusion of those people. In such a condition of society there could never have been peace for any length of time, for with a rapid growth of population the only alternatives would have been aggression or death from famine.

There was a difference in the disposition of individual Bushmen, though not to the same extent as is seen in civilised people. Towards the invaders that despoiled them of their game and their hunting grounds it was but natural that they should show vindictiveness and relentless cruelty; but they were fierce and passionate in their dealings with each other. Human life, even that of their nearest kindred, was sacrificed on very slight provocation.

They did not understand what quarter in battle meant, and as they never spared an enemy who was in their power, when themselves surrounded so that all hope of escape was gone, they fought till their last man fell. Yet after the colonisation of the country Europeans often observed that many of those who lived temporarily on farms at a distance from their former abodes were not insensible to acts of kindness, and were even capable of feeling gratitude. In this respect they were like those wild animals that in a state of restraint show attachment to their keepers. A pleasing trait in their character was fidelity in positions of trust. At the beginning of the nineteenth century many colonial farmers were in the habit of entrusting herds of cattle to the care of Bushmen in their neighbourhood, supplying them with food and tobacco in return, and seldom found them unfaithful. Another favourable feature was that no distress was so great as to induce them to devour human flesh, as so many Bantu were in the habit of doing.

Their manner of living was such as to develop only qualities essential to hunters. In keenness of vision and fleetness of foot they were surpassed by no people on earth, they could travel immense distances without taking rest, they could scale mountains and steep rocks with the agility of baboons, and yet their frames were so feeble as to be incapable of protracted labour. Their sense of smell was so dull that they experienced no discomfort from remaining for days together close to carrion, and their cave dwellings were disgustingly filthy. The stench from their persons was excessive, owing chiefly to their uncleanly habits and to their use of rancid grease when painting themselves for any festivity.

They possessed an intense love of liberty and of their wild animal way of life. Given only an abundance of food, especially of the flesh of game, and they were cheerful and merry in the highest degree. Mr. Stow states that before the intrusion of the stronger races they were governed by hereditary chiefs, and even down to our own times there have been claimants to such positions. But these chiefs were mere leaders in war and hunting exploits, and their rule did not extend to the exercise of judicial control. Far more than is the case among people possessing domestic cattle, each man was independent of every other. Even parental authority was commonly disregarded by a youth as soon as he could provide for his own wants.

Mr. Stow states that polygamy was common among the Bushmen in the days of their undisputed possession of the country. Kicherer, as already stated, affirms that they were polygamists. And Barrow asserts that at Kruger's farm at the Sneeuwberg he saw a Bushman with two wives and a little child. The same writer also, after coming by surprise upon a Bushman horde, remarks that it appeared customary for the elderly men to have two wives, one old and past childbearing and the other young. On this occasion he had a good opportunity of observing them closely, and he noticed that all the men had the cartilage of their noses bored, through which they wore a piece of wood or a porcupine's quill.*

The reverend John Campbell, too, when travelling in the country north of the Orange river in 1813, came by surprise upon a party of Bushmen, and states that their leader, whom he called Makoon, had two wives, each only about four feet in height.† The same traveller in 1820 was at a farm just beyond the mountains a short distance north of Beaufort West, where about fifty individuals, men, women, and children, of the Bushmen race were living. Mr. Smit, the owner of the farm, spoke their language with fluency. He gave Mr. Campbell much reliable information upon them, and stated :)" they make use of no form or ceremony at their marriages, if marriages they can be called. The men have frequently four or five wives, and often exchange wives with each other." ‡

* *Travels into the Interior of Southern Africa, in which are described the character and the condition of the Dutch Colonists of the Cape of Good Hope and of the several tribes of natives beyond its limits*, &c., &c., &c. By John Barrow. Two quarto volumes, published at London in 1801–4.

† *Travels in South Africa undertaken at the request of the Missionary Society*, by John Campbell, Minister of Kingsland Chapel. Demi octavo, 400 pages London, 1815. The incident referred to is mentioned on pages 235 and 236.

‡ *Travels in South Africa undertaken at the request of the London Missionary Society, being a Narrative of a Second Journey in the Interior of that Country.* By the Rev. John Campbell. Two octavo volumes, London, 1822. The statement transcribed above is on page 30 of the first volume.

With all this evidence to the contrary, it would be rash to assert that the Bushmen were strict monogamists. Circumstances would appear to have governed them in this respect. If the number of females in any locality was much greater than that of males, polygamy would be the natural result, for of course the men would have no qualms of conscience about the practice. But when the sexes were equal, or nearly equal, monogamy was the rule.

It is certain that in modern days the instances of a man living with more than one woman at a time have been exceedingly rare. Miss Lloyd, after long inquiry, could learn of but one such case, and Mr. Dunn and other investigators could hear of none whatever. That is not to say that one male and one female attached themselves to each other for life, though this may often have occurred; but that as long as they lived together a second man or a second woman was not admitted as a member of the family. Their passionate tempers prevented the presence of rivals in the same abode. Chastity, however, was unknown and uncared for, and any disagreement was sufficient to cause the separation of the man and woman, when new connections could immediately be formed by both. In general there was no marriage ceremony, the mere consent of both parties being all that was needed, but in some of the communities a youth who desired to take to himself a girl was obliged to prove himself a man by fighting with others for her and winning her by victory.

The Bushmen possessed several musical instruments, but all of the crudest kind. The most common was a bow, with a piece of quill attached in the cord, with which by blowing and inhaling the breath a noise agreeable to their ears was produced. Pieces of reed of different lengths were used as flutes, and a drum was formed by stretching a dried antelope skin over any hollow article. To their persons when dancing they attached rattles, made of hollow globes of dried hide containing pebbles, which added to the noise of the rude chant and the stamping of the feet.

They were fond of dancing by moonlight, after abundance of flesh had been obtained by the slaughter of some large animal.

There were various kinds of dances, each of which had its appropriate chant, but nearly all consisted of contortions of the body rather than of movements from place to place. Some of them were lascivious to the last degree, for the savages were devoid of all feeling of shame. Others, which perhaps must be considered the highest in order, were imitations of the actions of different animals. These dances caused much excitement, one especially, which was attended with great exertion of the body, frequently causing blood to flow from the noses of some of the performers and ending in the utter exhaustion of others.

The games that they practised were chiefly imitation hunts, in which some or all of them were disguised and represented animals. In this pastime they displayed much cleverness, whether they acted as men, or as baboons, or as lions in pursuit of antelopes. But it was not often that they engaged in play, for the effort to sustain existence was with them severe and almost constant.

At early dawn the Bushman rose from his bed of grass, and scanned the country around in search of game. If any living thing was within range of his far-seeing eye, he grasped his bow and quiver of arrows, and with his dog set off in pursuit. His wife and children followed, carrying fire and collecting bulbs and anything else that was edible on the way. They could pursue his track unerringly by indications that would escape the keenest European eye: a broken twig, a freshly turned stone, or bent blades of grass being sufficient to guide them aright. At nightfall, if they were fortunate, they collected about the body of an antelope, and there they remained till nothing that could be consumed was left. Or if a small animal was killed early in the day, it might be carried to the cave where they and others had their chief abode, to be generously shared with all the occupants, for in this respect the wild people were unselfish to the last degree. Such in general was their mode of existence, varied occasionally by either a great feast with boisterous revelry or a dire famine and tightened hunger belts. And so from day to day and year to year life passed on, without anything of an intellectual nature to ennoble it.

If the stone, horn, and bone implements, the weapons of the chase, the crude musical instruments, and the shell beads already mentioned be excluded, the Bushmen had little knowledge of manufactures. They had not advanced beyond the stage of making a coarse kind of pottery, and even this was extremely limited in use. But as they were artists, occasionally they attempted to decorate a jar by making a circle of lines or notches round it, which really had a neat effect. Add to this industry the plaiting of rush mats and net bags of fibres, in which their women carried ostrich egg-shells filled with water, and the list is exhausted.

They were firm believers in charms and witchcraft, and were always in dread of violating some custom—as for instance avoiding casting a shadow upon dying game—which they believed would cause disaster. A Bushman would not make a hole in the sandy bed of a river in order to obtain water, without first offering a little piece of meat, or some larvæ of ants, or an arrow if he had nothing else, to propitiate the spirit of the stream, that was imagined by him to have the figure of a man hideous in aspect, and capable of making himself visible or invisible at will. And so with every act of his life, something had to be done or avoided to avert evil, to bring game within reach of his arrows, or to make the wild plants appear.

Their reasoning power was very low. They understood the habits of wild animals better than anything else, yet they believed the different species of game could converse with each other, and that there were animals and human beings who could exchange their forms at will, for instance that there were girls who could change themselves into lions, and baboons that could put on the appearance of men. The moon, according to the ideas of some of them, was a living thing, according to the notions of others it was a piece of hide which a man threw into the sky. In the same way the stars were once human beings, or they were pieces of food hurled into the air. As well might one attempt to get reasons for their fancies from European children six or seven years of age as from Bushmen: the reflective faculties of one were as fully developed as of the other.

Dr. Bleek and Miss Lloyd obtained from several individuals prayers to the moon and to stars. But everything connected with their religion—that is their dread of something outside of and more powerful than themselves—was vague and uncertain. They could give no explanation whatever about it, and they did not all hold the same opinions on the subject. Some of them spoke indeed of a powerful being termed 'Kaang or 'Cagn, but when questioned about him, their replies showed that they held him to be a man like themselves, though possessing charms of great power. Many are supposed to have had a vague belief in immortality, because they buried a dead man's weapons with him and laid the corpse with its face towards the rising sun, and their custom of cutting off a joint of the little finger was imagined to be due to a belief that by doing so they would secure an abundance of food in the future life; but probably very few of them ever gave a thought to such a matter. The wants of the present day were sufficient to occupy all their attention.

They buried their dead in shallow graves, over which they piled stones to prevent wild animals scraping the bodies up. In a cavity scooped out of the western wall of the grave the corpse was placed on its side, either stretched to its full length or bent in a curve such as when sleeping it formed in life, with its face turned towards the east. The bones were not broken, as by some Bantu, and as well as can be ascertained, all human bodies were interred. It is remarkable that the Bushmen should have performed the labour of making graves and raising cairns over them, when the Hottentots, who were so much superior to them in civilisation, looked for an anteater's den or some natural cavity in which to lay their dead, and many tribes of Bantu, so much higher still, did not bury the corpses of common people at all, but left them exposed in solitary places to be devoured by beasts of prey.

It is difficult to conceive of a human being in a more degraded condition than that of a Bushman. In some respects, however, he showed considerable ability, and there was certainly an enormous gulf between him and the highest of the brute creation. He possessed extraordinary powers of mimicry. Enclosed in a framework covered with the skin and plumage of an ostrich, he was in the habit of stalking game, and by carefully keeping his prey to windward, was able to approach within shooting distance, when the poison of his arrow completed the task. This, though the commonest disguise assumed by a hunter, was but one of many, which varied according to circumstances. He could imitate the peculiarities of individuals of other races with whom he came in contact, and was fond of creating mirth by exhibiting them in the drollest manner.

In recent times travellers have noticed that the Bushmen are fond of showing their superiority to the large black men whenever they can do so. Thus in rainy weather when a number of Bakwena are endeavouring in vain to kindle a fire in the open air, a Bushman will look on with a smile of contempt until they desist, when he will produce his fire sticks and accomplish what they could not do. Or if they fail to find water on the border of the desert, he will wait till they are almost speechless from thirst, and then apparently by some instinct lead the way to a place where a little may be obtained by digging. In such cases he exhibits great satisfaction and pride.

He was also an artist. On the walls of caves and the sheltered sides of great rocks he drew rude pictures in profile of the animals with which he was acquainted. The tints were made with different kinds of ochre having considerable capability of withstanding the decay of time, and they were mixed with grease, so that they penetrated the rock more or less deeply according to its porousness. There are caves on the margins of rivers containing paintings which have been exposed to the action of water during occasional floods for at least a hundred years, and the colours are yet unfaded where the rock has not crumbled away.

In point of artistic merit, however, the paintings were seldom superior to the drawings on slates of European children eight or nine years of age, though there were occasional instances of game being delineated not only in a fairly correct but in a graceful manner, showing that some of the workmen possessed more skill than others. In none of them was any knowledge of perspective, and in only one or two of the very best any attempt at shading displayed.   Two or more colours were sometimes used, as, for instance, the head or legs of an animal might be white, and the remainder of the body brown, but—with extremely rare exceptions—each colour was evenly laid on as far as it went.   In short, the paintings might be mistaken for the work of children, but for the high positions of many of them on the rocks, and the scenes being chiefly those of the chase.   A peculiarity in them is that the human form is almost invariably grotesquely outlined. The lion also is never represented perfectly, probably from a superstitious fear of offending the formidable animal that often furnished food by leaving parts of the large antelopes uneaten, and that could when provoked do so much harm.   In only a few of the paintings are the feet of the animals shown.   Sometimes disguises are represented, usually a man's body with an animal's head, though these are rare.

In some places, where the rock was very smooth and hard, the Bushman drew an outline of a figure, and then chipped away the surface within it.   The labour required for such a task, without metallic implements, must have been great, and the workman was undoubtedly possessed of much patience.   He was a sculptor in the elementary stage of the art.   Mr. Stow believed that the engravers and painters were distinct branches of the race, and in his work he classified them as such.   Miss Lloyd, however, is of opinion that the method of delineating the figures depended merely upon the condition of the locality, the artists being the same, and with this view Messrs. Bain, Dunn, and other investigators agree.

These wild people possessed too a faculty—it might almost be termed an additional sense—of which Europeans are destitute. They could make their way in a straight line to any place where they had been before.   Even a child of nine or ten years of age, removed from its parents to a distance of several days' journey and without opportunity of carefully observing the features of the country traversed, could months later return unerringly. They could give no explanation of the means by which they accomplished a task seemingly so difficult.   Many of the inferior

ENGRAVING OF A ZEBRA ON A ROCK IN THE DISTRICT OF VRYBURG.

(From a Photograph of a cast in the South African Museum in Capetown.   The original is thirteen inches in length.)

[*To face p.* 52.

animals, however, have this faculty, as notably the dove, so that it is not surprising to find the lowest type of man in possession of it.

The life led by these savages was in truth a wretched one, judged from a European standard. They had no contact with people beyond their own little communities, except in war, for they carried on no commerce. If a pestilence had swept them all from the face of the earth, nothing more would have been left to mark where they had once been than the drilled stones, rudely shaped arrowheads, rough pottery, rock paintings, and crude sculptures. Their pleasures were hardly superior to those of dumb animals. But it is not correct to look at them from this standpoint, or to compare them with white people reduced to the same level of poverty. They knew of nothing better, they were all in the same condition and shared alike, so that envy was not felt, their cares were very few, and serious illness was hardly known among them. They probably enjoyed, therefore, more real happiness in life than the destitute class in any European city.

They had a rich stock of traditionary stories, which old women told to little children by evening fires, when food was plentiful and the able-bodied were enjoying themselves in other ways. In Miss L. C. Lloyd's book just published a number of these folklore tales can be found, and it must be remembered that even the grown-up people believed them to be true narratives, for they were as credulous in such matters as infants could be. But judging from the manner in which Bantu women tell such stories, a great deal of their interest is lost when they are read in print. A Xosa woman when narrating one of them displays all kinds of gestures, alters her voice in the dialogues, and sings the parts capable of such treatment, in short, puts life into the tale. It may be taken for certain that a Bushwoman did the same, and so even the endless repetitions of the same thing would not be wearisome, especially to children. The following are literal translations of two such stories, taken down by Miss Lloyd from the dictation of a Bushman named |han‡kass'ō, and published by her in the *Folklore Journal* of May 1880 :

"The Son of the Wind.

" The wind (the narrator explains the *Son of the Wind* is here meant) was formerly still. And he rolled (a ball) to !ná-ka-ti. He exclaimed, ' Oh !ná-ka-ti there it goes.' And !ná-ka-ti exclaimed, ' Oh comrade ! there it goes ! ' because !ná-ka-ti did not know his (the other one's) name. Therefore !ná-ka-ti said, ' Oh comrade ! there it goes ! ' He who was the wind, he was the one who said, ' Oh ! !ná-ka-ti ! there it goes '

" Therefore !ná-ka-ti went to question his mother about the other one's name. He exclaimed, ' Oh ! our mother ! utter for me yonder comrade's name ; for comrade utters my name ; I do not utter comrade's name. I would also utter comrade's name when I am rolling (a ball) to him. For I do not utter comrade's name ; I would also utter his name when I roll a ball to him.' Therefore his mother exclaimed, ' I will not utter to thee comrade's name. For thou shalt wait, that father may first strongly shelter the hut ; and then I will utter for thee comrade's name. And thou shalt, when I have uttered for thee comrade's name, thou must, when I am the one who has uttered for thee comrade's name, thou must scamper away, thou must run home, that thou mayest come into the hut, whilst thou feelest that the wind would blow thee away.'

" Therefore the child went away ; they (the two children) went to roll (the ball) there. Therefore he (!ná-ka-ti) again went to his mother, he again went to question his mother about the other one's name. And his mother exclaimed, |érriten-!kuan-!kuan it is ; !gau-!gaubu-ti it is. He is |erriten-!kuan-!kuan ; he is !gau-!gaubu-ti, he is |erriten-!kuan-!kuan.'

" Therefore !ná-ka-ti went away. He went to roll (the ball) there, while he did not utter the other one's name, because he felt that his mother was the one who had thus spoken to him. She said, ' Thou must not, at first, utter comrade's name. Thou must, at first, be silent, even if comrade be the one who is uttering thy name. Therefore thou shalt, when thou hast uttered comrade's name, thou must run home, whilst thou feelest that the wind would blow thee away.'

" Therefore !ná-ka-ti went away. They went to roll (the ball) there, while the other was the one who uttered his (!ná-ka-ti's) name ; while he felt that he (!ná-ka-ti) intended that his father might first finish sheltering the hut, and (when) he beheld that his father sat down, then he would, afterwards, utter the other one's name, when he saw that his father had finished sheltering the hut.

"Therefore, when he beheld that his father finished sheltering the hut, then he exclaimed, 'There it goes! Oh |érriten-!kuan-!kuan! there it goes! Oh !gau-!gaubu-ti! there it goes!' And he scampered away, he ran home; while the other one began to lean over, and the other one fell down. He lay kicking (violently) upon the flat ground. Therefore the people's huts vanished away; the wind blew away their (sheltering) bushes, together with the huts, while the people could not see for the dust. Therefore, his (the wind's) mother came out of the hut (*i.e.* of the wind's hut); his mother came to raise him up; his mother grasping (him), set him on his feet. And he was unwilling, (and) wanted to lie still. His mother, taking hold (of him), set him upright. Therefore, the wind became still; while the wind had, at first, while it lay, made the dust rise.

"Therefore, we who are Bushmen, we are wont to say, 'The wind seems to have lain down, for it does not gently blow = it blows very strongly).' For, when it stands (upright), then it is wont to be still, if it stands; for it seems to have lain down, when it feels like this. Its knee is that which makes a noise, if it lies down, for its knee does make a noise."

"THE WIND.

"The wind was formerly a person. He became a feathered thing (*i.e.* a bird). And he flew, while he no longer walked as formerly; for he flew, and he dwelt in the mountains (that is, in a mountain hole). Therefore he flew. He was formerly a person. Therefore he formerly rolled (a ball); he shot; while he felt that he was a person. He became a feathered thing; and then he flew, and he inhabited a mountain hole. And he was coming out of it, he flew about, and he returns home to it. And he comes to sleep in it; and he early awakes (and) goes out of it; he flies away; again he flies away. And he again returns home, while he feels that he has sought food. And he eats, about, about, about, about, he again returns home. And he, again, comes to sleep in it (that is, in his hole)."

The third story given here was taken down by Joseph M. Orpen, Esqre., British resident in Griqualand East, from the lips of a Bushman named Qing, who lived in the Maluti mountains. It was published by Mr. Orpen, with other tales and descriptive matter, in the *Cape Monthly Magazine* for July 1874, under the title of *A Glimpse into the Mythology of the Maluti Bushmen.*   Mr. Orpen does not use the usual signs for the clicks in the Bushman words, but the letters which in the Xosa dialect are employed to represent three of them.

"Story of Cagn.

" Cagn sent Cogaz (his eldest son) to cut sticks to make bows. When Cogaz came to the bush, the baboons (*co'gn*) caught him. They called all the other baboons together to hear him, and they asked him who sent him there.   He said his father sent him to cut sticks to make bows.   So they said, ' your father thinks himself more clever than we are ; he wants those bows to kill us, so we'll kill you,' and they killed Cogaz, and tied him up in the top of a tree, and they danced round the tree, singing (an intranscribable baboon song), with a chorus saying ' Cagn thinks he is clever.' Cagn was asleep when Cogaz was killed, but when he awoke he told Coti (his wife) to give him his charms, and he put some on his nose, and said the baboons have hung Cogaz.   So he went to where the baboons were, and when they saw him coming close by, they changed their song so as to omit the words about Cagn, but a little baboon girl said, ' don't sing that way, sing the way you were singing before.'   And Cagn said, ' sing as the little girl wishes,' and they sang and danced away as before.   And Cagn said, ' that is the song I heard, that is what I wanted, go on dancing till I return ; ' and he went and fetched a basket full of pegs, and he went behind each of them as they were dancing and making a great dust, and he drove a peg into each one's back, and gave it a crack, and sent them off to the mountains to live on roots, beetles, and scorpions, as a punishment.   Before that baboons were men, but since that they have tails, and their tails hang crooked.   Then Cagn took Cogaz down, and gave him canna, and made him live again."

It can now be asserted in positive language that the Bushmen were incapable of adopting European civilisation.   During the first half of the nineteenth century agents of various missionary societies made strenuous efforts for their improvement, and often believed they had in some cases succeeded and in others were in a fair way towards success. Men more devoted to their work than many of these missionaries have never existed, and it would be unjust to accuse them of wilfully misstating the results of their teaching, but the very excess of their zeal and their dwelling constantly upon the expression that the whole human family is of one blood, without reflecting that different branches of it even in Europe are incapable of thinking alike, led them to distort what they saw and heard, so that their reports are commonly misleading. In these reports Bushmen were represented as having become civilised and Christian. But no one else ever saw those transformed savages, and no trace of them exists at the present day. The wild people in the missionary writings are described as offshoots of a higher stock, degraded by oppression or neglect, and needing only instruction and gentle treatment to elevate them again. Some of the reasoning in favour of this theory is highly acute, but it is not borne out by the deeper investigations of our day.

Apart from missionary teaching also many persons tried during long years to induce families of Bushmen to abandon their savage habits, and there were even experiments in providing groups of them with domestic cattle, in order to encourage a pastoral life, but all were without success. To this day there has not been a single instance of a Bushman of pure blood having permanently adopted the habits of a white man, though a few mixed breeds are to be found among the least skilful class of labourers in some parts of the country. Even these are generally too feeble in body to endure anything like severe toil, and unless they intermingle with blacks—as in the instance of the degraded Batlapin tribe—quickly decrease in number. Those of unmixed blood who were not destroyed as noxious animals by the invaders of their hunting grounds could not exist in presence of a high civilisation, but dwindled away rapidly, and have now nearly died out altogether. It would seem that for them progress was possible in no other way than by exceedingly slow development and blending their blood in successive stages with races always a little more advanced.

CHAPTER III.

The Hottentots, termed by the Bantu of the eastern coast Amalawu, and by the Bantu of the south-western coast Ovaserandu.

The next section of the human species that claims the attention of a student of South African history is the people known to us as Hottentots. Long considered and termed aborigines by many writers, the not very remote ancestors of these people are now known to have been colonists in the same sense that the Dutch and English are, that is they came from another country and settled in those parts where they were found by the first European visitors, which localities had previously been occupied by earlier inhabitants. That this circumstance long remained unknown is a matter easy of explanation. Neither the Portuguese, nor the Dutch, nor the early English settlers took any trouble to make the necessary investigations, they were wholly occupied with other affairs, they found the Hottentots in the country, and that seemed sufficient for them to know.

Then, long before any real research was commenced, the Hottentots in those parts occupied by Europeans lost their own language and customs, and the blood of most of them became mixed with that of other races. Their traditions were forgotten, and no information of any value was to be obtained from them. At length the eminent philologist Dr. Bleek, by comparing the language of those who lived in secluded localities and retained their ancestral tongue, with the speech of sections of the inhabitants of Northern Africa, pronounced them to have close affinities. Already, in 1851, the reverend Dr. James Adamson had reported to the Syro-Egyptian Society a discovery he had made, that " the signs of gender were almost identical in the Namaqua and

PORTRAIT OF A HOTTENTOT.

(Copy of Le Vaillant's Portrait of his faithful Klaas.)

The headdress and the strings of beads are European additions to the costume, otherwise the portrait is an excellent one.

[*To face p.* 58.

the Egyptian, and the feminine affix might be considered the same in the Namaqua, Galla, and Old Egyptian." *   This was not known to Dr. Bleek, however, before he made the same discovery.

The question then arose how could the Hottentots, who differ as much from the present black inhabitants of Central Africa as they do from Europeans, have found their way to the south ?   Various answers were suggested, but as every one who attempted to solve this question regarded the black race as having occupied the whole of Central Africa from the most remote times, none were conclusive or satisfactory. The mystery remained unsolved, like that which veils from our knowledge the cause and the manner of the early migrations of our own race.

A satisfactory answer, however, has now been given, at least to part of what is implied in the question.   Mr. George W. Stow, who spent many years in research among the Korana clans, the purest Hottentots now existing—if some small sections of the Namaqua be excepted,—and who was aided in his investigations by missionaries and other inquirers, learned from the traditions of those clans that their ancestors had indeed moved down from the north, and that too at no very remote time.   These traditions, collected in different localities and from individuals who could have had no intercourse with each other, carried back the history of the Hottentots to a period when they were residing in a well watered region somewhere in the centre of the continent, from which they were driven by more powerful people, of a black colour, who came down from the north or north-east.   They do not go beyond that point, but there is strong reason to believe that the race had its origin in the country now termed Somaliland, and was formed there by the intercourse of men of a light-coloured hamitic stock with women of Bushman blood.

* The reverend James Adamson, D.D., first clergyman of the presbyterian church in Capetown, and for many years professor of mathematics in the South African college, was a man of great ability and of high education. Among the subjects to which he devoted much attention was philology, though he published nothing upon that subject except his addresses at the meetings of literary associations.   After a residence of twenty-two years in Capetown, he removed to the United States in 1850, but ten years later returned to South Africa, and remained here until his death on the 16th of July 1875, at the age of seventy-nine years.

Herodotus mentions that a large band of Egyptian soldiers, said by him to be two hundred and forty thousand in number, deserted and marched into Ethiopia at a date corresponding to about 650 before Christ, and were settled by the Ethiopian king as far beyond Meroë as Meroë was beyond Elephantine. These people he termed the Automoli or Deserters, but by succeeding writers they are called the Sembritæ or Sebritæ. The locality assigned to them was in about 13° to 14° north latitude, Meroë being not far above the junction of the Atbara with the Nile, or in latitude 17° north. This may not be correct,* and certainly, if there was any foundation for the statement, the number of the deserters must be enormously exaggerated, but it shows that such migrations were not deemed impossible at that time.

It is therefore not unlikely that at a much earlier date a small body of men, perhaps soldiers, did make their way from Egypt to Somaliland, and took to themselves there women of the Bushman race, there being no other females for them to associate with. All the difficulties of the problem are solved by this supposition, and to support it there are the following facts :—

1. The Egyptian picture of the queen of Punt is seen to be a correct portrait.

2. The Hottentot language, in its structure North African, and yet containing the four Bushman clicks most easily pronounced, is at once accounted for.

3. The possession by the Hottentots of horned cattle and Syrian sheep covered with hair and having very large tails is immediately explained.

4. The peculiarly shaped drilled stones found recently in considerable numbers by Germans in Somaliland, and now to be seen in the museum at Berlin, which are exactly similar to those used by Hottentots in South Africa and to one in the British museum found in Central Africa, also support this view.

The original Hottentots were therefore mixed breeds, but judging by analogy, there must have been a second intrusion of

* There is no mention of the Automoli in Egyptian history, nor any trace in the hieroglyphic inscriptions so far deciphered of the desertion of such an army. But nations do not usually record their own disasters.

males, who took consorts from the first cross and so obtained a preponderance of blood, or the newly formed race would not long have remained fertile. They must have been like the Griquas of modern times, who were originally half Hottentots, and who die out speedily if they intermarry only among themselves, but who have often large families if they take consorts of either of the races from which they have sprung.

How long these mixed breeds remained in Somaliland, and what caused them at length to leave that locality cannot be stated, but in all probability they were driven out by the arrival there of people more powerful than themselves. The date of their removal must have been earlier than the occupation of Central Africa by Bantu tribes, for they could not have passed through a region inhabited by any other people than Bushmen, especially as they had horned cattle and sheep with them. Their route was south-westward to the region of the great lakes, but whether they tarried at any place or places on the way, there are no means of ascertaining. Nor can it be even conjectured how long they remained at this new home, though probably it was a period of many centuries.

While they were there the Bantu tribes were increasing in the north and pushing their way down the continent, until they too reached the lake region, and then the Hottentots were compelled to move again. They were acquainted with the use of copper and iron, and were better armed than the Bushmen in advance of them, but they were too few in number to hold their own against the stalwart black men who had now come in contact with them. They had not the energy and alertness of the Bushmen either, for their mode of existence as herdsmen did not need the exercise of those qualities. Thus it is not likely that their resistance was protracted, if indeed they made any resistance at all. Before them the country was open, that is it had no other inhabitants than the pygmy aborigines, so they set out in quest of a place where they could live in safety. It is this point of their history that tradition reaches back to.

They turned their faces to the south-west. Eastward they could not go, because in that direction the Bantu were pressing down the coast, and probably were already far beyond the latitude they were in. Northward their way was blocked by the enemy they were endeavouring to escape from. Their choice of a route was thus limited, and even in the country apparently open to them, it was only to the south-west that they could proceed in safety. In migrations such as this, the line of least resistance is of course followed, but in the present instance that had to be determined by more than the usual considerations. It was not only the absence of enemies more powerful than themselves, and the physical features of the country to be traversed, its mountains and rivers, that the Hottentot fugitives had to take into account. The question was complicated to them by the existence of the tsetse fly in a broad belt of land to the south, which barred their retreat with cattle in that direction. That insect alone, whose sting is fatal to domestic animals, would have prevented them from crossing the Zambesi until they had travelled very far to the westward. The Bushmen could not oppose them with any chance of success, or they could not have journeyed with their women and children, much less have driven their flocks and herds, through the country, for no right is recognised by savages and barbarians but the right of the strong, even as men observe it to be among the lower animals.

Naturally, all details of the long journey have been lost, the only circumstance preserved by tradition being the point from which it commenced. That it must have been very slow after the danger of immediate pursuit was over, seems certain, however. Cows and sheep cannot be transferred hastily from one kind of pasture to another without heavy loss, and there could have been no motive for hurrying on when only Bushmen were in the neighbourhood. Probably many years were spent at each favourable halting place, though the design of a continued advance, once initiated, was never entirely lost sight of.

At length the shore of the Atlantic was reached, and then the wave of migration turned to the south. In some parts of this course, after the twentieth parallel of latitude is passed, the pasture is better at a distance inland than on the margin of the sea. The rainfall along the coast, owing to the prevailing

winds being offshore, is trifling compared with that of the thun‑
derstorms in the interior, and the sandy soil does not long retain
moisture. It is an arid, sterile belt of land, destitute of running
streams and fountains, where in places the sand hills blown about
by the wind are constantly changing their form. It is traversed
with difficulty even by those who are acquainted with the localities
where scanty pasture and a little water are to be found. Here
therefore the migrating horde, which must have been broken up
into small parties, moving on slowly at long intervals, turned
inland for a short distance and then kept on towards the south,
but as soon as possible it moved westward again and pursued its
course along the terrace nearest the ocean. Did the wanderers
expect that the shore would somewhere turn and lead them to
a fairer land, where they could rest at last ? No one can tell.
Perhaps they themselves did not know of an object in view, but
were merely impelled onward by a ruling desire for change. They
were not now driven forward by enemies stronger than them‑
selves, but still they advanced. Leaving a section behind in the
territory now termed Great Namaqualand, they crossed the Orange
river and entered the present Cape Colony.

During their march they must have had constant conflicts
with the Bushmen, the only earlier inhabitants of the land, who
could not look on unmoved while the country was thus invaded.
These puny savages were capable of causing much mischief,
though they could not prevent the strangers from either advancing
or taking possession of the choicest pastures along the shore.
The Hottentots did not regard them as human beings having
rights, but simply as noxious animals to be got rid of as quickly
as possible. In one respect, however, this was not the case.
Young girls of Bushman blood, when captured, were detained and
incorporated as inferior members of the families of those who slew
their kindred without the slightest feeling of remorse. In this
manner, probably from the first contact of the two peoples, a
mixture of blood took place, which, though slight in the beginning
of the journey from the centre of the continent, was considerable
by the time the intruding horde reached the Cape promontory.
On the other hand, there was no intercourse between Bushmen

and Hottentot women, either before or after this period. Their arrival at the southern shore of Africa must have preceded that of the first Portuguese explorers by only a very few centuries, certainly not more than two or three at most, and probably even less.

At different stages between the mouth of the Orange river and Table Bay sections of the horde were left behind, each of which took a tribal name, and thereafter carried on war with its nearest neighbours on its own account. As the majority of the Bushmen who had lived at these localities were either exterminated or forced to retreat farther inland, the incorporation of girls necessarily almost ceased, so that each tribe of Hottentots from north to south was of purer blood than the next in advance. Nearly all of the former dwellers on the coast, the people who raised the great shell heaps that cannot now be distinguished from natural mounds unless the materials of which they are composed are discovered by accident, must have been cut off at this time. A few only may have survived in situations favourable for concealment, and at a distance from localities where the invaders settled. All the others disappeared, and then dust and sand accumulated on the mounds, and plants began to grow upon them, and when centuries went by all traces of them were lost to view.

When the southern point of the continent was reached, the migratory movement did not end, but, turning eastward, a portion of the horde continued its march, still keeping close to the shore of the sea. At no point except the one mentioned on the long journey, which may have occupied several centuries, was any attempt made to penetrate the interior country. Yet these people did not possess the skill to make even a rough canoe, and only when they were without cattle resorted to catching fish for food. It was therefore not from any attachment to the ocean or from any benefit derived directly from it that they continued their course along its margin, but from the pastures, owing to the greater rainfall, being more luxuriant in its neighbourhood than farther inland.

The character of the country had now entirely changed. The south-east wind sweeping over the Indian ocean reached the land laden with moisture, which was deposited in abundance on the lowest terrace, in decreasing quantities on each succeeding plateau, and least of all on the vast plain in the interior. The farther to the north-east one proceeds the more is this perceptible, until the rich vegetation of the shore forms a striking contrast to the desert belt in the same latitudes on the Atlantic side.

As band after band was thrown off along the southern and south-eastern coast, and Bush girls were continually incorporated, the most advanced party at length probably contained more Bushman than pure Hottentot blood. It was so gradually absorbed, however, that it was assimilated, for these little tribes preserved the Hottentot customs and mode of living, and carried on hostilities with the Bushmen just as if they were wholly unconnected with those savages. Along this coast the Hottentots were never so numerous as along the shore of the Atlantic south of the Orange river. There were wide gaps between the various tribes or distinct bands, which were occupied solely by the aboriginal hunters. At the beginning of the sixteenth century of our era the Hottentots extended thus in a thin line, or rather a series of dots at varying distances from each other, from Walfish Bay on the western coast round to the mouth of the Umtamvuna river on the south-eastern, beyond which there is no indication that they ever advanced.

The cause of their being so thinly scattered along this line was their depending almost entirely upon milk for subsistence. They needed a large number of cows and ewes, and consequently a great extent of pasture for each separate community, as the cattle belonging to all the families composing it were herded together for reasons of safety, and were driven from place to place according to the state of the grass. As soon as a community became so large that this was impossible or even inconvenient, a swarm was of necessity thrown off, and moved to a distance in order to acquire a new pasture of sufficient extent for its use. The offshoot might for a time consider itself a dependency of the parent band, or a clan of the tribe, but the tendency would soon be towards perfect independence. There was no other way of extension, for a party moving needed to be strong enough to protect itself and its cattle from Bushmen and ravenous animals. For a single family, or even two or three families together, to settle separately on the pasture of a tribe and to keep up connection with the main body was not possible. Each Hottentot community was thus compact, but limited in number to a few hundred or at most to a couple of thousand souls. It occupied a single village, or kraal as now generally termed.

From the neighbourhood of the kraàl the Bushmen were cleared off as far as possible, but in many instances they still occupied the mountains and seized every opportunity to plunder cattle from the intruders and to put any stray individual of either sex to death. The feeling between the two peoples was in general one of intense animosity, though there were occasional instances of a compact between a Hottentot tribe and the Bushmen in its neighbourhood, under which the former provided food in times of great distress, and the latter acted as scouts and gave warning of any approaching danger. This was only the case, however, when the Bushmen were so reduced in number as to be incapable of carrying on war.

The great interior of the country was undisturbed by the intruders, but it did not always offer an asylum to the dispossessed people. Each little band of Bushmen had there its own hunting grounds, and resented intrusion upon them as much by individuals of kindred blood as by strangers. Then they were strongly attached to the localities in which they had lived from childhood, and in many instances preferred to die rather than abandon them. Still there were some who, under exceptional circumstances, made their way to localities far distant from the tracts they had lost, and established themselves anew on a wild mountain or an arid plain, dispossessing previous occupants as they had themselves been dispossessed of their former abode.

Such was the manner of the occupation of the South African coast by the Hottentots, and such were the effects of the invasion upon the earlier inhabitants.

The Hottentots termed themselves Khoikhoi, men of men, as they prided themselves upon their superiority over the savage hunters, and in fact they were considerably more advanced towards civilisation than the Bushmen, though a stranger at first sight might not have seen much difference in personal appearance between the two. A little observation, however, would have shown that the Bushmen were not only smaller and uglier, but that their faces were broader, their eyes not nearly as full and bright, their lobeless ears rounder in shape, and their chins less prominent. Their wild expression also was not observed in the Hottentot face.

The investigations of the late Dr. Bleek have shown that the languages of the two races were not only different in the words, except in such as were adopted by Hottentots from captive Bushman girls, but that they varied in construction. That of the Hottentots was of a high order, being of the same class as our own, and following grammatical rules as strictly as English does. Its vocabulary, however, was of a low type, as three-fourths of the syllabic elements began with clicks, though these sounds were not so extensively used as by Bushmen and did not vary so much, being only four in number. Further it was almost free of deep guttural or croaking sounds, except where there had been a large infusion of Bushman blood. Some words were composites, but most were monosyllables, as were all the roots, which invariably ended with a vowel. The sound of the liquid consonant *l* was wanting. In many instances the same monosyllabic word had different significations, according to the tone in which it was pronounced, when the context did not indicate its meaning. Thus !kaib pronounced in the lowest tone meant obscurity, pronounced in a medium tone meant a district or locality, and pronounced in the highest tone meant a particular article of clothing.*

* I am personally entirely unacquainted with the Hottentot language, and have taken the information upon it given here from Dr. Bleek's *Comparative Grammar of South African Languages*, *Eléments de la Grammaire Hottentote* by H. de Charencey, and *A Grammar and Vocabulary of the Namaqua-Hottentot Language* by the reverend Henry Tindall, Wesleyan missionary, a demi octavo volume published at Capetown in 1857. The first chapter of Dr. Theophilus Hahn's *Tsuni-||Goam, the Supreme Being of the Khoi-Khoi*, is exceedingly interesting in this respect, and his conclusions drawn from the structure of the language and its vocabulary fit in most accurately with the origin of the race and its migration from North-Eastern Africa as given in the preceding pages.

The nouns were divided into eight classes, three masculine in the singular, dual, and plural numbers, two feminine in the singular and plural numbers, and three common in the singular, dual, and plural numbers. The masculine denoted not only living creatures of the male sex, but whatever was large or prominent. The class was indicated by a suffixed letter, thus masculine *khoip* a man, feminine *khois* a woman, common *khoi* a person of either sex. There were three case forms : nominative, objective, and vocative, thus taras, a woman, was declined as follows :

	Singular	*Dual*	*Plural*
Nominative	taras	tarara	tarati
Objective	tarasa	tarara	tarati
Vocative	tarasi	tararo	taraso

The genitive or possessive and the dative were not formed by changes at the end of the noun itself, but by words corresponding to our prepositions, which, however, were placed after the noun, as the language did not admit of prefixes even of this kind.

The adjectives were as simple as in modern English, for they were not inflected to signify either gender, number, or case. They had the defect of not being changed in form to express degrees of comparison, and this had to be done in a roundabout way by the addition of other words less expressive than our more, most, less, least.

The system of notation was decimal, and was perfect at least up to a hundred, though it does not follow that every individual could count to high numbers. It was based upon counting by fingers, as is shown by the word for five meaning also the palm or full hand.

The personal pronouns were inflected for number and case, and except the first, *I*, for gender also.

The verb was as perfect as in any of the languages of Europe. Its root was the second person singular of the imperative mood, and its tenses were formed by means of an auxiliary. It had more forms than the English verb, as is shown by the following example : ordinary *mu* to see, relative *muba* to see for, reflective *musin* to see oneself, causative *mukci* to cause to see, reciprocal *muku* to see one another, diminutive *muro* to see a little, negative *mudama* not to see ; passive voice *muké* to be seen. It had all our moods and tenses. It was not inflected to express number or person, which were indicated by the noun or pronoun with which it was connected, just as in our common Cape Dutch.

Now here is a sex-denoting language of the same class as the languages of Europe and North Africa, and yet full of those primitive sounds called clicks. It forms a strong contrast to the speech of the Bantu in the same continent, though that is of a high order too. How can it have arisen ? There is only one way in which this can be satisfactorily explained, and that is by men of a light-coloured North African race consorting with women of Bushman blood. There is reason to believe that the men were more numerous than the women, as will be pointed out elsewhere, and therefore the form of their language was retained, while many Bushman words and the four Bushman clicks least difficult to pronounce were incorporated in it. In exactly the same manner, when the Amaxosa took modern Hottentot women to live with them, many Hottentot words and three of the Hottentot clicks were adopted, but the structure of the Xosa language underwent no change whatever. The new words were simply made to fall in grammatical line with those previously in use.

There were almost as many dialects as there were tribes, but these varied less than the forms of English spoken in different counties before the general diffusion of education from books. Towards the close of the seventeenth century an interpreter belonging to a tribe in the neighbourhood of the Cape peninsula, when accompanying Dutch trading parties, conversed without difficulty with even the most distant from his own home. This is a proof that the occupation of the country by these people and their spreading out along the coast must have been very recent. Unwritten languages change rapidly, especially in the vowel sounds, and tribes having no communication with each other, as for instance the Namaqua and the Gonaqua, in the course of only eight or ten generations would have developed differences greater than were found to exist. Another proof of their recent arrival is their acknowledgment down to the middle of the nineteenth century of the head of the Gei‖khauas as superior to all the other chiefs in rank, on account of his being the lineal representative of their ruling family when they crossed the Kunene river on their way southward.*

No difficulty has been experienced by European missionaries in reducing the Hottentot language to writing, and some religious literature has been printed in it. Words to express abstract ideas unknown before were formed from the roots of verbs and adjectives, and were at once understood by every one, just as meekness and meekly would be understood by any Englishman who had only heard the word meek used before. The reverend Mr. Waudres, Rhenish missionary in German Namaqualand, was kind enough to write to me how this is done. He says to the root of the verb or the adjective nothing more is necessary than to add the gender suffixes, and the word is at once understood. Thus, to the verb *gowa* to talk, if the masculine suffix *b* is added, the word *gowab* is obtained, which means language. If to the adjective *ama*, true, the same suffix is added, *amab* the truth is obtained.

The Hottentot language is now rapidly dying out, as the descendants of the people who once used it have long since learned to converse in Dutch, and by force of circumstances nearly all have forgotten their ancestral speech. A large admixture of blood—European, Asiatic, and particularly negro—that took place during the eighteenth and nineteenth centuries, contributed to this result, as well as the state of servitude to which many of these people were reduced. At the present day the language is only in common use by some of the Korana clans along the lower Vaal and Hart rivers and by some of the clans in German Namaqualand, and even they are year by year employing it less and less.

* The Gei‖khauas (the Cauquas of the early Dutch records) claim to be the oldest of the Hottentot tribes, and to be in a sense paramount over all the others. Dr. Theophilus Hahn asserts that this claim is well founded, and that it was recognised as correct by a clan of the Koranas not many years ago. The Gei‖khauas were living only two days' journey from Capetown at the close of the seventeenth century, but about 1811 as many of them as were left removed to Great Namaqualand to preserve their independence. They are the people who lived at Gobabis under the chief Amraal until his death in 1865, and later under the chief Andries Lambert.

The manner in which the various Hottentot tribes were formed has already been explained. They usually took their distinctive titles from the name of the chief under whose guidance they commenced to lead a separate existence, by adding to it the suffix qua, which signified those of or the people of, thus the Cochoqua were the people of Cocho, the Gonaqua the people of Gona. Sometimes, however, they called themselves after some animal, as the springbucks, the scorpions, or from some accidental circumstance, as the honey eaters, the sandal wearers. Many of the tribes consisted of several clans, more or less loosely joined together, though all tending to become independent in course of time. The tribes were almost constantly at war with each other, the object being to obtain possession of the cattle and girls of the opponent, and often the weaker ones were reduced to great poverty and distress. New combinations would then be formed, and the victors of one year frequently became the vanquished of the next. These internecine quarrels were not attended with much loss of life. There was never a slaughter of the whole of the conquered people, as was the case when a band of Bushmen was surrounded and overpowered.

Every tribe had its own hereditary chief, whose authority, however, was very limited, as his subjects were impatient of control. The succession was from father to son, and in the absence of a son to brother or nephew. The heads of clans not long formed recognised the supremacy in rank of the head of the community from which they had branched off, who was accounted the paramount chief, but unless he happened to be a man of more force of character than the others, he exercised no real power over them. The petty rulers, or heads of clans, were commonly jealous of each other, and only united their strength in cases of extreme danger to all. The government was thus particularly frail, and a very slight shock was sufficient to break any combination of the people into fragments. The powerful religious sentiment which binds the people of a Bantu tribe so strongly to their ruler was altogether wanting in a Hottentot community. The chief was not regarded as a divinity or the descendant of a divinity, but as a mere man like any of his followers. Riches commanded more respect than rank, and a man possessed of many cattle exercised as much influence as the nominal ruler, for the right of individuals to hold property apart from the community was recognised.

There were customs which had the same force as laws in civilised societies, and any one breaking them was subject to punishment. In such cases the whole of the adult males of the kraal discussed the matter and decided what was to be done, the chief, unless he happened to be a man of unusual strength of character, having little more to say than any one else. The moral code and the proportion of criminality ascribed to misdeeds were naturally very different from those of European nations.

The principal property of the Hottentots consisted of horned cattle and sheep, of which large numbers were possessed by some of the wealthiest tribes. They had great skill in training oxen to obey certain calls, as well as to carry burdens, and bulls were taught not only to assist in guarding the herds from robbers and beasts of prey, but to aid in war by charging the enemy on the field of battle. The milk of their cows was the chief article of their diet. It was preserved either in skin bags or in vessels made by hollowing a block of wood, and after coagulation formed healthy and nutritious food. The vessels used were commonly in a filthy state, as indeed was everything else in and about the huts, for in this respect the Hottentots were only slightly superior to Bushmen. They did not kill horned cattle for food, except on occasions of feasting, but they ate all that died a natural death.

Their usual method of cooking meat was to cut it in long strips, which were thrown upon embers and heated through, then one end was taken into the mouth, and it was gradually drawn in and devoured. The intestines of animals, after hardly any cleansing, were consumed in the same manner. Sometimes, however, flesh was boiled in clay pots, though it was not much relished in this way.

The ox of the Hottentot was an inferior animal to that of Europe. He was a gaunt, bony creature, with immense horns and long legs, but he was hardy and well adapted to supply the wants of his owner. He served instead of a horse for carrying burdens and for riding purposes, being guided by a riem or thong of raw hide attached to a piece of wood passed through the cartilage of his nose.

The sheep possessed by the Hottentots were covered with hair instead of wool, were of various colours, and had long lapping ears and tails three or four kilogrammes in weight. The tails were composed almost entirely of fat, which could be melted as easily as tallow, and which was relished as a dainty. Animals possessing such appendages were of course hardier than European sheep, and could exist much longer on scanty herbage in seasons of drought. The milk as well as the flesh was used for food. Children were taught to suck the ewes, and often derived their whole sustenance from this source.

The only other domestic animal was the dog. He was an ugly creature, his body being shaped like that of a jackal, and the hair on his spine being turned forward ; but he was a faithful, serviceable animal of his kind.

In addition to milk and the meat of oxen and sheep, of which they rejected no part except the gall, the food of the Hottentots consisted of the flesh of game obtained in the chase, locusts, and various kinds of wild plants and fruits. Agriculture, even in its simplest forms, was not practised by them. Like the Bushmen, they knew how to make an intoxicating drink of honey, of which large quantities were to be had in the season of flowers, and this they used to excess while it lasted. Like those savages also, they were acquainted with that powerful intoxicant, dacha or wild hemp, and whenever it was procurable they smoked it with a pipe made of the horn of an antelope. That its effects were pernicious was admitted by themselves, still they could not refrain from making use of it.

Their women were better clothed than those of the Bushmen, but the men were usually satisfied with very little covering, and had no sense of shame in appearing altogether naked. The dress of both sexes was made of skins, commonly prepared with the hair on. When removed from the animal, the skin was cleansed of any fleshy matter adhering to it, was then stretched and dried, and was afterwards rubbed with grease and worked between the hands till it became soft and pliable. The ordinary costume of a man was merely a piece of jackal skin suspended in front and a little slip of prepared hide behind. In cold weather he wrapped himself in a kaross or mantle of furs sewed together with sinews. The women wore at all times a headdress of fur, an under apron, and a wrapper or a girdle of leather strings suspended from the waist. In cold weather, or when carrying infants on their backs, they added a scanty kaross. Children wore no clothing whatever. Round their legs the females sewed strips of raw hide like rings, which, when dry, rattled against each other, and made a noise when they moved.

Both sexes ornamented their heads with copper trinkets, and hung round their necks strings of shells, leopards' teeth, or any glittering objects they could obtain. Ivory armlets were worn by the men. From earliest infancy their bodies were smeared with grease and rubbed over with clay, soot, or powdered buchu, and to this partly may be attributed the stench of their persons. The coat of grease and clay was not intended for ornament alone. It protected them from the weather and from the vermin that infested their huts and clothing.

Their dwellings were constructed by planting long pieces of supple undressed wood in the ground, and bending the upper ends inward, where they were attached by thongs to short pieces laid horizontally, so that the whole frame resembled approximately a rough hemisphere. Withes were then twisted round the structure and tied on outside, and the whole was covered with rush mats. The huts were so low that a tall man could not stand upright inside, and they had but one small opening through which the inmates crawled. In cold weather a fire was made in a cavity in the centre. The huts of a kraal were arranged in the form of a circle, the space enclosed being used as a fold for cattle. They could be taken to pieces, placed on pack-oxen, removed to a distance, and set up again, with very little labour and no waste. The furniture within them consisted merely of mats to sleep on, skins, weapons, cooking utensils, wooden milk dishes, and ostrich egg-shells used for carrying and containing water. Unlike the Bushman, who coiled himself to sleep on a little grass, the Hottentot stretched himself at full length on a mat in his hut.

A HOTTENTOT HUT.

(From a Drawing by William J. Burchell, Esqre.)

The weapons used by the Hottentots in war and the chase were bows and arrows, sticks with clubbed heads, and assagais. Mr. Stow asserts that at the time of their arrival in South Africa they were unacquainted with the use of poison, but if that be correct, they certainly acquired a knowledge of it shortly afterwards. It was not used by them so extensively, however, as by the Bushmen. The bow was larger and the arrow longer than those of the primitive inhabitants, still without poison the weapon would have been useless against large game. The assagai of the Hottentots was a light javelin, which could be hurled with precision to a distance of thirty or forty metres. The knobkerie, or clubbed stick, was almost as formidable a weapon. It was rather stouter than an ordinary walking cane, and had a round head six or eight centimetres in diameter. Boys were trained to throw this with so accurate an aim as to hit a bird on the wing at twenty or thirty metres' distance. It was projected in such a manner as to bring the heavy knob into contact with the object aimed at, and antelopes as large as goats had their legs broken or were killed outright with it.

The Hottentots were acquainted with the art of smelting iron, but were too indolent to turn their knowledge to much account. Only a few assagai and arrow heads were made of that metal. Horn and bone were ready at hand, were easily worked, and were commonly used to point weapons. Stone was also employed by some of the tribes for this purpose, but not to any great extent, though weights for digging-sticks were formed of it by them as by the Bushmen. Masses of almost solid copper were obtained in Namaqualand, and this metal was spread over the neighbouring country by means of barter and war, but was not used for any other purpose than that of making ornaments for the person.

At different places occupied by the Hottentots along the coast a very few polished stone implements have been found. They consist of arrow heads whose points have been ground, and disks like quoits with sharp edges, which are supposed to have been held in the hand and used in combat. No European has ever seen a Hottentot in possession of such implements, or ever heard them spoken of, and any remarks concerning them can only be founded on conjecture. But few as is the number of such ground stones as yet discovered, they are evidence that individuals, if not tribes, were in the neolithic stage of progress, though iron was in use at the same period.

The Hottentots manufactured earthenware pots for cooking purposes, which, though in general clumsily shaped and coarse in appearance, were capable of withstanding intense heat. This art was lost soon after Europeans came in contact with them and before observations upon their habits were made correctly and placed on record, so that it is only from specimens of their handiwork recently found that an opinion can be formed of the quality of such wares. Pots were useful at times, but were not much needed by people who seldom ate boiled food, nor were earthenware drinking vessels required where ox horns and ostrich egg-shells served that purpose. This may account for the small quantity and the coarse description of the utensils manufactured. Some of the pots found in recent shell heaps along the sea-shore have a number of holes neatly drilled in them, often near the bottom, probably in order to make them serve as strainers.

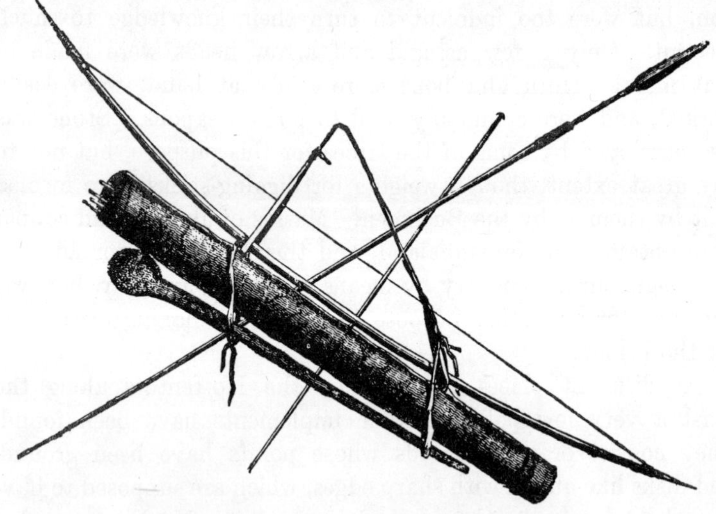

HOTTENTOT WEAPONS OF WAR AND THE CHASE.
(From a drawing by William J. Burchell, Esqre.)

CHAPTER IV.

The Hottentots or Khoikhoi (*continued*).

A few of the smallest and weakest clans of Hottentots who had lost their cattle in war or by disease, or who were the poorest members of tribes suffering from want, and had to abandon the communities to which they belonged and seek for means of existence elsewhere, lived chiefly upon the produce of the sea. They adopted from necessity the same means of obtaining a scanty supply of food as the earlier inhabitants who raised such enormous shell mounds as the one recently removed at East London had resorted to. They had neither boats nor hooks, but they managed to catch fish by throwing light assagais with lines attached to them from rocks standing out in deep water, and by making weirs in favourable situations along the shore enclosing considerable spaces which were left nearly dry at low tide. Shell-fish also formed a portion of their food, and occasionally a dead whale would drift ashore and furnish them with a feast. Further, they gathered all the edible plants in their neighbourhood, and captured as many wild animals as they could. Shell and ash heaps made by these people bearing signs of being quite modern, that is dating back only two or three hundred years, are found in several places along the coast from Walfish Bay to Natal.

The heaps contain ordinary Hottentot implements, in rare instances human skeletons, and bones of animals obtained in the chase, always broken in order that the marrow might be extracted. The perforated stone weights for digging-sticks found in them are usually of the shape of compressed spheres, nearly resembling in form those of Scotland referred to on a previous page. There is a good collection of specimens of various shapes and sizes in the South African museum in Capetown. It is supposed that the stones perforated by Hottentots were always of a distinct type from those drilled by Bushmen, but this is not certain, though as far as is known only spherical weights are picked up in tracts of country that were exclusively occupied by the aborigines, and compressed spheres wherever the later intruders or people connected with them lived, where also a few stones have been found that have first been perforated and then chipped into a convenient shape for use.

Hottentots, or it would be more correct to say mixed-breeds largely of Bushman blood who had been brought up at Hottentot kraals, who spoke the Hottentot language, and whose ideas and normal habits were those of Hottentots, were found living in the manner here indicated when Europeans first came to the country —one small band where Capetown now stands,—and on the coast of Namaqualand there were some existing in a similar state after the middle of the nineteenth century. As far as food, clothing, and lodging were concerned, they were in no better condition than the Bushmen who lived in a similar manner, though there was always the hope before them of acquiring cattle by a successful raid, in which case they would at once revert to the ordinary mode of living of the pastoral communities.

Only a few of the recent shell heaps on the South African coast, however, were made by Hottentot-speaking people. Much the greater number were made by Bushmen, as is proved by the articles found in them and by the paintings on rocks in their neighbourhood ; and these may be taken as forming a connected series with the most ancient mounds. A painting is the most positive evidence of the locality having been occupied by Bushmen, as the Hottentots did not practise that art, and the captives of the wild race living with them, being females only, could not introduce it.

The Hottentots, as observed before, did not form a continuous line of settlement, but a series of dots, frequently far apart, and between these stations Bushmen still lived, though the enmity between the two races was so strong that they were constantly seeking to destroy each other. This will account for shell mounds being formed by both people at the same time. But in point of fact those destitute Hottentots who lived as beachrangers, as the first European colonists termed them, in all probability had more Bushman than pure Khoikhoi blood in their veins, though they would have resented being termed Sana,* just as a mulatto prides himself upon his descent from a white man, and resents being termed a negro. In a pastoral clan the children of captive Bushman girls would be regarded as illegitimate, and would not inherit cattle from their fathers. The daughters of the next generation by Khoikhoi fathers might, and most likely did, occupy a better position, but the sons would remain paupers and dependents of some wealthy man. When fresh captives were made, their blood would become mixed with that of the half-breeds, and thus there would be men and women of only one-fourth Khoikhoi descent, and yet Khoikhoi in language, ideas, and habits.

This process having gone on for many generations, there must have been a mixture of blood in various proportions in the individual members of a clan. A raid would be made on a neighbouring tribe, and a herd of cattle would be secured, of which some of the mixed-breeds would obtain a share, when they would at once assume the position of honourable men and acquire all the rights of the purest Khoikhoi. But in the vanquished tribe there would be a similar class of mixed-breeds, and now that meat and milk had become so scarce that there was not sufficient food to keep all alive, the poorest of them would be compelled to separate from the others, and to seek subsistence along the shore until such time as chance placed an opportunity in their way of obtaining horned cattle or sheep by plunder. Their condition was more abject than that of pure Bushmen, who greatly excelled them as hunters, but as far as wild plants went, there was as great a quantity and as large a variety along the ocean shore as anywhere inland.

* Dr. Theophilus Hahn explained this word, not as a proper name, but as applied by the Hottentots to the Bushmen because it meant inhabitants or, as we should say, aborigines. The Hottentots often used opprobrious epithets when speaking of the wild people, but commonly called them by this name Sana.

The Hottentots were a superstitious people who placed great faith in the efficacy of charms to ward off evil. They even besought favours from certain pieces of root so used, and if their wishes were successful, they praised and thanked the charms. This superstition might in time have developed into idolatry, but it was arrested before it reached that stage. They believed that certain occurrences foreboded good or ill luck, and were always on the watch for omens. Their veneration of the mantis, an insect that bears so close a resemblance either to a withered leaf or to a dry stalk of grass that its presence cannot be detected except when it is in motion, has been asserted by many writers, some of whom have even termed it the Hottentot God, but it has been called in question by others. The reason of this contradiction is that their notions regarding the insect were acquired from their Bushman female captives, who had been taught by their parents that it was endowed with the power of exchanging its form for that of any other animal, and that it could confer good or bad fortune upon human beings. Clans in which Bushman blood was strong would therefore venerate the mantis, and others would pay little or no regard to it.

They lived in dread of ghosts and evil spirits, but with no more conception of the nature of such shadowy beings, or of the mode of receiving harm, than little children have. They invoked blessings from the moon, the harbinger of their festivities, to whose praise they sang and danced when it appeared as new. In later times those who had come in contact with Bantu prayed for blessings from dead ancestors, to whose shades sacrifices were offered by priests on important occasions, but this was evidently a custom of foreign origin. Generally they implored protection and favour from a mythical hero named Tsui‖goab or Heitsi-eibib, who was believed by them to have lived on the earth and to have died and risen again many times, and whose worship consisted in throwing a branch of a tree, a bit of wood, or an additional stone upon a cairn at a place where he was supposed to have been once buried. Tales of the wonderful deeds of this Heitsi-eibib were commonly narrated by old men, and were implicitly believed by every one who heard them.

All the actions ascribed to him were those of a man, but of one endowed with supernatural power.

Thus he was said on one occasion to have been pursued by an enemy, and with his family and his followers to have come to a large river. He said, " my grandfather's father, separate thyself that we may pass through, and close thyself afterwards." The river did so. Heitsi-eibib and his people passed through in safety, and when the enemy followed them, the river closed again and they were all drowned. This tale may seem to have had its origin in the teaching of missionaries, but it has been obtained from so many sources, some of which were never directly or indirectly under missionary influence, that it is beyond doubt original.

Another of the tales related of Heitsi-eibib is as follows : ‡Gā‡gorib sat by a large hole in the ground, and when people passed by he told them to throw a stone at his forehead. When they did this, the stone rebounded and stunned them, and they fell into the hole and died. Heitsi-eibib heard of this, so he went to the place, and ‡Gā‡gorib challenged him to throw a stone. He declined to do so, and they then began to chase each other round the hole, sayi " Push Heitsi-eibib down ! Push ‡Gā‡gorib down ! Push Heitsi-eibib down ! Push ‡Gā‡gorib down ! " At last Heitsi-eibib was pushed down, but he said " my grandfather's father, raise up thy bottom and let me out." The hole did so, and he came out. They began to chase each other round it again, saying " Push Heitsi-eibib down ! Push ‡Gā‡gorib down ! Push Heitsi-eibib down ! Push ‡Gā‡gorib down ! " and Heitsi-eibib was thrown in the second time. He said " my grandfather's father, raise up thy bottom and let me out." The hole did so. This happened many times, but at last when ‡Gā‡gorib was looking on one side, Heitsi-eibib struck him behind the ear and stunned him, so that he fell into the hole and could not get out again. From that time onward the people had rest, because ‡Gā‡gorib was conquered.

Still another of these tales is given, as it records one of the deaths of Heitsi-eibib, and of his coming to life again. It is in the words of the reverend G. Krönlein, as translated by him from the Nama original.

When Heitsi-eibib was travelling about with his family, they came to a valley in which the raisin-tree * was ripe, and he was there attacked by a severe illness. Then his young (second) wife said, " this brave one is taken ill on account of these raisins ; death is here at the place." The old man (Heitsi-eibib), however, told his son !Urisib (the whitish one), " I shall not live, I feel it ; thou must, therefore, cover me when I am dead with soft stones." And he spoke further, " this is the thing which I order you to do : of the raisin-trees of this valley you shall not eat, for if you eat of them I shall infect you, and you will surely die in a similar way."

His young wife said, " he is taken ill on account of the raisins of this valley. Let us bury him quickly, and let us go."

So he died there, and was covered flatly with soft stones according as he had commanded. Then they went away from him.

When they had moved to another place, and were unpacking there, they heard always from the side whence they came a noise as of people eating raisins and singing. In this manner the eating and singing ran :

> "I, father of !Urisib,
> Father of this unclean one,
> I, who had to eat the raisins, and died,
> And dying live."

The young wife perceived that the noise came from the side where the old man's grave was, and said, " !Urisib, go and look." Then the son went to the old man's grave, where he saw traces which he recognised to be his father's footmarks, and returned home. Then the young wife said, " it is he alone, therefore act thus :

> Do so to the man who ate raisins on the windward side,
> Take care of the wind that thou creepest upon him from the leeward ;
> Then intercept him on his way to the grave,
> And when thou hast caught him, do not let him go."

---

* A particular kind of tree in Namaqualand bearing a shrivelled wild fruit, for which Mr. Krönlein could think of no more appropriate name than the raisin-tree. I am unacquainted with it.

He did accordingly, and they came between the grave and Heitsi-eibib, who, when he saw this, jumped down from the raisin-tree, and ran quickly, but was caught at the grave. Then he said, " let me go, for I am a man who has been dead, that I may not infect you." But the young wife said, " keep hold of the rogue."

So they brought him home, and from that day he was fresh and hale.

Dr. Theophilus Hahn, the son of a missionary, who spent his youth among the Namaqua and learned to speak their language as soon as he did that of his parents, in his *Tsuni-‖Goam, the Supreme Being of the Khoikhoi,* published in London in 1881, states that the Namaqua believe Tsui-‖Goab, or Heitsi-eibib as otherwise called, to be a powerful and beneficent being, who lives in the red sky. There is also a powerful evil being, named ‖Gaunab,* who lives in the black sky and does harm to men, who on that account fear and worship him. In a series of combats with ‖Gaunab, Tsui-‖Goab was repeatedly overcome, but after every struggle grew stronger, till at last he killed ‖Gaunab by a blow behind the ear. He was, however, wounded in the knee, and has been lame ever since, whence his name, the wounded knee. At early dawn the Namaqua look towards the east, and implore blessings from him.

Dr. Hahn asserts his belief that this myth originated in the apparent conflict between light and darkness at dawn, and he gives the reasons that led him to this conclusion, which are mainly philological. If this be correct, the myth had an origin as lofty in ideal as that of many of the Aryans, but other inquirers are inclined to attribute it to the existence of some prominent man in olden time, whose exploits became magnified and distorted in legends. As they believe the moon dies and comes to life again, they may very easily have imagined this great man of their race to have done the same, or the deeds of different individuals at different times may have become blended under one name, as in some Bantu traditions.

---

* This is evidently another version of Heitsi-eibib and ‡Gã‡Gorib, cast in a more poetical mould.

Tsui-‖goab was also believed to have been the ancestor of the whole Hottentot race, and likewise to be the moon, for these people, with childlike simplicity, could not comprehend that such various suppositions were incapable of being reconciled with each other. In the corrupted form of Utixo, the first Protestant missionaries to the Bantu used the word Tsui-‖goab to signify God, and it is so employed to the present day.

Many cairns of considerable size, formed of small stones capable of being carried by one individual, have been found in various parts of South Africa, but only a few of these were raised by Hottentots at places where they supposed Heitsi-eibib to have been buried. The Bushmen erected cairns over some of their dead, and it is not unlikely that the Hottentots merely enlarged such of these as they found where they settled. Some of the Bantu also erected cairns over the bodies of their chiefs, but these are more massive and are well known, so that they cannot be confused with the graves of Heitsi-eibib. The adding a stone to such a heap, at first regarded merely as a mark of respect to the dead who lay there, might easily in course of time come to be considered as an act of worship.

The system of religion of the Hottentots could not be explained by themselves, what they understood being little more than that the customs connected with it had come down to them from their ancestors. They had not the faintest expectation of their own resurrection, or conception of a heaven or a hell. Sacred days or seasons were unknown to them, and if the graves of Heitsi-eibib be excepted, no places were set apart for worship of any kind.

A more improvident, unstable, thoughtless people never existed. Those among them who had cattle were without care or grief, and usually spent the greater part of the day in sleeping. They delighted, however, in dancing by moonlight to music, which they produced from reeds similar to those used by the Bushmen, but superior in tone and effect. Active in this exercise and in hunting, in all other respects they were extremely indolent. The labour of collecting wild plants and of building and removing huts was performed by the women. Their filthiness of person, clothing, and habitation was disgusting. They enjoyed eating food that would have turned the stomach of the least delicate of Europeans, for the sense of smelling with them—as with all people of a low type—was extremely dull. Still they were not without good qualities. Their tempers were in general mild; and their hospitality to peaceable strangers as well as to individuals of their own clan was unbounded. Even in the direst extremity of famine, cannibalism was never resorted to by people of their race.

They were in the habit of abandoning aged and helpless persons as well as sickly and deformed children, whom they allowed to perish of hunger. But they regarded this as mercy, not as cruelty. Better that a helpless wretch or a cripple should give up life at once than linger on in misery. For the same reason, when a woman giving suck died, the child was buried with its dead parent.

The Hottentots were polygamous in the sense that their customs admitted of a wealthy man having more wives than one, but the practice was by no means general. There were many kraals in which there was not a single case of polygamy. It was customary with them to take their wives not from their own but from another clan. The marriage customs required that cattle should be given by the bridegroom to the nearest relatives of the bride, but temporary unions were common, and indeed a system almost as bad as that of free love prevailed, for chastity on both sides was very lightly regarded. One of the principal objects in their wars with each other was to take females as prisoners, who were generally regarded as mere concubines, but were sometimes raised to the dignity of wives. The difference from a European point of view may seem obscure, but it involved a right over the distribution of the milk, and upon it depended the inheritance of the children. Female captives of Bushman blood occupied the lower position. There was no religious or moral scruple in operation against conduct of this kind, for they had no idea that it was in any way wrong. It was simply the natural right of the strong to take from the weak.

The women—excepting of course such captives as have been described—were more nearly the equals of the men, and were permitted to exercise much greater freedom of speech in domestic disputes, than among most barbarians. They were mistresses within the huts. The stores of milk were under their control, not under that of their husbands, as was the case with the Bantu. The men or their sons tended the cattle, but their daughters milked the cows.

Wherever men greatly preponderate in number over women, the females will enjoy extensive privileges, and if this is the case when a new nation is being formed, the custom regarding those privileges will become fixed. No census having ever been taken of these people in olden times, it is impossible to ascertain what the proportion of the sexes was where Europeans first became acquainted with them ; at present when the race is still comparatively pure they are believed to be about equal. They are not so prolific as white people, and very much less so than the Bushmen were or the Bantu are now. The probabilities are great that at the time of the origin of the race the females were few in number compared with the males who entered their country and induced or forced them to become consorts. Savages as those females were, they were yet able under these circumstances to occupy a position of influence in the household, which their descendants of the same sex never lost. Dr. Hahn says of them :

" All the Khoikhoi tribes use the expression *Taras* for woman. Taras is the woman, as ruler of the house, the mistress. The root *da* or *ta* means to conquer, to rule, to master, and the suffix *ra* expresses a custom or an intrinsic peculiarity. Taras is also a woman of rank, *a lady*. In every Khoikhoi's house the woman, or *taras*, is *the supreme ruler ;* the husband has nothing at all to say. While in public the men take the prominent part, at home they have not so much power even as to take a mouthful of sour milk out of the tub, without the wife's permission. In the house the wife always occupies the right side of the husband and the right side of the house.

" If a chief died, it often happened that his energetic wife became the gau-tas (contracted from gautaras), the ruling woman

PORTRAIT OF THE FAMOUS HOTTENTOT CHIEF JAN JONKER AFRIKANER,
IN EUROPEAN DRESS.
(*From a Photograph in the South African Public Library.*)

[*To face p.* 86.

—*i.e.* the queen of the tribe—in place of the son who was not of age. All the daughters are called after the father and all the sons after the mother. The eldest daughter was highly respected ; to her was entirely left the milking of the cows. This was in accordance with the respect shown to the female sex in general. There is a nice charming little song illustrating this :

> " My lioness !
> Art thou afraid that I will bewitch thee ?
> Thou milkest the cow with a fleshy hand (*i.e.* with a soft hand).
> Bite me ! (*i.e.* kiss me !)
> Pour for me (milk) !
> My lioness,
> Great man's daughter.

" The uncle always calls his niece, the brother's or sister's daughter, ' my lioness.'

" The highest oath a man could take, and still takes, was to swear by his eldest sister. A man can never address his own sister personally ; he must speak to another person to address the sister in his name, or in the absence of anybody, he says so that his sister can hear, ' I wish that somebody will tell my sister that I wish to have a drink of milk,' &c. The eldest sister can even inflict punishment on a grown-up brother, if he omits the established traditionary rules of courtesy and the code of etiquette."

Among some—not all—of the Hottentot clans there was a custom which, though described by many early observers, was regarded by most writers of the nineteenth century without sufficient investigation as so utterly incredible that they did not notice it. Yet it is practised at the present day by people who are certainly not of Hottentot blood, but who must have derived their language as well as many of their customs from Hottentot conquerors in bygone times. It stands to them in the same relation that circumcision does to many Bantu clans, that is, among them a youth cannot enter the society of men or take to himself a wife until he has become a *monorch* (μόνορχις). A custom so extraordinary shows what force habit and superstition have among barbarians.

With all their degrading habits, the Hottentots possessed large powers of imagination. They speculated upon objects in nature in a way that no Bantu ever did, and their ideas on these subjects, though seemingly absurd, at least bore evidence of a disposition to think. They had names for many stars and groups of stars, which they believed to be endowed with life. They were excellent story-tellers. Seated round fires of an evening, they repeated tales of the doings of men and of animals—usually the baboon or the jackal—which produced boundless mirth. These stories often contained coarse and obscene expressions, or what Europeans would regard as such, but their sense of delicacy in these matters was naturally low.

The first of the tales given here is one which with slight variants is told by Hottentots wherever they live in South Africa. It was taken down and translated by the late Mr. Thomas Bain, and was first published in the *Folklore Journal* of July 1879. The second is taken from the late Dr. Bleek's *Reynard the Fox in South Africa or Hottentot Fables and Tales*, published in London in 1864. It was taken down by the reverend G. Krönlein, Rhenish missionary in Great Namaqualand, from narrators in the Nama dialect, and with many songs, proverbs, and other tales was presented by him to the Grey Library in Capetown, where it was translated into English by Dr. Bleek. The last two were collected with many others by myself from people of the Xosa tribe between 1860 and 1879. The Xosas are of mixed Bantu and Hottentot descent, and the Hottentot women who during the seventeenth and eighteenth centuries were forced to become the consorts of Bantu men must have introduced these stories, for they are not current among pure Bantu elsewhere. They have a very slight Bantu colouring, but not more than the English colouring of the first and second, unavoidably due to translation from the language in which they were originally told.

The Animals and the Dam of Water.

There was a great drought in the land, and the lion called together a number of animals, that they might devise a plan for retaining water when the rains fell. The animals which attended to the lion's summons were the baboon, the leopard, the hyena, the jackal, the hare, and the mountain tortoise. It was agreed that they should scratch a large hole in some suitable place to hold water ; and the next day they all began to work, with the exception of the jackal, who continually hovered about in that locality, and was overheard to mutter that *he* was not going to scratch his nails off in making water-holes.

When the dam was finished, the rains fell, and it was soon filled with water, to the great delight of those who had worked so hard at it. The first one, however, to come and drink there was the jackal, who not only drank, but filled his clay pot with water, and then proceeded to swim in the rest of the water, making it as muddy and dirty as he could. This was brought to the knowledge of the lion, who was very angry, and ordered the baboon to guard the water the next day, armed with a huge knobkerie. The baboon was concealed in a bush close to the water ; but the jackal soon became aware of his presence there, and guessed its cause. Knowing the fondness of baboons for honey, the jackal at once hit upon a plan, and marching to and fro, every now and then dipped his fingers into his clay pot, and licked them with an expression of intense relish, saying in a low voice to himself, " I don't want any of their dirty water when I have a pot full of delicious honey." This was too much for the poor baboon, whose mouth began to water. He soon began to beg the jackal to give him a little honey, as he had been watching a long time and was very hungry and tired.

After taking no notice of the baboon at first, the jackal looked round, and said in a patronising manner that he pitied such an unfortunate creature, and would give him some honey on certain conditions, viz. that the baboon should give up his knobkerie and allow himself to be bound. He foolishly agreed, and was soon tied in such a manner that he could not move hand or foot. The jackal now proceeded to drink of the water, to fill his pot, and to swim, in the sight of the baboon, from time to time telling him what a foolish fellow he had been to be so easily duped, and that he (the jackal) had no honey or anything else to give him, excepting a good blow on the head every now and then with his own knobkerie. The animals soon appeared, and found the poor baboon in this sorry plight, looking very miserable. The lion was so exasperated that he caused the baboon to be severely punished and to be denounced as a fool.

The tortoise hereupon stepped forward and offered his services for the capture of the jackal. It was at first thought that he was merely joking, but when he explained in what manner he proposed to catch him, his plan was considered so feasible that his offer was accepted. He proposed that a thick coating of the sticky black substance found on beehives should be spread all over him, and that he should then go and stand at the entrance of the dam, on the water level, so that the jackal might tread upon him and stick fast. This was accordingly done, and the tortoise posted there.

The next day, when the jackal came, he approached the water very cautiously, and wondered to find no one there. He then ventured to the entrance of the water, and remarked how kind they had been in placing there a large black stepping-stone for him. As soon, however, as he trod upon the supposed stone he stuck fast, and saw that he had been tricked, for the tortoise now put his head out and began to move. The jackal's hind feet being still free, he threatened to smash the tortoise with them if he did not let him go. The tortoise merely answered, " Do as you like." The jackal thereupon made a violent jump, and found with horror that his hind feet were now also fast. " Tortoise," said he, " I have still my mouth and teeth left, and will eat you alive if you do not let me go." " Do as you like," the tortoise again replied. The jackal, in his endeavours to free himself, at last made a desperate bite at the tortoise, and found himself fixed both head and feet. The tortoise, feeling proud of his successful capture, now marched quietly up to the top of the bank with the jackal on his back, so that he could easily be seen by the animals as they came to the water. They were indeed astonished to find how cleverly the crafty jackal had been caught, and the tortoise was much praised, while the unhappy baboon was again reminded of his misconduct when set to guard the water.

The jackal was at once condemned to death by the lion, and the hyena was to execute the sentence. The jackal pleaded hard for mercy, but finding this useless he made a last request to the lion (always, as he said, so fair and just in his dealings) that he should not have to suffer a lingering death. The lion inquired of him in what manner he wished to die ; and he asked that his tail might be shaved and rubbed with a little fat, and that the hyena might then swing him round twice and dash his brains out upon a stone. This being considered sufficiently fair by the lion, was ordered by him to be carried out in his presence. When the jackal's tail had been shaved and greased, the hyena caught hold of him with great force, but before he had fairly lifted him from the ground, the cunning jackal had slipped away from his grasp and was running for his life, pursued by all the animals. The lion was the foremost pursuer, and after a great chase the jackal got under an overhanging precipice, and standing on his hind legs with his shoulders pressed against the rock, called loudly to the lion to help him, as the rock was falling and would crush them both. The lion put his shoulders to the rock, and exerted himself to the utmost. After some little time the jackal proposed that he should creep slowly out, and fetch a large pole to prop up the rock, so that the lion could get out and save his life. The jackal did creep out, and left the lion there to starve and die.

The Lion that took a Woman's Shape.

Some women, it is said, went out to seek roots and herbs and other wild food. On their way home they sat down and said, "let us taste the food of the field." Now they found that the food picked by one of them was sweet, while that of the others was bitter. The latter said to each other, "look here! this woman's herbs are sweet." Then they said to the owner of the sweet food, "throw it away and seek for other." So she threw away the food, and went to gather more. When she had collected a sufficient supply, she returned to join the other women, but could not find them. She went therefore down to the river, where the hare sat lading water, and said to him, "hare, give me some water that I may drink." But he replied, "this is the cup out of which my uncle (the lion) and I alone may drink."

She asked again : "hare, draw water for me that I may drink." But the hare made the same reply. Then she snatched the cup from him and drank, but he ran home to tell his uncle of the outrage which had been committed. The woman meanwhile replaced the cup and went away. After she departed the lion came down, and, seeing her in the distance, pursued her on the path. When she turned round and saw him coming, she sang in the following manner :

> My mother, she would not let me seek herbs,
> Herbs of the field, food from the field. Hoo !

When the lion at last came up with the woman, they hunted each other round a shrub. She wore many beads and armrings, and the lion said, "let me put them on." So she lent them to him, but he afterwards refused to restore them to her. Then they hunted each other again round the shrub, till the lion fell down, and the woman jumped upon him and kept him there. The lion said :

> "My aunt ! it is morning, and time to rise ;
> Pray rise from me ! "

She then rose from him, and they hunted again after each other round the shrub, till the woman fell down, and the lion jumped upon her. She then addressed him :

> "My uncle ! it is morning, and time to rise ;
> Pray rise from me ! "

He rose, and they hunted each other again, till the lion fell a second time. When she jumped upon him, he said :

> "My aunt ! it is morning, and time to rise ;
> Pray rise from me ! "

They rose again and hunted after each other. The woman at last fell down. But this time, when she repeated the above conjuration, the lion said :

> "He kha ! *Is* it morning, and time to rise ? "

He then ate her, taking care, however, to leave her skin whole, which he put on, together with her dress and ornaments, so that he looked quite like a woman, and then went home to her kraal.

When this counterfeit woman arrived, her little sister, crying, said, " my sister, pour some milk out for me." She answered, " I shall not pour you out any." Then the child addressed the mother : " Mama, do pour out some for me." The mother of the kraal said, " go to your sister, and let her give it to you." The little child said again to her sister, " please pour out for me ! " She, however, repeated her refusal, saying, " I will not do it." Then the mother of the kraal said to the little one, " I refused to let her (the elder sister) seek herbs in the field, and I do not know what may have happened ; go therefore to the hare, and ask him to pour out for you."

So the hare gave her some milk ; but her elder sister said, "come and share it with me." The little child then went to her sister with her bamboo (cup), and they both sucked the milk out of it. Whilst they were doing this, some milk was spilt on the little one's hand, and the elder sister licked it up with her tongue, the roughness of which drew blood ; this, too, the woman licked up. The little child complained to her mother : "Mama, sister pricks holes in me, and sucks the blood." The mother said, " with what lion's nature your sister went the way that I forbade her, and returned, I do not know."

Now the cows arrived, and the elder sister cleansed the pails in order to milk them. But when she approached the cows with a thong (in order to tie their fore legs), they all refused to be milked by her. The hare said, " why do you not stand before the cow ? " She replied, " hare, call your brother, and do you two stand before the cow." Her husband said, " what has come over her that the cows refuse her ? these are the same cows she always milks." The mother (of the kraal) said, " what has happened this evening ? These are cows which she always milks without assistance. What can have affected her that she comes home as a woman with a lion's nature ? "

The elder daughter then said to her mother, " I shall not milk the cows." With these words she sat down. The mother said therefore to the hare, " bring me the bamboos that I may milk. I do not know what has come over the girl." So the mother herself milked the cows, and when she had done so, the hare brought the bamboos to the young wife's house, where her husband was, but she (the wife) did not give him (her husband) anything to eat. But when at night time she fell asleep, they saw some of the lion's hair, which was hanging out when he had slipped on the woman's skin, and they cried, " verily, this is quite another being. It is for this reason that the cows refused to be milked."

Then the people of the kraal began to break up the hut in which the lion lay asleep. When they took off the mats, they said (conjuring them), " if thou art favourably inclined to me, o mat, give the sound *sawa* " (meaning making no noise). To the poles they said, " if thou art favourably inclined to me, o pole, thou must give the sound ‡*gara*." They addressed also the bamboos in a similar manner.

Thus gradually and noiselessly they removed the hut and all its contents. Then they took bunches of grass, put them over the lion, and lighting them, said, " if thou art favourably inclined to me, o fire, thou must flare up, *boo boo*, before thou comest to the heart." So the fire flared up when it came towards the heart, and the heart of the woman jumped upon the ground. The mother (of the kraal) picked it up, and put it into a calabash. The lion, from his place in the fire, said to the mother (of the kraal), " how nicely I have eaten your daughter." The woman answered, " you have also now a comfortable place."

Now the woman took the first milk of as many cows as calved, and put it into the calabash where her daughter's heart was ; the calabash increased in size, and in proportion to this the girl grew again inside it.

One day, when the mother (of the kraal) went out to fetch wood, she said to the hare, " by the time that I come back you must have everything nice and clean." But during her mother's absence, the girl crept out of the calabash, and put the hut in good order, as she had been used to do in former days, and said to the hare, " when mother comes back and asks who has done these things, you must say, I, the hare, did them." After she had done all, she hid herself.

When the mother (of the kraal) came home, she said, " hare, who has done these things ? they look just as they used to when my daughter did them." The hare said, " I did the things." But the mother would not believe it, and looked at the calabash. Seeing it was empty, she searched and found her daughter. Then she embraced and kissed her, and from that day the girl stayed with her mother, and did everything as she was wont in former times ; but she now remained unmarried.

Story of the Hare.

Once upon a time the animals made a kraal and put some fat in it. They agreed that one of their number should remain to be the keeper of the gate. The first one that was appointed was the coney. He agreed to take charge, and all the others went away. In a short time the coney fell asleep, when the inkalimeva (a fabulous animal) went in and ate all the fat. After doing this, he threw a little stone at the coney.

The coney started up and cried out: "the fat belonging to all the animals has been eaten by the inkalimeva." It repeated this cry several times, calling out very loudly. The animals at a distance heard it, they ran to the kraal, and when they saw that the fat was gone they killed the coney.

They put fat in the kraal a second time, and appointed the muishond to keep the gate. The muishond consented, and the animals went away as before. After a little time the inkalimeva came to the kraal, bringing some honey with it. It invited the keeper of the gate to eat honey, and while the muishond was enjoying himself the inkalimeva went in and stole all the fat. It threw a stone at the muishond, which made him look up. The muishond cried out: "the fat belonging to all the animals has been eaten by the inkalimeva." As soon as the animals heard the cry, they ran to the kraal and killed the muishond.

They put fat in the kraal a third time, and appointed the duiker to be the keeper of the gate. The duiker agreed, and the others went away. In a short time the inkalimeva made its appearance. It proposed to the duiker that they should play at hide and seek. The duiker agreed to this. Then the inkalimeva hid itself, and the duiker looked for it till he was so tired that he lay down and went to sleep. When the duiker was asleep, the inkalimeva ate up all the fat. Then it threw a stone at the duiker, which caused him to jump up and cry out: "the fat belonging to all the animals has been eaten by the inkalimeva." The animals, when they heard the cry, ran to the kraal and killed the duiker.

They put fat in the kraal the fourth time, and appointed the bluebuck to be the keeper of the gate. When the animals went away, the inkalimeva came as before. It said: "what are you doing by yourself?" The bluebuck answered: "I am watching the fat belonging to all the animals." The inkalimeva said: "I will be your companion, come, let us sit down and scratch each other's heads." The bluebuck agreed to this. The inkalimeva sat down; it scratched the head of the other till he went to sleep. Then it arose and ate all the fat. When it had finished, it threw a stone at the bluebuck and awoke him. The bluebuck saw what had happened, and cried out: "the fat belonging to all the animals has been eaten by the inkalimeva." Then the animals ran up and killed the bluebuck also.

They put fat in the kraal the fifth time, and appointed the porcupine to be the keeper of the gate. The animals went away, and the inkalimeva came as before. It said to the porcupine: "let us run a race against each other." It let the porcupine beat in this race. Then it said: "I did not think you could run so fast, but let us try again." They ran again, and it allowed the porcupine to beat the second time. They ran till the porcupine was so tired that he said: "let us rest now." They sat down to rest, and the porcupine went to sleep. Then the inkalimeva rose up and ate all the fat. When it had finished eating, it threw a stone at the porcupine, which caused him to jump up. He called out with a loud voice: "the fat belonging to all the animals has been eaten by the inkalimeva." Then the animals came running up, and put the porcupine to death.

They put fat in the kraal the sixth time, and selected the hare to be the keeper of the gate. At first the hare would not consent. He said: "the coney is dead, and the muishond is dead, and the duiker is dead, and the bluebuck is dead, and the porcupine is dead, and you will kill me also." They promised him that they would not kill him, and after a good deal of persuasion he at last agreed to keep the gate.

When the animals were gone he laid himself down, but he only pretended to be asleep. In a short time the inkalimeva went in, and was just going to take the fat when the hare cried out: "let the fat alone." The inkalimeva said: "please let me have this little bit only." The hare answered, mocking: "please let me have this little bit only."

After that they became companions. The hare proposed that they should fasten each other's tails, and the inkalimeva agreed. The inkalimeva fastened the tail of the hare first. The hare said: "don't tie my tail so tight." Then the hare fastened the tail of the inkalimeva. The inkalimeva said: "don't tie my tail so tight;" but the hare made no answer. After tying the tail of the inkalimeva very fast, the hare took his club and killed it. The hare took the tail of the inkalimeva and ate it, all except a little piece which he hid in the fence. Then he called out: "the fat belonging to all the animals has been eaten by the inkalimeva."

The animals came running back, and when they saw that the inkalimeva was dead they rejoiced greatly. They asked the hare for the tail, which should be kept for the chief. The hare replied : " the one I killed had no tail." They said : " how can an inkalimeva be without a tail ? " They began to search, and at length they found a piece of the tail in the fence. They told the chief that the hare had eaten the tail. He said : " bring him to me." All the animals ran after the hare, but he fled, and they could not catch him. The hare ran into a hole, at the mouth of which the animals set a snare, and then went away. The hare remained in the hole many days, but at length he managed to get out without being caught.

He went to a place where he found a bushbuck building a hut. There was a pot on the fire with meat in it. He said to the bushbuck : " can I take this little piece of meat ? " The bushbuck answered : " you must not do it." But he took the meat and ate it all. After that he whistled a particular tune, and there fell a storm of hail which killed the bushbuck. Then he took the skin of the bushbuck, and made for himself a mantle.

After this the hare went into the forest to get for himself some weapons to fight with. While he was cutting a stick the monkeys threw leaves upon him. He called to them to come down and beat him. They came down, but he killed them all with his weapons.

THE LION AND THE JACKAL.

Little Jackal one day went out hunting, when he met a Lion. The lion proposed that they should hunt together, on condition that if a small antelope was killed it was to be the jackal's, and if a large one was killed it was to be the lion's. The jackal agreed to this. The first animal killed was a large eland. The lion was very glad, and said to the jackal : " I will continue hunting while you go to my house and call my children to carry the meat home." The jackal replied : " yes, I agree to that." The lion went away to hunt. When he had gone, the jackal went to his own house and called his own children to carry away the meat. He said : " lion takes me for a fool if he thinks I will call his children while my own are dying with hunger." So the jackal's children carried the meat to their home on the top of a high rock. The only way to get to their house was by means of a rope.

The lion caught nothing more, and after a time he went home and asked his wife where the meat was. She told him there was no meat. He said : "did not Little Jackal bring a message to my children to carry meat ?" His wife replied : "no, he has not been here. We are still dying with hunger."

The lion then went to the jackal's house, but he could not get up the rock to it, so he sat down by the water and waited. After a time the jackal came to get water. He was close to the water when he saw the lion. He at once ran away, and the lion ran after him. He ran into a hole under a tree, but the lion caught his tail before he got far in. He said to him : "that is not my tail you have hold of, it is a root of the tree. If you do not believe me, take a stone and strike it, and see if any blood comes." The lion let go the tail, and went for a stone to prove what it was. While he was gone for the stone, Little Jackal went far into the hole. When the lion returned, he could not be found, so the lion lay down by the hole and waited. After a long time Little Jackal wanted to come out. He went to the entrance and looked round, but he could not see the lion. To make sure, he said : "ho ! I see you, my master, although you are in hiding." The lion did not move from the place where he lay concealed. Then Little Jackal went out, and the lion pursued him, but he got away.

The lion watched for him, and one day, when the jackal was out hunting, he came upon him in a place where he could not escape. The lion was just about to spring upon him, when Little Jackal said softly : "hush ! do you not see that bushbuck on the other side of the rock ? I am glad you have come to help me. Just remain here while I run round and drive him towards you." The lion did so, and the jackal made his escape.

At another time there was a meeting of the animals, and the lion was the chief at the meeting. Little Jackal wanted to go too, but there was a law made that no one should be present unless he had horns. So Little Jackal took wax out of a nest of bees, and made horns for himself with it. He fastened the horns on his head, and went to the meeting. The lion did not know him on account of the horns. But he sat near the fire and went to sleep, when the horns melted. The lion looked at him and saw who it was. He immediately tried to catch him, but the jackal was quick and sprang away. He ran under an overhanging rock and sang out : "help, help, this rock is falling upon me !" The lion went for a pole to prop up the rock, that he might get at the jackal. While he was away Little Jackal escaped.

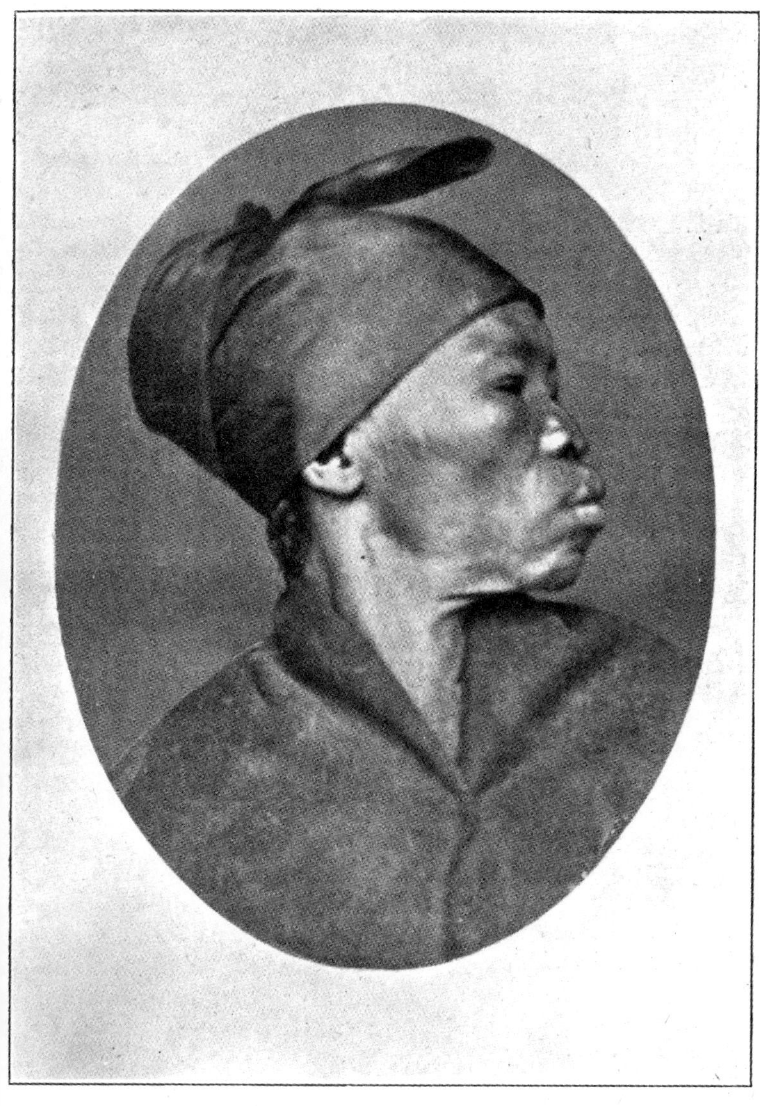

PORTRAIT OF A HOTTENTOT WOMAN, THE WIFE OF JAN JONKER AFRIKANER, SHOWING STRONG TRACES OF BUSHMAN BLOOD, IN EUROPEAN DRESS.

(From a Photograph in the South African Public Library.)

After that they became companions again, and went hunting another time. They killed an ox. The lion said : " I will watch it while you carry the pieces away." The lion gave him the breast, and said, " take this to my wife." Little Jackal took it to his own wife. When he returned, the lion gave him a shin, and said : " take this to your wife." Little Jackal took the shin to the lion's house. The lion's wife said : " I cannot take this, because it should not come here." Little Jackal thereupon struck the lion's wife in the face, and went back to the place where the ox was killed. The lion gave him a large piece of meat, and said : " take this to my wife." Little Jackal took it to his own wife. This continued till the ox was finished. Then they both went home.

When the lion arrived at his house he found there was weeping in his family. His wife said : " is it you who sent the jackal to beat me and my children, and is it you who sent this shin ? Did I ever eat a shin ? " When the lion heard that, he was very angry, and at once went to the jackal's house. When he reached the rock, Little Jackal looked down and said : " who are you, and what is your name, and whose son are you, and where are you from, and where are you going to, and whom do you want, and what do you want him for ? " The lion replied : " I have merely come to see you. I wish you would let the rope down." Little Jackal let down a rope made of mouse skins, and when the lion climbed a little way up, the rope broke, and he fell and was hurt. He then went home.

The evening with the Hottentots, as probably with all barbarians, was the time for enjoyment. What could be more cheerful than the dance in the bright moonlight or listening to a merry tale by a fire under a starry sky ? Then the young men tried their strength in wrestling matches, or in lifting one another from the ground, while the young women looked on and applauded the successful competitors. Then, too, they played games which, though apparently suited to the capacities of little children only, afforded them much amusement. The commonest of these games, very similar to one practised by the Bushmen, was adopted by the Bantu on the eastern border when they conquered the Hottentots there, and is performed by adults among them to-day, though the people with whom it originated have long since forgotten it.

It was played by two persons or any number exceeding two. The players sat on the ground, and each had a pebble so small that it could easily be concealed in a folded hand. If there were many players they formed themselves into sides or parties, but when they were few in number one played against the rest. This one concealed the pebble in either of his hands, and then threw both arms out against his opponent, at the same time calling out that he met or that he evaded. His opponent threw his arms out in the same manner, so that his right hand was opposite the first player's left, and his left opposite the first player's right. The clenched hands were then opened, and if the pebbles were found to meet, the first player won if he had called out that he met, or lost if he had called out that he evaded. When there were many players, one after another was beaten until only two were left. These two then played against each other, when the one who was beaten was laughed at and the winner was applauded. In playing, the arms were thrown out very quickly, and the words were rapidly uttered, so that a stranger might have fancied there was neither order nor rule observed. Young men and boys often spent whole nights in this childish amusement, which had the same hold upon them as dice upon many Europeans.

Probably, if intellectual enjoyment be excluded, the Hottentots were among the happiest people in existence. They generally lived until old age without serious illness. They did not allow possible future troubles to disturb them, and a sufficiency of food was all that was needed to make them as merry and lighthearted as children at play.

They were capable of adopting the habits of Europeans, though the process required to be so gradual that the training of two centuries and a half has been insufficient to complete it. They have learned to cultivate the ground, to use the same food as white people, to wear European clothing, and to act as rough handicraftsmen, but there is no instance on record of one of them having ever attained a position that required either much intellectual power or much mechanical skill. Since they came in contact with Europeans and African slaves, however, their blood has been so mixed that, except in Great Namaqualand and along the banks of the Vaal and Orange rivers near their junction, very few pure Hottentots are in existence now, and every successive generation sees the number become smaller.

CHAPTER V.

The Dark-skinned People termed by Europeans Bantu.

Far more important to a student of South African history than information upon either the Bushmen or the Hottentots is a knowledge of the people termed by us the Bantu, because the former are nearly extinct, while the latter to-day outnumber by more than threefold all the other inhabitants of the country put together, and are still increasing at a marvellous rate. The Bantu tribes of Africa south of the Zambesi vary so greatly in appearance, in speech, in customs, and in intellect, that it is evident they do not form one homogeneous race, still the manner of construction of the various dialects in use by them being the same, and one ruling tenet in the religion of them all being identical, they can be classed as a family group by themselves. Of late years a flood of light has been thrown upon the condition of their kindred in Central Africa, and by applying the knowledge thus gained to occurrences which have taken place since the settlement of Europeans in the southern part of the continent, the history of the Bantu family can be traced backward in general terms, though not in a detailed form.

There is only one way of accounting for the existence of the tribes as they are seen to-day all over Africa south of the equator and even some distance north of it. At some time not exceedingly remote a band of people speaking the parent language of the various dialects now in use, and having ancestor worship as their religion, must have entered North-Eastern Africa, as so many bands had done before. The hamitic family had long possessed the land from the valley of the Nile to the Atlantic ocean, and from the Mediterranean sea to the Sahara, negroes had entered the continent, perhaps not very long before, and had spread along the southern border of the desert, various lighter coloured communities of Asiatic blood had settled south-west of the Red sea, and Bushmen occupied the remainder of the continent, except perhaps where a little horde of Hottentots tended their flocks somewhere between the gulf of Aden and Lake Tanganyika, and maybe highly skilled people, Arab and Indian, were delving for gold in the Rhodesia of our day. This is no sketch of fancy, but what must have been, or the condition of Africa past and present is altogether unexplainable.

The band of immigrants conquered a section of the earlier inhabitants, and incorporated its girls, possibly some of its boys also, but destroyed all the others. Then, after a time, it separated into two or more tribes, each of which pursued a distinct career of conquest, one incorporating Asiatic girls, another negro girls, still another girls of Bushman blood. The tribes increased, and fought with each other, some were destroyed, others grew stronger and stronger, and pushed their way ever southward, where there were no other people than Bushmen to oppose them. The principal line of migration was down the eastern coast, and so when a tribe moving down the centre of the continent reached the region of the great lakes, the Hottentots were obliged to flee to the south-west. In that direction the advance of the Bantu was much slower than on the other side of the continent, for there is every indication that the lower bank of the Zambesi was reached long before the valley of the Congo was occupied.

It is possible that Arabic or Indian documents may some day be discovered which will throw light upon the migration of the Bantu down the eastern coast. At present much information from books concerning any part of the continent south of the Sahara, or of the people occupying it in ancient times, cannot be obtained. The following is all that the author of this volume has been able to gather :

Dr. Budge, in his valuable work on Egypt already mentioned, gives an account of the raising of an army of black men in the valley of the Nile above Nubia 3233 years before the commencement of the Christian era, but whether those black men had, or had not, any connection with the Bantu there are no means of ascertaining. In 2466 B.C. Nubia was conquered by Egypt, and again in 2433 and 2333. The Nubians, however, were certainly not near relatives of the Bantu.

There can be very little doubt that the eastern coast of Africa as far down perhaps as Cape Correntes was known to the inhabitants of Southern Arabia several thousand years ago. That they carried on commerce with India by sea is certain from various passages in the old testament, and it is most unlikely that they would expend all their energy on voyaging eastward and neglect at least to examine another coast quite as easy of access.*

They brought the spices to Egypt that were used in embalming the dead, and the great city of Thebes owed its grandeur largely to its being the distributing centre for Indian products brought in ships to the shore of the Red sea and thence conveyed overland by caravans of camels. In the very earliest times of this commerce probably a complete land route was followed, but people so far advanced as to carry on such traffic would speedily see the advantage of ocean transport, and creeping along the coast for short distances at first, they would soon learn to make use of the monsoons and steer boldly over from shore to shore. There is no other sea in the world that offers such facilities for safe navigation by small and crudely built vessels, nor one where facilities are so apparent to the people living on its shores. A single accident, such as a vessel being blown out to sea before the monsoon, would make the coast of Africa known to the people of India, and many accidents of this kind must have occurred. So it may be taken for certain that long before the dawn of written history Indians and Southern Arabians were well acquainted with the East African coast.

That there was little to be obtained in trade on that coast below the tenth degree of north latitude, compared with the products of India, is true, and there may have been nothing at all, for it is in the highest degree improbable that a race more advanced than Bushmen then inhabited the adjoining part of the continent. But if there was no trade, there was ivory to be

---

* A list of Indian spices that can only have been conveyed by them across the ocean is given in the thirtieth chapter of Exodus.

collected, and timber—an article of necessity to the Arabians; which their own country did not furnish—to be cut, and possibly gold to be gathered in the territory that now bears the name Rhodesia. There is no record of any kind in existence, however, from which information can be obtained concerning the inhabitants of Eastern Africa in those far-off times, and mere conjecture is valueless.

About the year 992 before Christ an event of importance took place. Solomon, ruler of Israel, had extended his kingdom southward, was in possession of Idumea and the isthmus of Suez, and had established a naval station at Ezion-geber on the gulf of Akaba at the head of the Red sea. He must have known of the existence of an extensive traffic on the shores of what we term the Indian ocean, and have resolved to secure a share of it, or he would not have done this. But his subjects were unused to the sea, and so he had recourse to his ally, Hiram, king of the great commercial city of Tyre, then the wealthiest community in the known world, whose riches were gained by water traffic with many distant peoples.

The Phœnicians may have kept up an uninterrupted trade on the Indian ocean from the time when their ancestors removed from its shore to that of the Mediterranean, though it would appear that in the tenth century before Christ they purchased most, if not all, of the eastern produce that they needed from Sabean merchants, conveyed it in vessels up the Red sea, and then transported it on camels to Tyre. But in whatever manner they acquired their knowledge, some of the subjects of Hiram certainly were acquainted with the sea to the south, and they went as officers just as they would have done in a fleet entirely their own, while sailors were engaged wherever fishermen could be found or recruits could be hired or purchased. This was the manner in which the commerce of Tyre was carried on, just as in modern times the army of the Netherlands East India Company consisted of Dutch officers and foreign soldiers.

So with the aid of Hiram, who had a large share of the profit and who was unable to carry on the trade alone on account of Solomon's possession of Idumea, fleets were built at Ezion-geber, of which every particle of the material must have been conveyed overland from the Mediterranean shore, and then they sailed southward to carry on commerce on a very large scale. Of this enterprise the following account is given in the ninth and tenth chapters of the first book of Kings :

"And king Solomon made a navy of ships in Ezion-geber, which is beside Eloth, on the shore of the Red sea, in the land of Edom. And Hiram sent in the navy his servants, shipmen that had knowledge of the sea, with the servants of Solomon. And they came to Ophir, and fetched from thence gold, four hundred and twenty talents, and brought it to king Solomon."

"And the navy also of Hiram, that brought gold from Ophir, brought in from Ophir great plenty of almug trees, and precious stones."

"Now the weight of gold that came to Solomon in one year was six hundred three score and six talents of gold, (equal to £3,646,350), beside that he had of the merchantmen, and of the traffic of the spice merchants, and of all the kings of Arabia, and of the governors of the country."

"For the king had at sea a navy of Tharshish with the navy of Hiram : once in three years came the navy of Tharshish, bringing gold, and silver, ivory, and apes, and peacocks."

Those Phœnicians must have known a great deal about Eastern Africa and its people, but they left absolutely nothing on record, and it is only from their brief connection with the kingdom of Israel that the information given in the sacred writings is obtained. They kept all their geographical knowledge carefully to themselves, for they did not wish to bring commercial rivalry into existence. And so the ships of Tharshish, which may be taken to mean the largest and best equipped vessels for long voyages then known, went up and down the coast ploughing the waters of the Indian sea, perhaps keeping the shore always in sight, or perhaps, like the South Arabian vessels, making direct courses from point to point with the sun and the stars for their guide, while the wisest men in Europe were ignorant of the existence of such a vast sheet of water or of the mass of land that closed it in on the western side.

Upon the death of Solomon his kingdom was divided into two sections, each too weak to carry on such great enterprises as he had engaged in, and though on one occasion subsequently the rulers of the separate states united to fit out and despatch a fleet from Ezion-geber, the attempt ended in failure and was never again repeated.

The extensive commerce of Tyre continued to be carried on, but whether she still maintained fleets in the Red sea is doubtful, for she may have needed foreign assistance to be able to do that. In the twenty-seventh chapter of Ezekiel, written about 588 years before Christ, there is a graphic account of her enormous trade, and from the twenty-second verse it would appear that her Indian wares were furnished by the merchants of Southern Arabia.

The splendid city was taken and destroyed after a siege of thirteen years by Nebuchadnezzar, king of Babylon, in the year 573 before Christ, but was soon afterwards rebuilt on an island close to the mainland, and partly recovered its commercial importance. It was taken again in 332 B.C. by Alexander the Great, of Macedon, after a siege of eight months, when its celebrity ceased for ever, as Alexandria, at the mouth of the western outlet of the Nile, took its place as the greatest commercial city of the world.

The Israelites and the Phœnicians not having supplied any information concerning the dark-skinned people of Africa, we turn now to the Greeks to ascertain whether they perchance knew and placed on record anything about them.

In the Homeric age, which is believed to have been somewhere between 1200 and 850 before Christ, the Greeks were aware that such people lived somewhere to the south, but of them, beyond their existence, they knew nothing. They considered the inhabited world to be a circular plane, with a great stream flowing round it, and farther away than the renowned city of Thebes in Egypt, on the border of this ocean stream, the Ethiopians were stated in the Iliad to dwell. The name Ethiopian was of course not that by which the people called themselves, but was that applied to them by the Greeks, and meant (αἰθίοψ) sun-burned, swarthy. They were described by Homer as a " blameless people, whom the gods themselves visit, and partake of their feasts." In the Odyssey they are mentioned further as divided into two sections, the most distant of men, some living where the sun sets and some where he rises.

It is evident from this that the Greeks had a dim knowledge that black men were occupying the valley of the Nile above Egypt, but whether the remote ancestors of the Bantu were among them it is utterly impossible even to make a conjecture. There is, however, reference to another race in the upper valley of the Nile, which, if it stood alone, would be regarded with justice as mythical, but as from this time onward for many centuries it was constantly repeated, must be considered as having a foundation in fact. The Greeks had heard vague rumours of pygmies living in the same part of the world as the Ethiopians, and the poet introduced them in his immortal work as veritable tom-thumbs, " men no bigger than your fist," whose mortal enemies were the cranes.

Probably no Greek of that age had ever seen a black man or a pygmy, and the vague knowledge that they had of the existence of such people must have been derived from Phœnician traders, who brought ivory among other things to them for sale, and who could have told them a great deal about Africa and its people, if they had not chosen to keep their knowledge to themselves and give fabulous accounts of everything beyond the immediate ken of those who listened to them. In this matter of the pygmies, we have the earliest reference by any European to the Bushman race, that must then have occupied wholly or partly all Africa south of the confines of Nubia.

The Homeric poems for many centuries were regarded by the Greeks as the repositories of all knowledge, and it was considered sinful to question the accuracy of Homer in such a matter as the locality of an island or the direction of a river. To so great a length did this reverence extend that even after the true form of the earth was known and its size approximately ascertained by Eratosthenes and others, the inhabited part was believed to be surrounded by an ocean stream, and Strabo, the most competent of all the ancient geographers, zealously maintained the authority of Homer.

In one matter only was it generally admitted that he had used the license of a poet, and that was in his description of the pygmies, who are pictured by later writers not as tom-thumbs but merely as men under the ordinary size.

The historian Herodotus, who was born in the year 484 before Christ, tells all that was known by the Greeks of his day of the people of Africa. With Egypt he was familiar, and his description of the Nile and its valley up to the first cataract is correct. From Elephantine just below the first cataract to Meroë, the principal town of the Ethiopians, the country is described from verbal information that he obtained and from traditions concerning the intrusion of an Egyptian army thus far.

Herodotus follows Homer in dividing the Ethiopians into two sections, but he is very much better acquainted with them than Homer was. The Eastern Ethiopians he placed along the southern coast of Asia, in a satrapy of Persia, extending from the mouth of the Indus to the entrance of the Persian gulf. And there to the present day a dark-skinned people extremely low in civilisation is to be found.

The Western Ethiopians he placed in the valley of the Nile south of Egypt. Above the first cataract there was an island inhabited partly by Egyptians and partly by Ethiopians, and beyond that were Ethiopians only, except the Automoli or Deserters settled farther south. Whether the Ethiopians in the valley of the Nile at this time were one people or whether they were composed of tribes of different origin, among whom were the progenitors of the Bantu, cannot be ascertained from any information that Herodotus gives. Not a word of the language or languages used by them has been transmitted to us, not an observation upon religion or peculiar customs that might lead to identification has been supplied.

Herodotus had no conception of the great extent of the

African continent to the southward, and holding the generally received opinion of the Greeks that it was bounded by the ocean stream not far from the land of the Automoli, he could not account for the volume of water in the Nile except by assuming that it flowed for a great distance from the west and then turned sharply to the north.

He had heard that Pharaoh Necho, who reigned in Egypt from 610 to 594 before Christ, had despatched a Phœnician fleet that sailed round Africa from the head of the Red sea through the pillars of Hercules or strait of Gibraltar to the mouth of the Nile, but of the particulars of the voyage he had obtained no account except that it occupied three years and that the voyagers during part of the passage had the sun on the north. The last statement is commonly regarded as a proof that such a voyage was really made, but it does not seem to be of much weight. It was then well known that only a short distance south of Elephantine on the Nile the sun was seen in the north for several days every year, and the natural inference could not be avoided that on the ocean stream farther south the duration would be longer.

The exact words of the statement are : " As for Libya, we know it to be washed on all sides by the sea, except where it is attached to Asia. This discovery was first made by Necôs, the Egyptian king, who on desisting from the canal which he had begun between the Nile and the Arabian Gulf, sent to sea a number of ships manned by Phœnicians, with orders to make for the Pillars of Hercules, and return to Egypt through them, and by the Mediterranean. The Phœnicians took their departure from Egypt by way of the Erythrean Sea, and so sailed into the southern ocean. When autumn came, they went ashore, wherever they might happen to be, and having sown a tract of land with corn, waited until the grain was fit to cut. Having reaped it, they again set sail ; and thus it came to pass that two whole years went by, and it was not till the third year that they doubled the Pillars of Hercules, and made good their voyage home. On their return they declared—I for my part do not believe them, but perhaps others may—that in sailing round Libya they had the sun upon their right hand. In this way was the extent of Libya first discovered." *

The Phœnicians were competent at that time to make voyages of considerable length, and they must have been acquainted by tradition at least with the East African coast a great distance down, but they never made their knowledge available for others. From them, if Africa had been circumnavigated, the Greeks would have heard nothing of it. But it was said to have been accomplished in the service of Necho, a king who favoured commerce, and who caused docks to be constructed at the head of the Red sea for the use of trading vessels. Is it possible that such a wonderful event as the discovery of a vast area of land previously unknown could have taken place without any record of it being preserved in Egypt, or is it not much more likely to have been just an idle tale told by people who believed the ocean stream to run round all the continents, and the Erythrean sea opening into it to provide a connection with the Atlantic far north of the equator? That this body of water was navigable was a matter of course, that it had been navigated from one side of Africa to the other was told of several expeditions beside this of the Phœnicians, and with as little probability of truth in any one instance as in any other.

Before the time that Herodotus wrote the West African coast had been explored a long way down, but he knew nothing of it. The voyage of discovery was made by a Carthaginian officer named Hanno, whose object was to plant trading stations and inspect the seaboard as far as he could. Hanno sailed with a fleet of sixty ships from Carthage some time between 520 and 470 B.C., and after passing the strait now called Gibraltar, kept close to the shore and made himself acquainted with as many particulars concerning it as possible. At a distance of several days' sail from the strait he landed and learned from some Libyan shepherds that the interior was occupied by people who lived in

---

* The extent of Libya, or the African continent, was not known, or even conjectured, by either the Egyptians or the Greeks in the time of Herodotus. If such a voyage had been made, there would certainly have been some mention of it in the Egyptian records.

caves and holes in the mountains, were of strange appearance, and swifter of foot than horses. Along the coast several trading stations were established, the last on the little island of Cerne, in a deep bay at the mouth of the river Do Ouro, in latitude 23° 50′ north.

From Cerne the explorer, now relieved of his passengers, and probably of his storeships, proceeded southward along the coast until he reached the mouth of the river Senegal. There something happened of which we have no information, that obliged the fleet to put back to Cerne, but setting out the second time Hanno kept on to Cape Verde, which he observed carefully and described accurately. South of that cape grass fires were seen, which terrified the crews, for the whole land seemed to be ablaze, just as it and other parts of the African coast are sometimes seen by modern voyagers at night. Still the fleet proceeded onward, until it reached Sherboro Sound, in latitude 7° 45′ north. Here some great apes resembling human beings were seen, and three of the females were killed, the skins of two of which were taken back to Carthage as curiosities. The explorers called them gorillas, and that name is now applied to the largest of the manlike apes found in Western Africa, though it is probable that the animals discovered by the Carthaginians were chimpanzees, as the males are stated to have taken to flight.

Sherboro Island was the farthest point reached by the expedition under Hanno. Here the coast trends to the south-east, but at no great distance turns abruptly to the east and forms the deep indentation known now as the gulf of Guinea. The general course from the strait of Gibraltar had been towards the south, but the old inaccuracy in the delineation of the African continent by the Greeks was not corrected after the discoveries made by Hanno were known. The Carthaginians were very careful not to impart useful knowledge to others, but an account of this voyage was inscribed on a tablet and placed in the temple of Moloch in their city, where it was copied, probably without the consent of the authorities. It was translated into Greek, and is known to have been extant in that language in the third century before Christ. But as Hanno kept no other reckoning than days' sail, and as anything resembling a compass was then unknown, though he distinctly stated that his course outward was towards the south, the Greek geographers, in their belief that the continent was bounded by the ocean stream far north of the equator, assumed that he must really have steered to the east, and marked his discoveries in that direction. The Portuguese explorers of the fifteenth century made known the true form and size of Africa, and only then was it possible to lay down the route of Hanno correctly and to fix with precision the places that he visited, which fortunately could be done from his accurate description of them.

Of the people of the African continent practically no information whatever is to be derived from the account of this expedition, but the event is a very interesting one.

The renowned scientist Aristotle, the tutor of Alexander the Great, who lived from 384 to 321 B.C., in his writings throws no light upon the subject of this inquiry. He believed that in the southern hemisphere there was a temperate belt corresponding to the one in the northern, but he expressed no opinion as to whether it was inhabited or not. Between these belts he held that there was a zone uninhabitable on account of intense heat. He knew of the existence of the pygmies in what we would term Northern Africa to-day, and described them as men under the middle height and black complexioned, but of any people corresponding to the Bantu he was quite ignorant.

In the time of Ptolemy Philadelphus, 285 to 247 B.C., the Greeks of Egypt must have known a great deal about the interior of Africa and its people, but they have left nothing on record that can lead to identification of the Bantu. That monarch founded a station named Myos-Hormus on the western shore of the Red sea, in about latitude 27° north, in order to carry on commerce in Indian products. Goods purchased by Greek merchants from Arabs at Aden, Saba, and other emporiums were conveyed by water to Myos-Hormus, and then transported overland to Koptos on the Nile, a distance of about two hundred miles or three hundred and twenty kilometres by the road. Far down the Red sea other stations were founded, from which elephant hunters went inland to capture young animals, that were taken to Egypt and trained to serve in war. That some of these hunters went a considerable distance inland south and south-west of Abyssinia is almost certain, but the information obtained from them is of elephants captured, not of tribes encountered.

In the year 30 B.C.; Egypt became a Roman province, and nine years later—in 21 B.C.—an army under Petronius entered Abyssinia, where such success awaited it that Kandákè, the queen of that country, was obliged to become a tributary. At that time it is evident that no Bantu were living so far north, but beyond this nothing is to be learned regarding them.

Passing by writers of less importance, we come now to the great geographer Strabo, of Amasia, in Pontus, who died about the year of our lord 21, and in whose work the highest knowledge of the Greeks and Romans concerning the earth and its inhabitants at the commencement of the Christian era is to be found.*

Strabo resided for some time at Alexandria, where he had access to everything on the subject that had previously been written, and he travelled up the Nile as far as Syene, close to the first cataract, nearly under the northern tropic, where three Roman cohorts were then stationed. His idea of the form of the earth and of its division into five zones—one torrid, two temperate, and two frigid—was that of the present day ; but he was the most orthodox of all the devotees of Homer, and everything in his geography is made to fit in with the expressions of the poet. So the Africa of Strabo is a continent bounded on the north by the sea now called the Mediterranean, on the east by the Arabian gulf or as we term it the Red sea, and on the

* See *The Geography of Strabo, literally translated, with notes.* By H. C. Hamilton, Esq., and W. Falconer, M.A. Three crown octavo volumes, published at London and New York in 1889–1893. Also *History of Ancient Geography among the Greeks and Romans from the Earlist Ages to the Fall of the Roman Empire.* By E. H. Bunbury, F.R.G.S. Second Edition. Two thick demi octavo volumes, published at London in 1883. *A History of Ancient Geography,* by H. F. Tozer, M.A., F.R.G.S., chiefly drawn from the work last named, was published in a small crown octavo volume at Cambridge in 1897.

south by the ocean stream which washed its coast first westward
and then north-westward from Cape Noti Keras, or Guardafui
as now termed, to the pillars of Hercules, the modern strait of
Gibraltar. His Africa is made the smallest of the three continents, and might be represented by the body of a plough, of
which the share was formed by the promontory ending in Cape
Noti Keras.

The Sembritæ he regarded as the most distant inhabitants
of Africa, living on the border of the ocean. How wide that
ocean was he could not even conjecture, but whether land or sea,
adjoining the equator was a belt so hot that it could not be
occupied or traversed, just as at the poles there were tracts that
were uninhabitable on account of the cold. Strabo believed
it possible that beyond the known part of the sea in the north
temperate zone there might be habitable land, so that a vessel
sailing westward from the coast of Europe might reach it. Of
the south temperate zone he thought it most probable that it
was inhabited, " but not by the same race of men as dwell with
us, and it must therefore be regarded as another habitable earth."

It seems strange to us who live in a time when communication is so rapid and easy, and when information is so widely
scattered by means of printed books, that Strabo was entirely
ignorant of the eastern coast of Africa below Cape Guardafui.
Something about it must have been known by an occasional
ship-captain that sailed beyond the gulf of Aden. The commerce
between the ports on the Red sea and Arabia had greatly
increased since the occupation of Egypt by the Romans, and
a direct trade with the coast of Malabar was now carried on by
the Greeks of Alexandria as well. Strabo states that " the
traffic of the Alexandrian merchants whose vessels pass up the
Nile and the Arabian gulf to India has rendered us much better
acquainted with these countries than our predecessors were.
I was with Gallus at the time he was prefect of Egypt and
accompanied him as far as Syene and the frontiers of Ethiopia,
and I found that about one hundred and twenty ships sail from
Myos-Hormus to India, although in the time of the Ptolemies
scarcely any one would venture on this voyage and the commerce

with the Indies." And yet the present Somali coast was entirely unknown to him.

Strabo's description of Ethiopia and the Ethiopians can be given in his own words as translated into English :

"But Egypt it (the Nile) traverses both alone and entirely, and in a straight line, from the lesser cataract above Syene and Elephantina (which are the boundaries of Egypt and Ethiopia), to the mouths by which it discharges itself into the sea. The Ethiopians at present lead for the most part a wandering life, and are destitute of the means of subsistence, on account of the barrenness of the soil, the disadvantages of climate, and their great distance from us."

"For formerly not even twenty vessels ventured to navigate the Arabian Gulf, or advance to the smallest distance beyond the straits at its mouth ; but now large fleets are despatched as far as India and the extremities of Ethiopia, from which places the most valuable freights are brought to Egypt, and are thence exported to other parts."

"For the mode of life (of the Ethiopians) is wretched ; they are for the most part naked, and wander from place to place with their flocks. Their flocks and herds are small in size, whether sheep, goats, or oxen ; the dogs also, though fierce and quarrelsome, are small. It was perhaps from the diminutive size of these people, that the story of the Pygmies originated, whom no person, worthy of credit, has asserted that he himself has seen.

"They live on millet and barley, from which also a drink is prepared. They have no oil, but use butter and fat instead. There are no fruits, except the produce of trees in the royal gardens. Some feed even upon grass, the tender twigs of trees, the lotus, or the roots of reeds. They live also upon the flesh and blood of animals, milk, and cheese. They reverence their kings as gods, who are for the most part shut up in their palaces.

"Their largest royal seat is the city of Meroë, of the same name as the island. . . . The inhabitants (of the island) are nomades, who are partly hunters and partly husbandmen. There are also mines of copper, iron, gold, and various kinds of precious stones.

"The houses in the cities are formed by interweaving split pieces of palm wood or of bricks. . . . They hunt elephants, lions, and panthers. . . .

"Above Meroë is Psebo, a large lake, containing a well-inhabited island. As the Libyans occupy the western bank of the Nile, and the Ethiopians the country on the other side of the river, they thus dispute by turns the possession of the islands and the banks of the river, one party repulsing the other, or yielding to the superiority of its opponents.

"The Ethiopians use bows of wood four cubits long, and hardened in the fire. The women also are armed, most of whom wear in the upper lip a copper ring. They wear sheepskins, without wool; for the sheep have hair like goats. Some go naked, or wear small skins or girdles of well-woven hair round the loins.

"They regard as God one being who is immortal, the cause of all things; another who is mortal, a being without a name, whose nature is not clearly understood.

"In general they consider as gods benefactors and royal persons, some of whom are their kings, the common saviours and guardians of all; others are private persons, esteemed as gods by those who have individually received benefits from them.

"Of those who inhabit the torrid region, some are even supposed not to acknowledge any god, and are supposed to abhor even the sun, and to apply opprobrious names to him, when they behold him rising, because he scorches and tortures them with his heat; these people take refuge in the marshes.

"Some tribes throw the dead into the river; others keep them in the house, enclosed in hyalus. Some bury them around the temples in coffins of baked clay. They swear an oath by them, which is reverenced as more sacred than all others.

"The following custom exists among the Ethiopians. If a king is mutilated in any part of the body, those who are most attached to his person, as attendants, mutilate themselves in the same manner, and even die with him. Hence the king is guarded with the utmost care."

Among the customs here mentioned are several that seem decidedly characteristic of Bantu, but by Strabo they were regarded as common to all the inhabitants of the Nile valley above Syene, and it is impossible from his account to determine whether there were or were not distinct races of men among them. Some must have been Nubians, others Abyssinians, and it is just possible that some of the most distant may have been

Bantu, but beyond this supposition all is vague and uncertain. The pygmies, it will be observed, have so entirely disappeared that their earlier existence even was doubtful.

Within three-quarters of a century from the time of Strabo a very great advance was made in the knowledge by the Greeks and Romans of the eastern coast of Africa. Exactly the same thing had happened as when the Portuguese appeared in the Indian sea more than fourteen centuries later : the Europeans, that is the Egyptian Greeks under Roman dominion, had almost driven the Arabs from the ocean and monopolised the eastern trade. About the year of our lord 47 a pilot named Hippalus became acquainted with the fact that the wind blew steadily from one quarter during certain months, and just as steadily from the opposite quarter during another season of the year. How it happened that the discovery of the monsoons was not made by the Greeks long before seems very strange, but so it was. They had not now to make a circuit along the coast of Asia, but could steer straight across the ocean, and without difficulty could visit any land that the Arabs had frequented before. Their ships were stronger than those of the Arabs, and in war they were superior to their naval rivals.

A few years after the discovery of Hippalus, which had such momentous consequences, the Arab emporium at Aden was destroyed by order of the emperor Claudius, though it was shortly afterwards occupied by the conquerors, and by them was termed the Roman port. The commerce of India with the dominion of the sea was then lost by those who had enjoyed it so long. Some of the coasting trade in small vessels appears to have been left to them for a time, but at length that too was taken from them, their commercial settlements on the African coast were abandoned, and for several centuries they were confined to their own country and to such trade as could be carried on by caravans. As the Roman power declined, however, the Arabs recovered some of the ocean commerce, and at length under the influence of a new religion they bounded into activity again, and with amazing vigour and energy brought into subjection a very large portion of the known world. The conquest of

Alexandria by Amrou in the twentieth year of the Hegira, the year 640 of the Christian era, carried with it the absolute destruction of the Greek trade in the Indian sea, and the Arabs had once more a monopoly of intercourse with Hindostan and Eastern Africa.

Just before the Egyptian Greeks succeeded in acquiring the full dominion of the Indian sea and ejecting the Arabs from it, a flood of light was thrown upon the condition of a large part of the eastern coast of Africa. About the year 80 of our era, or possibly a little later, appeared a very remarkable treatise on navigation termed *The Periplus of the Erythrean Sea,** which is believed to have been the production of a Greek merchant of Alexandria, who had inspected in person the greater part of the coasts he described. It contains a wonderful amount of information, and was the first treatise to make known to Europeans generally the extent of the African coast visited by the Arabs. In this periplus the coast is described from Myos-Hormus as far down as an island termed Menuthias, which Dr. Vincent is of opinion was the Zanzibar of our day, but which other investigators believe to be Pemba, as better answering the description of a low wooded island thirty miles or forty-eight kilometres from the coast. The distance named is greater than it is in reality, but for a conjecture without measurement it is not very inaccurate. Either Pemba, Zanzibar, or Mafia it must have been, and it is most unlikely to have been the last. Two days' sail south of the island of Menuthias was the commercial station of Rhapta on the mainland, the last of the kind on the seaboard of Azania. Dr. Vincent believed this place to be where Kilwa was afterwards built, but if Menuthias was Pemba, Rhapta must have been on or near the site of the present settlement of Bagamoyo. What the Arabs or the African inhabitants designated the place is not mentioned, Rhapta (from ῥάπτω to sew) being the Greek name given to it

* See *The Commerce and Navigation of the Ancients in the Indian Ocean,* by William Vincent, D.D., Dean of Westminster. Two large quarto volumes, published at London in 1807. The first volume is almost entirely devoted to the Voyage of Nearchus from the Indus to the Euphrates, and the second to the Periplus of the Erythrean sea.

on account of the vessels sewed together with coir which frequented the port.

The exports of Rhapta are mentioned as ivory, rhinoceros horns, tortoise shells, and shells for ornaments. It, as well as a few other commercial stations farther up the coast, was inhabited by Africans, but the Arabs had established fortified factories, by means of which they controlled the populace. Each station was absolutely independent of all others as far as government was concerned. Rhapta itself was subject, *in virtue of old-established right*, to the ruler of a district in Yemen, from whom the merchants of Muza on the south-eastern shore of the Red sea rented it, and they carried on a regular trade to it with their own ships. The traders spoke the language of the inhabitants, and were in the habit of forming alliances with their females.

The Arabs change not, as they were three thousand years ago, so they are to-day. The picture of the East African coast in the periplus is an almost exact counterpart of the same coast when the Portuguese discovered it at the close of the fifteenth century, except that real settlements, not mere trading stations, came into existence during the second period. That there were Indians mixed with the Arabs can hardly be doubted, as they would naturally be employed in carrying on the trade. And these foreigners, who must have numbered at least several hundreds, were mingling their blood with that of the Bantu inhabitants in the first century of the Christian era, how long before no one can say. It is unfortunate that no description of the inhabitants is given in the periplus, but there is one word of great significance to be found in it. The country along the coast to Rhapta from about latitude 5° north is termed *Azania*. This is to a certainty a Greek form of the Arabic name, and we are therefore justified in assuming that this territory was then occupied by Bantu tribes, and was regarded by the Arabs as the country of the Zendj.

The old theory of a zone uninhabitable on account of heat was now proved to be incorrect, for Greeks had advanced without difficulty to latitude 7° south. So far Bantu occupied the coast, but whether they extended farther at that time it is impossible to say. If they did, the question may reasonably be asked why the Arabs who had been there so long had not formed trading stations farther south? and to this no reply can be given. That they had explored the coast farther down cannot be doubted, but there may have been reasons, unconnected with the existence or non-existence of inhabitants so far civilised as to carry on commerce, for their not caring to fix themselves beyond Rhapta.

The information contained in the *Periplus of the Erythrean Sea* must have been quite new to learned men in all parts of the Roman empire except Egypt, for Pliny the elder was entirely unacquainted with Eastern Africa. Caius Plinius Secundus, who was born in A.D. 23, published in 77, two years before his death in the great eruption of Vesuvius which destroyed Herculaneum and Pompeii, an exceedingly comprehensive work, that can now be read in English as well as in the original Latin. The edition in our language is entitled *The Natural History of Pliny, translated, with copious notes and illustrations, by the late John Bostock, M.D., F.R.S., and H. T. Riley, Esq., B.A., Late Scholar of Clare Hall, Cambridge.* It is in six crown octavo volumes, published at London in 1855 to 1858.

Pliny believed Africa to be much the smallest of the three continents. His account of the Ethiopians is not only fabulous, but utterly absurd, such as a child might laugh at. He speaks of pygmies in different countries, among others some in India only twenty-seven inches (68·58 centimetres) in height. Of those in Africa his only remark is: "Some writers have also stated that there is a nation of Pygmies, which dwells among the marshes in which the river Nile takes its rise." The value of his work, as far as the subject of this inquiry is concerned, is purely negative, showing that Africa beyond Abyssinia was absolutely unknown to the most learned man of his day in Rome.

The next source of information that is available is the work of the renowned astronomer and geographer Ptolemy. Claudius Ptolemæus, of whose personal history nothing is known except that he was a native of Egypt, wrote at Alexandria about the middle of the second century of our era. The system which he introduced of laying down places on maps according to their latitude and longitude is the one still in use, and his map of the world is an enormous improvement upon all that preceded it, but as the position of very few places indeed was then accurately known from astronomical observations, he was obliged to have recourse to the crudest means for ascertaining the distance and direction of all other points, many of which it is evident he laid down by guesswork.

This is certainly the case with regard to the territory in Africa termed Agysimba, which he placed in the centre of the continent, on the parallel of 16° south of the equator. Two Roman officers, Septimius Flaccus and Julius Maternus, had been engaged in expeditions to the south, Flaccus from Cyrene and Maternus from Leptis. Flaccus reported that the Ethiopians of Agysimba were three months' journey south of the Garamantes, and Maternus stated that when he and the king of the Garamantes set out from Garama to attack the Ethiopians of Agysimba, they marched four months to the south. Rhinoceroses abounded in Agysimba. A preceding writer had stretched these distances to a fabulous length, and Ptolemy with these data and nothing more reduced the estimate of Marinus and fixed the position, giving as his reason that as black men and rhinoceroses were not found north of Meroë, Agysimba was probably the same distance south of the equator. The best commentators are now disposed to believe that Agysimba was in the Soudan, not far from the Sahara.

Of the eastern coast Ptolemy gave information similar to that of the periplus of the Erythrean sea, and stated that from Rhapta southward to Cape Prasum a gulf or shoaly sea extended, the shore of which was occupied by Ethiopians who were cannibals. It is conjectured that Cape Prasum is the Cape Delgado of our day. The Bantu are thus brought down to the tenth degree of south latitude, for there can be no doubt that the Ethiopian anthropophagi were of their family. Some terrible commotion must have taken place among them, and they had been compelled to resort temporarily to cannibalism and probably to migrate southward, as has more than once been the case in modern times. Ptolemy assigned latitude 15° south to Cape Prasum, but that is no guide to its position, as it was mere conjecture on his part.

But in one respect he made a wonderfully correct supposition with regard to Africa. The Greek traders who had supplanted the Arabs at Rhapta were in the habit of sending mixed breeds inland to collect ivory, and these men reported the existence of two large lakes and of mountains covered with snow in the lands that they visited. This information was communicated to Ptolemy, and though it was vague, he at once concluded that the lakes must be the sources of the Nile, and that the melting of the snow on the mountains was the cause of the periodical rising of the great river. In his map he laid down the lakes very nearly in their true position, and thus gained credit with many modern writers for knowledge which he did not really possess.

That he had no actual information concerning any part of Africa distant from the coast and south of Cape Prasum, wherever that was, is proved by the fact that he laid down the continent as making a sudden turn to the east just below his Mountains of the Moon at the sources of the Nile, and extending in that direction until it joined Asia beyond the Malay peninsula, thus making the Indian ocean, like the Mediterranean, an inland sea. From him therefore, great as was his merit in other respects, no knowledge concerning the Bantu can be derived beyond that which is here given.

CHAPTER VI.

Information given by Mohamedan Writers.

From the time of Mohamed to that of Vasco da Gama the Arabs
and Persians were the only traders on the Indian ocean, and
they must have been well acquainted with the inhabitants of
Eastern Africa even before they founded a chain of settlements
from Magadosho down to Sofala.* There may be Arabic documents in existence which would throw light upon the migrations of the tribes, but not much information is given by the
authors of books in that language which have been translated
and published in European speech. The following have been
consulted by the author of this volume, and all that they state
concerning the East African coast is given here, in the exact words
of the translator when the work has been rendered into English,
and in an English translation from the French when it has been
published in the latter tongue. It would of course be more
satisfactory if a direct translation from the original Arabic could
be given, but that is not possible, as the author is entirely
ignorant of that language.

Abou-Zeyd-Hassan, a native of Syraf, a town on the Persian
gulf, about the year 880 of our era wrote a book upon India
and China from accounts given by travelling merchants, principally by one named Soleyman. A copy of this work, transcribed
in 1199, was translated into French and published, with the Arabic

---

* Indians were largely employed in this trade, but usually, if not always,
in a subordinate capacity. Some of the vessels that plied between Hindostan
and the African coast were exclusively manned by them, and much of the
inland bartering was carried on through their agency. Mohamedan Indians
had extensive privileges, and it is possible that some of these may have traded
in Africa on their own account, but those who did not profess the creed of
Islam were not permitted to do so.

original, in two small volumes at Paris in 1845. It is entitled
*Relation des Voyages faits par les Arabes et les Persans dans
l'Inde et à la Chine dans le IXe siècle de l'ère chretienne. Avec
une traduction française par M. Reinaud, membre de l'Institut.*
This book gives no information regarding the migration of the
Bantu tribes, but it pictures them as at war with each other,
as subsisting chiefly on millet, as listening attentively to exhor-
tations to abide by ancestral customs made by seers clothed in
leopard and monkey skins, as bringing for sale the skins of spotted
and striped carnivora, then highly valued in eastern countries,
and as acknowledging the superiority of the Arabs. This is what
is stated :

THE COUNTRY OF THE ZENDJ.

The country of the Zendj is of great extent. The plants that
grow there, such as millet, which is the principal article of their
food, sugar cane, and other vegetable productions, are of a black
colour. The Zendj have many kings, who are at war with each
other. The kings have in their service men known by the title
of almokhazzamoun (those who have their nostrils drilled), because
they have holes pierced in their noses. To a ring placed in their
nostrils a chain is attached. In time of war these men march at
the head of the combatants, and the end of the chain is held by
some one, who pulls it when he desires to prevent the man from
going forward. Negotiators intervene close to the two parties ;
if they consent to an arrangement one party retires, if not, the
chain is rolled round the neck of the warrior, who is left to himself, and no one withdraws from his place, but all deal death at
their posts.

The Arabs exercise a great ascendancy over these people.
When a man of this nation sees an Arab, he prostrates himself
before him, and says : " Behold a man from the country which
produces dates," so fond are they of dates, and to such an extent
are their hearts smitten.

Religious discourses are pronounced before them ; in no nation
are preachers found so persistent as those of this people in their
language. Among them are men who have devoted themselves
to a pious life, who cover themselves with the skins of panthers
or of apes ; they have a staff in their hands, and proceed towards

the houses, when the inhabitants come together immediately. The devotee sometimes remains a whole day until evening upon his legs, occupied in preaching to them and recalling God to their remembrance, that he may be exalted! He explains to them the fate which has been undergone by those of their nation who are dead.

From this country zendjian panthers are exported, of which the skin of mingled red and white is very beautiful and very large.

Abou'l Hacan Ali el Masoudi was born at Bagdad towards the close of the third century after the hegira. In early manhood he was fond of travel, and visited India and many parts of the East, as well as the island of Kanbalou * and the African coast somewhere north of the equator. In later life he resided for a time at Antioch and at Bassorah, and died at Old Cairo in the year of our lord 956. In 943 he completed a great work, which has been translated into French by Messrs. C. Barbier de Meynard and Pavet de Courtaille, and was published in Paris for the Asiatic Society of France. The translation is entitled *Les Prairies d'Or*, and was issued with the original Arabic text in nine demi octavo volumes, in the years 1861 to 1877.

This great work contains more information upon the Bantu than all the other Arabic volumes yet translated put together. Those people were then found as far south as Sofala, which is mentioned not as a town or village, but as a territory.

The following is a translation into English from the French, of the complete account of the Zendj given by Masoudi:

These kingdoms (India) are constantly at war, and differ from each other as much in their language as in their religions. The greater number of these people believe in metempsychosis or the transmigration of souls, as we have already stated. But in their intelligence, their government, their philosophy, their robust constitution, as well as in the purity of their colour, the Indians

* The French translators of Masoudi's work were of opinion that the island of Kanbalou was the one now known as Madagascar, but they were not certain of it. It seems just as likely to have been Zanzibar or one of the Comoro islands, though there are as great difficulties in fixing upon one of these as upon Madagascar.

differ from all other black races, such as the Zendjes, the Demdemes, &c. Galien points out ten particular characteristics of the blacks, to wit : woolly hair, want of eyebrows generally, distended nostrils, thick lips, pointed teeth, offensive smell of the skin, blackness of colour, large size of the feet and hands, development of the genital organs, and excessive petulancy. This author attributes the last characteristic of the blacks to the imperfect organisation of their brains, from which the feebleness of their intelligence results. The vivacity of the negro, the hold that mirth has upon him, and the excessive petulancy which distinguishes the Zendjes among all the black races, have drawn forth the observations of other authors which we have inserted in our preceding works.

Yakoub, son of Ishak el-Kendi, in one of his treatises relating to the action of exalted bodies and of celestial spheres upon our earth, adds : " God has established a chain of causes in all parts of creation ; the cause exerts upon the creature that is acted upon an influence which it gives back in its turn ; but a purely subjective creature cannot react upon the cause or its agent. The soul being the cause and not the effect of the sphere, the sphere cannot react upon the soul, but it is in the nature of the soul to follow the temperament of the body as long as it meets with no obstacle, and it is this which takes place with the Zendj. Their country being very warm, the celestial bodies exert their influence in it, and attract the humours to the superior parts of the body. On this account the eyes are on a line with the faces of these people, their lips bulge out, their noses are flat and broad, and the development of the head arises from the ascending movement of the humours. The brain loses its equilibrium, and the soul can no longer carry on its full action ; the vagueness of perception and the absence of all acts of intelligence are the result."

The ancients as well as the moderns have discussed the causes of the conformation of the blacks and of their position with regard to the sphere. The question has been investigated whether one of the seven planets, the sun, the moon, or the five others, presides over their actions, and has a particular influence upon their birth and their physical development. But our work not being concerned in that kind of research, we cannot relate what has been said in regard to it ; the reader will find in our *Historical Annals* the theories and the arguments that have been brought forward ;

in it he will also find an account of the system of those ancient and modern astronomers who have regarded the negroes as under the influence of Saturn. Such is also the opinion of a poet and contemporary Moslem astrologer, very learned in that which relates to the spheres :

"The senior (of these stars) is sublime Saturn, majestic ancient of days, powerful monarch.

"His temperament is black and cold, black as the soul the prey of despair.

"His influence is exercised upon the Zendjes and the slaves, and also upon lead and iron."

Taous el-Yemani, companion of Abdallah, son of el-Abbas, would not touch the flesh of an animal killed by a Zendj, because, he said, the Zendj is a hideous being. I have heard it said that Abou'l Abbas er-Radi billah, son of el-Moktadir, would not receive anything from the hand of a negro, because he was a hideous slave. I do not know whether in acting in this manner he conformed to the doctrine of Taous, or whether he followed some particular philosophical precept. Amr, son of Bahr el-Djahiz, has written a book *Upon the Superiority of the Blacks, and their Struggle with the White Race.*

I have seen in the Geography (of Ptolemy) a plan representing the Nile issuing from the foot of the mountain el-Komr. Its waters, which burst forth at first from twelve sources, flow into two lakes like the ponds (of Bassorah) ; they unite when issuing thence, and flow through sandy and mountainous regions. The Nile pursues its course across that part of the Soudan which adjoins the country of the Zendj, and from it issues a branch which flows into the sea of Zendj. This sea washes the island of Kanbalou, an island well cultivated, and inhabited by Mohamedans who speak the language of the Zendj. They made themselves masters of the island by taking captive all the Zendj population, at the time of the conquest of the island of Crete in the Mediterranean by the Mohamedans, at the commencement of the Abbaside dynasty and about the close of the reign of the Ommiades.

Concerning the branch of the Nile which, as we have said, flows into the sea of Zendj, this is nothing but a channel which issues from the great basin of the Zendj, and separates that country from the frontiers inhabited by the Abyssinian races. Had it not been for this channel, the great deserts, and the drifting sands, the turbulent and innumerable hordes of the Zendj would have driven the Abyssinians from the land of their birth.

The Indian sea forms upon the borders of Abyssinia a channel which projects into the country of Berbera, a part of the territory inhabited by the Zendjes and the Abyssinians. This channel, known by the name of *Berberi*,* is five hundred miles long, and its breadth from one shore to the other is one hundred miles. The territory of Berbera must not be confounded with the country of the Berbers, situated in the land named Ifrikiyah, a land quite distinct from that of which we are speaking, and which has nothing in common with it except the name. The pilots of Oman sail down this channel to reach the island of Kanbalou, which lies in the sea of Zanguebar, and is inhabited by a mixed population of Mohamedans and of pagan Zendjes. These same sailors of Oman maintain that this channel of Berberi, that they designate the sea of Berbera and of the country of Djafouna, is of much greater extent than we have indicated ; they add that its billows are like high mountains, and they term them *blind billows*, without doubt because after having been swollen like high mountains, they sink into the form of deep valleys ; but they never break, nor are they covered with foam, as one observes in other seas. They give them also the name of *foolish billows*. The sailors who frequent these parts are Arabs of Oman and of the tribe of Azd. When they have reached the open sea, and are willingly going up and down the rolling billows, they sing in harmony the following refrain :

> " Berbera and Djafouna, may your billows be foolish !
> Djafouna and Berbera, those are their billows."

The termination of their passage on the sea of Zendj is the island of Kanbalou, of which we have already spoken, and the country of Sofala and of the Wakwaks, situated upon the border of Zanguebar and at the extreme end of this branch of the sea. The people of Siraf also make this passage, and I myself have sailed upon this sea when I left Sendjar, the capital of Oman, in company with several nakhoda or pilots of Siraf, among others Mohamed, son of Zeïdboud, and Djewher, son of Ahmed, surnamed Ibn Sirah, who was lost there afterwards with all his crew. My last passage from the island of Kanbalou to Oman took place in the year 304 (A.H.). I was on board a vessel belonging to Ahmed

* Now termed the gulf of Aden.

and Abd es-Samed, two brothers of Abd er-Rahim, son of Djâfar
of Siraf, a resident of Mikan, which is one of the quarters of Siraf,
and these same two men, Ahmed and Abd es-Samed, sons of Djâfar,
perished afterwards with their property in this sea. At the time
of my last voyage the emir of Oman was Ahmed, son of Helal,
son of a sister of el Kaïtal. Indeed I have sailed upon many seas,
the sea of China, of Roum, of Khazars, of Kolzoum, and of Yemen,
I have gone through dangers without number, but I have known
none more full of perils than this sea of Zendj, of which we have
been speaking.

We return to the different kings of the country and to the
enumeration of the kingdoms which remain to be described upon
the border of the sea of Abyssinia. The king of the Zendj is called
Flimi.

Behind the country of Alawah (Lowata) there is a large
population of blacks living, called Bekneh (Bedjneh). They go
naked like the Zendj. Their country contains mines of gold.
It is in this kingdom that the Nile is divided, and from it issues
a large channel which when it leaves the Nile takes a greenish
colour. The principal stream, the true Nile, has no other offshoots, and its course is towards the country of the Nubians. But
at certain times the great branch of the Nile is diverted into this
channel, and takes a whitish colour, when the little arm turns
green. This channel divides into several streams of water and
canals crossing inhabited valleys ; afterwards it reaches the deserts
of the south towards the shore of the Zendjes, and it discharges
its waters into the sea of Zendj.

When the posterity of Noah spread themselves out over the
earth, the sons of Kouch, son of Kanaan, directed their steps
towards, and crossed over the Nile. There they separated ; some,
that is to say the Nubians, the Bedjah, and the Zendjes, turned
to the right, between the east and the west ; the others, in great
numbers, marched towards the west, in the direction of Zagawah,
of Kanem, of Markab, of Kawka, of Ganah, and other parts of
the country of the blacks and of the Demdemeh. Those who
went towards the right, between the east and the west, separated
in their turn, and formed several nations : the Mékir, the Meckkir,
the Berbera, and the other tribes of the Zendjes.

The country of the Zendjes furnishes skins of tawny panthers ;
the inhabitants use them to clothe themselves, or send them to

a Mohamedan country. They are the largest panther skins and the most beautiful to make saddles of. The sea of Zendj and of Abyssinia is on the right side of the sea of India, though these two seas join each other. Tortoise shells are also exported from this country, of which combs are made, in the same way as horn is used for this purpose.

As we have already stated, the Zendjes and the other tribes of Abyssinia spread themselves out along the right bank of the Nile to the extremity of the sea of Abyssinia. Alone among all the tribes of Abyssinians, the Zendjes proceeded along the channel which flows from the larger stream of the Nile and empties itself in the sea of Zendj. They established themselves in this country, and spread out to Sofala, which is the most distant frontier of the territory and the terminus of the navigation of the vessels of Oman and of Siraf in the sea of Zendj. Just as the sea of China reaches to the country of Sila (Japan), of which we have already had occasion to speak, so are the limits of the sea of Zendj the country of Sofala and of the Wakwak, a country which produces gold in abundance and other wonderful things. The climate is hot, and the land is fertile. It is there that the Zendjes built their capital ; afterwards they chose a king whom they named Waklimi. This name, as we have already seen, has always been that of their sovereigns. The Waklimi has as dependents all the other Zendjian kings, and has command of three hundred thousand fighting men. The Zendjes employ the ox as a beast of burden, because in their country there are neither horses, nor mules, nor camels, and they do not even know of such animals. Snow and hail are unknown to them, as to all the Abyssinians. Among them are some tribes who have their teeth very sharp and who are cannibals. The country of the Zendjes commences at the channel which is derived from the upper Nile, and extends to the country of Sofala and of the Wakwak. Their habitations are spread out over an area of about seven hundred parasangs * in length and in breadth.

This country is formed of valleys, mountains, and sandy deserts ; it contains many wild elephants, but not even a single tame one is found there. The Zendjes do not employ them in war or for other purposes, and they hunt them only to kill them. When they wish to capture them, they throw into the water the leaves,

---

* A parasang was a measure of length equal to about five kilometres and a half.

the bark, and the branches of a tree which grows in their country, then they place themselves in ambuscade until the elephants come to drink. The water burns and intoxicates them, they fall down and cannot rise again, their legs, as we have said, being deprived of movement. The Zendjes attack them, armed with long darts, and kill them in order to take their tusks. It is their country which furnishes those tusks of ivory of which each one weighs one hundred and fifty *menn* and more. They are usually taken to Oman, and are sent to China and India. That is the course which they follow, and if they were not so forwarded, ivory would be very abundant in the Mohamedan country.

But returning to the subject of which we were treating at the beginning of this chapter, the Zendjes, the description of their country, and of the other tribes of Abyssinia. The Zendjes, although constantly occupied in hunting elephants and collecting ivory, do not employ this material for domestic purposes. Instead of gold and silver they use iron for making ornaments for their persons, just as they use oxen, as we have already stated, as beasts of burden or for war, instead of camels and horses. These oxen are harnessed like horses, and run with the same speed.

In reverting to the Zendjes and to their kings, the name of the kings of this country is *Waklimi*, which signifies son of the supreme lord ; they designate their sovereign thus because he was chosen to rule over them with equity. Therefore if he exercises a tyrannical power and if he departs from the rules of justice, they put him to death and exclude his posterity from the accession to the throne, for they maintain that by conducting himself in that way he ceased to be the son of the master, that is to say of the king of heaven and earth. They give to God the name of *Maklandjalou*, which means the sovereign master.

The Zendjes express themselves with elegance, and there are among them orators in their language. Frequently a devout person of the country, standing in the middle of a numerous concourse of people, addresses an exhortation to his audience in which he calls upon them to do that which is pleasing to God and to be submissive to his commands. He represents to them the chastisements they will make themselves liable to by disobedience, and cites the example of their ancestors and their ancient kings. These people have no religious code ; their kings follow custom, and in governing they conform to certain political rules. The Zendjes use as food the banana, which is as plentiful with them as it is in India ; but the principal article of their diet is millet and a plant called kalari,* which is drawn from the ground like the truffle and the root of the elecampane. It is found in abundance at Aden and in the district of Yemen which adjoins this town, it resembles the colocasie of Egypt and Syria. They consume also honey and flesh. Each one worships whatever he pleases, a plant, an animal, or a mineral. They possess a large number of islands in which the cocoa palm grows, the fruit of which is one of the articles of food of all the tribes of Zendjes. One of these islands, situated at a distance of one or two days' journey from the coast, contains a Mohamedan population among whom royalty is transmitted, This is the island of Kanbalou, of which we have had occasion to speak in this work.

Masoudi also gives the following account, which completes all that he says about the Zendj in any part of his work :

Under the caliphate of Moutazz, in the year 252 of the hegira, the first symptoms of discord between the Bellalites and the Saadites appeared at Bassorah, and the revolt of the chief of the Zendj was the consequence of these troubles.

The history of Ahmed, son of Moudebbir, that of Ibrahim, his brother, and the transactions of the latter with the chief of the Zendj when he made him prisoner, present a view of facts of great interest.

The revolt of the chief of the Zendj broke out at Bassorah in the reign of Mouhtadi, in the year of the hegira 255. This man claimed to be Ali, son of Mohamed, son of Ahmed, son of Yça, son of Zeïd, son of Ali, son of El-Huçeïn, son of Ali, son of Abou Talib ; but in the general opinion this genealogy was false

---

* I have been unable to ascertain what this plant is. All sections of the Bantu that I am acquainted with use many varieties of wild plants for food, and are much more expert in finding them than Europeans are. I once asked a Xosa youth who was out in the veld with me if he knew what a nongwe (Hypoxis, p. 385 *Harvey's Gen. S. A. Plants*) was. I wanted to know, because the word occurred in a tale I had recently heard. He stooped down, and drew one from the ground, observing " if I had not eaten so much maize this morning I would be eating them now." They were to be found at our very feet and all around us, but I was quite ignorant of that. In his *Lake Regions of Central Equatorial Africa*, London, 1860, Captain (afterwards Sir Richard) Burton mentions among the vegetables of Ujiji the roots of a white arum, somewhat resembling the Jerusalem artichoke, but almost without flavour.

and should be rejected. He was a native of a village named Verzenên, which was a dependency of the province of Rey. His conduct proved that the accusation against him of belonging to the sect of the Kharédjites named Azrakites was well founded; indeed he killed women, little children, old men, and all those whose lives should have been spared, which proves that the charge was correct. . . . Placing himself at the head of the Zendj, he raised the standard at *Bir Makhl* (the well of the palm tree), between Medinet el-Fath and Kerkh-Basrah, on Thursday the third day before the end of ramadan in the year of the hegira 255. He made himself master of Bassorah in 257, and was killed on Saturday the second of safer, in the caliphate of Moutamid-Alallah.

On Thursday the first day of the moon of rébi I in the year 258 of the hegira, he (Moutamid-Alallah) bestowed a vestment of honour upon his brother Abou Ahmed Mouaffak and on Mouflih, after which he sent them to Bassorah to fight against the chief of the Zendj. Mouflih, the Turk, gave battle to this chief on Tuesday the twelfth day before the end of djemadi I of the same year. Struck by an arrow in the temple, Mouflih died on Wednesday the next day. His body was conveyed to Samarra, and was buried in that town. Mouaffak then ceased to carry on the contest with the chief of the Zendj.

In the month of safar in the year of the hegira 267 Mouaffak renewed the campaign against the chief of the Zendj. In rebi II he detached his son Abou 'l Abbas to march upon Souq el-Khamîs, or Chârani, one of the towns devoted to the Alevide, that is to say the chief of the Zendj, who was entrenched with a large body of Zendj. Abou 'l Abbas made himself master of the place and of all the spoil that it contained, he took several other towns, and put to death all the Zendj that he encountered. On his side Mouaffak entered the province of Ahwaz (Susiane), and repaired there the damages caused by the enemy. He returned afterwards to Bassorah, and did not cease to fight against the chief of the Zendj until he killed him. This rebel, whose power lasted fourteen years and four months, had massacred without pity children and aged people, men and women, everywhere he had spread fire and pillage. In a single battle fought near Bassorah, he killed three hundred thousand men.

Mohallebi, one of the principal officers of Ali ben Mohamed (the name of the chief of the Zendj), remained at Bassorah after this battle. . . . As those of his party who remained at Bassorah still held firmly to the opinions of Mohallebi and continued to assemble on certain Fridays, they were outlawed. Some succeeded in saving themselves, the others were killed or were drowned. A large number of them concealed themselves in the houses and the wells ; they came out only at night, and hunted for dogs, rats, and cats, which they killed for food ; but this resource was soon exhausted, and they found nothing more to eat. Then they devoured the corpses of their companions who died, they watched one another, each waiting for the death of the other, the strongest killed their comrades and devoured them. To these evils the want of fresh water was added.

The insolence of the army of the Zendj was such that they sold by auction the women of the family of Haçan, of Huçein, and of Abbas, the descendants of Hachem, of Koreïch, and of the noblest Arab families. A young girl was sold for two to three dirhems. Every black owned ten, twenty, and even thirty of these women ; they served as concubines to the blacks, and in comparison with their wives performed the work of the humblest slaves.

In the foregoing account of Masoudi, it will have been noticed that an arm of the Nile emptying into the Indian ocean is more than once mentioned, and that the Zendj or Bantu are asserted to have migrated to the south along it. This geographical feature was for centuries regarded as correct, though at the time of the entrance of the Portuguese into the Indian ocean it was believed that the stream did not issue from the Nile itself, but from one of the two lakes which were the common source of it and the Nile. A little later it was supposed that there were several lakes connected with each other in the centre of the continent, and every stream of importance that empties itself along the eastern coast was regarded as issuing from one or the other of them. We have in the name Delagoa Bay a result of this belief. The name da lagoa was first given by the Portuguese to the river on which the town of Lourenço Marques is now built, because it was held to flow from the great lake, and by the English and the Dutch, but not by the Portuguese, the name was transferred to the bay.

Masoudi terms that part of the Indian ocean adjoining the African coast the sea of Zendj, because the Bantu lived along it. He estimated it at seven hundred parasangs or thirty-five degrees of latitude in length from the gulf of Aden to Sofala, which is very nearly correct, though his numbers, such as three hundred thousand fighting men at the disposal of the ruler at Sofala or the same number of men killed in one battle near Bassorah, are utterly fabulous.

The use by the Bantu of the ox as an animal of burden, the method of hunting and killing elephants for their tusks, the use of iron instead of gold or silver for ornaments, and the clothing made from skins are all correctly described. The account of the barter with the Arabs of ivory, skins of carnivora, and tortoise shells, is an item of interest.

But far more important is the information that Bantu were then living as far south as Sofala, though what is stated of the position and power of the chief there must be rejected as a wild flight of imagination, perhaps not of Masoudi himself, but of his informants, for he never was there. When or how the tribe crossed the Zambesi and settled in what is now the northern part of Mashonaland and the territory between it and the coast is not related, still the cause of the migration can be conjectured almost to a certainty. There was a constant pressure southward, and there was never ceasing war among the tribes along the coast. The people who had inhabited the country adjoining the ancient trading station of Rhapta, and who had the blood of Arabs and Persians, of Indians and even of Greeks, mixed with that of Bantu in their veins, had been compelled to leave their former home, and had by some means managed to make their way so far and to place a great unfordable river between them and their foes. Their superior intelligence, due to their better blood, had enabled them to do this. They knew the value of gold for trading purposes, though they made no use of that metal themselves, and so they collected it in their new settlement, and the Arabs followed them by sea to obtain it from them by barter, as Masoudi states.

From the territory in which they settled the Bushmen were of course expelled, but the area cannot have been large, for centuries later they had not crossed the Sabi, and to this day Bushman paintings found in many easily accessible places testify that they did not extend their occupation into what is now known as Matabeleland. Masoudi does not define their border, he merely says that the Wakwak or Bushmen adjoined them, and indeed he could not have ascertained more.

Abi l'Cassem Abdallah Ebn Haukal, a native of Khorasan, wrote an account of the world as known to him between the years of our era 902 and 968, probably completed about A.D. 950. The original Arabic was translated into Persian, and it is from the latter text that the edition in English has been obtained. This was published in a quarto volume in London in 1800, and is entitled: *The Oriental Geography of Ebn Haukal, an Arabian Traveller of the Tenth Century. Translated from a Manuscript in his own Possession, collated with one preserved in the Library of Eton College, by Sir William Ouseley, Knt., LL.D.*

Possibly the reason why the Mohamedan writers give so little information upon the Bantu was not their ignorance, but their scorn. Ebn Haukal, at any rate, asserts this to be the case with him. He says: " As for the land of blacks, in the west (Africa), and the Zingians, Æthiopians, and such tribes, I make but slight mention of them in this book; because, naturally loving wisdom, ingenuity, religion, justice, and regular government, how could I notice such people as those, or exalt them by inserting an account of their countries ? " And all he says of Eastern Africa is the following :

Between *Yajouge* and Majouge, and the northern ocean, and between the deserts of the Blacks and the other limits of the ocean, all is desolate and waste, without any buildings. I know not what are the roads or stages of those two deserts which are on the coasts of the ocean, because it is impossible to travel in them on account of the excessive heat, which hinders the building of houses, or the residing there. Thus, also, in the south, no animal can exist, so excessive is the heat, nor any person dwell there.

On the sea-coast there is a place called Zeilaa, which is the port for those who go to Yemen and Hejaz. Then begin the deserts of Nubia. The Nubians are Christians ; and their country is wider than that of the Abyssinians ; and the Ægyptian Nile passes through their territories, and goes on to the land of the Zingians (Æthiopia) ; and one cannot proceed beyond that.

The sea continues to the land of Zingbar, Æthiopia, opposite Aden : thence it departs from the regions of Islam. Æthiopia is a dry country, with few buildings, and very little cultivated ground. The leopard skins, and other spotted skins which are brought into *Yemen*, come from this place. The inhabitants are at war with the Mussulmans. There is in *Zingbar* a race of white people, who bring from other places articles of food and clothing. This country produces little : the inhabitants are not much inclined to the cultivation of arts and sciences.

So far we have spoken of those countries bordering on the Persian Sea : now we proceed to describe the regions of the West.

The greatest of the Arab geographers was Abou Abdallah Mohammed el Edrisi, a native of Spain, who lived from A.D. 1100 to A.D. 1154, and who wrote his valuable book under the patronage of Roger, Christian king of Sicily, the most enlightened monarch of his age. There is a translation into French of part of this work by R. Dozy and M. J. de Goeje, published at Leyden in 1866, but it does not contain the sections relating to Eastern Africa. The complete work, however, exists in French in two quarto volumes, in which the translation—the original Arabic text is not given—occupies one thousand and fifty-one pages. These volumes were published at Paris in 1836 and 1840, at the expense of the French government, and are entitled *Géographie d'Édrisi traduite de l'Arabe en Français d'après deux manuscrits de la Bibliothèke du Roi, et accompagnée de Notes, par P. Amédée Jaubert, Professeur de Turk a l'école royalé et spéciale des langues orientales vivantes, etc., etc., etc.*

Edrisi followed Ptolemy in the belief that Africa stretched away to the east, but of that part he professed to know nothing. What he did know and relate, as of the exportation of iron, of the abundance of gold obtained at Sofala, of the Bantu using copper ornaments in preference to gold, and, above all, of

Bushmen alone occupying the country beyond Sofala, is of high interest. The following is an English translation of the French of Professor Jaubert, and is all the information that Edrisi gives upon the Bantu and the country they were occupying:

First Climate.*—Seventh Section.

This section contains the description of a part of the Indian sea and of all the islands that are found there, and that are inhabited by people of different races. In the middle of the region comprised in this section are the rest of the territory of the black Kaffirs and various countries bordering on the sea. Our intention is to describe all these subjects clearly. We say then that this sea is the sea of the Indies, and that upon its shore is situated the town of Merouat, at the extreme end of the country of the Kaffirs, people without a faith, who worship nothing but stones smeared with fish oil, such is the degree of stupidity in which they are sunk and the absurdity of their vile beliefs. Part of this country is subject to the king of the Berbers, the other part is a dependency of Abyssinia. From Merouat, situated upon the coast, to Medouna, is reckoned three days' journey by sea. The last named town is in ruins, almost deserted, filthy, and unpleasant to live in. Its inhabitants subsist upon fish, shellfish, snakes, rats, lizards, and other loathsome reptiles. These people carry on fishing in the sea without boats, and without living constantly on the shore. They fish by swimming or by diving with little nets made by them of vegetable fibres. They fasten these nets to their feet ; by means of lines and of running knots which they hold in their hands they close the net as soon as they feel that a fish has entered it, and that with a skill in which they excel and with ruses of which they have long experience. To attract the fish they make use of land reptiles. Although they live in such a condition of distress and of profound misery, still these people (God loves those who cling to their domestic hearths) are satisfied with their lot, and are content with that which they have. They are under the government of the Zendj.

From the town of Medouna, following the coast, Melinde, a town of the Zendj, is reached by sea in three days and three nights.

* The zones of Edrisi are climatic, not measured by degrees from the equator as ours are.

Melinde is situated on the border of the sea, at the mouth of a river of fresh water. It is a large town, of which the inhabitants occupy themselves in hunting and fishing. On land they hunt the tiger and other ferocious animals. In the sea they catch different kinds of fish, which they salt, and with which they carry on commerce. They possess and work mines of iron, and this is with them an article of commerce and the source of their greatest profits. They claim to understand the art of charming the most venomous snakes, and making them harmless to every one except to those to whom they wish evil, or to those on whom they desire to execute vengeance. They claim also that by means of enchantments tigers and lions cannot do them any harm. Such enchanters bear in the language of these people the name of el-Mocnefa. From this town to Manisa, along the coast, is two days' journey. This is a small place, and is a dependency of the Zendj. Its inhabitants are occupied in working mines of iron and hunting tigers. They have dogs of a reddish colour that fight with and conquer every kind of wild animal, even lions. This town is situated upon the border of the sea, and close to a great gulf which vessels go up for two days' sail, upon the shores of which there are no habitations on account of the animals of prey that live there in the forests, where the Zendjes go to hunt them, as is reported. It is in this town that the king of Zenghebar resides. His guards are footmen, because there are no horses in this country, as they cannot live there. From Manisa to the town of el-Banes is by land six days' journey, and by sea a hundred and fifty miles. El-Banes is a very large and populous town. The inhabitants venerate a drum called errahim, as large as . . . , covered with skin on one side only, and to which is attached a cord by means of which the drum is beaten. This results in a frightful noise, which can be heard at a distance of three miles or thereabouts.

El-Banes is the last dependency of the Zendj. It borders on Sofala, the country of gold. From el-Banes to the side of the town named Tohnet is by sea a hundred and fifty miles, and by land eight days' journey, as between these places there is a great gulf which, extending towards the south, compels travellers to turn from a straight course, and a high mountain named Adjoud, of which the flanks have been worn into deep ravines on all sides by the waters which course down with a frightful noise. This mountain draws towards it the vessels that approach it, and the sailors take care to keep away from it and to flee from the locality.

The town of Tohnet is also a dependency of the country of Sofala, and borders on that of the Zendjes. There are a good many villages, and they are all built upon the banks of rivers. In all the country of the Zendjes the principal productions are iron and the skins of tigers of Zenghebar. The colour of these skins is reddish, and they are very pliant. As these people have no beasts of burden, they are obliged to carry upon their heads and their backs the articles destined for the two towns of Melinde and Molbasa, where they make their sales and their purchases. The Zendjes have no ships in which they can make voyages, but vessels from the country of Oman visit them, and others bound to the islands of Zaledj, which are dependencies of India; these strangers sell their merchandise at Zenghebar, and purchase the productions of the country. The inhabitants of the islands of Zaledj go to Zenghebar in large and small ships, and they make use of them for commerce with their merchandise, as they understand the languages of each other. The Zendjes have at the bottom of their hearts great respect and a good deal of veneration for the Arabs. For this reason when they see an Arab, whether he is a traveller or a trader, they prostrate themselves before him, magnify his dignity, and address him in their language: " you are very welcome, o son of Yemen ! " Travellers who go into this country steal children, and delude them by means of dates which they give them. They entice them away here and there, and end by taking possession of their persons and conveying them into their own country, for the inhabitants of Zenghebar form a numerous population, and are wanting in resources. The prince of the island of Keich, situated in the sea of Oman, with his vessels undertakes military expeditions against the Zendj, and makes a good many of them captives.

Opposite the shores of the Zendj are the islands of Zaledj; they are numerous and large.

EIGHTH SECTION.

This section contains the description of the remainder of the country of Sofala.

To begin with, two towns, or rather two burghs, are found there, between which are villages and camping places like those of the Arabs. These burghs are called Djentama and Dendema. They are situated upon the border of the sea, and are not of great size. The inhabitants are poor, wretched, and have no other means of existence than iron. There are a good number of mines of this metal in the mountains of Sofala. The inhabitants of the islands of Zanedj and of other neighbouring islands come to seek iron there to transport it to the continent and the islands of India, where they sell it at a good price, for it is an important article of trade and is much used in India, and although it is found in the islands and in the mines of that country, it is not equal to the iron of Sofala, either in abundance or in quality and malleability. The Indians excel in the art of manufacturing it, in that of preparing the ingredients by means of which, by fusion, the soft iron is obtained which is commonly called iron of India. They have manufactories in which the most highly valued sabres in the world are made. It is thus that the irons of Sind, of Serendib, and of Yemen are estimated according to the account of the quality resulting from the local atmosphere, as well as according to that of skill in manufacture, in smelting, in forging, in the beauty of polish and of brightness, but it is impossible to find any capable of taking a sharper edge than the iron of India. This is a matter universally recognised, and that no one can dispute.

From Djentama to Dendema is reckoned two days' journey by sea, seven days' journey by land.

Dendema is one of the principal towns of Sofala, three others adjoin the territory of this country. One of these is Siouna, a town of medium size, of which the population consists of Indians, Zendjes, and others. It is situated upon a gulf where foreign vessels come to anchor. From Siouna to Boukha, upon the border of the sea, is three days' journey; from the same place to Dendema of Sofala towards the west is three days' journey by sea, and by land about twenty days' journey, because there lies between them a great gulf which extends towards the south, and which necessitates a considerable detour. From Boukha to Djentama is by sea one day's journey, by land four days' journey. In all the country of Sofala gold is found in abundance, and of excellent quality. Notwithstanding this the inhabitants prefer copper, and they make their ornaments of the last-named metal. The gold that is found in the territory of Sofala exceeds in quantity as well as in size (of the nuggets) that of other countries, for pieces are found of one or two mithcals, more or less, and sometimes even of a rotl. It is smelted in waste places by means of fire made of cowdung, without which it would be necessary to have recourse to quicksilver, as is done in Western Africa, for the inhabitants of the latter country put together their pieces of gold, mix them with quicksilver, fuse the mixture by means of charcoal fire, so that the quicksilver evaporates and nothing remains but the mass of pure gold. The gold of Sofala does not need to be treated in this manner, but it is smelted without any contrivance that alters it. We shall conclude afterwards what we have to say of this country, if it pleases God.

NINTH SECTION.

This section contains the description of the part of the sea of India known by the name of the sea of China, and of a part of the sea named Darlazouï. In this sea are various islands of which we shall make mention hereafter.

We say then that to the south of this sea is a part of Sofala, of which we have already spoken, and that among the number of inhabited places in the country is the town of Djebesta, of some importance. A quantity of gold is found there; gathering it is the sole industry and the principal resource of the inhabitants. They eat sea turtles and shellfish. Millet is fairly plentiful with them. The town is situated upon a great gulf into which ships can enter. The inhabitants of Djebesta having neither ships nor beasts to carry their burdens, they are compelled to bear them themselves, and to assist each other reciprocally. Those of Comor and the traders of the country of Mehradj visit them, are well received, and traffic with them. From the town of Djebesta to that of Daghouta is three days and three nights by sea, and to the island of Comor one day.

The town of Daghouta is the last in Sofala, the land of gold, it is situated on a great gulf. Its inhabitants go naked, nevertheless they conceal their sexual parts with their hands when the traders from the neighbouring islands approach them. Their women have a feeling of shame, and do not show themselves in the paths or in places of meeting, on account of their nudity; for that reason they confine themselves to their dwellings. Gold is found in the town and in its territory in greater abundance than anywhere else in Sofala. This country borders on that of the Wakwak, where there are two towns wretched and poorly peopled, on account of the scarcity of subsistence and of the slender resources of all kinds. One is called Derou, and the other Nebhena. In its neighbourhood is a large burgh Da'rgha. The natives are blacks, hideous in appearance, with ill-favoured dispositions; their language is a kind of whistling. They are absolutely naked, and are seldom visited by strangers. They live upon fish, shellfish, and tortoises. They are (as it is said) in the neighbourhood of the island of Wakwak, of which we shall speak again, if it pleases God. Each of these countries and of these islands is situated on a great gulf. Neither gold, nor commerce, nor ship, nor beast of burden is found there. As for the island of Djalous, its inhabitants are Zendjes, they go naked, and live, as we have said, on whatever falls into their hands.

TENTH SECTION.

In the part of the islands of Wakwak near it, the places are isolated by islets and mountains inaccessible to travellers, owing to the extreme difficulty of communication. The inhabitants are infidels who know nothing of religion, and who have not received the law. The women go entirely naked, wearing only combs of ivory adorned with mother of pearl. A woman wears sometimes up to twenty of these combs. The men cover the head with a head dress like that which we call alcaanès and which is termed in the Indian language el-bouhari. They remain protected in their mountains, without leaving them, and without allowing any one to visit them, nevertheless they show themselves upon their heights along the shore to watch the vessels, and sometimes they call out to them in an unintelligible language. Such is always their manner of existence. Close to this country is the island of Wakwak, beyond which nothing is known of what there is.

The geographer known in Europe as Aboulfeda was born at Damascus in the year of the hegira 672, or A.D. 1273, and died at Hamat in October 1331. The name given to him when he was circumcised was Ismaël, and on arriving at the age of manhood he took the surname Emad-eddin. He became prince of Hamat, when the sultan of Egypt gave him the title Almalek-almovayyad, so that Aboulfeda is only a nickname. He travelled through Egypt, Northern Arabia, Syria, and the territory eastward to the Euphrates, but the information he gives upon other countries consists of quotations from earlier authors. His work was translated into French, and was published at Paris in two quarto volumes in 1848 at the expense of the government. The translation is entitled *Geographie d'Aboulféda traduite de l'Arabe en Français et accompagnée de Notes et d'Eclaircissements par M. Reinaud, membre de l'Institut de France, Professor d'Arabe, etc.* Upon South Eastern Africa the only information given in this work is the following quotation from Ibn-Sayd :

Melende is a town in the country of the Zendjes, in longitude 81° 30′ and latitude 2° 50′ south. To the west of this town is a large gulf, into which a river flows that courses down from the mountain of Comr. The extensive settlements of the Zendjes are upon the borders of this gulf, the settlements of the people of Comr are found to the south. To the east of Melende is Alkherany, a mountain very celebrated among travellers ; this mountain projects into the sea for a distance of about a hundred miles towards the north-east, it also extends upon the continent in a straight line towards the south to a distance of about fifty miles. Among other peculiarities which this mountain presents these are noticeable : the part which is on the continent contains a mine of iron, and that which is in the sea a mine of loadstone which attracts the iron. The tree of zendj is found at Melende. The king of the Zendjes lives in the town of Melende. Between Monbase and Melende there is about a degree of distance. Monbase is situated upon the border of the sea. To the west is a gulf which vessels penetrate to a distance of about three hundred miles. Close by, on the eastern side, the desert appears which separates the country of the Zendjes from that of Sofala.

Among the towns of the country of Sofala is Batyna, situated at the extreme end of a great gulf which runs into the land, distant from the equinoctial line 2° 30′, and in longitude 87 degrees. According to Ibn-Sayd to the west of Batyna is Adjred, a mountain that projects into the sea towards the north-east to a distance of a hundred miles ; the waves which the sea forms in this place make a great noise. To the east of this mountain are the habitations of the people of Sofala, of which the capital is named Seyouna, in ninety degrees of longitude and two degrees and a half south latitude. This town is situated upon a large gulf, into which flows a river that descends from the mountain of Comr. The king of Sofala lives at this place. Next to it, the town of Leyrana is reached. Ibn-Fathima, who has visited this town, says that it is a place where ships arrive and from which they set sail. The inhabitants profess the creed of islam. The longitude of Leyrana is a hundred and two degrees, and its latitude about thirty minutes ; it is situated upon a large gulf. The town of Daghouta is the last in the country of Sofala and the most distant of the inhabited part of the continent on the southern side. Its longitude is a hundred and nine degrees, and its latitude twelve degrees south of the 'equator.

Sofala. According to the *Canoun* in 50 degrees and 3 minutes longitude and 2 degrees latitude south of the equinoctial line. Sofala is situated in the country of the Zendjes. According to the author of the Canoun, the inhabitants are Mohamedans. Ibn-Sayd states that their principal means of existence depends on the extraction of gold and iron, and that their garments are leopard skins. According to Masoudi's account, horses do not thrive in the country of the Zendjes, so that the warriors march altogether on foot, or fight upon oxen. I will observe that Sofala is also a country in India.

Abou Abdallah Mohamed, commonly known as Ibn Batuta, a native of Tangier, born in February 1304, travelled over the known world from the Atlantic coast to China during the twenty-four years from A.D. 1325 to A.D. 1349, and from A.D. 1351 to 1354 he was engaged in exploring the Soudan. He went down the East African coast as far as Kilwa. His account of the countries he visited was translated into French, and was published in four octavo volumes at Paris by the Asiatic Society from 1853 to 1858. It is entitled *Voyages d'Ibn Batoutah, texte Arabe, accompagné d'une Traduction par C. Defrémery et le Dr. B. R. Sanguinetti.* All that is related of Eastern Africa is the following :

I embarked at the town of Makdachaou, proceeding towards the country of the Saouâhil and the town of Couloua (Kilwa) in the country of the Zendj. We arrived at Manbaça (Mombasa), a large island, at a distance of two days' journey from the land of the Saouâhil. This island has no dependency on the continent, and its trees are of the banana, the lemon, and the citron. Its inhabitants gather also a fruit which they call djammoûn (*Eugenia Jambu*), which resembles the olive. It has a stone like that of the olive, but the fruit has an extremely sweet taste. The people do not apply themselves to agriculture, and grain is imported from the Saouâhil. The greater part of their food consists of bananas and of fish. They profess the doctrine of Châfi'y, and are religious, chaste, and virtuous. Their mosques are constructed very solidly of wood. Near each entrance of these mosques there are one or two wells of the depth of one or two arms' length; the water is drawn up by means of a wooden basin, to which is attached a slender stick of the length of an arm. The ground around the mosque and the wells is quite smooth. Whoever wishes to enter the mosque begins by washing his feet, and there is near the entrance a piece of very coarse matting with which he dries them. He who desires to perform his ablutions takes the dish between his legs, pours the water upon his hands, and then washes. Everyone there goes barefoot.

We passed one night in this island, after which we embarked again to proceed to Kilwa, a large town situated upon the coast, of which the inhabitants are for the most part Zendjes of an extremely black colour. They are marked with incisions, like those which the Lîmiîn of Djenâdah have. A merchant informed me that the town of Sofala is situated at a distance of half a month's journey from Kilwa, and that from Sofala to Yoûfi in the country of the Lîmiîn is a month's journey. From Yoûfi gold dust is brought to Sofala. Kilwa is one of the handsomest and best built towns; it is entirely built of wood; the roofing of its houses is of dîs (*ampelodesmos tenax*), and rain is plentiful there. Its inhabitants are devoted to the holy war, for they occupy a country contiguous to that of the infidel Zendj. Their leading characteristics are piety and devotion, and they profess the doctrine of Châfi'y.

The Sultan of Kilwa.

When I reached this town, it had as its sultan Abou'lmozhaffer Haçan, also surnamed Abou'lmewâhib, on account of the great number of his gifts and acts of generosity. He made frequent incursions into the country of the Zendjes, attacked them, and took booty from them, of which he deducted the fifth part, which he dispensed in the manner fixed in the koran. He deposited the portion of the relatives of the prophet in a separate chest, and when the cherifs came for it he delivered it to them. They resorted to him from Irâk, Hidjâz, and other countries. I found at his court several from Hidjâz, among them Mohamed, son of Djammâz, Mansoûr, son of Lebîdah, son of Abou Nemy, and Mohamed, son of Chomaîlah, son of Abou Nemy. I have seen at Makdachaou Tabl, son of Cobaïch, son of Djammâz, who intended to visit him also. This sultan is extremely humble, he sits and eats with the fakirs, and respects pious and noble men.

Account of one of his generous actions.

I was close to him one Friday, when he was returning to his house from prayer. A fakir of Yaman presented himself before him, and addressed him : " O Abou'lmewâhib ! " " I am here," he replied, " what is your desire ? " " Give me those garments you have on." " Very well, I will give them to you." " This hour ? " " Yes, certainly, at once." He returned to the mosque, went into the house of the preacher, took off his garments, put on others, and said to the fakir " go in and take them." The fakir entered, took them, put them in a napkin, placed them on his head, and went away with them. The attendants extolled the sultan's gracious act, on account of the humility and the generosity he had shown. His son and successor designate took back this dress from the fakir, and gave him ten slaves in exchange for it. The sultan having ascertained that his subjects applauded his action, ordered that ten other slaves and two loads of ivory should be sent to the fakir, for in this country most of the presents consist of ivory, and gold is rarely given.

When this virtuous and liberal sultan died, his brother Daoud became king, and conducted himself in a totally opposite manner. When a poor man desired anything of him, he said " he who gave is dead, and left nothing to give." Visitors remained at his court many months, and then he only gave them something of trifling value, so that no one came again.

We embarked at Kilwa for the town of Zhafar.

The work of Hassan el Ouazzan ibn Mohamed, of Grenada, born about 1491, who was named John Leo Africanus by Pope

Leo X when he professed to abandon the creed of Islam, being written after the entrance of the Portuguese into the Indian sea, need not be referred to here beyond giving the title of the French edition, which is *Description de l'Afrique, tierce partie du Monde, escrite par Jean Leon African premièrement en langue Arabesque, puis en Toscane et à present mise en Français.* The new edition, with notes by Ch. Schefer, is in three quarto volumes, and was published at Paris in 1896, 1897, and 1898.

CHAPTER VII.

Settlement of Bantu tribes south of the Zambesi and Kunene rivers.

As has been seen, the territory of Sofala was occupied by Bantu in the tenth century of our era, but how far south that territory extended cannot be ascertained with precision. It is certain, however, that it did not pass the Sabi river, and beyond it the only inhabitants were Bushmen, the Wakwak of the Arab writers. Westward its limit was short of the Mashonaland of our day, for down to much more recent times Bushmen alone occupied that border. Whether the tribe mentioned by Masoudi was the modern Karanga is uncertain, though in all probability it was, still it is possible that the first immigrants may have been conquered and exterminated by later intruders.

These Bantu of Sofala were the first of their family to occupy land south of the Zambesi. When they arrived it is most improbable that on the opposite coast the Hottentots had reached the Kunene.

Some centuries must have elapsed before they were followed by others of their kin. The centre and the western portion of the continent was being gradually occupied, and at length either pressure or war forced other bands to cross the Zambesi and make their way south. These people were the ancestors of the Bakalahari and Balala of our day, and they settled somewhere about the head waters of the Molopo river, which was then a much larger stream than it is now. From the time of their arrival until the middle of the eighteenth century of our era bands frequently came down from the north, but even now, though they have multiplied at an amazing rate since they have been under the protection of Europeans, the whole number south of the Zambesi and the Kunene does not exceed seven millions, who represent all the offshoots from the great mass of Bantu in the central zone of the continent.

If tradition can be relied upon, the first immigrants who settled in the territory now called Betshuanaland had large herds of cattle in their possession. They formed a number of little bands independent of each other, who came down in succession. These pioneer parties, being small and weak, tried to fraternise with the Bushmen, and were not molested to any serious extent by those savages. Their quarrels were principally with each other. They built kraals at distances far apart, and cultivated the ground about them, leaving the aborigines in undisturbed possession of the open spaces between. With these they to some extent mixed their blood, and numbers of Masarwa or Betshuana-Bushmen came into existence.

After a time another horde came down from the north. These were the ancestors of the people known to early European visitors, from the name of one of their chiefs, as the Leghoyas, of whom the Bataung living in Basutoland are the present representatives. They were more numerous and better armed than the pioneer bands, upon whom they had no scruple in falling, with the object of seizing their cattle and garden produce. Many of the little communities were broken up and dispersed, some seeking refuge in the desert, where they have since been known as Bakalahari, others remaining as slaves, who were termed Balala or the paupers. The Leghoyas then settled in the country, built villages, and made gardens, just as the pioneers had done.

The hordes migrated slowly, often remaining for two or three years at favourable localities on the way. Some of these stations are mentioned in their traditions, others can be recognised by the materials found on their sites. The Bataung, for instance, used stone for building their huts to a much greater extent than any of the other tribes, and Mr. R. N. Hall has recently discovered close to Bulawayo the ruins of a station of those people that must have been occupied for many years. When the next body of invaders made its appearance, if it was stronger the preceding horde was obliged to move on, but sometimes it migrated from pure love of change, as many of the Betshuana clans have done down to our own times.

The next to make their appearance in Southern Betshuanaland were the Batlapin, closely followed by the much more powerful Barolong, who settled for a couple of generations on the northern bank of the Molopo. The antiquaries of this tribe state that their ancestors, in the time of a chief whose name and lineage from father to son to the present day are preserved, left a country on the border of a great lake where at one time of the year shadows were cast towards the north, and gradually migrated southward.* About the middle of the eighteenth century the Barolong crossed the Molopo and dispersed the Leghoyas or Bataung, who, however, were able to retreat to the eastward with their cattle, and then the newcomers settled in the country, where some of their descendants are still living. They made their principal kraal at first on the Setlagoli river, but after a few years moved much farther on, and occupied the bank of the Hart, where their chief Tao (Lion) established his head quarters at the place ever since called after him Taung, that is the place or residence of Tao. This was the commencement of a feud between the Leghoyas and the Barolong, which was carried on without intermission until after the middle of the nineteenth century, and which was one of the leading difficulties of the government of the Orange River Sovereignty, when Molitsane on the one side and Moroko on the other could not be brought to observe peace.

These Batlapin and Barolong completed the destruction of the pioneer bands, those who had escaped the attacks of the Leghoyas being now compelled to become Bakalahari or Balala, and to live after the manner of Bushmen. They were in the most miserable condition to which human beings can be reduced, they could not even own a jackal's skin, and their lives were regarded by their tyrants as of no more value than the

---

* I had a unique opportunity of learning particulars concerning this tribe when investigating rival claims to land made by one of its chiefs and the chief of another tribe for the high commissioner Lord Loch. In a case of this kind facts were brought out which would not have been made known in any other way.

lives of dogs. Whether they were originally less intelligent than other Betshuana, or whether they became stupid and spiritless from oppression and degradation, is uncertain ; but when Europeans first visited these wretched people they were found to be the most abject of all the dwellers in South Africa.

There was now no attempt to conciliate the Bushmen, for the newcomers were too strong to fear their hostility. Girls of that race were taken by the Batlapin in the same manner as by the Hottentots, but against all others relentless warfare was waged. The Betshuana were armed with strong bows, and soon learned to poison their arrows ; they used also the assagai and battle-axe, and protected their bodies with a diminutive shield. In a fight on the open plain the aboriginal savages had no chance whatever, though when attacked on a mountain or among rocks they often managed to beat off their assailants. Still the country was so large, the Bantu invaders were as yet so few in number, and their settlements were so far apart, that the Bushmen could not be entirely exterminated. At the beginning of the nineteenth century they were still numerous in the territory that then began to be known as Betshuanaland, and there are still a few to be found in the desert.

In the fifteenth, sixteenth, and seventeenth centuries, when these events were taking place, the climate of the country north of the Orange and east of the Kalahari was moister than it is at present. For some unknown reason it has gradually become drier since Europeans became acquainted with it, and the process must have been going on long before the first white man made his appearance there. The traditions of the Betshuana are not needed to confirm this fact : the dry beds of ancient rivers and the remains of a luxuriant vegetation are ample evidence. It is very possible indeed that the Betshuana, by frequently burning the grass and destroying the great forests of camelthorn trees they found in the territory, hastened the process of desiccation.

After the Barolong other tribes of the same family came down, notably the Bakwena, whose branches in course of time spread over the whole country south of the Waterberg and the

Olifants' river eastward to the Kathlamba and down nearly to the Orange. These people, whose siboko is the crocodile and who in former times venerated that reptile because they believed that the spirits of their ancestors appeared to them in its form, constitute the largest section of the Bantu family in South Africa at the present day. The majority of the Basuto tribe of our time are Bakwena, so are the Bahurutsi, the Bangwaketse, the Bamangwato, and very many others. The present Bakwena tribe is merely a small section of this great family, and took its name not from that circumstance, but from its chief at the time of its formation as an independent body being named Kwena. At the close of the sixteenth century there were Bakwena living north of the Zambesi, but whether they were the pioneers of that branch of the Bantu family, or stragglers left behind on the march southward, cannot now be ascertained. The Dominican friar Dos Santos,* who was living on the Zambesi at that time, gives the following particulars :

" Below these mountains of Lupata, close to the river on the eastern side facing the lands of Mongas, is a fine lake, three leagues in circumference and very deep, in the middle of which is an island very lofty and craggy, about a thousand yards in circumference. . . . The Kaffirs call this lake Rufumba. It is of fresh water, abounds with good fish, hippopotami, and very large crocodiles. On its edge is a grove called by the Kaffirs Tshipanga, thickly wooded with shady trees. The Kaffirs who live in the vicinity of this grove bury their dead there, and it is looked upon by all as a very sacred place, the principal reason of this being that the crocodiles of the Rufumba stretch themselves in the sun on its borders according to their custom, and the Kaffirs imagine that the souls of their dead go into the crocodiles and frequent this lake, for which reason they frequently throw food to them on the borders of the grove."

The various tribes who settled in the country along the eastern border of the Kalahari were constantly at war, plundering one another of cattle, yet they increased in number at a

---

* See the *Ethiopia Oriental* of João dos Santos, the whole Portuguese text of which with my English translation is to be found in the seventh volume of the *Records of South-Eastern Africa* printed for the Cape government. The extract given above is from the sixth chapter.

marvellous rate. Their battles were not attended with much loss of life, and every female on arriving at the age of womanhood began to bear children. Each tribe lived by itself in a town of from five to fifteen thousand inhabitants, around which extended to a great distance gardens of millet, beans, watermelons, and sweet cane. Beyond these their horned cattle, sheep, and goats were herded, many of which were also kept at distant stations and brought in as needed. The towns required to be removed frequently. The garden ground would become less productive after three or four crops had been taken from it, and owing to the want of even the simplest sanitary arrangements the town itself would become offensive. Then another site would be selected, and on a fixed day the whole population would march to it and begin to erect huts and enclosures, each family taking its position in the new village exactly as in the place abandoned.

After the Bakwena the next to come down along the central plateau were the Bavenda group of tribes, who arrived on the southern bank of the Limpopo about the close of the seventeenth or the beginning of the eighteenth century. According to their own traditions they migrated from the lower basin of the Congo, but there is sufficient evidence in their language and their customs to prove that they do not belong to the western branch of the Bantu family. Their affinities with the Bakwena group are in many respects so close that they must have separated from them at no very remote time, and it is impossible to doubt that they were first driven to the lower Congo basin from some region far to the east. The scattering of the remnants of tribes in the destructive wars towards the close of the sixteenth century, as related in the records of the Portuguese on the Zambesi, must have been in every direction, east, west, north, and south, just as in the dispersions caused by Tshaka.

It is not improbable that these people were the same as those termed by the Portuguese Cabires, who laid waste the territory between the Zambesi and the Limpopo soon after the Abambo and some of the Amazimba passed southward through it. This is mere conjecture, however, for there are no means of tracing either the origin or the fate of those Cabires who were so destructive to the Makaranga. If they and the Bavenda were the same, they must have roamed about the southern portion of what is now Mashonaland for many years before crossing the Limpopo. According to their traditions, the Makaranga were subject to the greatest of their chiefs, which seems to point in that direction.

Before the wars of Tshaka the Bavenda occupied the whole of what is now the district of Zoutpansberg. In those wars they were dispersed, but after the emigrant farmers from the Cape Colony drove Moselekatse to the north, the fugitives who survived began to collect together again under the chief Mpofu and others, and settled once more in parts of the district from which they had fled. On the death of Mpofu, his sons Ramovana and Ramapulana fought for the chieftainship. The emigrant farmers under Commandant-General Hendrik Potgieter assisted Ramapulana, and secured the position for him, but as a vassal of their government. From that time that section of the Bavenda has been commonly known as the Baramapulana, but it was of hardly any importance until the accession in 1864 of Magadu, son of Ramapulana, to the chieftainship, which he held until his death in 1895.

Among many other sections of less note of this branch of the Bantu family are the tribes which have as their chiefs men with the dynastic titles of Pafuri and Tshivasa, and which also occupy land in the Zoutpansberg district.*

The reverend Mr. Hofmeyr, a missionary for twenty years among these people, states in his volume issued in 1890 that they are able to make out the meaning of an address in Sesuto, and that he has seen among them wooden images, such as are

---

* I am personally unacquainted with this section of the Bantu family, and am therefore entirely indebted to other authors for the information here given concerning the Bavenda, or Batsethla as sometimes termed. My principal authorities are : *Twintig jaren in Zoutpansberg : een verhaal van twintig jarigen arbeid onder de heidenen in de Transvaal, door den eerwaarden Stefanus Hofmeyr, zendeling der Nederduitsch gereformeerde kerk ;* a volume of 322 pages, published at Capetown in 1890 ; and *History of the Native Tribes of the Transvaal*, a bluebook of 67 pages, published by the Transvaal government in 1905.

found in use by some of the Betshuana. This establishes their affinity with the Bakwena, and proves them to be of East African origin. But he has also ascertained that they venerate sticks stuck in the ground, such as those used by the Ovaherero to represent their ancestors, which seems to prove that their traditions of having migrated from the lower basin of the Congo are correct. Their religion is ancestral spirit worship, like that of all other Bantu, but sacrifices to the shades of the dead are more frequent, and food is commonly placed upon graves. Some other differences exist between these people and the Bakwena, but none of much importance.

The last to move down from the distant north to the territory below the Limpopo was the little tribe termed the Bakwebo, which arrived, it is supposed from the lower Congo basin, shortly after the middle of the eighteenth century. This is the tribe governed in our time by the chieftainess Madjaji, about whom there was supposed to be much mystery, as she was kept carefully concealed from strangers. There is no special difference, however, between these people and their neighbours, and their language is merely a link between Tshevenda and Sesuto.

The eighteenth century was far advanced before the Betshuana crossed the Vaal river. The Bataung, who had been compelled to flee from the Barolong, set their faces south-eastward from their former home on the Setlagoli, crossed the Hart and the Vaal, and took up their residence along the upper course of the Vet river. In their new settlement they were attacked by some offshoots of the Bakwena, by whom they were robbed of many of their cattle. These enemies passed onward, however, without completely destroying them, and settled along the upper banks of the Caledon, where they were joined at a later date by many others.

In 1505, when the Portuguese formed their first settlement on the south-eastern coast, the Makaranga tribe occupied the territory now termed Mashonaland and the seaboard between the Zambesi and Sabi rivers. Before the commencement of the eighteenth century that tribe was broken up by war, and about that time a considerable immigration began to set in from the north. The immigrants, who were the ancestors of most of the people now called by Europeans Mashona, came down from some locality west of Lake Tanganyika in little parties, not in one great horde. The first to arrive was a clan under a chief named Sakavunza, who settled at a place near the present town of Salisbury.

The details of this immigration were not placed on record by any of the Portuguese in the country, who merely noticed that there was a constant swirl of barbarians, plundering, destroying, and replacing one another ; and when recent investigators, like Mr. R. N. Hall, of Zimbabwe, and Mr. W. S. Taberer, the government commissioner, endeavoured to gather the particulars from the descendants of the immigrants, it was found impossible to obtain more accurate information from them concerning the events of distant times than the general fact that their ancestors came down from the north about two centuries ago. Messrs. Hall, Taberer, and other inquirers state that their proper designation is Baroswi, or Barotsi, and that they constitute a very large proportion of the population of what is termed Mashonaland at the present day.

The larger number settled in the territory now termed Matabeleland, where they remained until 1834, when Moselekatse began to send raiding parties in their direction. Then all those nearest the Matabele kraals, without waiting to be attacked, fled eastward, those farther north, that is the section now under Lewanika, having already been conquered by the Makololo under Sebetoane, who had taken part in the murderous career of the Mantati horde, and subsequently forced their way up from the Bakwena country. The unfortunate Makaranga, who had suffered terribly under the iron rod of the Angoni and the Matshangana, were then still further crushed until they and the Baroswi alike were brought under subjection by the Matabele.

After their arrival in the territory south of the Zambesi the Baroswi not only carried on war against the earlier inhabitants, but among themselves one clan was constantly pillaging another, so that discord and strife were perpetual. There was no paramount power over all, every chief who was strong enough to hold his own being absolutely independent of every other. In this turmoil the aborigines almost completely disappeared, for the Bantu, at variance with each other concerning other matters, were united in endeavouring to exterminate them.

Clans of the Baroswi family continued to migrate from the distant north into the territory that is now Rhodesia until the close of the eighteenth century. In some respects, though not in any matters of importance, they differed from the earlier Bantu immigrants. Thus their custom was to dry the dead bodies of men of note before enclosing them in hides for burial, which made the corpses appear like mummies. Girls, when mere infants, were contracted in marriage, though the husband could not claim them until they were capable of bearing children.

Some other customs which are commonly considered as peculiar to them are observed by many other Bantu in South Africa. Such, for instance, is the putting to death of twin children, through fear that if they were allowed to live they would try to displace the chief, and of girls who cut their upper teeth first, under the belief that if they were permitted to grow up any man marrying them would immediately die. Their law of inheritance also, which provides that when a man dies his principal son takes all of the widows except the one who bore him, is common to many other of the interior tribes. So is their skill in weaving loin cloths of wild cotton or making them of bark, and in carving wood, as well as their knowledge of building rough walls of unhewn stone.

They differ from the Makaranga in personal appearance, having coarser features and being blacker in colour and somewhat stouter in build. There is no other tribe in South Africa which has so many individuals bearing traces of Arab, Persian, and Indian blood as the Makaranga, which is due to the long continuance of Asiatic intercourse with them in past times. All who have dealings with them state that, though now spiritless and degraded from constant strife and oppression during more than two centuries, they possess greater latent power of advancement, especially in mechanical arts, than any other Bantu in the country.

On the eastern coast, south of the Makaranga and extending now even farther than the Fish river, are to be found the sturdiest and most warlike of all the Bantu in South Africa.   The numerous tribes into which they have been divided since Europeans became acquainted with them are so closely related to each other in language and customs that they must have formed a community by themselves at no very distant date, and as some of them crossed the Zambesi only a little before the close of the sixteenth century, the others cannot have long preceded them.   This section of the Bantu came from some locality on or near the western coast, so that its route of migration crossed that of the Betshuana like that of the letter X.

It is not only from the traditions of these people that it is known they came down from the country beyond the Zambesi in recent times.   Tradition can never be entirely depended upon in such matters, and from it no dates could be obtained, five hundred years or three hundred years would be indistinguishable from each other.   It is exceedingly vague also, and no antiquary among the tribes is able to give any particulars whatever concerning events during the migration.   They can give the names of chiefs for a period of perhaps three hundred years, but are quite ignorant of what the earlier ones did or where they lived and died.   In short, any occurrence that they give an account of dating back longer than a century and a half must be regarded as doubtful, unless supported by other evidence, and even their relations of more recent events must be carefully looked into and compared with those from rival tribes.

Fortunately other evidence is available in this case.   In 1498 the first Portuguese fleet that crossed the Indian sea touched at the mouth of the Limpopo river, and on board one of the ships was a man, Martin Affonso by name, who could speak several dialects of the tribes on the western coast.   This man was able to make himself understood by some of the people on shore, who, as the chronicler Damião de Goes states, must have been strangers from some part of Guinea.*

---

* " que se entẽdeo cõ algũs delles (q̃ deuião ser estrãgeiros das partes de Guinê)."—*Chronica do Felecissimo Rei Dom Emanuel,* por Damião de

Recent immigrants they certainly must have been, and they must have come from the western coast, or a man understanding only dialects in use there could not have conversed with them. They were Batonga, and on their way across the continent they dropped sections behind, particularly on the southern bank of the Zambesi, where the descendants of those offshoots are to be found to-day. That is all the information obtainable now upon the first billow of Bantu invaders that rolled over the continent from north-west to south-east, and that subsided on the shore of the Indian sea between the Sabi river and Delagoa Bay. What set that billow in motion, what havoc it wrought on its way, what time it took on its course, are all among the unknown particulars of the past. Nothing more can be said with certainty than that the Batonga of the Zambesi valley and of the eastern coast arrived there some time during the fifteenth century.

The whole number of these immigrants was very small, but they were strong enough to exterminate or drive away the aborigines from the localities where they settled. They practised agriculture, though not so extensively as the Betshuana, depending for sustenance more upon their cows and goats than upon vegetable food. They smelted iron, which they wrought into implements such as assagai heads, axes, knives, and hoes, coarser and clumsier than those made by the Makaranga and Betshuana tribes.

Of the next Bantu to make their appearance on the eastern coast very little definite information can be given. As they spoke the same dialect, however, as those that arrived towards the close of the sixteenth century, as their siboko was the same, and as all their leading customs were similar, they must have been members of the same community proceeding in advance

Goes. Primeira Parte, Capitulo XXXVI. Castanheda also says that Martin Affonso understood the language. "Martim Afonso porque entendia a lingoa foy aq̃la noyte á pouoação deste senhor."—*Descobrimento e Conquista da India pelos Portuguezes*, por Fernâo Lopez de Castanheda. Livro Primeiro, Capitulo IV. For full particulars of this event see my *Records of South-Eastern Africa*, in which the Portuguese text and English translations are given.

of the main body. Such migrations can only be accomplished slowly, as halts are made for years at convenient places along the line of march. Then a party coming on behind arrives, and the one in advance is obliged to move on. At last the shore of the ocean is reached, and as progress in the previous direction is now barred, the future line of advance must be either up or down the coast. When the ancestors of the Xosas, Tembus, and Pondos reached the sea, the coast to the north was already occupied by the Batonga, so they turned to the south, and entered the territory now known as Natal. Vestiges of their sojourn in that region could be found there after the middle of the nineteenth century.*

They had scattered themselves thinly along the coast as far south as the mouth of the Umzimvubu river when, towards the close of the sixteenth century their numbers were greatly increased, and an impetus was given to the movement southward by an irruption from the far distant north-west into the lower valley of the Zambesi of devastating bands that pillaged and destroyed all the weaker clans in their line of march. When other food could not be procured, these invaders resorted to cannibalism, and at length became so accustomed to eat human flesh that they consumed it as an ordinary article of diet. One of the largest of these bands was termed the Amazimba, and to this day the word zim with the southern Bantu denotes a cannibal. It enters largely into folklore tales, and is commonly used to frighten disobedient children. This band drove before it a horde of fugitives composed of the remnants of numberless tribes

* The first account of the southward migration of the Zulu, Tembu, and Xosa tribes that I am acquainted with is that given by the reverend J. L. Döhne, of the American board of missions, in the introduction to his *Zulu-Kafir Dictionary*, published at Capetown in 1857. In 1852 he found a small section of the Amaxosa, that had been left behind when the main body moved on, still living in Natal. He believed these tribes to have come from some place along the Mozambique coast, but of course he knew nothing of the invasion from the north-west and the terribly destructive wars towards the close of the sixteenth century, of which the Portuguese on the Zambesi have left accounts. Those narratives picture the events to which all the dim traditions of the tribes along the south-eastern coast collected during the nineteenth century point, and solve questions that could not be answered satisfactorily before they were published in accessible form.

plundered and partly destroyed on the way from the Atlantic shore, and that collectively was known as the Abambo.

Just as with the Mantati horde and the Amangwane two centuries and a quarter later, the Abambo and the Amazimba were partly destroyed by starvation and partly by incessant war, but some remnants forced their way in murderous marches through the earlier settlements to distant localities, where they remained and built permanent kraals. A considerable remnant of the Abambo horde in this manner cut its way through the western part of the territory occupied by the Makaranga, and finally settled in the valley of the Tugela and in the territory farther south. On its march it had incorporated a large number of Karanga girls, and probably of boys also, so that at least one section of it was largely affected by this mixture of blood. To the present day this section—the Amazizi—show abundant signs of Karanga ancestry, and are as a rule more intelligent than any of their neighbours. By other tribes they were even often termed Amalanga on this account. The occupation of Natal by the Abambo compelled the pioneers of their family to move farther along the coast, and very likely these were joined by many little offshoots from the main body. The Xosas, Tembus, and Pondos still term Natal Embo, that is the country of the Abambo.

Some time after its settlement in Natal the horde broke up into many communities independent of each other, between which rivalries and feuds broke out just as everywhere else among the Bantu. These new tribes were probably the remnants of older ones that had been broken up and pressed into the horde on its long journey across the continent, but which still retained their former titles and regarded their separate existence as a matter of common usage and right.

The Portuguese, who occupied stations at Sofala, Sena, and Tete at this time, give no direct information upon the occupation of Natal by the Abambo. Very likely they knew nothing of what was going on at a distance from their forts, just as the Cape government and colonists knew nothing at the time of the career of the Mantati horde or of Sotshangana or Moselekatse.

Or if rumours of terrible destruction being caused inland by a horde of ferocious invaders ever reached them, they were too much taken up with their own disasters to pay attention to them. Even of the section which they termed the Cabires, that gave them much trouble, they placed very little information on record. It is from them, however, that we learn that in 1570 the Abambo horde made its first appearance on the northern bank of the Zambesi above Tete, that there were then very few Bantu inhabitants south of the Umvolosi river, and that after 1600 Natal had a considerable population. The traditions of all the tribes that they came down from the north may not count for much, but they cannot be altogether passed over. A much stronger proof of the recent occupation by Bantu of the country south of the Sabi river is the fact that the Arabs never attempted to form a station there. They were among the very keenest traders in the world, but south of the Sabi were only Wakwak or Bushmen, so nothing was to be bought or sold there. In 1505 the Portuguese wrested Sofala from them, but they never thought of sending a trading party south of Delagoa Bay before the irruption of the Abambo, and then the days of their enterprise and vigour were gone for ever.

The remaining tribes on the south-eastern coast, that is those between Natal and Delagoa Bay, may have occupied that territory at the same time as the Abambo settled in Natal, or they may have arrived there at a little later date. They are the same in language and generally in customs, and there is nothing unlikely in the supposition that they were part of the same horde that had lagged somewhat behind. But it is possible that they were connected with the Amazimba, who, though pursuing the Abambo, were themselves fugitives from some stronger power in the locality from which they set out on their murderous career. Before the time of Tshaka the Abatetwa were the most prominent people in that part of South Africa, and at the beginning of the nineteenth century they were under a chief of note named Dingiswayo.

A man who claimed to be a grandson of Dingiswayo by one of his inferior wives, and who had received sufficient education to be able to write English fluently, in 1883 drew up an account of this tribe, which was forwarded to the author of this volume by a friend interested in South African history. It assigns to the Abatetwa a position of greater importance than they really filled, inasmuch as it claims paramountcy for them from the time of their arrival in Zululand over every other tribe in South-Eastern Africa, including even the sections of the Abambo. But this is in perfect keeping with all narratives of the kind from Bantu antiquaries, who invariably represent their own chiefs as more glorious than any others, and it need not be taken into consideration.

The writer of the account says that the Abatetwa were driven across the Zambesi from some place far away in the north or north-west by their neighbours the Komanti and the Ashongwa, and he puts their arrival in Zululand in the time of the great-grandfather of Dingiswayo. Of the earlier history of the tribe, or even the names of its remote chiefs, his own ancestors, he had been unable to obtain any information that he could depend upon. Of its career on the march he says nothing, but pictures it as conquering all around it upon its arrival in Zululand, which country he is therefore of opinion ought to be regarded as rightly belonging to it. Such a narrative, however, is not to be strictly depended upon, and in some of the particulars given, such as, for instance, the date of the arrival of the Abatetwa, it is certainly erroneous ; but it corroborates the general tradition of a not very remote migration of the tribes now living in Zululand from some far distant locality.

When the pioneers of the Bantu crossed the Umtamvuna they encountered the earlier Hottentot occupants, who were themselves recent immigrants, and who had largely mixed their blood with that of the aboriginal Bushmen. These were too feeble to resist the advancing wave from the north, and there-fore met with the fate of the weaker everywhere in Africa. The males were exterminated, and the females were incorporated with the conquerors. Through this amalgamation the language of the tribes in advance was greatly affected, three of the Hottentot clicks being introduced—chiefly in words pertaining to the occupations of women,—and even the character and appearance of the people underwent a change. It is this mixture of Hottentot and Bushman blood that makes the difference between the Xosa or Tembu and the Hlubi of our day. Originally they were in every respect identical.

Along the coast the Bantu settlements were denser than in the interior, but south of the Tugela river in general only the terrace adjoining the sea and the one next to it were occupied. From these the Bushmen were entirely driven, but in advance of the migrating Bantu they massed in as great numbers as could obtain food, and held their own until the beginning of the eighteenth century, some indeed until nearly a hundred years later. They were numerous in the territory between the Kei and the Keiskama when Rarabe (pron. Khàkhábăy), a chief who was well known to the Europeans on the eastern frontier of the Cape Colony, entered that district. They stole and killed his favourite racing ox, which so incensed him that he gave orders for their destruction, and was not appeased until none were left. On the plateau adjoining the Kathlamba from the Tugela to the Fish river they were not disturbed, except by occasional parties of men sent to punish them for committing robberies in the lowlands, and there they remained until long after the British conquest of the Cape Colony.

On the western coast the Bantu occupation is still more recent than on the south-eastern. The first small horde that appeared there was subdued by the Hottentots, and forced to adopt the language and customs of its conquerors. These are the people now called Berg Damaras by Europeans and Ghou Damara (masculine, singular, nominative, Damup) by the Nama-quas—Haukoin they term themselves,—who are Bantu or possibly negro by blood, but Hottentot by speech, religion, and many customs, and live like Bushmen almost entirely on game, insects, reptiles, and wild plants. They hardly ever attempt to cultivate the ground, and when they do, it is only to plant watermelons of the wild variety and dacha for smoking, which they use to great excess. Their habitations are made of a few branches of trees or shrubs, not always covered with

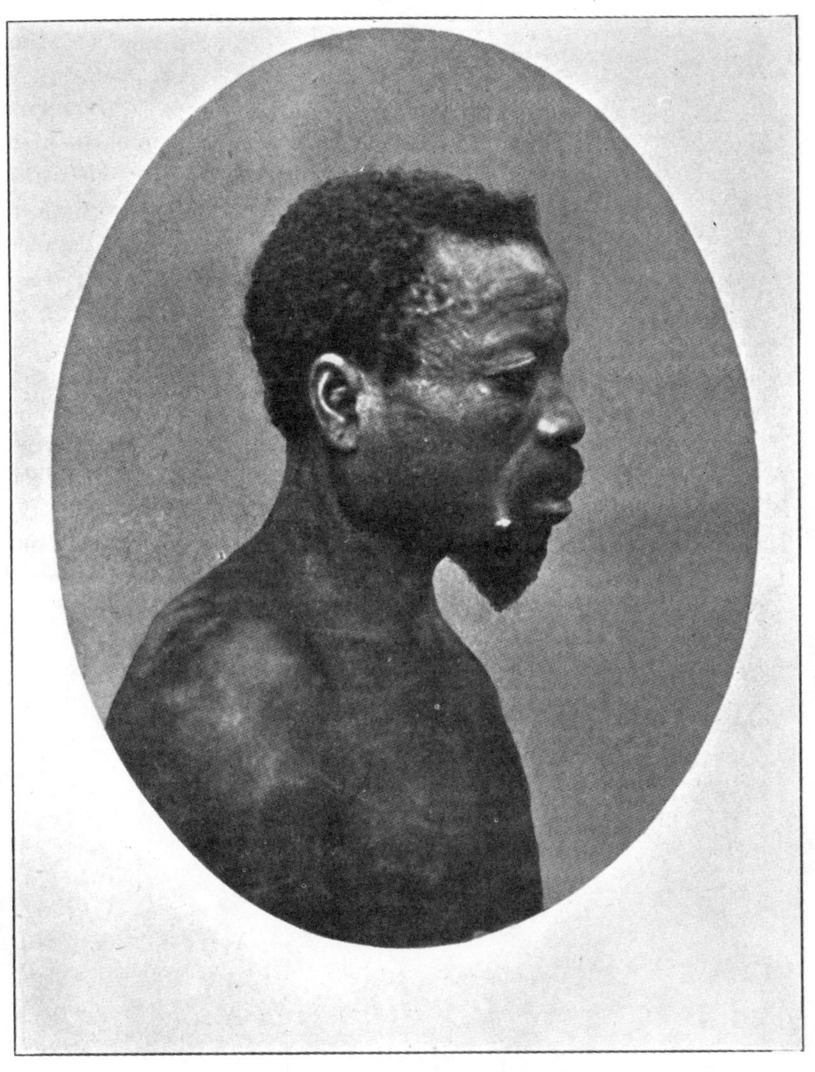

PORTRAIT OF A BERG DAMARA.
(*From a Photograph in the South African Public Library.*)

[*To face p.* 166.

mats, and their weapons and implements are of the crudest kind.

At length the Hottentots moved farther southward, and left them behind. They were then attacked by the Ovaherero, a purely pastoral and nomadic tribe, who came down from the north, drove them into the mountains of what is now Southern Damaraland, and occupied the plains themselves. The reverend C. Hugo Hahn, of the Rhenish missionary society, who was for many years a resident with the Ovaherero and collected their traditions, states that they can only with certainty be traced back to a locality somewhere in the neighbourhood of the Zambesi below the Victoria falls. From that locality they migrated westward with great herds of cattle and flocks of sheep, and then turned to the south, crossing the Kunene a little before the middle of the eighteenth century. After passing the Kaoko, they met the Haukoin or Ghou Damara, who fled from them to the mountains. They next encountered clans of the Namaqua Hottentots, whom they fought with and gradually drove far to the southward.

This war with the Hottentots lasted many years, and occasionally the Ovaherero would be beaten and driven back for a time, as was found to be the case in 1792 by the expedition from the Cape Colony which penetrated the country in that year. But occasional reverses were followed by successes until Oasib, chief of the Hottentot tribe called the red nation, applied to Jonker Afrikaner for assistance. Jonker was the son of that Jager Afrikaner who was a widely dreaded freebooter at the beginning of the nineteenth century, and who was more widely known at a later date as having in his old age become a convert to Christianity. Jonker followed the career of his father very closely. At this time he was living on the bank of the Orange river, but as soon as the request of Oasib reached him, he and his followers set out to join in the fray. The tide of fortune then turned, and the Ovaherero were speedily driven back to the Zwakop, which river bed was afterwards regarded as the boundary between the two peoples. This was the condition of things when in 1814 the reverend H. Schmelen, of the London missionary society, arrived in the country and commenced work there among the Namaquas.

After they crossed the Kunene the Ovaherero threw off a section, which took the name Ovambanderu and became quite independent, and from both of the tribes numbers of individuals who were without property of any kind moved away to seek food like Bushmen. These destitute persons are called Ovatyimba, and form distinct communities. Of all the inhabitants of South Africa, the Ovaherero and their offshoots have the reputation of being the most heartless and unfeeling towards each other, hence the condition of the Ovatyimba. These people differ in many respects from the Bantu of the interior and the eastern coast, though they are of the same family and speak a dialect of the same language. They do not practise agriculture, but depend for sustenance upon wild plants and their horned cattle and sheep. Some of their peculiar customs will be described farther on, which will show them to be less advanced than the other members of their family.

The Ovaherero were preceded by the Avare group, of which the Ovambo tribe is the best known. This group consists of eleven distinct tribes, who occupy a small tract of land south of the Kunene river some distance from the coast. These people are industrious agriculturists, breeders of cattle, and workers in iron. They sink wells, sometimes thirty metres in depth, manufacture many useful articles, and are altogether far in advance of their southern neighbours. They are believed to have migrated from the valley of the Congo river, but the exact locality is unknown. Their dialect differs considerably from that of the Ovaherero, though there are strong reasons for supposing that the last-named people migrated from the same valley to the neighbourhood of the Zambesi some time before their removal to their present home. North of the Avare group the tribes need not be mentioned, as they live beyond the territory to which these pages are limited.

Along the western coast, north of the Zwakop river, the Ovaherero, like all the other invaders, attempted to exterminate or drive out the Bushmen. Pastoral communities and wild hunters could not exist side by side. But they did not entirely succeed, for the nature of the country is such that escape to barren and almost waterless parts was comparatively easy. The Kalahari desert lay on the east, into which the weaker party could retreat when hard pressed, without danger of successful pursuit. And so it happens that Bushmen are still to be found in what is now German South-West Africa, though not in any considerable number.

The invasion of the Bantu did not at first affect the Hottentots, except at the extremities of the thin line they occupied along the coast, for nowhere else did they come in contact.

All of the tribes and people dealt with in this chapter, together with their kindred who possess a vast extent of Africa north of the Kunene and Zambesi rivers, are now usually termed the Bantu, in accordance with a proposal of the late Dr. Bleek. They had no word except tribal names to distinguish themselves from other races, *ntu* * in their language meaning a human being or person of any colour or country ; but ethnologists felt the want of a specific designation for them, and adopted this as a convenient one. In the division of mankind thus named are included all those Africans who use a language which is inflected principally by means of prefixes, and which in the construction of sentences follows certain rules depending upon harmony of sound.†

* In the dialect of the Tembu, Pondo, Zulu, and other coast tribes : *um-ntu* a person, plural *aba-ntu* people ; diminutive *um-ntwana* a child, plural *aba-ntwana* children ; abstract derivative *ubu-ntu* the qualities of human beings, diminutive *ubu-ntwana* the qualities of children. In the Herero dialect : *omu-ndu* a person, plural *ova-ndu* people. In the dialect of the Basuto : *mo-tho* a person, plural *ba-tho* persons. The pronunciation, however, is nearly the same, the *h* in *batho* being sounded only as an aspirate, and the *o* as *oo*, *baat-hoo*.

† This definition is of course only a general one, and must be subject to exceptions, because people cannot be grouped by means of language alone. Thus the people called Berg Damaras, who have already been referred to and who live in the tract of country along the western coast north of Walfish Bay, are Bantu or perhaps negro by blood, though they speak a Hottentot dialect, and resemble Bushmen in their habits. After their subjugation they were forced to adopt the language of their conquerors. This may also have been the case with tribes in the northern part of the continent, as it certainly was with females.

Before the Bantu tribes migrated to Africa south of the Zambesi great differences existed between them, and there was a tendency for these differences to increase after their settlement where Europeans found them. Intercourse between the different sections was restricted, as in general each tribe regarded its neighbour with jealousy, and each group of tribes of recent common origin looked upon every other such group as enemies. Besides the change which takes place in all unwritten languages in the course of even a few generations, there was a habit with some of these tribes which hastened the variation, and therefore made intercourse more difficult. This was the *hlonipa* custom, by which women were obliged constantly to invent new words, so that each dialect changed in a different manner from all others. The structure of the dialects remained the same, but the words used by a Tembu, for instance, could not be understood by a Morolong or an Omuherero. An educated European can at once see that the great majority of the roots in all the dialects is the same, and that there is consequently but one language ; but the people who used those dialects were unable to detect this.

A change of speech was followed, though much more slowly, by change of customs and ceremonies, and even by dissimilar modifications of religious belief. Long intercourse with Arabs, Persians, and Indians resulted in a great advance in the mental condition of the eastern tribes over those of the west.

For general purposes the tribes can be classified in the three groups already mentioned as migrating to the southern portion of the continent by separate routes—from the coast of Guinea south-eastward, from what is now German East Africa south-westward, and from the Congo basin southward,—though there are many trifling differences between the various branches of each of these. In the first group can be placed those along the eastern coast south of the Sabi river, and those which in recent times have made their way from that part of the country into the highlands of the interior. The best known of these are the Amaxosa, the Abatembu, the Amampondo, the Amabaca, the Amamfengu or Fingos, the whole of the tribes in Natal, the

PORTRAIT OF MOSHESH, THE FOUNDER OF THE PRESENT BASUTO TRIBE, IN EUROPEAN DRESS.

(From a Photograph in the South African Public Library.)

Moshesh was the most intelligent Bantu chief ever known in South Africa.

[*To face p.* 170.

Amazulu, the Amaswazi, the Amatonga, the Magwamba, the Matshangana, and the Matabele. This group can be termed the eastern coast tribes, though some members of it are now far from the sea.

The second group can include the tribes that at the beginning of the nineteenth century occupied the greater part of the interior plain north of the twenty-ninth parallel of latitude, and came down to the ocean between the Zambesi and Sabi rivers. It will include among many others the Batlapin, the Batlaro, the Bakatla, the Barolong, the Bahurutsi, the Bangwaketse, the Bakwena, the Bamangwato, the Batawana, the Bavenda, the Bapedi, the Makaranga, the Baroswi, and the Basuto. This group can be termed the interior tribes.

The third will comprise the Bantu living between the western part of the Kalahari desert and the Atlantic ocean, who may be termed the western coast tribes. These are very recent immigrants, and before the beginning of the twentieth century had no influence upon South African history. They differ in many respects from their eastern kindred, being blacker in colour, coarser in appearance, and duller in intellect than the others, if an average be taken. The dialects spoken by them are also more primitive. It will not be necessary to describe the people of this section as fully as the others, but the principal points of difference will be given for comparison.

CHAPTER VIII.

General Description, Form of Government, and Religion of the Bantu.

Observations made during the sixteenth century by Portuguese missionaries and travellers in South Africa throw much light upon the origin of several customs which to other, though more recent, observers of Bantu habits, were involved in obscurity. With the Hottentots or the Bushmen the Portuguese rarely came in contact, and of these people they give no information of any value. But with sections of the Bantu they lived in as close intimacy as Dutchmen or Englishmen have ever done, they learned the language of these people, studied their customs, and several of the best informed recorded what they observed. They tell of no golden age of peace and happiness disturbed by the intrusion of white men, but of almost constant strife and cruelty and misery. From them we learn that long before the time of Tshaka despots as clever and as ruthless as he spread desolation over wide tracts of land, that cannibalism as practised in Basutoland and in Natal during the early years of the nineteenth century was no new custom with sections of the Bantu family, that the military organisation and mode of attack employed by Dingiswayo and Tshaka were not inventions of those chiefs, but were known long before their time. Much besides can be learned from their writings, so that since the translation and publication of many of those documents any description of the dark-skinned tribes south of the Zambesi previously written can be considerably amplified.

The various sections of the Bantu, while they have much in common, have also many differences. There can be no doubt that these differences arise from their descent from females of

blood varying as greatly as hamitic from negro or from Bushman, and from the intercourse of large numbers of Arab, Persian,
and Indian males with the eastern tribes in bygone times.ʹ If
an extreme example be taken, such as that of a Damara with
thick projecting lips, a broad flat nose, a narrow forehead, a square
chin, a massive pelvis, and great splay feet with projecting heels,
and on the other side a Karanga with features almost resembling
those of a European, with an oval chin, light pelvis, and well
formed feet, any one would say that they did not belong to the
same race, and in truth *race* is not a correct word to use in connection with the Bantu. But it is not necessary to compare
men of such different tribes to show their different descent:
this can be seen in the same tribe, often even in the same family.
Atavism sometimes produces two full brothers with hardly a
point of resemblance to each other. This is especially the case
mentally, and the instances are very rare of a highly intelligent
man among them having equally able sons.

In general it can be said of them that they have great power
of imitating, but very little of inventing, so that they are highly
conservative in character. But they are emotional and impul-
sive, so that they seldom continue long in the same pursuit.
They can learn strange languages much more quickly than most
Europeans, and they have very retentive memories.

The Bantu vary in colour from chocolate brown to deep black.
Those who occupy the land along the south-eastern coast are in
general large without being corpulent, strong, muscular, erect
in bearing, and with all their limbs in perfect symmetry. Many
of them are haughty in demeanour, and possess a large amount
of vanity. The men are usually handsomer than the women,
owing to the girls being often stunted in growth and hardened
in limb by carrying burdens on their heads and toiling in gardens
at an early age. The people of the interior are in general somewhat smaller than those of the coast, though they are far from
being diminutive specimens of the human species.

In some respects a description of the Bantu in South Africa
as they are to-day would not be a correct representation of them
as they were when Europeans first became acquainted with them,

or even as they were in the middle of the nineteenth century. Their government by white men, missionary teaching, commerce, and particularly their employment in large numbers in mines and on farms, have tended to alter their habits and even their ideas, though there are very few of them who would not gladly have remained as their ancestors were. With some tribes this is the case to a much greater extent than with others, but as all are more or less affected, the description that follows will be of them before European influence had brought about any change.

Though at times the Bantu presented the appearance of a peaceable, good-natured, indolent people, they were subject to outbursts of great excitement, when the most savage passions had free play. The man who spent a great part of his life gossiping in idleness, not knowing what it was to toil for bread, was hardly recognisable when, plumed and adorned with military trappings, he had worked himself into frenzy with the war dance. The period of excitement was, however, short. In the same way their outbursts of grief were violent, but were soon succeeded by cheerfulness.

They were subject to few diseases, and were capable of undergoing without harm privations and sufferings which the hardiest Europeans would have sunk under. Occasionally there were seasons of famine caused by prolonged drought, when whole tribes were reduced to exist upon nothing else than wild roots, bulbs, mimosa gum, and whatever else unaided nature provided. At such times they became emaciated, but as long as they could procure even the most wretched food they did not actually die, as white people would have done under similar circumstances. Nor did pestilence follow want of sustenance to the same extent as with us.

One cause of their being a strong healthy people was that no weak or deformed children were allowed to live long. There was no law which required an end to be put to the existence of such infants, but it always happened that they died when very young, and public opinion was opposed to any inquiry into the mode of their death. Every one, even the parents, believed that it was better they should not live, and so they perished from neglect. But owing to the prevalence of this custom in preceding generations, the number of weaklings born was very small indeed. For some reason an exception was occasionally made in the case of albinos, who, though regarded as monstrosities, were not always destroyed in childhood. These hideous individuals, with features like others of their kindred, were of a pale sickly colour, and had weak pinkish eyes and hair almost white. Very few, however, were to be seen in any tribe, and in some none at all.

Under natural conditions the Bantu were a longer-lived people than Europeans. The friar Dos Santos found several women at Sofala who perfectly remembered events that had taken place eighty years before, and modern observers in other parts of the country have noticed the same circumstance. A man of this race placed beside a white colonist of the same age invariably looks the younger of the two, and wherever they reside individuals can be found with personal knowledge extending over the ordinary span of life in Europe or America.

They were probably the most prolific people on the face of the earth. All the females were married at an early age, very few women were childless, and in most of the tribes provision was even made by custom for widows to add to the families of their dead husbands. In some parts the brothers of the deceased took them, in others male companions were selected for them by their late husband's friends, in each case the children born thereafter being regarded as those of the dead man. In the Makaranga and most of the tribes whose remnants now form the Basuto, the principal son inherited his own father's widows for whom the full bohadi had been paid, except the one who bore him, but it was a custom with them to lend their superfluous wives to their retainers or to men who were in their service temporarily. The object of all was to have as many children as possible, to lose no productive power whatever.

The census of the Cape Colony in 1904 compared with that of 1891 shows an increase of Bantu, excluding those in the territory annexed between those dates, from 838,136 to 1,158,980, or at the rate of 25·24 per thousand yearly. According to these census returns they double in number in a little less than twenty-eight years. But there were circumstances in operation in 1904 which tended to reduce the rate of increase much below that of the middle of the nineteenth century, when the people of tribes that were not at war were doubling in number in less than twenty-five years.

The form of government varied from that of a pure despotism established by a successful military ruler, to a patriarchal system of a simple order. In the former everything centred in the person of one individual, at whose word the lives of any of his subjects were instantly sacrificed, who was the owner of all the property of the tribe, and who appointed officials at his pleasure. He was served by attendants in the most abject attitudes, could only be approached by a subject unarmed and crouching, and arrogated to himself a form of address due to a deity. He was absolute in every respect, and by his will alone his subjects were guided, though to retain such power for any length of time it was necessary for him not to counteract any strong desire of the warriors of his tribe. This purely despotic form of government was rarely found among the people of the interior, who were in general more peaceably disposed than those of the coast. It ended as a rule when great reverses were sustained, or when a man of feeble intellect succeeded in the direct line of the one who established it.

The more common system, the one indeed that may be termed normal except when interfered with by a chief possessing great military genius, was of a milder character. Under it a tribe was composed of a number of sections which may be termed clans, each under its own chief, but all acknowledging the supreme rank and to some extent the authority of one particular individual. Sometimes the heads of the clans were members of the family of the paramount chief, more or less distantly connected with him by blood, in which case, unless there was a quarrel between brothers or between uncles and nephews, the tribe was a compact body, every individual in it having a common interest with every other ; but it often happened that clans broken in war, though retaining their own chiefs, were adopted as vassals by a powerful ruler, and in these cases the cohesion of the different sections, owing to the object of their worship being different, to jealousy, and to rival views, was much less firm.

Among the interior tribes, owing to the misconduct or incompetency of individual chiefs, this system sometimes broke down, when a condition of greater freedom resulted. Here the common people acquired sufficient power to make their wishes respected to some extent, and nothing of importance was undertaken without a general assembly of the men of the tribe being first held, when each one was at liberty to express his views. But even in these cases the opinion of a member of the ruling family was regarded as of vastly greater weight than that of a commoner. Merit was of small account against privilege of blood in the estimation of any branch of the Bantu family.

Among the tribes under the normal system of government the rule of the paramount chief in times of peace was hardly felt beyond his own kraal. Each clan possessed all the machinery of administration, and in general it was only in cases of serious quarrels between them or of appeals from judicial decisions that the tribal head used his authority. In war, however, he issued commands to all, and on important occasions he summoned the minor chiefs to aid him with advice.

The members of the ruling families, even to the most distant branches, were of aristocratic rank, and enjoyed many privileges. Their persons were inviolable, and an indignity offered to one of them was considered a crime of the gravest nature. Even the customs of the people were set aside in favour of the chiefs of highest rank. A common man of the coast tribes, for instance, could not marry certain relatives by blood, no matter how distant, but a great chief could, though connections nearer than fourth or fifth cousins were very rare. Such a marriage was strictly forbidden to a commoner, but was allowed in the chief's case, in order to obtain a woman of suitable birth to be the mother of the heir in the great line.

Portuguese writers relate that the principal chiefs in the territory between the Sabi and Zambesi rivers took their own sisters and daughters as their wives of highest rank, but perhaps this statement arose from their attaching the European meaning to the words sister and daughter, which when used by people of the Bantu family applied equally to cousins and nieces on the father's side. No marriages with sisters or daughters in the European sense is permitted at the present day, but with cousins—sisters in the Bantu sense—they are common among the interior tribes.*

With regard to the common people, the theory of the universal Bantu law was that they were the property of the rulers, consequently an offence against any of their persons was atoned for by a fine to the chief. Murder and assaults were punished in this manner. When a man died, his nearest relative was required to report the circumstance to the head of the clan, and to take a present of some kind with him as consolation for the loss sustained.

But while the government of all the tribes was thus in theory despotic, the power of the chiefs in those which were not under military rule was usually more or less restrained. In each clan there was a body of counsellors—commonly hereditary—whose

---

* The following words in the Xosa dialect will further illustrate the difference between European and Bantu ideas as to relationship. *Bawo* is the word used in addressing father, father's brother, or father's half-brother. Little children say *Tata*. But there are three different words for father, according as a person is speaking of his own father or uncle, of the father or uncle of the person he is speaking to, or of the father or uncle of the person he is speaking of. Speaking of my father, *bawo* is the word used ; of your father, *uyihlo ;* of his father, *uyise*. *Ma* is the word used in addressing mother, any wife of father, or the sister of any of these. The one we should term mother can only be distinguished from the others, when speaking of her, by describing her as *uma wam kanye, i.e.* my real mother ; or *uma ondizalayo, i.e.* the mother who bore me. Speaking of my mother, *ma* is the word used ; of your mother, *unyoko ;* of his or her mother, *unina.* *Malume* is the brother of any one called mother. A paternal aunt is addressed as *dadebobawo, i.e.* sister of my father, showing a distinction between relatives on the paternal and maternal side. *Mnakwetu* is the word used by females in addressing a brother, half-brother, or male cousin. Males when addressing any of these relations older than themselves, use the word *mkuluwa ;* and when addressing one younger than themselves, say *mninawe.* A sister and a female cousin are alike termed *odade wetu, our* sister—the pronoun being always used in the plural form ;—though sometimes the word *mza,* an abbreviation of *umzalwana, i.e.* of our family, is applied to a cousin on the mother's side by females older than the one addressed. *Mtakama* is an endearing form of expression, meaning child of my mother.

advice could not always be disregarded. A great deal depended upon the personal character of the chief. If he was a man of resolute will, the counsellors were powerless ; if he was weak they possessed not only influence, but often real authority. Then there was a custom that a fugitive from one clan was entitled to protection by the chief of another with which he took refuge, so that an arbitrary or unpopular ruler was in constant danger of losing his followers, although they remained in the same tribe, for no misconduct on the part of a paramount chief could weaken the religious tie that bound his people to him. This custom was an effectual check upon gross and unrestrained tyranny by the minor chiefs or heads of clans.

The law of succession to the government favoured the formation of new tribes. The first wives of a paramount chief were usually the daughters of some of his father's principal retainers, but as he grew older and increased in power his alliance was courted by great families, and thus it generally happened that his consort of highest rank was taken when he was of advanced age. Usually she was the daughter of a neighbouring ruler, and was selected for him by the counsellors of the tribe, who provided the cattle required by her relatives. She was termed the great wife, and her eldest son was the principal heir.

Another of his wives was invested at an earlier period of his life, by the advice of his counsellors and friends, with the title of wife of the right hand, and to her eldest son some of his father's retainers were given, with whom he formed a new clan. The government of this was entrusted to him as soon as he was full grown, so that while his brother was still a child he had opportunities of increasing his power. If he was the abler ruler of the two, a quarrel between them arose almost to a certainty as soon as the great heir reached manhood and was also invested with a separate command. If peace was maintained, upon the death of his father the son of the right hand acknowledged his brother as superior in rank, but neither paid him tribute nor admitted his right to interfere in the internal government of the new clan.

In some of the tribes three sons of every chief divided their father's adherents among them. In the latter case the third heir was termed the representative of the ancients or the son of the left hand.

In this manner new tribes, entirely independent of the old ones from which they sprang, were frequently formed. This was especially the case when the adjacent territory was thinly occupied by a weak people like the Bushmen, affording means for the ruler of lower rank without difficulty to remove to a distance from his brother. The disintegrating process was to some extent checked by frequent tribal wars and feuds, which forced chiefs of the same family to make common cause with each other, but whenever there was comparative peace it was in active operation, and so a steady and rapid expansion of the Bantu communities was effected.

Sometimes it was necessary to set aside the heir to a chieftainship, as in cases of insanity, weakness of character, gross misconduct, or other cause that made him unfit for the duties of a ruler. This was considered a matter of such weight that the chief could not act upon his own authority, though he might, and usually did, initiate the proceedings. The whole tribe assembled, and the matter was discussed, often for days together, before a final conclusion was arrived at. When a great son was in this manner set aside, the next in the line of descent was invariably chosen to fill his place. It sometimes happened that a chief died without having married a great wife, and consequently without leaving a recognised principal heir. In such a case the counsellors and leading men met and decided which of the widows should hold that position, when her eldest son became the head of the tribe. If a chief died leaving a great wife childless, and the woman bore a son even years afterwards, the boy was regarded as the legitimate heir, though he usually had some trouble in displacing rivals who were actual sons of the dead man. Among some of the tribes in the Zambesi valley the chiefs were succeeded not by their own sons, but by the sons of their eldest sisters, a custom unknown farther south.

With the limitations that have been mentioned, in the life of the people the chief was everything, his wishes were the guide of their conduct, his orders were implicitly obeyed, the best of all they had was at his disposal. To every one else they could tell the grossest falsehoods without disgrace, but to him they told the simple truth, and that in language which could not bear two meanings. They could not even partake of the crops in their own gardens until he gave them leave to do so. In this case, when the millet was ripe the chief appointed a day for a general assembly of the people at his residence, that was known as the great place ; he then went through certain rites, among which was the offering of a small quantity of the fresh grain to the spirits of his ancestors, either by laying it on their graves or by casting it into a stream, after which ceremony he gave the people permission to gather and eat.

Every people has its own standard of virtue, which if it does not live up to, it at least respects. The Bantu had theirs, which consisted in fidelity to the chief. A man might be a thorough scoundrel according to European ideas, cruel, lascivious, intemperate, mean : all this mattered nothing if he was devoted to his chief, in which case in the estimation of his tribe he was virtuous. There was a reason for this, as will presently be seen.

The most solemn oath that a man could take was by either some great legendary ruler or the one then living, though he did not regard even that as binding if he believed that by speaking falsely the interest of the chief would be advanced. Portuguese writers state that the people near the Zambesi swore *by Mambo*, which was rather one of the titles of the head of a great tribe than his proper name, but the individual or his line of ancestors was meant. At present the form of oath varies slightly in different places, the most common expression being I call to witness or I point to, as *Ki supa ka Mokatshane*, the usual oath of a Mosuto, I point to Mokatshane.

The amount of taxes paid by the people for the maintenance of government was not fixed, as it is in European states. The ordinary revenue of a chief was derived from confiscations of property, fines, and presents, besides which his gardens, that were usually large, were cultivated by the labour of his people. The right of the ruler to the personal service of his subjects was everywhere recognised, and it extended even to his requiring them to serve others for his benefit. The Portuguese engaged carriers from a chief, who took a considerable portion of their earnings, just as the tribal heads at present send their young men to a distance to work for them. Men who would not think of assisting in the cultivation of their own gardens went willingly, when called upon to do so, to labour in those of their chief. The breast of every animal killed, which was regarded as the choicest meat, was sent to him as his right, and certain furs were his alone. When he felt so disposed, he made a tour through his tribe, when each kraal visited provided food for him and his attendants, and if he was in need, made him a present of cattle. The oxen, often from fifty to a hundred, needed to procure his principal wife—who was to be the mother of the future ruler —were contributed by his retainers.

In some of the tribes the chief might be said to be the owner of everything. Cattle taken in war were his property, and though the cows were distributed among the people, who had the use of the milk, he could demand their restoration at any time. All trade with strangers passed through his hands, and he kept as much of the gains as he chose. Though this system was confined to the military tribes, even in those less highly organised it was usual for the chiefs to exact heavy dues upon commercial transactions between their subjects and others. When, for instance, the first fairs were established by the British authorities on the Xosa border, the chiefs fixed the quantity of beads or other merchandise to be received for every ox or tusk of ivory, and commonly took about half for themselves, without the people raising any objection.

The charges upon the government, except in the case of the military tribes, were limited to the cost of entertainment of attendants and visitors, and of presents to favourites or for services performed. There were no salaries to be paid, and no public works to be provided for. In all the country from the Zambesi to the utmost limit of the Bantu border there was not so much as a road, nothing better than a footpath, which, though leading towards a fixed point, wound round every obstacle in the way, great or small, for no one cared to remove even a puny boulder to obtain a more direct line. Many of these foot-paths were worn deep by constant use for years, but they were never repaired. The simplest bridge over a stream was unknown, nor was there any other public work, if barricades of stones in the approaches to hill tops are excepted.

The religion of the Bantu was based upon the supposition of the existence of spirits that could interfere with the affairs of this world. These spirits were those of their ancestors and their deceased chiefs, the greatest of whom had control over lightning. When the spirits became offended or hungry they sent a plague or disaster until sacrifices were offered and their wrath or hunger was appeased. The head of a family of com-moners on such an occasion killed an animal, and all ate of the meat, as the hungry ghost was supposed to be satisfied with the smell. In case of the chief or the community at large being affected, the sacrifice was performed with much ceremony by the tribal priest, an individual of great influence, who had as other duties to ward off from the ruler the malevolent attacks of wizards and to prepare charms or administer medicine that would make the warriors who conducted themselves properly and bravely invulnerable in battle.

An instance may be given to illustrate the operation of this religion. Upon the death of Gwanya, a chief of great celebrity in the Pondomsi tribe, he was buried in a deep pool of the Tina river. The body was fastened to a log of wood, which was sunk in the water and then covered with stones. The sixth in the direct line of descent from this chief, Umhlonhlo by name, to save himself from destruction by an enemy became a British subject at his own request, but in October 1880 his clan treacherously murdered three English officials, and went into rebellion, which resulted in his being obliged afterwards to take shelter in Basutoland.* In 1891 one of Umhlonhlo's sons

* After eluding capture for twenty-three years, Umhlonhlo was at length arrested, though he made a desperate resistance. In 1904 he was put upon his trial for murder, but was acquitted, as it could not be proved, though it was morally certain, that he had personally taken part in the crime. In the interim through the agency of a Roman catholic missionary he had become a convert to Christianity. During his confinement and when on his trial he

ventured into the district where his father had lived, and there committed an assault, for which he was arrested and sent before a colonial court to be tried. It was a time of intense heat and severe drought, which the tribe declared were caused by the spirit of Gwanya, who in this manner was expressing displeasure at the treatment accorded to his descendant. As a peace-offering therefore, cattle were killed on the banks of the pool containing his grave, and the flesh was thrown into the water, together with new dishes full of beer. The prisoner was sentenced to pay a fine, which was at once collected by the people for him. A few days later rain fell in copious showers, which of course confirmed the belief of the tribe that what was right had been done, and that the spirit of Gwanya was appeased.

In all such cases the conception of the spirit was that it manifested its power by doing harm, and must therefore be propitiated. The idea of a God of love was foreign to the Bantu mind until introduced by the teaching of Christian missionaries, and even then the converts were very prone to reflect more on the anathemas than on the invitations contained in holy writ. It was a peculiar turn of mind, which was not quickly diverted to an opposite direction.

The Bantu had no idea of reward or punishment in a world to come for acts committed in this life, and thus there was no other restraint of religion upon their actions than was connected with loyalty to their chiefs dead and living. Except when compelled by circumstances to do so, they thought as little as possible of their own after fate, and seldom allowed reflection of any kind to disturb them.

A belief in the existence of spirits would seem to have as its consequence a belief in some special place where they resided, but the Bantu power of reasoning in such matters did not extend so far. Their minds in this respect were like those of little children, who are content to credit marvellous things told to them, without attempting to investigate any of the particulars.

conducted himself with such dignity as to win the admiration of every one, a feature of character, however, that most Bantu chiefs would display under similar circumstances.

It is only since European ideas have been disseminated among them that such a question has arisen, and that one has said the spirits resided in the sky, another that their place of abode was a cavern under the earth. They acted as if the ghosts of the dead remained at or near their habitations when in life, and they were constantly fearful of meeting them at night. In all parts of the country there were localities, usually wild or secluded glens, which had the reputation of being haunted, and where no one would venture to appear alone after dusk. This might be said, however, of almost every part of Europe as well, so that in it the Bantu did not differ from the most highly civilised section of mankind.

No man among them, upon being told of the existence of a single supreme God, ever denies the assertion, and among many of the tribes there is even a name for such a Being, as, for instance, the word Mukuru used by some, or Unkulunkulu the Great Great One, used by the Hlubis and others. From this it has been assumed by some investigators that the Bantu are really monotheists, and that the spirits of their ancestors are regarded merely as mediators or intercessors. But such a conclusion is incorrect. The Great Great One was once a man, they all assert, and before our conception of a deity became known to them, he was the most powerful of the ancient chiefs, to whom tradition assigned supernatural knowledge and skill.

When a person was killed by lightning no lamentation was made, as it would have been considered rebellion to mourn for one whom the great chief had sent for. In cases of death within a kraal the relatives and friends of the deceased often exhibited the most passionate symptoms of grief, which, however, seldom lasted long, though they generally shaved their heads as a sign of mourning. There was an idea that something connected with death attached to the personal effects of the deceased, on which account whatever had belonged to him that could not be placed in the grave, his clothing, mats, head rest, &c., was destroyed by fire. The hut in which he had lived was also burned, and no other was allowed to be built on the spot. If he had been the chief, the whole kraal was removed to another site. Those who touched the corpse or any of the dead man's effects were obliged to go through certain ceremonies, and then to bathe in running water before associating again with their companions. Except in cases of persons of rank, however, very few deaths occurred within kraals. As soon as it was seen that any one's end was near, the invalid was carried to a distance and left to die alone,.in order to avert the danger of the presence of the dreaded something that could not be explained.

If it happened that a common person died within a kraal, the corpse was dragged to a distance, and there left to be devoured by beasts of prey ; but chiefs and great men were interred with much ceremony. A grave was dug, in which the body was placed in a sitting posture, and by it were laid the weapons of war and ornaments used in life. When the grave was closed, such expressions as these were used : " Remember us from the place where you are, you have gone to a high abode, cause us to prosper." To prevent desecration of any kind, watchers were then appointed to guard the grave, who for many months never left its neighbourhood. In some instances it was enclosed with a fence large enough to form a fold, within which selected oxen were confined at night. These cattle were thenceforward regarded as sacred, were well cared for, and allowed to die a natural death. The watchers of the grave were also privileged men ever afterwards.

The funeral customs of the Ovaherero were somewhat different from those of the other tribes. The backbone of a dead man was broken, to prevent his spirit from practising mischief, and the body was then doubled up and buried in a deep grave with the face towards the north, the home of his ancestors. These people believed that the eyes of the spirit of a dead man were in the back of the head. They slaughtered the favourite oxen of the deceased, in order that the shades of these might accompany him to the spirit world, but they did not eat the flesh of the dead animals, as was the practice with other Bantu. In such cases the Ovaherero killed the oxen by shedding their blood, whereas cattle killed by them on all other

PORTRAIT OF HERERO MEN.

(*From a Photograph in the South African Public Library.*)

[*To face p.* 186.

occasions were bound fast and suffocated, with their faces turned towards the north.

Before the interment of the paramount chief of a powerful tribe, especially of a great military ruler, a number of his attendants were killed, and their bodies were placed around his in the grave in such a way as to keep it from contact with the earth. The object was to provide him with servants in the spirit world. His principal wives either took poison voluntarily or were killed, to serve him as companions. If he had a favourite dog, ox, or other animal, that was also slaughtered, to give him pleasure. It does not follow that such animals were regarded as immortal, but there was something unexplainable connected with them that the dead chief could enjoy, just as there was with his assagais and his metal bracelets. Afterwards, especially when drought occurred or any disaster overtook the people, sacrifices were offered at the grave, and prayers were made to him for assistance. When a number of chiefs had thus been interred, a tacit selection was made of the one who had been the wisest and most powerful in his day, and the others were neglected and gradually forgotten except by the antiquaries who preserved their names.

The custom of slaughtering wives and attendants upon the death of a great chief was not observed by the less important tribes, nor upon the death of mere chiefs of clans or of other individuals of position ; but a practice carried out to the present day shows that it must at one time have been general. When a man of what may be termed aristocratic rank died his widows betook themselves to forests or lonely places, where they lived in seclusion as best they could for a month or longer, according to the time of mourning customary among their people. During this period no one even spoke to them, and when, as sometimes —but not always—happened, they were supplied with food, it was done by leaving a little millet in a place near their haunts where they would probably find it. Death from exposure and starvation was frequently the result of this custom. At the end of the time of mourning the emaciated creatures returned to their kraals, when ceremonies of purification were observed, their clothing and ornaments were burned, and their relatives supplied them with the new articles that they needed. This method of mourning must have been developed from the practice of slaughtering such wives of a man of rank as could not make their escape when he died, in order that they might accompany him to the land of spirits.

The slaughter of attendants upon the death of a chief proves a belief in the continued existence of his spirit, but the burial of the weapons and ornaments of a warrior with his corpse is by no means such conclusive evidence. The fear of the mysterious power death was such that every one dreaded to come in contact with the personal effects of the individual smitten down, lest these also should partake of the infection. Whatever could be deposited in a grave was therefore disposed of in this manner, and the hut, mats, clothing, and everything else belonging to the deceased were destroyed by fire. To keep anything whatever as a memento of a departed relative or friend was an idea utterly foreign to the Bantu mind.

The tribes farthest in advance on the south-east had a dim belief in the existence of a powerful being, whom they termed Qamata, and to whom they sometimes prayed, though they never offered sacrifices to him. In a time of danger one of them would exclaim: " O Qamata help me," and when the danger was over he would attribute his deliverance to the same being. But of Qamata nothing more was known than that he was high and mighty, and that though at times he helped individuals, in general he did not interfere with the destinies of men. Recent investigations have shown that this belief did not extend far among the Bantu tribes, and it is now known to have been acquired from the Hottentots. Not that the Hottentots venerated a deity thus designated, but that a knowledge of some other object of worship than their own ancestral shades having been obtained through Hottentot females whom they took to themselves, this name was given to the unknown divinity.

To obtain information upon the religion of any barbarous people long observation is necessary, and nothing that can be depended upon is ever obtained by direct questions to comparative strangers. The relationship of the author of this volume to a Gaika clan was, however, once of such a nature that knowledge possessed by its members was freely communicated, and in a discussion upon religion with a group of old men, their opinions were given, though negatively rather than positively.

Question. Was Qamata once a chief, such as Xosa or Tshawe ?

Reply. No.

Q. Was he the first man, the father of the nations, the one whom some of the old Fingos call Unkulunkulu ?

R. No, not at all ; Qamata was never a man.

Q. Was he the creator of all things that we see, the mountains, and the sun, and the stars ?

R. Perhaps he was, we don't know.

Q. Where is he ?

R. Everywhere.

Q. Does he see all things ?

R. We think he does.

Q. Does he help people ?

R. We ask him to sometimes, and we believe he does.

Q. Is he altogether good, or altogether bad, or partly good and partly bad ?

R. We don't know about that ; but we think he is altogether good.

Q. Are there any others like him ?

R. No, he is all alone.

Q. Is there any other name for him ?

R. In the olden times that was the only name, but now he is called by some u-Tixo (a name for God introduced by missionaries).

In various parts of the Xosa and Tembu country there are artificial heaps of stones, and a man, when travelling, may often be seen adding one to the number. He repeats no words, but merely picks up a stone and throws it on the heap. Why does he do it ? That good fortune may attend him, that he may not be carried away by the river spirit when crossing a stream, that he may find food prepared for him where he is to rest, that he may be successful in the business he is engaged in, or something of the kind he is thinking of at the time. It is an act of superstition. The old men said "it was for Qamata." How? They did not know; but their ancestors had done the same thing and said it was for Qamata, and so they did it too.

Here then is an instance of a foreign belief adopted by a section of the people, for the above is simply the worship of Heitsi-eibib, and must have been introduced by the Hottentot women who were incorporated in the Xosa and Tembu tribes when they were advancing south-westward. But it was further modified by the percolation of missionary teaching, as is shown by the answers of the old men, though not one of them was a professed Christian.

The Bantu believed that the spirits of the dead visited their friends and descendants in the form of animals. Each tribe regarded some particular animal as the one selected by the ghosts of its kindred, and therefore looked upon it as sacred. The lion was thus held in veneration by one tribe, the crocodile by another, the python by a third, the bluebuck by a fourth, and so on. When a division of a tribe took place, each section retained the same ancestral animal, and thus a simple method is afforded of ascertaining the wide dispersion of various communities of former times. For instance, at the present day a species of snake is held by people as far south as the mouth of the Fish river and by others near the Zambesi to be the form in which their dead appear.

This belief caused even such destructive animals as the lion and the crocodile to be protected from harm in certain parts of the country. It was not indeed believed that every lion or every crocodile was a disguised spirit, but then any one might be, and so none were molested unless under peculiar circumstances, when it was clearly apparent that the animal was an aggressor and therefore not related to the tribe. Even then, if it could be driven away it was not killed. A Xosa of the present time will leave his hut if an ancestral snake enters it, permitting the reptile to keep possession, and will shudder at the thought of any one hurting it. The animal thus respected by one tribe was, however, disregarded and killed without scruple by all others.

The great majority of the people of the interior have now lost 'the ancient belief, but they still hold in veneration the animal that their ancestors regarded as a possible embodied spirit. Most of them take their tribal titles from it, thus the Bakwena are the crocodiles, the Bataung the lions, the Baputi the little blue antelopes. Each terms the animal whose name it bears its *siboko*, and not only will not kill it or eat its flesh, but will not touch its skin or come in contact with it in any way if that can be avoided. When one stranger meets another and desires to know something about him, he asks " to what do you dance ? " and the name of the animal is given in reply. Dos Santos, a Portuguese writer who had excellent opportunities of observation, states that on certain occasions, which must have been frequent, men imitated the actions of their siboko ; but that custom has now almost died out, at least among the southern tribes.

Frequently two or more different animals were held in veneration by a tribe. This circumstance arose in some instances from the community being composed of fragments of others blended together, in a few instances from the name of its founder having been that of an animal. Thus from the crocodiles a section might separate and become independent under a chief named the baboon. The people would then in all probability venerate the baboon as well as the crocodile, for the twofold purpose of honouring their founder and giving themselves a distinctive title. Occasionally in recent times an inanimate object has been venerated, thus the Barolong have iron as their siboko, the Bamorara the wild vine. The sun, the sky, rain, etc. are thus used as the siboko of different tribes that have long since lost all knowledge of the belief of their remote ancestors. Owing to the many terrible convulsions these people have gone through, only a glimmering remembrance of the faith and practice of the distant past has remained to some sections of them.

The tribes along the south-eastern coast, though separated into distinct communities absolutely independent of each other since the beginning of the seventeenth century, as far back as their tradition reaches, are of common stock. They all regard the same species of snake as the form in which their ancestral shades appear. Further, their tribal titles, with few exceptions, are derived from the chief who left the parent stock, thus the Amahlubi are the people of Hlubi, the Abatembu the people of Tembu, the Amaxosa the people of Xosa, Hlubi, Tembu, and Xosa being the chiefs under whom they acquired independence. The exceptions are derived from some peculiarity of the people, but in these cases the titles were originally nicknames given by strangers and afterwards adopted by the tribes themselves.

Nearer than the spirits of deceased chiefs or of their own ancestors was a whole host of hobgoblins, water spirits, and malevolent demons, who met the Bantu turn which way they would. There was no beautiful fairyland for them, for all the beings who haunted the mountains, the plains, and the rivers were ministers of evil. The most feared of these was a large bird that made love to women and incited those who returned its affection to cause the death of those who did not, and a little mischievous imp who was also amorously inclined. Many instances could be gathered from the records of magistrates' courts in recent years of demented women having admitted their acquaintance with these fabulous creatures, as well as of whole communities living in terror of them.

The water spirits were believed to be addicted to claiming human victims, though they were sometimes willing to accept an ox as a ransom. How this belief works practically may be illustrated by facts which have come under the writer's cognisance.

In the summer of 1875 a party of girls went to bathe in a tributary of the Keiskama river. There was a deep hole in the stream, into which one of them got, and she was drowned. The others ran home as fast as they could, and there related that their companion had been lured from their side by a spirit calling her. She was with them, they said, in a shallow part, when suddenly she stood upright and exclaimed, " It is calling." She then walked straight into the deep place, and would not allow any of them to touch her. One of them heard her saying "Go and tell my father and my mother that it took me." Upon this, the father collected his cattle as quickly as possible, and went to the stream. The animals were driven into the water, and the man stood on the bank imploring the spirit to take the choicest of them and restore his daughter.

On another occasion a man was trying to cross one of the fords of a river when it was in flood. He was carried away by the current, but succeeded in getting safely to land some three or four hundred metres farther down. Eight or ten stout fellows saw him carried off his feet, but not one made the slightest effort to help him. On the contrary, they all rushed away frantically shouting to the herd boys on the hillsides to drive down the cattle. The escape of the man from the power of the spirit was afterwards attributed to his being in possession of a powerful charm.

Besides these spirits, according to the belief of the Bantu, there are people living under the water, pretty much as those do who are in the upper air. They have houses and furniture, and even cattle, all of their domestic animals being, however, of a dark colour. They are wiser than other people, and from them the witchfinders are supposed to obtain the knowledge of their art. This is not a fancy of children, but the implicit belief of grown-up men and women at the present day. As an instance, in July 1881 a woman came to the author of this volume, who was then acting as magistrate of a district in the Cape Colony inhabited by Bantu, and asked for assistance. A child had died in her kraal, and the witchfinder had pointed her out as the person who had caused its death. Her husband was absent, and the result of her being *smelt out* was that no one would enter her hut, or so much as speak to her. If she was in a path every one fled out of her way, and even her own children avoided her. Being under British jurisdiction she could not be otherwise punished, but such treatment as this would of itself, in course of time, have made her insane. She denied most emphatically having been concerned in the death of the child, though she did not doubt that some one had caused it by witchcraft. The witchfinder was sent for, and, as the matter was considered an important one, a larger number of people than usual appeared at the investigation. On putting the ordinary tests to the witchfinder he failed to meet them, and when he was compelled, reluctantly, to admit that he had never held converse with the people under the water, it was easy to convince the bystanders that he was only an impostor.

By some of the Bantu tribes great regard was paid to fire. The Makaranga when first visited by Europeans four centuries ago were in the habit of extinguishing all the fires throughout their country on a certain day named by the chief, and lighting them again from a flame produced at his residence by friction of two pieces of wood, which observance was attended with much ceremony. The Ovaherero keep a fire constantly burning at the place where cattle are sacrificed to the spirits of the dead at the principal ruler's kraal, which flame is considered sacred, and is guarded by the eldest unmarried daughter of the chief. When the kraal is removed the sacred fire is put out, and is lit afresh at the new place of settlement with much ceremony, when pieces of wood to represent their ancestors are set up. Symbolic figures of their ancestors are kept in their huts and are held in veneration by some of the Betshuana also, but the sacred fire, if ever it existed among them, has long since died out.

Of the origin of life or of the visible universe the Bantu never thought, nor had any one of them ever formed a theory upon the subject. There was indeed a story told in all the tribes of the cause of death, but it is in itself an apt illustration of their want of reasoning power in such matters. The chameleon, so the tale was told, was sent to say that men were to live for ever. After he had gone a long time the little lizard was sent to say that men were to die. The lizard, being fleet of foot, arrived first at his journey's end, and thus death was introduced. But in whom lay the power of forming these decisions, and of sending the animals with the messages, they did not trouble themselves to inquire, nor did it strike them that the narrative was incomplete without this information until Europeans questioned them concerning it.

Some of the eastern Bantu had a legend that men and animals formerly existed in caverns in the bowels of the earth, but at length found their way to the surface through an opening in a marsh overgrown with reeds. They always pointed to the north as the direction in which this marsh lay. The Bantu of the interior believed that men and animals first made their appearance from a fissure in a large rock far away in the north. Wizards had power to cause this rock to open and shut at will, but whether it was the entrance to a cavern, or merely itself hollow, no one could say. The legends collected in different parts vary greatly in detail as to the manner in which the men and animals made their appearance, the special gifts bestowed on each—by whom is never stated,—and the mode of their dispersion subsequently. The Bushmen in these tales are not included in human beings, they were already in existence when the men and cattle appeared.

The Ovaherero and their kindred believe that the first man and woman came out of a tree similar to a particular species found in the country they now inhabit. From this couple were born the ancestors of the Hottentot and Bantu tribes, but not of the Bushmen, the Berg Damaras, or the baboons, classifying the three latter as equal. Cattle also and game animals first came from the same tree, but emerged from it in herds, not in couples. They pay such respect to every tree of this species that they will not even lop a twig from it, but when passing by one make an offering to it by throwing a bunch of grass or some sticks at its foot. For this reason it is now commonly called by the Europeans in the country the Damara mother tree, Damara being the Hottentot name of all the black people living north of Walfish Bay, who are distinguished merely as Cattle Damaras, that is Ovaherero, and Berg Damaras, or those who live like Bushmen.

This belief of the Ovaherero is possibly of Hottentot origin; for the people that hold it have strangely mixed up the worship of Heitsi-Eibib with that of their own ancestral shades. Wherever barbarous races intermingle, even as enemies as in this instance, each derives something from the beliefs of the other. Mr. Stow gives a legend of some of the Bushmen near the mouth of the Orange river, that men and animals first came forth from a hole in the ground at the foot of a great tree, which may also have had a Hottentot origin.

Dos Santos states that the people of his time in the Zambesi basin observed certain fixed days as holy, and abstained from labour upon them; but this custom was certainly not universal, and very likely the friar was mistaken. At any rate modern observers in that part of the country as well as in the south have noticed that no days or seasons are considered more sacred than others, though there are times marked by particular events when it is considered unlucky to undertake any enterprise, and even movements in war are delayed on such occasions.

Still it must be observed that, though no days were considered holier than others, or were specially dedicated to religious observances, with the Bantu, as probably with all uncivilised people, the time of a new moon was one of special rejoicing. Next to the apparent course of the sun through the sky, the changes of the moon are those which to every one are most striking. This is particularly so in a country like South Africa, where a moonlit evening, when the winds are lulled and the air is deliciously fresh and cool, is to Europeans the pleasantest part of the twenty-four hours, far more so to people who know of no other artificial light than that of burning wood. It is no wonder therefore that the new moon was hailed with shouts of joy, that its praises were chanted in set words, and that among some of the tribes dances and other ceremonies took place in its honour. With all this, however, the moon was not regarded as a deity, nor was the evening of rejoicing considered more holy than any other. After the crops were gathered, many of the tribes were accustomed to offer special sacrifices to the spirits of their dead chiefs, though there was no fixed day in every year set apart for the purpose, and indeed they did not even know how to reckon time as we do. A chief who considered that his people, male or female, needed rest. might issue an order that no work was to be done on a particular day, but that did not cause it to be regarded as holy.

Each ruling family had an individual connected with it, one of whose duties can properly be described as that of a priest, for it was he who in times of calamity sacrificed cattle for the tribe to the spirits of its dead chiefs. Another of his duties was by means of charms and incantations to ward off evil influence of every kind from the reigning ruler. When a community was broken in war and compelled to become a vassal clan of some other tribe, it retained its priest until by time or circumstances a thorough incorporation took place. That was a process, however, not usually completed until several generations had passed away.

As a factor in the government of a Bantu tribe religion was more powerful than in any European state, for the fear of offending the spirits of the deceased chiefs, and so bringing evil upon themselves, kept the clans loyal to their head. He was the representative, the descendant in the great line, of those whose wrath they appeased by sacrifices. A tribe all of whose clans were governed by offshoots of the family of the paramount chief was thus immensely stronger in war than one of equal size made up of clans brought together by chance. In the one case the religious head was the same as the political, in the other they were separate.

The belief in witchcraft was deep-seated and universal. The theory was that certain evil-disposed persons obtained power from the demons to bewitch others, and so to cause sickness, death, or disaster of some kind. They were believed often to use snakes, baboons, and other animals as their messengers. They could only be discovered by individuals who went through a very severe novitiate, and to whom the necessary knowledge was imparted by people who lived under water. Undoubtedly some of the witchfinders were impostors; but many of them were really monomaniacs, and had the firmest conviction in their ability to do what they professed.

Occasionally a person believed that he had received revelations from the spirit world. If his statements were credited, his power at once became enormous, and his commands were implicitly obeyed. Crafty chiefs sometimes made use of such deranged beings for the purpose of exciting the people to war, or of inducing them to approve of measures which would otherwise have been unpopular.

Among tribes varying from each other in blood as much as the different Bantu communities south of the Zambesi and the Kunene, it might be expected that there would be great differences in religious belief. Ancestral worship was common to them all, and so was fetishism, or a trust in certain charms to ward off evil or to bring about good. But fetishism was much more prevalent with some tribes than with others, so that it is only in general terms that the religion of these people can be described. To go more closely into detail would need the treatment of each section separately, which would tend more to confusion than to enlightenment.

The large number of stone phalli found in the ruins of great buildings in Rhodesia has caused some persons to suppose that phallic worship may once have prevailed among a section of the Bantu. But the ruins and the phalli found at the bottom of the rubbish in them were there before a tribe of this family crossed the Zambesi, and there is not a trace of such worship existing at present, or having ever existed, among the dark coloured people in any part of the country, unless the occasional use of imitation phalli as charms by individuals belonging to some of the interior tribes can be regarded in that light. Among the Basuto and some of the Betshuana a childless woman procures charms from a man professing to be a doctor, which she carries about with her in hope that through their efficacy she may become a mother. These are sometimes, but not always or even commonly, imitations of phalli, such as the neck of a calabash elaborately adorned with beads. But in no case are they regarded in any other light than as charms to be employed for a particular purpose, and among most of the tribes they are quite unknown.

CHAPTER IX.

Superstitions and Customs of the Bantu.

Among all the sections of the Bantu there were individuals who professed to be able to make rain, and whose services were frequently called into use when any part of the country suffered from drought. If it happened that rain fell soon afterwards they received credit for it, and were amply rewarded, while if the drought continued they asserted that some unknown powerful wizard was working against them, a statement that was in most cases believed. Sometimes, however, the chief and people lost faith in them, when they were pronounced guilty of imposture, and were tied hand and foot and thrown over a precipice or into a stream.

This belief in the power of certain individuals to cause or to prevent rain was universal, and in our own times has been shown to exist even among people who were supposed to have made long strides towards European civilisation. As an instance, a few years ago the Cape government, under the guidance of the right honourable Cecil J. Rhodes, caused a large area of land at Glen Grey to be surveyed into small farms, and allotted to Tembus who were believed to be so far advanced as to be able to appreciate the advantages of individual tenure. After a time it was found that some of the stone boundary beacons had been thrown down, and upon inquiry it was ascertained that the owners of the farms had been directed by a rainmaker to plant poles in the ground when they wanted rain and take them out when they desired it to cease. They thought the stone beacons would have the same effect, and consequently broke them down to prevent floods.

There were also among them persons who were skilful in the use of herbs as remedies for diseases, and who were well acquainted with different kinds of poison. This knowledge was transmitted in certain families from father to son, and was kept profoundly secret from the mass of the people. Some of their medicines were beyond doubt of great efficacy, such as those used for the cure of dysentery, for causing virulent sores to heal, and to counteract snake bites.* But with these, and classified as of equal value, they professed to have medicines that would cause love from a woman, favour from a chief, etc. The writer of this was once so fortunate as to come into possession of the whole stock in trade of a famous Xosa herbalist. Each article in it was afterwards submitted to different practitioners, under exceptionally favourable circumstances for eliciting information, when most of them were at once recognised and their uses pronounced. Some were cures for various diseases, one was a love philter, and one was a piece of wood which was to be burned and the smoke inhaled, when the person using it would find favour in the eyes of his superior. But there were several whose use no one would divulge, their properties being regarded as secrets upon the strictest maintenance of which the fortunes of the herbalist families depended. In every case, in addition to the medicine, charms were made use of, and the one was as much relied upon as the other by the people at large.

The remedies used by these people would have been more efficacious if they had understood how to prepare them in proper doses, but this was never considered as of consequence, nor had they any knowledge necessary to repeat the doses at

* A valuable pamphlet, in which the botanical, Xosa, and colonial names, and the uses of a great many of these medicinal plants are given, was not long ago prepared and published by the late Andrew Smith, Esqre., M.A., for many years a teacher in the higher department of the Lovedale Missionary Institution, who expended a great deal of time and thought in the investigation of this subject. My friend the reverend Dr. W. A. Soga, a medical missionary with the Bomvanas in the district of Elliotdale, informed me a few years ago that a remedy for one form of cancer was certainly known to some herbalists of his acquaintance, but though he had long been endeavouring to acquire their secret, he had been unable to do so.

regular intervals. Very often when a man of importance was ill, instead of taking the medicine himself he would require one of his attendants to swallow it, in the full belief that if it was taken by some one about him it would answer as well as if taken by himself. Of course in such cases faith, or the influence of the mind upon the body, was the real healer.

It often happened that the three offices of witchfinder, rain-maker, and herbalist were combined in the same person, but this was not always the case, and the occupations were distinct. When practising, these individuals attired themselves fantastically, being painted with various colours, and having the tails of wild animals suspended around them.

Charms were largely depended upon to preserve the wearers against accident or to produce good luck. They were merely bits of wood or bone, which were hung about the neck, and were regarded just as lucky pennies and fortunate days are by some silly Europeans. But the belief was firm in charms and medicines which would give to an assagai the property of hitting the mark, to an individual the property of winning favour, and such like. The issue of warlike operations was divined by revolting cruelties practised on animals. At the commencement of hostilities, and often before an engagement, two bulls were selected to represent the opposing parties. These were then skinned alive, and success was foretold to the combatant represented by the one that lived longest. By some means, however, each band of warriors was made to believe that the result denoted victory to its side. While this was taking place pieces of flesh were cut from other living bulls, which the warriors devoured raw, in the supposition that by this means their courage in battle would be increased. Cruelty of so dreadful a kind shocked no heart among the spectators, for the Bantu in general were utterly indifferent to the sufferings of animals, except favourites such as a man's own race-ox or his pet dog.

The tribes of the interior were more superstitious than those of the coast, as they were guided in nearly all their actions by the position in which some pieces of bone or wood of the character of dice fell when they were cast on the ground. The largest made of wood were oblong tablets, about fifteen centimetres in length, five centimetres in width, and a centimetre and a half in thickness, but usually those of wood, and almost invariably those of bone, were smaller, the commonest being about six centimetres long, two centimetres and a half wide, and a third of a centimetre in thickness. On each tablet a different pattern was carved, and each had a signification different from the others. Sometimes instead of tablets pieces of bone or of ivory carved in various shapes were used, in the manufacture of which a great deal of patient labour was expended. The usual number employed was five, but more were sometimes found in a set. If an ox strayed the *daula* was thrown to ascertain in what direction it had gone, if a hunt was to take place it was consulted to indicate in what quarter game was most readily to be found, in short it was resorted to in every case of doubt. Each individual carried with him a set of these mystic articles strung on a thong, to be used whenever required. This superstitious practice, just as it was described more than three hundred years ago by the friar Dos Santos, is still prevalent and firmly believed in.

With many of the tribes there was a custom upon the accession of a chief to kill the commoner with the largest head among the people, in order that his skull might be used by the priest as a receptacle for the charms against witchcraft employed in the protection of the ruler. Such a receptacle was regarded as requisite for that particular purpose. Only a generation ago a man was killed with this object by a section of the Xosa tribe that was not then under British rule, but that had been to some extent for many years under European influence. The writer has heard his grandchildren speak of the event without the slightest feeling of horror, with as much indifference, in fact, as if they were relating any ordinary occurrence.

The belief in witchcraft was a part of the very nature of these people, and to the present time in very few instances has it been eradicated by the adoption of Christianity. Instances have come under the observation of the author of this volume of young men who were not only professing Christians themselves, but whose parents and even grandparents were also

Christians, on some emergency showing that the old ideas were still in full force. One bright, cheerful, intelligent youth of eighteen years of age in particular may be mentioned. He was giving promise of a life of usefulness, when suddenly on a slight attack of illness he became morose, and persisted in declaring that " the river had bit him."

In a pamphlet issued in February 1910 * a teacher at Lovedale says :

" But it is not so generally recognised that up to the present Christian teaching and our educational systems have failed to dislodge this terrible enemy to progress and happiness. When I first went to Lovedale nothing impressed me more forcibly with the futility of much of the educational work than the sight of boys in the senior classes learning Latin and reading Shakespeare while their minds were steeped in the crudest superstitions. There was one boy in particular whose name I may mention. He was in the matriculation class, a Christian, and a member of the Christian Association, in connection with which he used to go out to preach on Sundays to the ' red ' Kaffirs in the surrounding kraals. Through overwork his health broke down, and seeing no ostensible cause of his illness he immediately thought he was bewitched, a belief shared by all his friends at the Institution. He consulted a native witchdoctor in the district, who advised him that he was being bewitched by an enemy in Basutoland, and a few days later he left the school to seek out his would-be murderer. In Christian congregations, in Christian villages, people still attribute sickness to the work of some witch, generally a neighbour, whose life is often rendered unbearable because of social or other persecution."

The Bantu had a system of common law and perfectly organised tribunals of justice, which, however, were sometimes set aside by the great military tribes. Their laws came down from a time to which even tradition did not reach, and those which related to ordinary matters were so well known to every

---

* *Native Higher Education. The proposed inter-colonial Native College. An address delivered at Durban before a meeting of the Natal Native Affairs Reform Committee.* By K. A. Hobart Houghton, M.A., of Lovedale.

member of the community that trials were mere investigations into statements and proofs of occurrences. When complicated cases arose, precedents were sought for, antiquaries were referred to, and celebrated jurists even in other tribes were consulted. If all these means of ascertaining the law failed, and the chief before whom the case was being tried was not a man of generally recognised ability, it often happened that no judgment was given, for fear of establishing a faulty precedent. From the decisions of the minor chiefs there was a right of appeal to the head of the tribe.

The law held every one accused of crime guilty, unless he could prove himself innocent. It made the head of a family responsible for the conduct of all its branches, the kraal collectively in the same manner for each resident in it, and the clan for each of its sub-divisions. Thus if the skin of a stolen ox was found in a kraal, or if the footmarks of the animal were traced to it, the whole of the residents were liable to be fined. There was no such thing as a man's professing ignorance of his neighbour's doings : the law required him to know all about them, or it made him suffer for neglecting a duty which it held he owed to the community. Every individual was not only in theory but in practice a policeman.

In general principles the law was the same in all the Bantu tribes, but in details there were almost as many variations as there were distinct communities. The law was simply the recognised custom of each, fixed by time as in a mould. Since they have come under European government, some attempts have been made to frame codes applicable to certain areas inhabited by several distinct tribes, but none have been fully successful, though a vast amount of trouble has been taken in their preparation. The same punishment for a particular offence of a man in tribe A, and which was regarded by his fellows as just and correct, would be resented by tribe B as altogether oppressive if applied to one of its members. Their standards of degrees of offences were different. Then their customs in many matters, regarded by us as trifling, were different, and each would consider itself slighted if these were disregarded.

A lawsuit among these people was commonly attended by all the men of the kraal where it took place. Nothing was more congenial than to sit and listen to the efforts of the querists to elicit the truth, or for the ablest among them to assist in the investigation. The trial took place in the open air. The person charged with crime or the defendant in a civil suit underwent a rigorous examination, and anything like warning him against criminating himself was held to be perversion of justice.

The accuser or plaintiff or a friend prosecuted, and a friend of the individual on trial conducted the defence ; the counsellors, who acted as assessors, or any individual of recognised legal ability who happened to be present, put any questions they chose ; and the mass of spectators observed the utmost silence and decorum. At the conclusion of the trial, the counsellors expressed their opinions, and the chief then pronounced judgment.

There were only two modes of punishment, fines and death, except in cases where an individual was charged with having dealt in witchcraft, when torture, often of a horrible kind, was practised. In this class of trials every one was actuated by fear, and was in a state of excitement, so that the formalities required on other occasions were dispensed with. The whole clan was assembled and seated in a circle, the witchfinder, who was fantastically painted and attired, went through certain incantations, and when all were worked into a state of frenzy he pointed to some individual as the one who had by bewitch-ment caused death or sickness among the people, murrain among cattle, blight in crops, or some other disaster. The result to the person so pointed out was confiscation of property and torture, often causing death. The number of persons who perished on charges of dealing in witchcraft was very great. The victims were usually old women, men of property, persons of eccentric habits, or individuals obnoxious to the chief. Any person in advance of his fellows was specially liable to suspicion, so that progress of any kind towards what we should term higher civilisation was made exceedingly difficult by this belief.

No one except the chief was exempt, however, from being charged with dealing in witchcraft. The cruelties practised on the unfortunate individuals believed to be guilty were often horrible, but a single instance, which occurred in July 1892, will be sufficient to exemplify them. A wife of the Pondo chief Sigcawu being ill, a witchfinder was directed to point out the person who caused the malady. He declared that Ma Matiwane, sister of the Pondomsi chief Umhlonhlo and widow of Sigcawu's father, was the guilty person, and that she had a lizard and a mole as her servants in the evil work. By order of Sigcawu, a number of young men then seized Ma Matiwane, stripped her naked, fastened her wrists and ankles to pegs driven in the ground, and covered her with ants irritated by pouring water over them. She suffered this torture for a long time without confessing, so they loosed her, saying that her medicines were too strong for the ants. They then lashed her arms to a pole placed along her shoulders, and taking her by the feet and the ends of the pole, they held her over a fire. Under this torture she confessed that she was guilty, but as she could not produce the lizard and the mole, she was roasted again three times within two days. No European could have survived such a burning; but she was ultimately rescued by an agent of the Cape government, and recovered. This woman had taken care of Sigcawu after the death of his own mother, yet on the mere word of a witchfinder she was thus horribly tortured. And instances of this kind were common events in the olden times.

Frequently, when a great calamity had occurred, or the life of a chief was believed to be in danger, not only the individual pointed out by the witchfinder, but his or her whole family was exterminated, and even entire kraals were sometimes wiped out of existence on such occasions. So strong was the belief in witchcraft and in the power of witchfinders to detect those guilty of practising it that instances were not rare of persons accused admitting that the charge against them must be correct and that they ought to suffer death, because some evil emanation over which they had no control must have gone forth from their bodies and caused the disaster, though they had done nothing directly to produce it.

The Bantu were seen in the most favourable light at ordinary lawsuits before the chiefs and counsellors, and in the most unfavourable light at trials for the discovery of wizards and witches. In the one case men were found conducting themselves with the strictest gravity and propriety, in the other case the same people were seen as a panic-stricken horde, deaf to all reason, and ready to perform most atrocious acts of cruelty, even upon persons who just previously were their companions.

The sentences pronounced in ordinary cases were often such as would have seemed unjust to Europeans, but that was because our standard of comparative crime is not the same as theirs, and because with us there is supposed to be no difference of punishment according to the rank of the criminal. With them the ruling families in all their branches had the privilege of doing many things with impunity that commoners were severely punished for. Bribery was not unknown, but in courts as open as theirs, and where there was the utmost freedom of inquiry, it could not be practised to any great extent. When a case was talked out, every one present was usually acquainted with its minutest details.

Among the northern tribes trial by ordeal was resorted to in cases where personal or circumstantial evidence was wanting, and in appeal from decisions of witchfinders. The form of ordeal varied. In some instances the accused person was required to lick or to pick up a piece of red-hot iron, and if he was burnt he was condemned as guilty. In other cases he drank the poisonous juice of a certain herb, and if it had effect upon him he was doomed to immediate death. In others again he was forced to drink a huge basin of hot water mixed with a bitter emetic, and if he could not retain it the charge against him was regarded as proved. Yet so confident were innocent persons that no harm would come to them from the iron, the poison, or the emetic, that they accepted the ordeal with alacrity. Among the southern tribes this practice was not common, though it was well known.

The Bantu knew of no other periods in reckoning time than the day and the lunar month, and could describe events only as happening before or after some remarkable occurrence, such as the death of a chief, a season of famine, or an unusually heavy flood. The rising of the Pleiades shortly after sunset was regarded as indicating the planting season. To this constellation, as well as to several of the prominent stars and planets, they gave expressive names. They formed no theories concerning the nature of the heavenly bodies and their motions, and were not given to thinking of such things. In later times, if questioned by a European, they might venture to remark that the sky was smoke which had risen from fires, but in such cases it would be evident that the effort to find a solution to a query of this kind was new to them.

They had no knowledge of letters or of any signs by which ideas could be expressed. There were old men who professed to be acquainted with the deeds of the past, and who imparted their knowledge to the young, but their accounts of distant times seldom corresponded in details. They touched lightly upon defeats sustained by their own tribe, but dilated upon all its victories. In the traditions of each independent community a particular chief, usually the second or third in descent from the founder, was invariably represented as having conferred extraordinary benefits upon his people. He was the inventor of iron weapons, the one who decorated them with copper ornaments, and who taught them to use millet for food. Thus among the Barolong at the present day all this is attributed to Noto, son of Morolong; among the Amaxosa to Tshawe, great grandson of Xosa; among the Abatetwa to Umyambosi, son of Umtetwa. Now it is absolutely certain that long before the time of Morolong, Xosa, and Umtetwa, who founded these modern tribes, iron, copper, and millet were in general use by almost all sections of the Bantu. But in praise of chiefs who probably gained some important victory, or under whose rule there was unusual prosperity, whatever the succeeding generations could think of as being great improvements was ascribed to their wisdom, and has been handed down as tribal history from one antiquary to another. Thus these narratives convey incorrect impressions, and little is beyond question except the genealogies of the great chiefs, which have been carefully preserved for ten or twelve generations.

Every chief of highest rank in the military tribes was attended by individuals whose duty was to act as official praisers. These persons were attired in the most fantastic costumes, thus one might have his head and every part of his body covered with the skin of a lion, another with that of a leopard, and so on. On any appearance of the chief, they shouted in a kind of chant a poem in which greatness of every kind was attributed to him, using such terms as great elephant, great despoiler, great ravisher, great conqueror, and great soothsayer. Very often at the same time drums were beaten and horns were sounded, making a din gratifying to the Bantu ear, but intolerable to that of a European. The chiefs of tribes in the ordinary condition had also official praisers, who were, however, more modest in their words, and whose chants were seldom accompanied by such a deafening noise of discordant instruments.

The heads of the independent communities along the eastern coast from the Zambesi river to Kosi Bay had dynastic names, which they assumed upon succeeding to the chieftainship, and by which they were afterwards known, just as all the rulers of ancient Egypt were termed Pharaoh. Thus the paramount chiefs of the tribe that occupied the south-eastern shore of Delagoa Bay took the name Nyaka, those of the adjoining tribe to the westward Kapela, and those of the tribe living along the lower course of the Limpopo river Manisa. Each of these dynastic names originally had a special signification, and was derived from some occurrence connected with the founder of the ruling family or one of the most distinguished of his descendants. The custom applied only to paramount chiefs. South of Kosi Bay dynastic names were not used, owing probably to the manner in which the tribes were formed and their recent origin.

The names given to children at birth were often changed at a later age, especially in the case of chiefs who performed any noteworthy act, or with a view to flattery, a custom that makes research into their history somewhat difficult. It frequently happened also that a chief was known to his own people by one name, and to neighbouring tribes by another very different. In our own day there are many instances of this custom. Thus a chief of a Barolong clan, Montsiwa as his own people called him, is termed Seyangkabo (meaning intruder in a bad sense) by some of his immediate neighbours, and Motshele oa Maaka (the fountain of lies) by others. Some of the names given to notable persons were very expressive, and of these also there are many instances at present. Thus Sigcawu (the great spider), the paramount Xosa chief, was so named on account of his supposed cleverness, Dalindyebo (creator of wealth, from roots uku dala to create and indyebo riches), the paramount Tembu chief, on account of his having been born during an exceedingly abundant harvest, Ngonyama (the lion), a Gaika chief, on account of his personal bravery, Uzwinye (one word, from roots izwi a word and nye one), the reverend Mr. Hargreaves, on account of his constantly recommending peace. When a woman is married, her husband's parents give her a new name, by which she is known to his family afterwards. Upon the birth of her first child, whether son or daughter, she is usually called by every one else after the name given to the infant, Ma * *, the mother of * *.

When about fifteen or sixteen years of age boys in nearly all the tribes were circumcised. The rite was purely civil. By it a youth was enabled to emerge from the society of women and children, and was admitted to the privileges of manhood. Its performance was attended with many ceremonies, some of a harmless, others to European ideas of a criminal nature. At a certain period in every year, unless it was a time of calamity or the chief had a son not ready, all the boys of a clan who were old enough were circumcised. Thereafter for a couple of months or longer they lived by themselves, and were distinguished by wearing a peculiar head-dress and a girdle of long grass about the loins, besides having their bodies covered with white clay. During this period they had license to steal freely from their relatives, provided they could do so without being caught in the act. After returning to their homes, they were brought before the old men of the tribe, who lectured them upon the duties and responsibilities which they had taken upon themselves. Presents of cattle and weapons were afterwards made by their friends to give them a start in life, and they could then indulge in immorality without let or hindrance from their elders.

In case a scion of the ruling house was growing up, the performance of the rite of circumcision was generally allowed to stand over for a year or two, so that he might have a large number of companions. These were all supposed to be bound to him by a very strong tie. In after years they were to be his counsellors and attendants, and in case of danger were to form his bodyguard. In modern times no instance has been known of any one who was circumcised at the same time as a chief afterwards proving unfaithful to him, but numerous instances have come under the notice of Europeans where such persons have sacrificed their lives for him.

With some—if not all—of the interior tribes at the time of circumcision the youths were formed into guilds with passwords. The members of these guilds were bound never to give evidence against each other. The rites of initiation were kept as secret as possible, but certain horrible customs connected with them were known. One of these was the infusion of courage, intelligence, and other qualities. Whenever an enemy who had acted bravely was killed, his liver, which was considered the seat of intelligence, the skin of his forehead, which was considered the seat of perseverance, and other members, each of which was supposed to be the seat of some desirable quality, were cut from his body and baked to cinders. The ashes were preserved in the horn of a bull, and during the circumcision ceremonies were mixed with other ingredients into a kind of paste and administered by the tribal priest to the youths, the idea being that the qualities which they represented were communicated to those who swallowed them. This custom, together with that of using other parts of the remains of their enemies for bewitching purposes, led them to mutilate the bodies of all who fell into their hands in war, a practice which infuriated those whose friends were thus treated, and often provoked retaliation of a terrible kind.

Among the Ovaherero and kindred tribes boys were generally circumcised between the ages of four and seven years, and therefore the rite had not the same signification as it had with other Bantu. From it they dated their age, naming the most important event at the time of their circumcision as their starting point in life, just as other Bantu name the most important event at the time of their birth. These people differed further from their eastern kindred by mutilating themselves in a peculiar manner. When a child was eight or ten years of age its four lower front teeth were broken out, and the corresponding upper front teeth were filed with stones into the shape of triangles with the base downwards. This was their national mark, as the mode of wearing the hair is with many other tribes.

Among the tribes along the eastern coast females who arrived at the age of puberty were introduced into the state of womanhood by peculiar ceremonies, which tended to extinguish virtuous feelings within them. Originally, however, the very worst of the observances on these occasions was a test of discipline. The object of the education of the males was to make them capable of self-restraint. They were required to control themselves so that no trace of their emotions should appear on their faces, they were not to wince when undergoing the most severe punishment. In olden times a further test was applied, which has now degenerated into the most abominable licentiousness. It will be sufficient to say that the young women who attended the revels on these occasions were allowed to select temporary companions of the other sex, and if they declined to do so, the chief distributed them at his pleasure. As the first edition of this chapter was being prepared, a chief, who was regarded as being more advanced towards civilisation than most of his people, came into legal collision with the European authorities for distributing a large number of girls in this manner in a district within the Cape Colony.

But degrading as this rite was among the Bantu of the coast, among some of those of the interior it was even more vile. All that the most depraved imagination could devise to rouse the lowest passions of the young females was practised. A description is impossible.

The other ceremonies observed on this occasion varied among the tribes, but an account of those of the Amaxosa at the present day will give a general idea of all. When a girl of this tribe arrives at the age of puberty, messengers are sent by her father to all the neighbouring kraals to invite the young women to attend the "ntonjane." The girl in the meantime is kept secluded in the hut of an aunt, or other female relative, and her father does not see her. Soon parties are seen coming from all sides, singing as they march. The first that arrive halt in front of the cattle kraal, where they are joined by those who come later. When the girls are all assembled, the father selects an ox to be slaughtered, and the meat is cooked for a feast. The women then dress the girls for a dance, and when this is done they are ranged in rows in front of the cattle kraal. They are almost naked, having on only a girdle round the loins, and a little apron called *cacawe*, made for the occasion out of the leaves of a certain plant. In their hands they hold assagais, using them as walking sticks.

When all is ready, four of the girls step out of the front row and dance, the rest singing ; and when these are tired four others step out, and so on, until all the girls present have danced. The spectators then applaud the best dancer, or if they do not at once fix upon the same person, the girls dance until all present agree. The girls then give room to the men and women that in the meantime have arrived, who form themselves in lines in the same manner, and dance until it is decided which of them surpass the others. The dancing is continued until sunset, when the men and women return home, leaving the party of girls, called the *jaka*, who remain overnight. Next day dancing is resumed in the same order, the guests usually arriving very early in the morning.

If the girl's father is a rich man three oxen are slaughtered, and the ntonjane is kept up for twelve days. On the thirteenth day the young woman comes out of the hut where she has all the time been living apart from her family. If the girl is a chief's daughter the ntonjane is kept up for twenty-four days. All the counsellors send oxen to be slaughtered, that there may be plenty for the guests to eat.

The following ceremony takes place on the occasion of a chief's daughter coming out of the house in which she was concealed during the twenty-four days :—

A son of her father's chief counsellor puts on his head the two wings of a blue crane (the indwe), which are regarded as an emblem of bravery only to be worn on this occasion and by veterans in time of war. He goes into the hut where she is, and when he comes out she follows him. They march towards the kraal where the dancing took place, the girl's mother, the jaka or party of young women, the girl's father, and his counsellors, forming a procession. More cattle are slaughtered for the *indwe*, and then dancing is renewed, after which the girl drinks milk for the first time since the day when she was concealed in the hut. Large skin bags containing milk are sent from different kraals to the place where the ntonjane is held. Some milk is put into a small vessel made of rushes, a little of it is poured on the fireplace, the aunt or other female relative in whose charge the girl was takes the first mouthful, then she gives the milk to the girl, who, after having drunk, is taken to her mother's house. The people then disperse, and the ntonjane is over.

This ceremony acts as an advertisement to people far and wide that the girl can now be applied for in marriage.

The Bantu were polygamists, and women occupied a lower position than men in their society. Marriage was an arrangement, without any religious ceremony, by which in return for a girl cattle were transferred to her relatives by the husband or his friends. It did not make of a woman a slave who could be sold from hand to hand, nor did it give her husband power to maim her. In its best aspect this method of marriage was a protection to a woman against ill usage, as well as a guarantee to the husband that she would study his interests. If he maimed her, or treated her with undue severity, she could return

XOSA GIRL IN DANCING COSTUME.
(From a Photograph in the South African Public Library.)

[To face p. 214.

to her father or guardian, who was allowed in such cases to retain both the woman and the cattle, but if she abandoned him without sufficient cause he could reclaim the cattle he had transferred and she lost caste in the eyes of every one. In its worst aspect it permitted a parent or guardian to give a girl in marriage to the man who offered most for her, without the slightest reference to her inclinations. A woman was a drudge, upon whom the cultivation of the ground and other severe labour fell, she could inherit nothing, and she was liable to moderate castigation from her husband, such as a parent is at liberty to inflict upon a child, without protection from the law. Wealth was estimated by the number of wives and cattle that a man possessed, and the one was always made use of to increase the other. The husband was head or lord of the establishment, and the wives were required to provide all the food except meat and milk. Each had a hut of her own, which she and her children occupied, and the husband used his caprice as to which of them he associated with at any time.

Though the transfer of cattle alone made a marriage binding, it was customary to engage in festivities in connection with it. Those ordinarily observed in the Xosa tribe at the present day are fairly typical of all. Among these people the whole of the marriage ceremonies are included in the term *umdudo*, a word derived from the verb *uku duda*, which means to dance by springing up and down, as *uku xentsa* means to dance by moving the upper parts of the body. The dance at a marriage is considered of more importance than any of the others except the war dance, and is therefore frequently practised until skill in its performance is attained.

The marriage of a young woman is arranged by her father or guardian, and she is not legally supposed to be consulted in the choice of a husband. In point of fact, however, matches arising from mutual love are not uncommon. In such cases, if any difficulties are raised by the guardians on either side, the young people do not scruple to run away together, after which their relatives usually come to an arrangement. Yet instances are not wanting of girls being compelled against their wishes to marry old men, who have already perhaps five or six wives. In practice the umdudo is often deferred to a convenient season, but the woman is considered not less a wife, and her children not less legal, providing always that the transfer of cattle has taken place according to agreement.

Marriage proposals may come from the father or guardian of the young woman, or they may first be made by the man himself or the relatives of the man who wishes to take a wife. The father of a young man frequently selects a bride for him, and intimates his wish by sending a messenger to make proposals to the girl's father or guardian. In this case the messenger takes some cattle with him, when, if the advances are favourably received, an assagai is sent back, after which the relatives of the young people discuss and finally arrange the terms of the marriage. If the proposal comes from the girl's father, he sends an assagai, which is accepted if the suit is agreeable, or returned if it is not.

When the preliminary arrangements are concluded, unless, as sometimes happens, it is considered expedient to permit tho marriage at once to take place, but to postpone the festivities to a more convenient season, a bridal procession is formed at the young woman's kraal, to escort her to her future home. It consists of her relatives and all the young people of both sexes who can get away. It leaves at such a time as to arrive at its destination after dark, and tries to reach the place without attracting notice. The bridal party takes with it a cow, given by the bride's father or guardian to confer fortune upon her, and hence called the *inqakwe*. This cow is afterwards well taken care of by the husband. The party has also an ox provided by the same person, as his contribution towards the marriage feast. On the following morning at daylight the ox is killed, when a portion of the meat is taken by the bride's party, and the remainder is left for the people of the kraal. The bridegroom's friends then send messengers to invite the people of the neighbourhood to the feast, and as soon as these arrive the dancing commences.

In the dance the men stand in lines three, four, or more rows in depth, according to their number, and at a little distance behind the women stand in the same order. The men stand with their heads erect and their arms locked together. They are nearly naked, but wear ornaments of brass around their waists. The trappings of the war dance are altogether wanting. The women are, however, in full dress, for their part consists only in singing. When all are ready, a man who has been selected for the purpose commences to sing, the others immediately join in, and at a certain note the whole of the men rise together from the ground. The dance consists merely in springing straight up and coming down with a quivering of the body ; but when the men warm to it, it gives them great satisfaction. The song is very monotonous, the same note recurring at every rise from the ground. This dancing, with intervals of rest and feasting, continues as long as the bridegroom's relatives supply oxen for slaughter. A day suffices for a poor man, but a rich man's marriage festivities may last a week or upwards.

On the closing day the bridegroom and his friends march from one hut, while the bride and her party march from another, so as to meet in front of the entrance to the cattle kraal. The bride carries an assagai in her hand, which she throws so as to stick in the ground inside the kraal in an upright position. This is the last of the ceremonies, and the guests immediately begin to disperse, each man taking home the milk-sack which he had brought with him. In olden times ox-racing usually took place on the closing day, but this custom has of late years fallen into neglect.

There were different restrictions with regard to the females whom a man was at liberty to marry. No man of any coast tribe would marry a girl whose relationship by blood to himself on his father's side could be traced, no matter how distantly connected they might be. So scrupulous was he in this respect that he would not even marry a girl who belonged to another tribe, if she had the same family name as himself, though the relationship could not be traced. A man, for instance, whose family title was the Amanywabe * might belong to the Dushane clan of the Xosa tribe. Among the Tembus, the Pondos, the Zulus, and many 'other distinct communities, are people with this same family title. They cannot trace any relationship with each other, but wherever they are found they have ceremonies peculiar to themselves. Thus the customs observed at the birth of a child are exactly the same in every part of the country among people of the same family title, though they may never have heard of each other, while neighbours of the same clan, but of different family titles, have these customs altogether dissimilar. This indicates that the tribes and clans of the present day are combinations of others that were dispersed before their traditional history commenced. No marriage between the Amanywabe is permissible.

In some tribes, as at present in the Pondos, Tembus, and Xosas, the same rule was applied to relatives by blood on the mother's side also. Children take the family title of the father, and can thus marry those of the same family title as the mother, provided their blood relationship cannot be traced. Every man of a coast tribe regarded himself as the protector of those females whom we would call his cousins, second cousins, third cousins, and so forth, on the father's side, while some had a similar feeling towards the same relatives on the mother's side as well, and classified them all as sisters. Immorality with one of them would have been considered incestuous, something horrible, something unutterably disgraceful. Of old it was punished by the death of the male, and even now a heavy fine is inflicted upon him, while the guilt of the female must be atoned by a sacrifice performed with due ceremony by the tribal priest, or it is believed a curse will rest upon her and her issue.

Of late years this feeling has become less operative than formerly among those Bantu of the coast belt who have long

---

* The Amanywabe must at some distant date have been a tribe or a clan of a tribe, which was broken up, when its members were dispersed and subsequently joined different communities. The old tribal title then became a kind of family name. And so with all the other family names in every Bantu tribe, they indicate that the existing communities are formed of the fragments of others long since broken up.

been in contact with Europeans, still immorality between persons related to each other as above described is extremely rare. It is still more so among those who have learned little or nothing from white men. Shortly after the annexation of Pondoland to the Cape Colony the principal chief of the western division of that territory instituted an inquiry into one such case, which he reported to a magistrate, and wished the usual punishment to be inflicted. The common ancestor was found on investigation to be seven generations back, still in public opinion the crime was enormous.

In contrast to this prohibition the man of the interior almost as a rule married the daughter of his father's brother, in order, as he said, to keep property from being lost to his family. This custom more than anything else created a disgust and contempt for them by the people of the coast, who term such inter-marriages the union of dogs, and attribute to them the insanity and idiocy which in recent times have become prevalent among the inland tribes.*

With the Ovaherero and their near kindred marriage was a much looser union than among other Bantu, for it could be more easily dissolved by either party. There was practically very little property at stake in the matter. Custom required that when a woman went to live with a man he should transfer to her father or guardian a large ox, a heifer, a large fat sheep, a ewe with a lamb, and a young ewe, but the most valuable of these animals were at once strangled and eaten at the feast which was the only ceremony attending the alliance. A rich man or a man of rank gave no more than a poor one.

With the Makaranga infant girls could be contracted as wives, but they remained with their parents until they attained

---

* Among the tribes within the Cape Colony at the present time the differences are as follows :—

Xosas, Tembus, and Pondos : marry no relative by blood, however distant, on either father's or mother's side.

Hlubis and others commonly called Fingos : may marry the daughter of mother's brother and other relatives on that side, but not on father's side.

Basuto, Batlaro, Batlapin, and Barolong : very frequently marry cousins on father's side, and know of no restrictions beyond actual sisters.

the age of puberty. With these people a custom revolting to our sense of morality was common. A young man too poor to acquire a wife by the transfer of cattle would make an arrangement with the father of a girl to live with her and to serve him, when, as children do not belong to their father until the full ikazi * has been transferred, the father of the woman had sole control over all that were born, and enriched himself by the disposal of the females.

In no section of the Bantu was there any restriction in regard to marrying a wife's blood relatives. Thus a man might marry two sisters, though not at the same time, and of course two brothers might marry two sisters. Sometimes it happened that a man and his wife could not agree, and that he could bring some substantial charge against her, when, if she had a young unmarried sister, an arrangement was usually made by which she returned to her parents and her sister took her place, on the husband's making a small addition to the cattle that had been transferred on the first occasion.

This was also the case when, as sometimes happened, a woman was childless. Such a person finds little favour in Bantu society, so that on becoming a mother a wife who has been married some time may say from the bottom of her heart, with Elizabeth of old, that " her reproach is taken away from among men." A childless woman is usually exchanged for a marriageable sister, but the husband is required first to perform a ceremony which can be illustrated by a case tried before the writer when acting as a border magistrate in 1881. A sued B

---

* *Ikazi*, Sesuto *bohadi*, means the cattle transferred to the father or guardian of a woman for her. When this has been delivered in full, she becomes a member of her husband's family and her children are legally his, but until that is done she is a member of her father's family and any children she may give birth to are wholly or partly under his control. An attempt to prevent the endless contention and litigation that arises from this rule was made by the colony of Natal, which provided by law that in the case of a common man the ikazi should not exceed ten head of cattle, that it should be paid in full before the marriage, and a declaration to that effect be made by the woman's father or guardian before an official witness. As no action can be brought before any court thereafter for any portion of the ikazi, litigation is prevented, but immorality of the grossest kind has greatly increased.

to recover the value of a heifer supplied to him two years before under these circumstances. B's wife, who was distantly related to A, had been married more than a year without bearing a child. B thereupon applied to him for a heifer, the hair of which was needed by the doctor of the clan to make a charm to put round the woman's neck. He had supplied one for the purpose, and now wanted payment for it. The defence was that A, being the woman's nearest relative who had cattle, was bound to furnish a heifer for the purpose. The hair of the tail was needed, the doctor had made a charm of it and hung it round the woman's neck, and she had thereafter given birth to a son. The heifer could not be returned after being so used. In this case, if the plaintiff had been so nearly related to the defendant's wife as to have participated in the benefit of the cattle given by her husband for her, he could not have justified his claim under Bantu law; but as he was very distantly connected, he got judgment. The feeling entertained by the spectators in court in this instance was that B had acted very ungratefully towards A, who had not even been present at the woman's marriage feast, but who had cheerfully acted in conformity with the custom which requires that a charm must be made out of the hair of the tail of a heifer belonging to a relative of a childless wife, in order to cause her to bear children.

If it happened that a woman had such a repugnance to her husband that her life with him was miserable, her father or guardian had the power of releasing her by sending back to the husband the portion of the ikazi that had been transferred, which was equivalent to a legal divorce. Such instances, however, were extremely rare.

Far the greater number of lawsuits among the Bantu arose from their marriage customs. The cattle to be transferred to the family of a woman were seldom or never fully paid until long after the union, and in the meantime if the husband died disputes were almost sure to arise as to what family the widow and her children belonged, whether she had a right to return to her parents, if so whether she could take any of her offspring with her, and so on. The nearest relative of a deceased man had it in his power to settle the matter at once by paying the cattle still due, but he did not always follow that course. If there were any daughters, an arrangement was possible that of the cattle to be received for them when they should marry the number due on account of the mother should be paid. But even in this case disputes were sure to arise. One party would fix the number very differently from the other, and then the case would have to be tried, when every little particular from first to last was entered into, and much patience was needed before a decision could be arrived at. Sometimes these cases depended upon the payment or non-payment of cattle three generations back, for in Bantu opinion if a grandmother had not been fully incorporated into the family of her husband, that is if the full number of cattle had not been transferred for her, the position of her descendants was doubtful, two distinct families having claims upon them. In their expressive way of speaking, such cases did not die.

In most of the tribes the eldest brother of a married woman exercised greater influence over his sister's children than any of her husband's brothers until all the cattle to be given for her had been transferred. The reason is obvious : the woman did not fully belong to her husband's family until that time, and her children were in the same position. Her eldest brother was considered their natural guardian. Except with chiefs, in whose case it was necessary that there should be no question whatever as to the family each child belonged to, it very seldom happened that the whole, or even the greater number of the cattle were transferred until many years after the marriage. It might almost be said it never happened, because at the birth of a child a claim was made upon its father by the father or brother of its mother for an ox or a cow, and this claim was recognised as one of right. Thus it was usually the case that a woman of the commoner class was well advanced in life before the guardianship of her brother over herself and her children ceased and she and they were entirely incorporated in her husband's family. In the meantime her sons grew up, when this maternal uncle of theirs had the right of control over them to a considerable extent, with the corresponding duty of giving protection and assistance if necessary. Her daughters grew up and got married, when some of the cattle given for them went to this maternal uncle, who had been in a way their guardian and had kept them supplied with clothing if they needed it. With some tribes the principal *malume*, that is the eldest full brother of the mother of any one, had much more authority over his sister's children than with others. But with all it rested upon the principle that a woman was a member of the family of her father—provided of course that her mother had become so—until she was fully incorporated in the family of her husband. But there was a long period of her life when her position was not perfectly assured, and it was for this time, when protection was most needed, that Bantu law provided by the custom here described. It was when the position of a woman's mother, or even her grandmother, was uncertain, that complications arose which taxed the ingenuity of a court of Bantu law to clear.

Chastity in married life was exceedingly rare among the coast tribes. By custom every wife of a polygamist had a lover, and no woman sank in the esteem of her companions on this becoming publicly known. The law allowed the husband a fine from the male offender, and permitted him to chastise the woman, provided he did not maim her; but in the opinion of the females the offence was venial and was not attended with disgrace. Favoured guests had female companions—who were, however, generally widows—allotted to them. Still, chastity had a value in the estimation of the men, as was proved by the care with which the harems of a few of the most powerful chiefs were guarded. It might be thought that the framework of society would fall to pieces if domestic life were more immoral than this, but in point of fact a kraal on the coast was a scene of purity when compared with one in some parts of the interior.

There it was a common occurrence for a chief to secure the services and adherence of a young man by the loan of one of his inferior wives either temporarily or permanently. In either case the children belonged to the chief, who was regarded by the law as their father. Another revolting custom among them was that of polyandrous marriages. A man who had not the requisite number of cattle to procure a wife, and whose father was too poor to help him, obtained assistance from a wealthy individual on condition of having joint marital rights.

CHAPTER X.

Description of the Bantu (*continued*).

The Bantu were agriculturists. Millet of several varieties, all now called by Europeans kaffir-corn, was the grain exclusively grown. They raised large quantities of this, which they used either boiled or bruised into paste from which a very insipid kind of bread was made. In good seasons much millet was converted into beer. It was steeped in water until it began to sprout, then dried in the sun, and afterwards partly crushed in wooden mortars made by hollowing the end of a block of wood about seventy or eighty centimetres high. Two women, standing by the mortar, stamped the contents with heavy wooden pestles, keeping time with the strokes and usually lightening their labour by chanting some meaningless words. The malt was then boiled, and leaven mixed with it to cause it to ferment. Sometimes a bitter root was added to flavour it. It could be made so weak as to form a harmless and refreshing beverage, or so strong as to be intoxicating. In the latter case unmalted corn was crushed and mixed with water, which was then boiled, and malt was added afterwards until it was almost as thick as gruel, and to a European palate would have been nauseating. Millet beer was largely consumed at feasts of all kinds. It was used as soon as it ceased fermenting, for it speedily became sour. Some women were reputed to be able to make it much better than others, and on that account their services were largely in demand. In some parts of the country an intoxicating drink was also made from honey, which was plentiful in the season of flowers.

More pernicious was the custom of smoking dried leaves of wild hemp, which had the effect of producing violent coughing, followed by stupefaction. The usual pipe was a horn, but sometimes the smoke was inhaled through a clay tube made on the surface of the ground, and sometimes it was drawn through a vessel partly filled with water. A number of men would sit round the smoking apparatus, and each in turn make use of it until all were helpless. Another means of intoxication was afforded by the same leaves of wild hemp, which, when dried and reduced to powder, were mixed with water and drunk. The practice, however, either of smoking or drinking bangue was necessarily limited to a few men in each community, and the baneful plant was only obtainable at certain seasons of the year. In the form of snuff the stalks as well as the leaves and fibres, dried and beaten into powder, could be preserved, and were more generally used.

The individuals, whether male or female, among the Bantu who could resist the temptation of using intoxicants to excess were so few in number, that their amazing fertility must have been checked, if the opportunities for indulging the vicious taste had not been so limited. Nature is pitiless in her mode of strengthening the will and the minds of men. Europeans would not be what they are to-day if in past times intoxication had not destroyed so many of the feeblest-willed of their race, and the Bantu have not gone through that strengthening process.

Tobacco is believed to have been introduced by the Portuguese in the sixteenth century, but there is no account extant of the importation of the plant, nor any tradition of its first appearance, as there is of maize. Wherever it came from, and at whatever time it was brought into the country, it spread among the Bantu with great rapidity, for all the tribes visited by the Dutch in the seventeenth and eighteenth centuries were found cultivating and using it.

Among the coast tribes a supply of millet was preserved from attacks of weevil by burying it in air-tight pits excavated beneath the cattle-folds. When kept for a long time in these granaries, the grain lost the power of germinating, and acquired a rank taste and smell, but it was in that condition none the less agreeable to the Bantu palate. The interior tribes preserved their grain either in huge earthenware crocks or in enormous baskets, which were perfectly watertight, and which could be exposed to the air without damage to their contents.

But even after the best seasons the grain rarely lasted longer than a few months, as it was recklessly wasted in making beer, which might almost be said to have been common property as long as it lasted. Frugality is not a virtue of barbarians, and the thought that a time of scarcity might arrive was not allowed to trouble their minds while the means of gratifying their appetites to excess were at hand. Thus at one season of the year a clan would be revelling in abundance, every member of it being fat and strong and happy, and six months later the same people would be stinted with hunger, dejected, and miserable.

Different kinds of gourds, a cane containing saccharine matter in large quantities, and a sort of ground nut were the other products of their gardens. In the country between the lower Zambesi and Sabi rivers rice and various foreign vegetables had been introduced by the Arabs long before the beginning of the sixteenth century, but the cultivation of these had not extended beyond that area. Everywhere wild bulbs and plants, the pith of certain shrubs, and different kinds of indigenous fruit formed no inconsiderable part of the vegetable diet of the people, being almost entirely depended upon when the millet stores were exhausted. Children at a very early age were taught to look for edible plants, and soon acquired such extensive knowledge in this respect that they were able to support themselves easily where Europeans would have perished.

As food they had also milk and occasionally flesh, though domestic cattle were seldom slaughtered except for sacrifices and feasts. The flesh of all that otherwise died was, however, eaten without hesitation. Milk was kept in skin bags, where it fermented and acquired a sharp acid taste. As it was drawn off for use by the master of the household, who was the only one permitted to touch the bag, new milk was added, for it was only in the fermented state that it was used. Amasi, or fermented milk, was exceedingly nutritious, and at the present day is relished by most Europeans. In warm weather, especially, it is a pleasant and wholesome beverage. The art of making butter and cheese was unknown.

Fish was consumed only by the tribes living along the large rivers in the interior and those on the eastern coast from Delagoa Bay northward. South of Delagoa Bay it was not used, except by offshoots from the northern tribes that had settled at a few places along the sea shore, possibly because in ancient times it may have been regarded as connected with the snake in whose form the ancestral spirits appeared. This, however, is mere conjecture, as the people themselves at the present day can give no other reason for not eating fish than that their fathers did not do so.

Occasionally large quantities of meat were obtained by means of the chase. The chief would select a day, and give instructions for all his people to assist in the hunt. A large tract of country would then be surrounded, and the game would be driven towards a deep pit, with a strong hedge extending some distance on each side of it. The pit was made in such a way that no animal forced into it by pressure of the herd behind could escape until it was full. By the warlike tribes the pit was often disdained as a means of capturing such game as antelopes and zebras, and they preferred gradually to contract the circle of hunters and drive the animals towards the centre, killing with their assagais all that could not break through the ring. After one of these hunts feasting was continued until not a particle of meat was left, as the palates of the people did not reject what Europeans would regard as carrion.

Very large animals, such as the elephant, the hippopotamus, and the rhinoceros, were generally captured either by means of snares that caused a heavily weighted spear to fall upon them as they passed under a tree, or by means of carefully covered pits with sharp stakes in them, made in the beaten tracks of the animals towards water. Sometimes, however, men were found sufficiently courageous to lie in ambush beside the paths and hamstring the animals as they went by, when their destruction was easy. North of the Sabi river the tusks of the elephant and the hippopotamus were always sale-able to the Mohamedan traders along the coast, and everywhere among the Bantu ivory arm-rings were esteemed as ornaments. The flesh of all these animals was much prized, especially that of the hippopotamus.

Another occasional article of food was dried locusts. Swarms of these destructive creatures sometimes appeared, when every one engaged in capturing and preserving them, the legs, when dried, being regarded as not only nutritious, but pleasant to the taste. By the people of the interior a species of caterpillar was considered a special dainty, and the little field mouse was eagerly sought for as another. Boys before being circumcised were permitted to eat any kind of meat, even wild cats and other carnivora, but after that ceremony was performed the flesh of animals of prey was usually rejected.

Ordinarily two meals were eaten every day : a slight break-fast in the morning, and a substantial repast at sunset. Any one passing by at that time, friend or stranger, provided only that he was not inferior in rank, sat down without invitation or ceremony, and shared in the meal. So great was the hospitality of the people to equals and superiors that food could almost have been termed common property.

When reduced to great extremity of want by the ravages of enemies, sections of the Bantu sometimes resorted to canni-balism, but the horrible practice was by no means common. Portuguese writers indeed mention tribes whose habitual food was human flesh, still everything related concerning them shows that they were war-stricken hordes driven from their homes and wandering about with their hands against every man and every man's hands against them. In just the same manner in the early years of the nineteenth century parties of absolutely destitute people in Basutoland and in Natal, driven into the forests and mountains by the devastations of Tshaka, preyed upon their fellows, whom they pursued as game ; but as soon as a condition of comparative peace was restored, most of them returned to their normal way of living. A few indeed, who had acquired a taste for human flesh, though they were held in execration by all others, continued to exist as cannibals until they died out or were exterminated. It must have been the same in olden times with the tribes along the Zambesi of whom information is given by Dos Santos and other Portuguese writers : it was the direst necessity, not by any means their own choice, that led them to adopt a mode of maintaining life so different from that of the Bantu in general. They may have continued longer in that condition than those in the south in the days of Tshaka, but it is certain that no tribe depended permanently upon human flesh for its subsistence.

The Bantu had an admirable system of land tenure for people in their condition. The chief apportioned to each head of a family sufficient ground for a garden according to his needs, and it remained in that individual's possession as long as it was cultivated. He could even remove for years, with the consent of the chief, and resume occupation upon his return. He could not lend, much less alienate it. But if he ceased to make use of it, or went away for a long time without the chief's permission, he lost his right. Under the same conditions he had possession of the ground upon which his huts stood, and of a yard about them. All other ground was common pasture, but the chief had power to direct that portions of it should be used in particular seasons only. No taxes of any kind were paid for land, air, or water.

The gardens were not enclosed by hedges or fences, and they were very irregular in outline, as were also the different cultivated plots within them, for the eyes of the women were indifferent as to straight rows of plants. If the crops were damaged by cattle at night, the owner of the cattle was required by law to make good the loss, because he should have seen that his herds were either confined in a fold or guarded on a pasture so distant that they could do no harm. But if the damage was done in the daytime there was no redress, because some member of the family of the owner of the garden was then supposed to be watching it.

Sometimes a tree was left standing at a kraal, and the men would sit in its shade during the heat of the day, but in general all others in the neighbourhood were ruthlessly destroyed for fuel, and not one was ever planted to take their place. The havoc wrought in a patch of natural forest by a Bantu kraal being built in its vicinity was so great that in the course of a very few centuries the whole land would have been denuded of trees, if the population had not been kept very limited by strife and slaughter for alleged dealing in witchcraft, and if European influence following so speedily after the arrival of the tribes in the localities which they now occupy had not prevented the waste. The Bantu were so thoughtless and so indifferent to the wants of future generations that such a thing as the preservation of a forest never occurred to them.

Kraals were usually built in situations commanding an extensive view of the surrounding country, and always on ground with good natural drainage. The brow of a hill, with a clear flowing stream at its base and fertile garden ground beyond, was the site most favoured. Sanitary arrangements, even of the simplest kind, were unknown and uncared for, as the sense of smell was much duller with these people than with Europeans, and an impure atmosphere did not affect their health. Their superstition too required them to remove their residences whenever a man of importance died, so that kraals seldom remained many years on the same site.

Clans exposed to sudden attack by powerful enemies had naturally little or no choice in selecting sites for kraals. They were under the necessity of constructing their habitations in the best possible defensive position, which was usually the crown of a steep hill difficult of approach. Such hills are found in different parts of the country, often with sides so precipitous that the top can be reached by only one or two paths. When these were barricaded with rough stone walls, the space above became a fortress, impregnable or nearly so. Such sites for kraals were, however, only resorted to as a last means of defence, on account of the occupants being cut off from gardens and pasture for their cattle as well as from easy access to water. Along the Zambesi some clans lived in stockaded enclosures, but these were unknown farther south.

The huts of the tribes along the coast were shaped like domes or beehives, and were formed of strong frames, thatched with reeds or grass. They were proof against rain or wind. The largest were about seven or eight metres in diameter, and from two metres and a fifth to two and a half in height at the centre. They were entered by a low, narrow aperture, which was the only opening in the structure. A hard and smooth floor was made of antheaps, moistened with water and then kneaded with a round stone. When this had set, it was painted with a mixture of cowdung and water, which was the material used afterwards for keeping it in good order. In the centre of the floor a fireplace was made, by raising a band three or four centimetres in height and a metre or so in diameter, and slightly hollowing the enclosed space. Many women bestowed a great deal of attention upon their firecircles, often enclosing them with three bands, a large one in the centre, and a smaller one on each side of it, differently coloured, and resembling a coil of large rope lying between concentric coils of less thickness. Against the wall of the hut were ranged various utensils in common use, the space around the firecircle being reserved for sleeping on. Here in the evening mats were spread, upon which the inmates lay down to rest, each one's feet being towards the centre. Above their heads the roof was glossy with soot, and vermin swarmed on every side. It was only in cold or stormy weather that huts were occupied during the day, for the people spent the greater portion of their waking hours in the open air.

The habitations of the people of the interior were much better than those of the people of the coast. With them the hut had perpendicular walls, and consisted of a central circular room, with either a broad verandah or three or four small apartments outside, each being a segment of a circle. It was surrounded by a courtyard enclosed with a high wall of reeds or wattles, in the case of one or two of the tribes with a fairly built wall of uncut stone. Within this enclosure stood also the granary and frequently two or three subsidiary huts, and the ground was levelled and was usually kept perfectly clean. The

HUT OF THE BANTU OF THE INTERIOR.

(*From a Drawing by William J. Burchell, Esqre.*)

[*To face* p. 232.

interior of the principal hut was smoothly plastered, and was often coloured red, or white, or blue, occasionally decorated with simple patterns or rude figures of animals. It was destitute of chimney or window, or as a habitation it would have been equal, if not superior, to the abodes of many European peasants. On the coast no effort was made to secure privacy.

Horned cattle constituted the principal wealth of the Bantu, and formed a convenient medium of exchange throughout the country. Great care was taken of them, and much skill was exhibited in their training. They were taught to obey signals, as, for instance, to run home upon a certain call or whistle being given. Every man of note had his racing oxen, and prided himself upon their good qualities as much as an English squire did upon his blood horses. The horns of the animals were trained into the most fantastic shapes, and were often divided into two, three, or more parts, which was effected by slitting them as soon as they appeared on the young animal. The intelligence displayed by some of these oxen was as wonderful as the patience and skill shown by their trainers. They were taught to lie down at an order, to run in a circle, or to dance in rows. Ox racing was connected with all kinds of festivities. The care of cattle was considered the most honourable employment, and fell entirely to the men. They milked the cows, took sole charge of the dairy, and would not permit a woman so much as to touch a milk-sack.

The other domestic animals were goats, dogs, and barnyard poultry everywhere, and in the north sheep of the large-tailed hair-covered breed. Eggs were never used as an article of diet, and poultry very rarely except by young children.

The descent of property was regulated in the same manner as the succession to the chieftainship, and disputes could not easily arise concerning it. Every head of cattle a man acquired was immediately assigned to a particular branch of his family, that is either to the house of his great wife, to that of his wife of the right hand, or to that of his wife of the left hand. If he had more wives than three, the remainder were in a subordinate position in one or other of these houses. When he died, the eldest son of each of the three principal wives inherited everything that belonged to his mother's house. But the distribution of wealth was more equal than in any European society, for each married man had a plot of garden ground, and younger brothers had a recognised claim upon the heirs of their father for assistance in setting them up in life.

The heir was in fact regarded as the representative of his dead father, and as having taken upon himself the duties and responsibilities as well as the property and privileges of the head of the establishment. Among the interior tribes this idea was carried so far that he inherited even his father's widows, except the one who bore him, though it was usual for him to distribute most of them to other men. Daughters born to them afterwards, however, no matter who their fathers were, were under his control only, and the bohadi given for them went to enrich him. Following out this principle, he was supposed to assist his brothers in raising the bohadi needed by them when they married, so that he might really be regarded as a trustee as well as an heir of his deceased father's estate. In some tribes along the coast the brothers of the dead man distributed his widows among them, but even then the heir claimed the offspring, as they were held to be the children of his deceased father.

There was thus a simple but perfect law of inheritance, which regulated the succession of three heirs or representatives at most, but usually two, the great son and the right hand son. Among common people the first wife married was usually, though not always, the great wife, which further simplified the matter. A man, however, had the right of disinheriting any of his sons for gross misconduct, but this could only be done in open court with the sanction of his chief and the counsellors of his clan, when the next in order of succession took the place of him who was dispossessed, just as if death had occurred. In case the great wife had no son, the eldest male child born in her establishment would be adopted by her, and become the heir of that branch of the family. The same was the case with the right hand wife.

Polygamy was the cause of many evils, but it had its advantages too. Low as was the state of morality among the Bantu, it would have been infinitely lower if monogamy had been their rule, and a large number of women, who regarded it as folly to restrain their passions, had been unable to obtain the status even of inferior wife in the establishment of a rich man. Their constant feuds and wars caused the number of women to be much greater than that of men, even if the sexes were at birth nearly equal, which is doubtful. The census of the Cape Colony in 1904, when war had long ceased to have any effect upon the Bantu inhabitants, showed the number of males to be 692,728 and of females 732,059, that is for every hundred men and boys there were nearly one hundred and six women and girls. By force of circumstances, in many parts of South Africa polygamy is greatly decreasing among these people at the beginning of the twentieth century, but for their own sakes it may almost be hoped that it will not quite cease until they learn to have more command over themselves than is the rule at present.

The Bantu of the coast were more warlike in disposition and braver in the field than those of the interior. The universal weapons of offence were wooden clubs with heavy heads and assagais or javelins, and shields made of oxhide were carried, which varied in size and pattern among the tribes. The assagai was a slender wooden shaft or rod, with a long, thin, iron head, having both edges sharp, attached to it. Poising this first in his uplifted hand, and imparting to it a quivering motion, the warrior hurled it forth with great force and accuracy of aim. The club was used at close quarters, and could also be thrown to a considerable distance. Boys were trained from an early age to the use of both these weapons. To those above named the northern and central tribes added the battle-axe and bow and arrow, which, though known to, were not used by the men of the south.

In the most warlike of the Bantu communities the men were formed into regiments, and were trained to act in concert and to go through various simple military evolutions, but in the others the warrior knew nothing but the use of his weapons. With these a battle was a series of individual engagements, in which it sometimes happened that a man would challenge a noted adversary by name, and a duel would take place in presence of the others on both sides as mere spectators. In such cases the victor was presented by his chief with a crane's feather to be worn on his head, and he was thereafter a man of note among his people. A classification thus arose of the plumed and the unplumed in the following of a chief, though the former did not thereby become leaders or officers, that distinction being reserved exclusively for members of the ruling house and their counsellors. It was a custom for a man to be marked, usually with a scar from a gash or a brand, for every adversary slain, and warriors prided themselves relatively upon the number of these.

Among the military tribes reviews in presence of the chiefs and mock combats were of frequent occurrence. The warriors were in full dress on such occasions, with their kilts of animals' tails around them, and their ornaments on their persons. Everything was conducted with as much order and ceremony as were observed by our own ancestors in their tournaments. At the command of the chief one regiment would be pitted against another, and each would attack, retreat, skirmish, and go through all the evolutions of a real battle until the weaker side became exhausted, when the other was pronounced the conqueror. Or it might be a general skirmish of the whole army against an imaginary enemy, or an attack upon a hill supposed to be fortified, or simply a march of the regiments past the commander in chief. Sometimes oxen were brought to take part in the manœuvres and to prove the skill of their trainers. A feast and a dance invariably followed the review, but often jealousies had been roused by the events of the day which led afterwards to engagements in real earnest between different regiments.

The dress of the people between the lower Zambesi and Sabi rivers at the beginning of the sixteenth century was partly composed of skins of animals and partly of cloth either obtained in barter or manufactured by themselves of wild cotton or the fibres of a certain bark. The home made cloth was coarse but strong, and was woven in the simplest manner in squares large enough to be fastened round the loins. The art of weaving, though not much more difficult than mat making, was not practised by all the clans, but by certain of them who traded with their productions. At a much earlier date the Arabs and Persians had introduced Indian calico, and squares of this material, obtained in exchange for ivory and gold, were in common use in that part of the country.

Elsewhere the ordinary dress of men when the air was chilly was composed of skins of wild animals formed into a square mantle the size of a large blanket, which they wrapped about their persons. The skin of the leopard was reserved for chiefs and their principal counsellors, but any other could be used by common people. Married women wore a leather wrapper like a petticoat at all times, and big girls at least an apron of leather strings, usually much more. In warm weather men and little children commonly went quite naked.

They were fond of decorating their persons with ornaments, such as necklaces of shells and teeth of animals, arm-rings of copper and ivory, head-bands, etc. They rubbed themselves from head to foot with grease and red ochre, which made them look like polished bronze. Their clothing was greased and coloured in the same manner.

Some of the attires of the women on festive occasions were grotesque in the extreme, and to a European eye made them appear perfectly hideous. Thus the Herero women wore a headdress with three large leather ears attached to it in an upright position, and carried on their persons leather thongs and bands with pieces of iron attached to them often weighing ten or twelve kilogrammes.

Many of them worked lines and simple patterns on different parts of their bodies—chiefly the breasts, shoulders, cheeks, and stomachs—by raising the skin in little knots with a sharp iron awl and burning it, a process that to European eyes disfigured them much more than tattooing would have done, but which

they regarded as ornamental. Each community that adhered
to this custom favoured a form of cicatrice different from that
of its neighbours, but there were numerous tribes that were
without such markings. So with the front teeth: some clans
filed them to a point, a few removed the two upper, but most
allowed them to remain in their natural state. The hideous
boring and plugging the lips and cheeks, so common north of
the lower Zambesi, was not practised south of that river.

More attention was bestowed upon the hair than upon any
other part of the body. Each tribe had its own fashion of
wearing it, so that at first sight the nationality of an individual
was known. Some worked it with wax and strings into imitations of horns, others into arches, others into circles, and so
on. This necessitated the use of a peculiar head rest when
sleeping, to prevent the hair from becoming disordered. The
rest was made of a single piece of wood, according to the fancy
of its owner. Some were forty-five centimetres long, six or
seven centimetres wide, and as many deep, with a slightly
concave surface. Others were only fifteen or twenty centimetres
long, ten to twenty centimetres high, and five to eight centimetres wide, with a deep concave surface for the head to lie
in. Some of these were beautifully carved out of a block of
hard wood, and were highly polished by being frequently rubbed
with grease. In no other manufacture of wood was so much
ingenuity displayed in designing patterns. An elaborate head
rest used by a chief, for instance, might be a carved band supported by two, three, four, or even six columns standing on an
oval or oblong base, each column fluted or otherwise decorated,
and the base covered with little knobs or marked with a herring-
bone pattern. Or it might be of almost any conceivable design
between that and a plain block of wood of the requisite shape.
It was never more than seven or eight centimetres wide, because
it was necessary for the head to project beyond it, in order that
the horns or other forms into which the woolly hair was trained
might remain undisturbed.

Their manufactures, however, were not of a very high order
when judged by a European standard of the present day.

HERERO WOMEN IN FULL DRESS.
(*From a Photograph in the South African Public Library.*)

[*To face p.* **238.**

Foremost among them must be reckoned metallic wares, which included implements of war and husbandry and ornaments for the person. In many parts of the country iron ore was abundant, and this they smelted in a simple manner. Forming a furnace of clay or a boulder with a hollow surface, out of which a groove was made to allow the liquid metal to escape, and into which a hole was pierced for the purpose of introducing a current of air, they piled up a heap of charcoal and virgin ore, which they afterwards covered in such a way as to prevent the escape of heat. The bellows by which air was introduced were made of skins drawn from the animal with as little cutting as possible. These were inflated by opening the ends, which were then closed, when the air was pressed through horns of large antelopes tightly fixed at the other extremities. Two skins were worked by one man, using his hands alternately, and thus a continuous current was kept up.* The molten iron, escaping from the crude yet effective furnace, ran into clay moulds prepared to receive it, which were as nearly as possible of the same dimensions as the implements they wished to make. These were never of great size, the largest being the picks or heavy hoes required for breaking up ground for gardens.

The smith, using a boulder for an anvil and a hammer of stone, next proceeded to shape the lump of metal into an assagai head, an axe, a pick, or whatever was wanted. The occupation of the worker in iron was hereditary in certain families, and was carried on with a good deal of mystery, the common belief being that it was necessary to employ charms unknown to those not initiated. But the arts of the founder and the blacksmith had not advanced beyond the elementary stage. Instead of an opening for inserting a handle in the hoe, it terminated in a spike which was driven into a hole burnt through the knob of a heavy shaft of wood. The assagai was

---

* The double bellows are identical in form with those used by the Malays, Papuans, and Polynesians, which may be accidental, or it may indicate that the principal ancestral tribe of the Bantu had close affinity with those people. Standing alone, it would not have much weight, but, as will be seen farther on, there is another and stronger reason for believing that the last named alternative may be correct.

everywhere in use, and in addition the interior tribes made crescent-shaped battle-axes, which were fastened to handles in the same manner as the hoes. On these implements of war they bestowed all their skill, and some of them really produced neatly finished articles. They worked the metal cold, and were unable to weld two pieces together.

Knives, or more properly daggers, for the ends were pointed and both edges were sharp, were also made of iron. The handles, which were of wood, bone, horn, or even occasionally of ivory, were frequently ornamented, as were also the sheaths of wood or bone in which they were carried. The amount of labour required to make one of these implements and its sheath was very considerable, so that its value relatively to other articles was high, and it was not every man who was so fortunate as to possess a knife. It was carried about by means of a thong round the neck, and lay on the chest a little lower than the charms and strings of teeth and other ornaments, so that it was always ready for use. It was not regarded as a weapon of war, and indeed was unfit for much real service in combat.

Copper was found in several parts of the country, and was distributed over it by means of barter. It was used only for making such ornaments for the person as large beads, earrings, and armlets. Much less skill was employed in working this metal than in manufacturing iron implements, the articles produced being of a very rough kind, not to be compared in point of finish with a battle-axe or an assagai. The armlet was a mere bar bent until its ends met, and the earring was of no better workmanship. The beads were nothing more than drilled lumps of metal globular in shape, and were strung with bits of wood and teeth of animals on a thong. The neater ornaments of copper and brass wire now in use, and exhibited in various museums as specimens of Bantu industry, are of modern date, made of materials obtained from Europeans.

To a people acquainted with the use of iron, bronze could not be of much importance except for making ornaments, and its use appears to have been unknown to the Bantu before the arrival of Europeans. In all the inquiries made by and for the writer among various tribes, no individual was ever found acquainted with the art of mixing copper and tin to make bronze, nor have implements of that metal—with possibly one exception—as yet been discovered in any other part of the country than at Zimbabwe, where those collected are certainly not of Bantu manufacture. The exception is an implement now in the South African museum, something like a spearhead with deeply indented edges, obtained in the Barotsi country and supposed to be of Barotsi manufacture, though this is doubtful. Yet there is ample evidence that some individuals in recent times acquired the knowledge of mixing copper and tin, both of which are to be obtained in different parts of South Africa, though it is evident they had been instructed by strangers how to do it. In the instance mentioned by the reverend Dr. Moffat, quoted farther on, the description of the hammer and the cold chisel proves contact with some more highly civilised people. The only other authority for the use of bronze by Bantu gives the locality as the neighbourhood of Delagoa Bay, where Portuguese had then been trading nearly a century and a half.

This authority, Jan van de Capelle, an official of the Dutch East India Company at Delagoa Bay, reported to the governor and council of policy at the Cape on the 3rd of August 1723 that some blacks had brought a quantity of copper and also of tin for barter, and that all the inhabitants there used the tin of the country as well as what they obtained from the Dutch to mix with copper for the purpose of making neck and arm rings.*

* "In laatste van 't jongst gepasseerde jaar aan la goa neegers sijn geweest, uijt de landschappen paraotte en machicosje die niet alleen koper, maar ook tin met haar bragten om aldaar te verruijlen ; het koper was seer mooij van couleur . . . ; het tin is meede mooij van couleur dogh wat weekelijk en ligt, gelijk uijt twee stukjes van staafjes gesien kan werden : het eene is veel harder van specie, dan het andere, gelijk sulx bij omsmelting hebbe gevonden. Dit thin seggen sij gevonden te werden in de landstreek machicosje, aan de kanten der rivier, in mandjes opgeraapt, gesuijvert van het zand, en dan door de negers tot staafjes gebragt om te verruijlen, alle de inlanders gebruijken dit thin, ook het geene zij van ons inkoopen, om onder haar kooper, tot hals en armringen te smelten : waar door 't sonder twijffel komt, dat haare ringen, sô een glans hebben, en buijgsamer zijn dan d'Comps ringen, die daar sijn geweest." In a report dated 17th of February 1732 Mr. Van de Capelle informed the governor and council of policy that he had purchased from blacks at Delagoa Bay fifty-six bars (staven) of tin. Quite

In 1826 the reverend Robert Moffat visited the Barolong near the Molopo, and at Kongke, one of their kraals, he saw a Mohurutsi making bronze. He says on pages 466 to 468 of his *Missionary Labours and Scenes in Southern Africa* :

"Having occasion to mend the linchpin of my wagon, I inquired for a native smith, when a respectable and rather venerable man, with one eye, was pointed out. Observing, from the cut of his hair, that he was a foreigner, and inquiring where he practised his trade, I was affected to hear him reply, 'I am a Mohurutsi, from Kurrechane.' I accompanied him to his shop, in an open yard at the back of his house. The whole of his implements consisted of two small goat-skins for bellows, some small broken pots for crucibles, a few round green stone boulders for his anvil, a hammer made of a small piece of iron about three-quarters of an inch thick, and rather more than two by three inches square, with a handle in a hole in the centre, a cold chisel, two or three other shapeless tools, and a heap of charcoal. 'I am not an ironsmith,' he said ; 'I work in copper,' showing me some of his copper and brass ornaments, consisting of ear-rings, arm-rings, etc. I told him I only wanted wind and fire. He sat down between his two goat-skins, and puffed away. Instead of using his tongs, made of the bark of a tree, I went for my own. When he saw them he gazed in silent admiration ; he turned them over and over , he had never seen such ingenuity, and pressed them to his chest, giving me a most expressive look, which was as intelligible as 'Will you give them to me ? ' My work was soon done, when he entered his hut, from which he brought a piece of flat iron, begging me to pierce it with a number of different-sized holes, for the purpose of drawing copper and brass wire. Requesting to see the old one, it was produced, accompanied by the feeling declaration, 'It is from Kurrechane.' Having examined his manner of using it, and formed a tolerable idea of the thing he

recently tin mines, worked at some former, but not very remote, period, have been discovered at and near the Rooiberg, in the district of Waterberg, south of the Limpopo river. These have been abandoned for many years, and there are no traditions among the present inhabitants concerning them. But the tribes in that part of the country settled there so recently that no information can be expected from them, and most probably it was from this locality that the tin taken to Delagoa Bay in 1732 was obtained. How Bantu acquired a knowledge of this metal, and how to smelt it, remains a mystery.

wanted, I set to work ; and finding his iron too soft for piercing holes through nearly an half-inch iron plate, I took the oldest of my two handsaw files to make a punch, which I had to repair many times. After much labour, and a long time spent, I succeeded in piercing about twenty holes, from the eighth of an inch to the thickness of a thread. The moment the work was completed, he grasped it, and breaking out into exclamations of surprise, bounded over the fence like an antelope, and danced about the village like a Merry-Andrew, exhibiting his treasure to every one, and asking if they ever saw anything like it. Next day I told him, that as we were brothers of one trade, (for, among the Africans, arts, though in their infancy, have their secrets too,) he must show me the whole process of melting copper, making brass, and drawing wire. The broken pot or crucible, containing a quantity of copper and a little tin, was presently fixed in the centre of a charcoal fire. He then applied his bellows till the contents were fused. He had previously prepared a heap of sand, slightly adhesive, and by thrusting a stick about two-eighths of an inch in diameter, like the ramrod of a musket, obliquely into this heap, he made holes, into which he poured the contents of his crucible. He then fixed a round, smooth stick, about three feet high, having a split in the top, upright in the ground, when, taking out his rods of brass, he beat them out on a stone with his little hammer, till they were about the eighth of an inch square, occasionally softening them in a small flame, made by burning grass. Having reduced them all to this thickness, he laid the end of one on a stone, and rubbed it to a point with another stone, in order to introduce it through the largest hole in his iron-plate ; he then opened the split in the upright stick, to hold fast the end of the wire, when he forced the plate and wire round the stick with a lever-power, frequently rubbing the wire with oil or fat. The same operation is performed each time, making the point of the wire smaller for the less hole, till it is reduced to the size wanted, which is sometimes about that of thick sewing-cotton. The wire is, of course, far inferior in colour and quality to our brass-wire. These native smiths, however, evince great dexterity in working ornaments from copper, brass, and iron."

In the manufacture of wooden articles, such as spoons, bowls, fighting sticks, mortars, etc., they were tolerably expert. Each article was made of a single block of wood, requiring much time and patience to complete it, and upon it was frequently carved some simple pattern or the figure of an animal. Standing on the handle of a spoon might be seen a lizard, an ox, or an elephant, though always stiff in attitude ; encircling the fighting stick might be seen two or three snakes with spots burnt upon them to make them resemble the living reptiles.

The tribes bordering on some of the rivers of the interior and along the eastern coast north of Delagoa Bay were able to construct canoes out of the trunk of a single tree, and knew how to propel them with paddles, but this simple art was not practised elsewhere. No means for crossing a swollen river, other than carrying a stone under each arm if the water was not too deep, had been devised by the Bantu of the coast below Delagoa Bay, and ocean navigation was of course unthought of.

A product of some ingenuity was a little vase used for various purposes. It was made of the scrapings of skins which when soft were spread over clay moulds, and when dry became solid cases. The clay was then taken out with an *isilanda* or large iron pin which every man carried about with him to extract thorns from his feet, and the vessel was ready for use. Some were in the shape of animals, others of gourds, or whatever else the moulders desired. Usually while the gluey matter was still soft it was creased, or raised in ridges, or pricked all over with a sharp piece of wood, which greatly improved its appearance. Some of these articles, especially those in the form of European vases or decanters, were really extremely neat and pretty.

Skins for clothing, when the fur was preserved, were prepared by scraping them carefully and then thumping them with the hand and rubbing them for a length of time with a very smooth stone, by which means they were made nearly as soft and pliable as cloth. The interior tribes excelled in the art of dressing skins, and were able to make beautiful fur robes, which they stitched with sinews by the help of an awl. When the hair was removed from skins to make wrappers for women the process of preparing them was different. They were steeped in water, scraped on both sides, then dried, and afterwards beaten and rubbed with grease till they were soft. Finally they were cut into shape and sewed together with sinews to the required size, when the wrapper was coloured with red ochre and was ready for use.

In one comparatively small district of South Africa,—the territory between the lower courses of the Zambesi and Sabi rivers,—men were sometimes engaged in an occupation altogether unknown to their kindred elsewhere. This was the collection of gold. The chiefs were induced by the Mohamedan traders of the coast to employ bands of their subjects in searching for the precious metal, principally by alluvial washing in the rainy season, though sometimes by extracting quartz from reefs near the surface by the aid of fire. The quartz was crushed, and the gold was then obtained by washing. As the Makaranga knew of no other artificial light than burning wood they could not mine beneath the surface, and consequently very little gold was obtained in this manner. This gold was inferior to the other in quality, and was known by a different name. According to Dos Santos the diggers were termed botonghi, which is evidently an approximation to the Tshikaranga word for gatherers, from the root *uku buta*, to collect or gather.

The industries above mentioned were confined to males, but in other departments the women were equally skilful. Earthenware vessels containing from a quarter of a litre to three hectolitres were constructed by them, some of which were almost as perfect in form as if they had been turned on a wheel. Though they were frequently not more than a third of a centimetre in thickness, they were so finely tempered that the most intense heat did not damage them. These vessels were used for beer pots, grain jars, and cooking utensils. The potter's art has now become nearly, if not wholly, lost by the Bantu of South Africa, owing to the cheapness of importations from abroad. The women have found by experience that with much less labour they can earn sufficient money to purchase earthenware crocks, iron pots, and wooden kegs, and so contact with European civilisation has had the effect in this respect of diminishing their former skill.

Baskets for holding corn, rush mats for sleeping on, small mats used like plates to serve food on, and grass bags were made by the women. The bags were so carefully and strongly woven that they were used to hold water or any other liquid. In general none of these articles were dyed, nor was any attempt made to ornament them, though by a few of the people of the interior simple patterns were occasionally worked in the best of their mats with materials of different colour.

Of the use of stone for building purposes, the coast tribes knew nothing, and the interior tribes very little. None of them ever dressed a block, but the cattle-folds, which along the coast were constructed of branches of trees, in parts of the interior were made of round stones roughly laid together to form a wall. A few of the enclosures of courtyards among the Betshuana were also made of rough stones, and the walls of the huts of the Bataung were usually made of that material. The quern, or handmill for grinding corn, which was in common use, consisted of untrimmed stones, one flat or hollow and the other round or oval.

When not engaged in the industries that have been mentioned, the men were habitual idlers. A great portion of their time was passed in visiting and gossip, of which they were exceedingly fond. They spent days together engaged in small talk, and were perfect masters of that kind of argument which consists in parrying a question by putting another. Though not pilferers, they were inveterate cattle thieves. According to their ideas, cattle stealing except from people of their own clan was not so much a crime as a civil offence, and no disgrace was attached to it, though if it was proved against a man the law compelled him or his connections to make ample restitution. But any one detected in the act of lifting cattle might be killed with impunity by the owner, and a chief punished with death any of his subjects whose conduct as a robber from other clans had a tendency to involve his own people in war.

A custom of the Bantu everywhere which irritated the first Europeans who came in contact with them was their persistency in begging for everything that a stranger had, no matter how indispensable it was to him. From the chief down to his poorest subject, the cry was nothing but give, give. Every artifice was employed to get from him whatever they saw, and among some of the most degraded of the communities he might consider himself fortunate if really violent means were not used to effect the purpose. This habit made it very difficult to explore the parts of the country that they occupied, added to which every tribe invariably represented the next in advance as dangerous to deal with, the object being to keep all gain for themselves. A very strong party could of course make its way onward without being subjected to annoyances, and a little party of perfectly destitute people, such as a band of shipwrecked sailors, might traverse the country and be assisted with food on the journey, but an ordinary traveller, unless under exceptionally favourable circumstances, had to pay a very heavy toll.

The interior tribes were the more advanced in skill in such handicrafts as were common to them all, and many of them had greater latent power of mind, owing to the large mixture of blood of higher stock in their veins. Their males sometimes aided the females in agriculture, though the hardest and most constant labour was by them also left to the women. But with these exceptions, all comparisons between the tribes must be favourable to those of the coast. The Bantu of the interior were smaller in stature and less handsome in appearance than the splendidly formed men who lived on the terraces facing the sea. In all that is comprised in the word manliness they were vastly lower.

Truth is not a virtue of barbarian life. In general if a man could extricate himself from a difficulty, escape punishment, or gain any other advantage by telling a falsehood, and did not do so, he was regarded as a fool. Many of the chiefs of the coast tribes, however, prided themselves on adhering faithfully to their promises; but the word of an interior chief was seldom worth anything.

The deceptive power of all these people was great. But there was one member which a man of the coast could not entirely control, and while with a countenance otherwise devoid of expression he related the grossest falsehood or the most tragic event, his lively eye often betrayed the passions he was feeling. When falsehood was brought home to him unanswerably, he cast his glances to the ground or around him, but did not meet the eye of the person he had been attempting to deceive. The man of the interior, on the contrary, had no conception whatever of shame attached to falsehood, and his comparatively listless eye was seldom allowed to betray him.

The man of the coast was brave in the field ; his inland kinsman was in general an arrant coward. The one was modest when speaking of his exploits, the other was an intolerable boaster. The difference between them in this respect was great, and was shown in many ways, but a single illustration from an occurrence of the present generation will give an idea of it. Faku, son of Gungushe, chief of the Pondos, by no means the best specimen of a coast resident, once wished to show his regard for a white man who was residing with him. He collected a large herd of cattle, which he presented with this expression : "You have no food to eat, and we desire to show our good will towards you, take this basket of corn from the children of Gungushe." An inland chief about the same time presented a half-starved old goat to his guest, with the expression " Behold an ox ! " *

Among the coast tribes the institution of slavery did not exist, but there could be no more heartless slave-owners in the world than some of the people of the interior. Their bondsmen were the descendants of those who had been scattered by war, and who had lost everything but life. They could not

---

* This was unquestionably the case when Europeans first came into contact with the different tribes and placed on record the peculiarities of each, but it is not so in all instances at the present day. The chief of our time who possesses the highest moral qualities of any in South Africa is Khama, ruler of the Bamangwato. Bathoen, chief of the Bangwaketse, and Sebele, chief of the Bakwena, are also superior to most of the other Bantu rulers. All of these are heads of interior tribes. It is not only from the observations of others, but from personal experience, that the writer of these pages is able to state that the chiefs here named are capable of acting with such generosity and good feeling as would do credit to any European. But they are exceptions to the general rule, and unfortunately few of their followers come up to their standard.

own so much as the skin of an antelope, and upon any caprice of their masters they were put to death with as little compunction as if they were vermin.

In a state of society in which women were drudges performing all the severest labour, in which a man carrying only an assagai and a knobbed stick walked in front of his wives and daughters all bearing heavy burdens on their heads, it might be supposed that the females were unhappy. Such a supposition, however, would be erroneous. Freedom from care to anything like the extent that is common to most individuals of our own race tended to make Bantu females as well as males far happier on the whole than white people.

The women were quite as cheerful as the men, and knew as well as Europeans how to make their influence felt. In times of peace, after working in her garden a great part of the day, towards evening a woman collected a bundle of sticks, and with it on her head and a child on her back, trudged homeward. Having made a fire, she then proceeded to grind some soaked millet upon a quern, humming a monotonous tune as she worked the stone. When sufficient was ground, it was made into a roll, and placed in the hot ashes to bake. Meantime curdled milk was drawn by the head of the household from the skin bags in which it was kept, and the bags were refilled with milk just taken from the cows. The men made a hearty meal of the milk and the bread, with sometimes the flesh of game and different vegetable products, and after they had finished the women and children partook of what was left. Then the men gathered round the fire and chatted together, and the young people sat and listened to the stories told by some old woman till the time for sleep arrived. Different games were also played occasionally, but as the only artificial light was that of burning wood, they were usually carried on in the daytime.

At a very early age boys commenced trials of skill against each other in throwing knobbed sticks and imitation assagais. They enjoyed this exercise in little groups, those of the same age keeping together, for there was no greater tyrant in the world than a big lad over his younger fellows. Commencing

with an antheap at a distance of ten or fifteen metres for a
target, they gradually became so perfect that they could hit
an object thirty centimetres square twice or even three times
as far off. The knobbed stick and the imitation assagai were
thrown in different ways, the object with the first being to inflict
a heavy blow upon the mark aimed at, while that with the last
was to pierce it. This exercise strengthened the muscles of the
arms and gave expansion to the chest. The result was that
when the boys were grown up they were able to use their weapons
without any further training. When practising, they kept up
a continual noise, and if an unusually successful hit was made
the thrower uttered a cry of exultation.

Boys above the age of nine or ten years were fond of sham
fighting with sticks. They stood in couples, each with a foot
advanced to meet that of his antagonist, and with a cudgel
elevated in the right hand. Each fixed his eye upon the eye
of his opponent, and sought to ward off blows as well as to inflict
them. In these contests pretty hard strokes were sometimes
given and received with the utmost good humour.

A game of which they were very fond was an imitation hunt.
In this, one of them represented a wild animal of some kind,
a second acted as a hunter, and the others took the part of dogs
in pursuit. A space was marked off, within which the one
chased was allowed to take breath, when he was said to be in
the bush. He tried to imitate as closely as possible the animal
he was representing. Thus if he was an antelope he simply
ran, but if he was a lion he stood and fought.

The calves of the kraal were under the care of the boys, and
a good deal of time was passed in training them to run and to
obey signals made by whistling. The boys mounted them when
they were eighteen months or two years old, and raced about
upon their backs. When the boys were engaged in any sport,
one of the number was selected by lot to tend the calves. As
many blades of grass as there were boys were taken, and a knot
was made on the end of one of them. The biggest boy held
the blades between the fingers and thumb of his closed hand,
and whoever drew the blade with the knot had to act as herd.

They had also a simple game called hide and look for, exactly like our own. As a training for the eye and hand nothing could be better than their method of playing with little round pebbles. Each boy had a certain number, which he threw into the air one after another, catching them on his hand by turns as they fell, and throwing them up again before any touched the ground. He who could keep the whole longest in the air was the winner. Or they would try who could keep the greatest number of pebbles in the air at once.

If they chanced to be disinclined for active exercise, they amused themselves by moulding clay into little images of cattle, or by making puzzles with strings. Some of them were skilful in forming knots with thongs and pieces of wood, which taxed the ingenuity of others to undo. The cleverest of them sometimes practised tricks of deception with pebbles. They were so sharp that although one was sure that he actually saw the pebble taken into the right hand, that hand when opened would be found empty, and it would be contained in the left, or perhaps it would be exhibited somewhere else.

The above comprised the common outdoor sports of boys up to the age of fourteen or fifteen years. At that time of life they usually began to practise the different dances which they would be required to take part in when they became men. These dances differed from one another almost as much as those practised by Europeans.

The commonest indoor game of the extreme southern tribes at the present time is the *iceya*, but this is of Hottentot origin, so need not be described here. A game of Bantu children everywhere was the *imfumba*. One of the players took a pebble or any other small substance in his hands, and pretended to place it in the hands of the others, who were seated in a circle around him. He might really give it to one of them, or he might keep it himself. One after another then guessed in whose possession it was. A variation of this game was played by men in rows of holes in the ground, but it was much more complicated.

Another common indoor game of children was called *cumbulele*. Three or four little ones stood with their closed hands on top of each other, so as to form a column. They sang *cumbulele, cumbulele, pangalala,* and at the last *la* they drew their hands back sharply, each one pinching with his thumb nail the hand above.

Toys as playthings were few in number, and were almost confined to clay oxen, wooden darts, bows and arrows, and the *nodiwu.* This was a piece of wood about fifteen or twenty centimetres long, four or five centimetres wide, and a third or half a centimetre thick in the middle. Towards the edges it was bevelled off, so that the surface was convex, or consisted of two inclined planes. At one end it had a thong attached to it by which it was whirled rapidly round. The other end of the thong was usually fastened to a small round piece of wood used as a handle. The *nodiwu,* when whirled round, gave forth a noise that could be heard at a considerable distance. Besides the use which it was put to by the lads, when a little child was crying inside a hut, its mother or nurse would sometimes get a boy to make a noise with it outside, and then induce the child to be still by pretending that a monster was coming to devour it. There was a kind of superstition connected with the *nodiwu,* that playing with it invited a gale of wind. Men would, on that account, often prevent boys from using it when they desired calm weather for any purpose. It was much in evidence when the millet crops were ripening, and women and children were engaged from early dawn until darkness set in keeping the birds away. Little stages were then erected in the gardens, and on the appearance of a flock of finches each watcher shouted, clapped hands, whirled a *nodiwu,* or otherwise made as much noise as possible.

The form of greeting when people met varied greatly among the tribes. In the north clapping hands was the commonest form, accompanied by prostration of an inferior before a superior. " I see you " was the expression used by others on the coast. Among some of the interior tribes one person on meeting another asked the question " what are you eating ? " and received as a conventional reply " nothing at all." In the south, on meeting a chief the salutation was " ah ! " There was no general custom observed in this respect by all the branches of the Bantu family.

CHAPTER XI.

Description of the Bantu (*continued*).

The language of the Bantu was exceedingly expressive, but its construction was quite different from that of any European people. It was broken up into a great number of dialects, which differed from each other so much that the men of one group could not understand the men of another. On analysing the words, an educated European can see that the roots of those used by the coast tribes and frequently the full words are the same as those of some of the dialects of Guinea, which arises from their separation only a few hundred years ago. Between the coast dialects and those of the interior the difference consists not only in the words used, but even in some of the roots, while in the extreme case of the Tshikaranga the bulk of the roots vary considerably from those of all others in the country. This follows from one ancestral branch of each group of tribes being different from that of the other groups, though there has been much mixture also among these.

But while the words, and even some of the roots, vary, the structure of the sentences is the same in all, thus testifying to the fact that the original Bantu band, which afterwards conquered a variety of people, and incorporated females of such different blood as hamitic, semitic, Bushman, and negro, spoke a prefix-pronominal language. The noun is the governing word in each sentence. There are classes of nouns, in some dialects more numerous than in others, and each class is distinguished by the prefix before the root. This prefix is changed to form the plural, except in the case of abstract nouns, which are used in the singular form only. Thus in the dialect of the Amaxosa tribe *in-doda*, a man, *ama-doda*, men, *um-fazi*, a woman, *aba-fazi*, women, *is-andla*, a hand, *iz-andla*, hands.*

Here alone are six prefixes, and every adjective and every verb connected with one of these nouns must take before it a corresponding prefix, so that the other words in a sentence may agree with it in that syllable, as *abafazi bané*, women four, *izandla ziné*, hands four. Until this rule was discovered, a Bantu dialect could not be reduced to writing, and was regarded as formless, but now it can be studied as easily as French or German. Its system of notation is decimal, and is complete up to a very high number, but it is cumbersome for arithmetical purposes. The language has a very copious verb, and abstract nouns can be formed readily where they are not already in common use, so that any idea whatever can be expressed in it. As nearly every word ends in a vowel, and the enunciation of the people is clear and distinct, with the voice nicely modulated, the language is musical to the ear. Many individuals, especially among the chiefs and counsellors, display great ability in public speaking. In some dialects the sound of our *r* is not heard, in others the sound of our *l*, in others again *r*, *l*, and *d* are interchangeable. Dr. Bleek has pointed out that the language has close affinities with the Malayan, Papuan, and Polynesian tongues. When brought under European rule, the members of one tribe learn the dialect of another very quickly, as they do also English or Dutch, their power in that respect being like that of young white children.

Besides the change which takes place in all unwritten languages in the course of even a few generations, some of the tribes had a habit which hastened the variation, and therefore made intercourse between them more difficult. This was the

---

* As excellent grammars of various dialects, in which the medium of explanation is English, can be procured without difficulty, it is not necessary for me to give more than the very barest outline of the structure of the language in this chapter. Among the best of the grammars published at an early date are *A Grammar of the Zulu Language*, by Rev. Lewis Grout, demi octavo, 432 + lii pages, London, 1859, and *A Grammar of the Kaffir Language* by the Rev. William J. Davis, demi octavo, 183 pages, London, 1872. Dr. Bleek's valuable *Comparative Grammar of South African Languages* has already been mentioned.

hlonipa custom, by which women were obliged constantly to invent new words, in which the principal syllable of their husband's name or that of any of his male relatives in the ascending line was avoided, and as some of those words came into general use, the dialect had a tendency to change in a different manner from all others. This custom of *hlonipa* extended so far that if a stranger were to ask the daughter-in-law of the head of a kraal whose place it was, she was obliged to call some one else to tell him, as she could not pronounce his name herself.

There were clicks in only a few of the dialects spoken by the Bantu family. They were three in number, and were derived in the south chiefly from Hottentot, and elsewhere from Bushman sources. They were introduced by females who were spared when the hordes to which they belonged were conquered, as is evident not only from tradition, but from the words in which the clicks occur being chiefly those pertaining to the occupations of women.

The reverend J. L. Döhne, in the introduction to his *Zulu-Kafir Dictionary*, was the first to make known to English students a fact with which every one conversant with any Bantu dialect is now acquainted, that the language contains a considerable number of words whose roots are identical with those of words with the same or nearly the same meaning in other tongues. He gives a list of over forty akin to words in Hebrew, Arabic, Greek, Latin, English, Dutch, and German, though the identity of some of them is not very clear. Mr. I. Bud-M'belle, in the introduction to his excellent *Kafir Scholar's Companion*, published at Lovedale in 1903, gives a list of fourteen words— eleven of them verbs,—which have the same meaning and almost the same sound in Zulu as in English. Among them are *uku-beta* to beat, *uku-kala* to call (out), and *uku-lala* to lie (down). A gentleman long resident among the Xosas and Tembus occupied much time in making a similar list of Xosa and Latin words with the same roots, and he informed the writer that he had succeeded in obtaining over thirty. The early French missionaries in Basutoland were astonished to find the people there sacrificing to the *Barimo*, a word identical with *Baalim*, the *l* in other dialects being often changed by the Basuto to *ɹ*, and the noun requiring a vowel ending. How can these facts be explained? As to the last, the identity of words is probably accidental. The Barimo are the spirits of the dead, Baalim are forms of the sun god. The meaning is thus not the same. Then Barimo is found only in a highly specialised dialect of the Bantu language, and before any certainty can be arrived at, it will be indispensable to know what the primitive form was, that is the form in use by the original conquering band.

As for the numerous words with roots common to many languages, the only explanation that can be offered seems to be this. Taking the human species as of one origin, no matter where that origin may have been, there must have been a time, however remote, when all mankind, then a small community, used the same language. That language was probably very limited in words. Then a division of the people took place, when some migrated in one direction, some in another. Each section added new words to the old vocabulary to express new ideas, and each put the words together to form sentences in a different manner. Very soon there would be many distinct languages, varying from each other not only in the words used, but in grammatical construction. But is it not allowable to suppose that the original words common to mankind would be retained by all to express the same meanings, and that though modified and distorted, abraded in some instances, enlarged in others, many of these primitive words may have come down even to the present day in such a form that their identity can be recognised by diligent observation? Is it not possible at least that when a Zulu or a Xosa says *ngena* and an Englishman says *enter*, the *en* in both instances is a relic of a far-off age, when a little group of human beings, perhaps in Southern Asia, perhaps in some land now buried beneath the ocean waves, could look around in every direction without seeing others of their kind, and could claim the whole world as their own?

Many of the proverbs in common use among all sections of the Bantu conveyed excellent practical lessons of prudence and wisdom. The following are a few of those collected by the writer when residing with the Xosas, and they might be extended to fill many pages :—

A brand burns him who stirs it up, equivalent to our English one Let sleeping dogs lie.

Like the marriage feast of Mapasa, used to denote anything unusually grand. The marriage festivities of one of the ancients, Mapasa by name, are said to have been carried on for a whole year.

Misfortune of soup made of shanks and feet, applied to any person who never does well, but is always getting into trouble. The kind of soup spoken of is very lightly esteemed.

One fly does not provide for another, a saying of the industrious to the idle, meaning that each should work for himself as the flies do.

Bakuba is far away, no person ever reached it. Bakuba is an ideal country. This proverb is used as a warning against undue ambition, or as advice to be content with that which is within reach. It is equivalent to our English saying It is no use building castles in the air.

They have slaughtered at Kukwane, where much meat is obtainable. According to tradition, there was once a very rich chief who lived at Kukwane, and who entertained strangers more liberally than any who went before or who came after him. This proverb is used to such persons as ask too much from others, as if to say : It was only at Kukwane that such expectations were realised.

It is not every one who is a son of Gaika. Gaika was at the beginning of the nineteenth century the most powerful chief west of the Kei. This proverb signifies that all are not equally fortunate.

I rejoice that Kolomba's mother is dead. The mother of Kolomba was, according to tradition, a very disagreeable person. This saying is used when anything that one dreads or dislikes has passed away.

You will shed tears with one eye like a monkey. A warning used to deter any one from being led into a snare of any kind.

It is said that when a monkey is caught in a trap he cries, but that tears come out of one eye only.

It is the seed of the umya (a species of wild hemp). This saying is applied to any thing or person considered very beautiful. The seed referred to is like a small jet black bead.

He is ripe inside, like a water-melon. Said of any one who has come to a resolution without yet expressing it. From its appearance it cannot be said with certainty whether a water-melon is ripe or not.

You will find out what Hili of the Amambala experienced. This saying is applied as a warning to people to avoid doing wrong, lest the punishment of Hili overtake them. Hili, or Tikoloshe, is, according to the belief of the Xosas, a mischievous being who usually lives in the water, but who goes about as a human dwarf playing tricks upon people. He milks the cows when no one is watching them. He causes women to fall in love with him, for he is of a very amorous disposition towards the female sex. There are few Xosas even at the present day who doubt the existence of such a being. It is said that a long time ago there was a man of the Amambala who had good reason to suspect that his wife had fallen in love with Hili. He accordingly pretended to go upon a journey, but returned in the middle of the night and fastened his dogs at the door of his hut. He then went inside and kindled a fire, when, as he anticipated, he found Hili there. The man called his neighbours, who came with sticks and beat Hili till he was unable to move. They then tied him up in a bundle, fastened him to the back of the woman, and sent her away to wander wherever she liked.

A spy for both. Said of a talebearer.

The shield turned the wrong way. This saying is applied to any one who goes over from one party to another. It is a common expression for one who turns evidence against accomplices in crime.

It is a cob stripped of grain in an ashpit. Said of a worthless character.

You will prefer roasted meat. This saying is applied to any one who is boasting immoderately, as a warning that if he does not take care he will get into trouble, when he will be glad to take whatever comes to hand. He will prefer roasted meat because it is easily cooked, and he will have neither time nor means to boil it. This saying is also used as a threat, as if one said, I will punish you thoroughly.

Throats are all alike in swallowing. This proverb is used when one asks another for anything, and implies, if you do not give to me now, I will not give to you when I have anything that you would like a share of.

The people who rescue and kill. This saying is applied to Europeans. It first arose from the heavy demands made by Lord Charles Somerset upon the Gaikas in return for English protection, but the Xosas maintain that we have acted up to the description ever since. It is sometimes put in this form, The people who protect with one hand and kill with the other.

The coming of Nxele. This saying implies anything long expected, but which never occurs. Nxele (the lefthanded), or Makana, one of the most remarkable men that the Xosa tribe has produced, rose by his own merits from a private station to be the leader of the Ndlambe clans in the second decade of the nineteenth century. It was he who united them against the English when Lord Charles Somerset invaded their country with a view of compelling them to recognise a chief whom they detested. He led in person the attack upon Grahamstown, and only retreated after the flower of his forces was swept away. To obtain peace for his people, he voluntarily surrendered to the English troops, and was sent as a prisoner of state to Robben Island. In attempting to make his escape from the island in a boat, he was drowned. But the Xosas would not believe that Makana was dead, for they deemed him immortal. All through the wars of 1835, 1846–7, and 1851–2, they looked for his reappearance to lead them to victory. In 1872 his personal ornaments were still in preservation at a kraal near King-Williamstown, but about that date the hope of his return was generally abandoned.

He has drunk the juice of the flower of the wild aloe. Said of a dull, sleepy person. This juice when drunk has a stupefying effect, and benumbs the limbs so as to make them powerless for a time.

The walls have come into collision, said of any dispute between persons of consequence.

A person who will not take advice gets knowledge when trouble overtakes him.

You have cast away your own for that which you are not sure of, equivalent to the English proverb A bird in the hand is worth two in the bush.

He is a buck of an endless forest, a saying applied to a shiftless person, one who never continues long in any occupation.

You are lighting a fire in the wind, said to any one who favours strangers in preference to relatives, or to their disadvantage.

There is no beast that does not roar in its den, meaning that a man recognises no superior in his own establishment. Equivalent to Every cock crows on his own dunghill.

A dog of the wind, a saying applied to any one who has no settled plan of living.

I, the adhesive grass, will stick fast to you. This proverb is used as a warning to any one to avoid a bad habit or an unworthy companion that cannot easily be got rid of.

The sun never sets without fresh news.

They are people of experience who do not sleep at a strange place, said in praise of one who is smart in going a message, or who performs any duty at a distance quickly.

The land is dead, a saying which implies that war has commenced.

One does not become great by claiming greatness, used to incite any one to the performance of noble deeds. It means that a man's actions, not his talk and boasting, are what people judge of his greatness by.

The wonderful and the impossible have come into collision. A saying applied to any intricate question.

The mist and the sun are together. A saying denoting a very great number.

It is the foot of a baboon. A saying denoting a treacherous person.

We shall hear, we are on the side towards which the wind blows. This saying denotes, we shall soon know all that is going on.

He has gone in pursuit of the (fabulous) birds of the sea. A saying applied to one whose ambitious aspirations are not likely to be realised.

They prevent us from getting red clay from the pit, and they do not use it. This saying is used of Europeans, to denote that they act as the dog in the manger towards the Xosas. It has unfortunately become a very common expression.

You drink out of the old cup. The indebe is a drinking vessel made of rushes. The saying is used to a wealthy man, and means, you use a vessel handed down to you from your ancestors.

You are creeping on your knees to the fireplace. This saying is used as a warning to any one who is following a course that must lead to ruin. It is as if one said, you are like an infant crawling towards the fire-circle, who is sure to get burnt.

To skin a mouse. A saying which implies to do anything secretly. A mouse can be skinned without any one seeing it, but an ox can not.

It has stuck fast by one of the front legs. This saying is used when one has committed oneself to any matter of importance. An animal cannot extricate itself easily when fast by one of its front legs.

One who eats the remains of a meal without first obtaining permission. This saying is used of an uncalled-for expression of opinion.

You disturb monkeys on their way to drink. This saying is used to express uncalled-for interference.

It dies and rises like the moon. Said of any question that springs up again after it is supposed to be settled.

There is no wormwood that comes into flower and does not wither. A proverb descriptive of the life of man.

The foot has no nose. This proverb is an exhortation to be hospitable. It is as if one said, give food to the traveller, because when you are on a journey your foot will not be able to smell out and avoid a man whom you have turned from your door, but to your shame it may carry you to his.

You have exposed yourself. This saying is applied as a warning not to give anything to an importunate person, as he would very likely be encouraged thereby to continue asking for more.

The crab has stuck fast between the stones at the entrance of its hole. Said of any one who is involved in difficulties of his own creation, or of one who raises an argument and is beaten in it.

He has fastened a dog to a shrub. This saying is used to denote a very greedy person, one who is so greedy as to fasten his dog to a shrub that the animal may not beg for food while he is eating. The shrub denoted is the very common one that is covered with yellow flowers at midsummer.

Guluwe's two of yesterday. This is a saying of any one who goes away promising to return, and does not do so. It had its origin in an event which happened six generations back. Guluwe was a hunter of great renown, who crossed the Kei with Khàkhábay, the great-grandfather of the late Sandile. No man was ever so skilful and successful in the pursuit of game as he. But when Khàkhábay took possession of the Amatola mountains, which he purchased from the Hottentot chieftainess Hoho, he found them infested by great numbers of Bushmen. One day Guluwe, who had two young men with him, killed an eland, but while he was still shouting his cry of triumph: " Tsi ! ha ! ha ! ha ! ha ! the weapons of Khàkhábay ! " he was surprised by a number of these inhuman abatwa. They said : " Look at the sun for the last time, you shall kill no more of our game." Guluwe offered them a large quantity of dacha for his ransom. One of the abatwa was unwilling to spare him, but all the rest agreed. They kept him with them while he pretended to send the two young men for the dacha, but privately he told them not to return. The Bushmen then commenced to eat the eland. They ate that day, and all that night, never ceasing to watch

Guluwe. The next morning they asked him when the young men would be back with the dacha, and he replied that he did not expect them before sunset. The abatwa, gorged with meat, then lay down to sleep, all except the one who advised that Guluwe should not be spared. That one watched a little while longer, but at length he too was overcome by drowsiness. Guluwe then with his assagai put one after another to death, until, forgetting himself, he shouted his cry: "Tsi! ha! ha! ha! ha! Izikali zika Rarabe!" This awakened the Bushman who had advised that he should be killed; he now sprang to his feet and escaped, calling out as he ran with the speed of the wind: "I said this Guluwe of the Khàkhábays should be destroyed; you who are dead have perished through not following my advice."

Of poetry the Bantu had a fairly rich store, but there was nothing particularly grand in it. It was chanted by men on special occasions, and consisted chiefly of adulation of chiefs, deeds of war, and actions of animals. Thus a favourite ox might have a chant in its praise. The war chants, in certain parts of which the whole of the men present joined, were certainly impressive, but those in ordinary use were monotonous and disagreeable to a European ear. All were distinguished by a note of sadness. These people, though their voices were rich and melodious, had no conception of such vocal music as we are accustomed to: they had neither rhymic hymn, nor song, nor glee. Their musical instruments were of the rudest kind, mostly calculated to make noise rather than melody, those in ordinary use being capable of producing only a monotonous thrumming sound. The best consisted merely of pieces of wood or iron for keys, with calabashes attached to them, arranged on stretched strings, and struck with a small round-headed cane, or of thin iron keys fastened over a gourd or hollow block of wood, and touched by the hand. Of these there were several kinds, but all were constructed on the same principle.

The description given in the preceding pages is that of the Bantu in general south of the Zambesi when Europeans first became acquainted with them at the beginning of the sixteenth century, and of the sections of their family when they arrived at a later date. It is also a description of a very large proportion of them as they are to-day, though the customs of many have been more or less modified by the authority or the influence of white people. With blood of such different origins in their veins, some are far more intelligent than others, but the opinion of those who have most to do with them now—four hundred years after their first contact with Caucasian civilisation—is that occasional individuals are capable of rising to a high standard, but that the great mass shows little aptitude for European culture.

In mission schools children of early age are found to keep pace with those of white parents. In some respects, indeed, they are the higher of the two. Deprived of all extraneous aid, a Bantu child is able to devise means for supporting life at a much earlier age than a European child. But while the European youth is still developing his powers, the Bantu youth in many instances is found unable to make further progress. His intellect has become sluggish, and frequently he exhibits a decided repugnance, if not an incapacity, to learn anything more. The growth of his mind, which at first promised so much, has ceased just at that stage when the mind of the European begins to display the greatest vigour.

Numerous individuals, however, have emerged from the mass, and have shown abilities of no mean order. A score of ministers of religion might now be named as earnest, intelligent, and devoted to their calling as average Europeans. Masters of primary schools, clerks, and interpreters, fairly well qualified for their duties, are by no means rare. One individual of this family has translated Bunyan's *Pilgrim's Progress* into the dialect of the Xosa tribe, and the translation is as faithful and expressive as any that have been made in the languages of Europe. Plaintive tunes, such as the converts at mission stations love to sing, have been composed by another for a considerable number of hymns and songs in the same dialect. Still another edits a newspaper, and shows that he has an intelligent grasp of political questions. One of the very best clerks the writer of this volume ever had was a Xosa who served him in that capacity when he was magistrate of a border district, and who was industrious, painstaking, and thoroughly trustworthy. But unfortunately these men are exceptions to the general rule, though it may be hoped that their number will increase as time goes on and the effect of education becomes more generally felt. As might be expected, they are very weak in everything that relates to finance, and are consequently incapable of conducting any but the simplest commercial transactions. The position of a merchant, or even of a large storekeeper, is quite beyond them, for they would not be able to calculate profit or loss.

As mechanics they do not succeed very well, though an individual here and there shows an aptitude for working with iron. No one among them has invented or improved a useful implement since white men first became acquainted with them. And the strong desire of the greater number is to live as closely like their ancestors as the altered circumstances of the country will permit, to make use of a few of the white man's simplest conveniences and of his protection against their enemies, but to avoid his habits and shut out his ideas. Compared with Europeans, their adults are commonly children in imagination and in simplicity of belief, though not unfrequently one may have the mental faculties of a full-grown man.

As this is a matter of great importance for the future of South Africa, the opinions of the most competent men in the country, as supplied by them in evidence before a committee of the parliament of the Cape Colony appointed in 1908 to investigate the question of the education of these people, are given here : *

Dr. Thomas Muir, C.M.G., LL.D., M.A., F.R.S., Superintendent General of Education in the Cape Colony.

Question. You could not express an opinion as to the theory which is often advanced about the inability of the native † to go beyond a certain stage in mental development ?

---

* *Report of the Select Committee of the House of Assembly of the Cape Colony on Native Education.* Demi octavo, 709 pages, Capetown, 1908.

† By *native* an individual belonging to the Bantu family is meant throughout these inquiries.

Answer. Yes, I think I have had evidence of that. With boys who become pupil teachers it is noticeable that when they reach a certain stage of development their mental growth rather comes to a stop.

Q. Does that apply to girls also, or not so much ?

A. I have not the same experience in reference to girls, but if you compare a white boy and a coloured boy from the ages of twelve onwards you will find that a white boy goes on growing mentally, whereas a coloured boy seems for a while almost to come to a stop. I believe there are physiological reasons given for it.

Q. You believe that is really the essential thing in the physiology of the native ?

A. Yes. There are exceptions.

Q. Do you think the evidence on this point has advanced so far that we can say it is established ?

A. If you take the case of writers on Kafirs, you will find it considered an established thing. I only notice it in connection with examinations that there is not that rapid growth over twelve years of age that you have in the early stages, and more especially in reference to anything requiring initiative—that a native has very considerable imitative powers, and those parts of his education that call upon the imitative powers make progress, whereas those requiring real fresh thought or initiative do not.

Q. You see no reason for thinking that the system of education is in any way responsible for that, or for thinking that some improved system might remedy that defect ?

A. I do not think so ; I think it is inherent.

Q. Going back to the opinion you expressed about the mental growth seeming to stop at the age of twelve years or thereabouts, do not you think it is to a very large extent a question of their home life and environment ? Up to that age their education would consist very largely of all matters with which they have come into contact in their home life ?

A. Yes.

Q. When they begin to get beyond a certain stage they go away from questions that they come into daily contact with, and come, as it were, into a foreign world, so that they are there, as it were, with nothing that they can lay hold of. It is all a new field to them, and therefore they are at a disadvantage to European children, to whom that is not a foreign field, owing to their contact with it in their life ?

A. I think that is quite possibly a partial explanation ; and then it must be remembered, too, that the African who has settled in the United States of America does not show that to any appreciable extent. Whether it is the difference in the surroundings in America during these generations or not I do not know, but there are plenty of American negroes who progress in mental development steadily as a European does.

Q. Do you hold there is an inherent lack of capacity beyond that ?

A. Not an inherent lack of capacity ; I would not say that, because one cannot very well judge of that. When I said there was something inherent, I meant it was more of a physiological reason than anything else.

Q. Do you mean unalterable ?

A. It would be alterable under different circumstances— different surroundings.

Q. But then would it not be incorrect to say it is physiological ?

A. I do think it is connected with physiology.

Q. I did not quite understand you to say that they stopped in mental development, but that they were slower ?

A. Yes, that is the point : they do not stop ; they simply do not progress at the same rate.

Q. The evidence you have given as regards America would rather militate against the statement that it is dependent upon physiology, would it not ?

A. Not quite ; because I do not say if they were brought under totally different circumstances their bodily habits and so forth would not be affected to the same extent.

Q. So that if we continued our present line of education, especially in parts of the country where the natives do not continue to live in their kraals, it is quite possible that in a century or two that race might not be so backward ?

A. That is exactly what I wanted to suggest by bringing forward the case of America.

Mr. Newton Ogilvie Thompson, Resident Magistrate of Kentani.

Q. With regard to the actual teaching and the effects of education, we have had evidence on the question whether the native mind is specially limited and unable to progress beyond a certain age. Have you any opinion upon that question ?

A. Well, I had the idea myself that the native mind was not limited, and with proper teaching would be able to go on, and on making inquiries they lead to the confirming of those conclusions. I have often heard the question discussed, but I have never heard it conclusively proved to my own mind.

Q. That is just your opinion ?

A. I still think so.

Q. And it is an opinion which is not only a theoretical opinion, but which squares with your experience of the natives ?

A. Yes, as far as my experience goes.

Q. But is it not a fact that with many of the educated natives there is a want of initiative ?

A. Yes, there is, but then of course one cannot expect that it should be otherwise. If one looks back and counts time, as you would do in the history of a people, I do not think we can expect any very great results at this day.

Q. You ascribe that defect to the fact that the native starts a long way behind ?

A. Yes.

Q. Do you think the environment of native home life has a considerable effect in that way ?

A. Oh yes, I do think so. Now, for instance, I think the rising generation and the next generation will lend itself more to education than the past generation, because of the parents in their home life, and the conversation and everything, and the education that they are getting will help matters.

The reverend William Charles Willoughby, Principal of the Tigerkloof Native Institution in Betshuanaland.

Q. You say that the Betshuana are lacking in intelligence as compared with English people. Do you think their civilisation has advanced far enough for us to be able to say that it is a radical defect or is it perhaps curable ?

A. I do not think I quite said he was lacking in intelligence : I should say his intelligence is of a different order. In many cases he excels us ; in many others—and those we are apt to think most essential to civilisation—he is most distinctly our inferior.

Q. Is that due to something ineradicable, or is it due to circumstances and surroundings ?

A. I dare say environment has a very great deal to do with it. It is very difficult to say physiologically how much hereditary influence and environment respectively have to do with the peculiar twist of a native's mind, or of a tribal mind. I dare say if one studied it carefully one would come to the conclusion that it is more generally due to environment than anything else. At the same time, the true capacity of the native mind is just now occupying the attention of a good many scientists. Statistics are being prepared in the Soudan, and especially the age at which the fissures of the skull close up is being studied, and we may have some light on that in a few years : I do not think we have any now.

Q. As far as you have seen, does the native in the district with which you are acquainted stop developing in a remarkable way at a particular standard ?

A. Yes ; natives in school, you mean.

Q. Does he develop faster in the lower than in the higher standards ?

A. Yes. I should say upon the whole the advantage is in favour of the lower standards. . . . It is a fact that the lower standards are easier in proportion than the higher standards. I have not seen anything along the lines of your question to lead me to the conclusion that there is any cessation of growth in the native mind. I have watched it, as the question is being asked in a good many quarters, and I have seen nothing at all that enables me to make any dogmatic statement on the subject.

Q. Have you found them (big boys) quick to learn in these directions (building with stone, bricks, and wood) ?

A. Of course there is considerable difference between them, as between all other boys. They are very quick to learn to a certain point, but when you get to the point needing more care and exactness a certain number are almost unable to appreciate it. About one-third seem to stick at that point. They can all do a certain amount of rough work, and then in anything a little finer you lose about a third of your class as far as advance is concerned.

Mr. James M‘Laren, M.A., Inspector of Schools in Fingoland.

Q. Do you think that the natives show a capacity for advance at the higher standards as much as at the lower standards ?

A. A capacity to benefit by instruction in the higher standard ?

Q. Yes.

A. I have been very much surprised to find how many of my teachers were able successfully to teach Standard V and Standard VI, and how well the pupils, on the whole, were able to meet the requirements of these standards.

Q. It is sometimes said that the native mind is incapable of advancing beyond a certain very limited standard. Have you found that so in your experience ?

A. No, not in the elementary school course, up to Standards IV, V, and VI, but I find that the children of the second and third generations of civilised natives are considerably more intelligent than the children of the raw natives ; that is to say, the children of men who have been brought up in an atmosphere of civilisation have much less difficulty in appreciating the work of the higher standards than the ordinary native child has.

Q. From that you would be inclined to infer that any want of intelligence there may be is due to environment and circumstances quite as much as to any physiological difference ?

A. I think it is due to heredity—that the child of the civilised parent actually acquires at birth some slightly improved mental capacity.

Q. It is heredity which only depends on the parents ; it does not depend on the race ? If the parents are civilised the children will be born civilised, so to speak, according to your theory ?

A. If the parents have been educated I think the children are born with a rather better intelligence.

Q. So even if you take a raw native, if you educate him his child will have a better chance ?

A. Certainly.

Reverend James Henderson, Principal of Lovedale Missionary Institution.

Q. Have you seen any reasons to suppose that the native is constitutionally incapable of developing beyond a certain stage, as is sometimes stated ?

A. There is, I think, a great deal of what one might call " cant " written and spoken about natives, and one of the doctrines of this cant is about native boys and girls at the age of puberty. At the age of puberty, on general grounds, we should expect that pupils would show increased mental activity and greater capacity for responsibility. Now, it is impressed upon us, as if it were an established fact, that the average native at that age goes back —that that is the critical period of his development, and in the great majority of cases it is the point at which his advancement ceases. Now, this degeneration at puberty is not an established fact. Experienced men I have come in contact with do not recognise that there is this break in development at puberty. What does happen is that in European and native schools—I am not aware in native schools any more than in European schools— there is a small percentage of pupils who from that date do not make normal progress, but I do not think the number is any greater in native schools than in European schools. What does occur in native schools is this. When pupils—and this is a much more serious problem in the newer fields than in districts of the country which have long been under the influence of civilisation —begin school-work at the age of ten or twelve they are liable to come to a dead-stop later on, and probably more so beginning later on ; it is more marked with pupils beginning, in many cases, after puberty. In these new fields we have grown-up men and grown-up women coming for education. Now, what has repeatedly been the experience in regard to these is that when education has been pressed with these people grown beyond mere boyhood or girlhood there has been a liability to mental trouble ; the pupils become saturated and incapable of mental effort, and in some cases a form of temporary insanity appears.

Reverend Canon Cyril Edwin Earl Bulwer, Principal of an Institution for training Native Teachers.

Q. Is there steady progression, or do they come to a point at which they seem to stop ?

A. Individual children ?

Q. Take the average.

A. It depends so much on the age. We find the young boys especially are very sharp, and go right to the end of their course without a break. If a boy comes at the age of nineteen or twenty in Standard IV or V it is very rarely that he will get beyond the first year. They seem above that age to have come to the end of their intelligence, and get very dull and heavy. We always encourage the younger boys ; they seem much more successful.

Q. What is your explanation of this ?

A. It is hard to say. I think it is a natural dullness which comes to this kind of native character. They begin to think about different things more than their school work, I think. You know what they are. They think of getting married, and leaving school, and so on, and it seems to affect their brains in some way, so that they get very dull and heavy at that age.

Reverend David Duncan Stormont, M.A., B.D., L.C.P., LL.B.,
Principal of Blythswood Missionary Institution.

Q. Is there anything in the theory that a native child seems to lack capacity for development when he gets to a certain age, say about twelve or thirteen years ?

A. Well, I examined that question practically many years ago, and I have not examined it recently. I find your age is wrong, but there is something in the theory. The stop in development comes later. It may come at seventeen ; it may not come till twenty-one. But, speaking from my enquiries made practically a dozen years ago, I should say when the sexual feelings begin to be very powerful, especially in the men, the moral and intellectual faculties degenerate, as we would say, and if the native gives way to the sexual feeling he is gone.

Q. That would apply also to a European ?

A. The surroundings of the European save him from collapse, and then I believe the sexual feelings, physiologically and psychologically, come later in Europeans than natives.

Q. You mean the native gives way altogether ?

A. And they come earlier with him.

Reverend Richard Fraser Hornabrook, Governor of the Wesleyan
Training Institution, Healdtown.

Q. Have you, in your experience, seen any reason to suppose that the native mind is incapable of advancing beyond a certain stage ?

A. No.

Q. You think the opinions which are sometimes expressed with considerable confidence on this subject are not warranted, according to your experience ?

A. I think not.

*Dr. Neil Macvicar, M.D., D.P.H., Medical Officer to the Lovedale
Mission.*

I should like to say that my experience does not in any way
support the theory put forward by some writers that the native's
mental development is arrested at puberty. I know that at
Blantyre many of the highest boys in school were from seventeen
to twenty years of age. And the same is the case in Lovedale.
There are some native boys, it is true, who fall into evil habits
at that age, and so injure their health. But this happens even
at the best English public schools. Such boys in an institution
like Lovedale are a trifling minority, perhaps five per cent of the
whole number of big boys. The others, the great majority that
is, at the age in question throw themselves into their lessons with
increasing earnestness. At a later age, about twenty-three or
twenty-four, I have noticed some native young men suffering from
mental exhaustion. I attribute this partly to the long number
of years some of these boys had been at school, but chiefly to the
fact that they were carrying on all their studies in a difficult foreign
language which even the most intelligent among them understood
very imperfectly.

*Reverend William Allerton Goodwin, who had been nine years
Principal of the Training College, Umtata, and five years
doing similar work in Natal.**

Q. Will you tell us how the Zulus compare in intelligence with
the Europeans; taking the raw native at the age of twelve and edu-
cating him properly, how would he compare with the white boy?

A. In subjects like arithmetic, reading, or writing, he will be
equal to any European, but if you put him to anything that requires
abstract thought, he is absolutely beaten. Furthermore, he has
no power, as far as I have known, of initiative. He is a splendid
pupil, but is no good at all as a master.

Q. He does not realise, for instance, in argument, that he has
been beaten?

A. I do not think so, in abstract matters. He is a past master
in arguing concrete facts, but he has no idea of abstract reasoning.

* This gentleman's evidence was not given before the Committee on Native
Education, but on the 12th of May 1904 before the Native Affairs Commission.
See *Report of the South African Native Affairs Commission* 1903–5, *with Minutes
of Evidence.* Five Foolscap folio volumes, together 3979 pages, Capetown,
1904–5.

CHAPTER XII.

Specimens of Bantu Folklore.

Among a people without knowledge of letters, legends and traditional tales occupy the same place as books with Europeans, and thus form perfect guides as to their powers of expression and thought. The greater part of the folklore of the Bantu was neither of a moral character, nor did it convey any useful lessons. The actors in it were animals that spoke as human beings, persons who were bewitched and compelled to appear as beasts, individuals with magical powers, fantastic creatures, imps, cannibals, young chiefs, girls, &c., &c. There was nothing that led to elevation of thought in any of these stories, though one idea, that might easily be mistaken on a first view for a good one, pervaded many of them : the superiority of brain power to physical force. But on looking deeper it is found that brain power was always interpreted as low cunning ; it was wiliness, not greatness of mind, that won in the strife against the stupid strong. Such an idea was in full accord with the life of the people, and it may have been on this account that the tales were so much liked.

Where force is directed as mercilessly as it is among brutes, the weak were compelled to scheme against the strong. The little boy, who lived in constant terror of larger ones, the woman, who was the drudge, not the companion, of her husband, the petty clan, that felt the exactions of a powerful neighbour, all were obliged to scheme, and no people on earth ever learned the art of deception more thoroughly than the Bantu. Thus these traditional tales, many of which must have been those of the original or parent band of the Bantu, as they are found with little variation among tribes using dialects that are not understood by each other, gave a large amount of pleasure to those among whom they passed current, though to European minds there is nothing amusing or interesting in them. Readers must bear in mind that full-grown men and women who have never been under European influence really believe many of the actors in these tales to have had an existence, so that they are not merely stories to amuse children.

The tales which follow, with one exception, were collected by the author of this volume from individuals of the Xosa tribe nearly forty years ago, and were revised for him by ancient dames to whose ears they were familiar. They are not indeed exact literal translations, but they are as nearly such as they could be made while at the same time they were put into English that can be easily read and understood. The original of the first one is given, as a specimen of the language.

Intsomi ka Nyokalide.

Yati intombi etile yemka kowayo yaya emzini ka Nyokalide. Ifikileke kulomzi ka Nyokalide yahlala kona, kodwa engeko umninimzi. Kupela umntu okoyo kulomzi ingunina.

Kute ngokuhlwa unina ka Nyokalide wanika lentombi amazimba ukuba iwasile. Emveni kokuba iwasilile yenze isonka. Sati sakuvutwa wati unina ka Nyokalide " yisa esisonka kulandlu ka Nyokalide."

Kuteke kusemzuzwana lentombi ingene kulendlu wafika umninimzi. Yaza yamnika isonka namasi, wadlake. Bate bakugqiba ukudla baya kulala. Kute kusasa wemka u-Nyokalide, ngokuba emini uhlala endle.

Ite ke nentombi yaya kokwayo. Waza unina ka Nyokalide wayivatisa ngengubo ezinhle kakulu. Emveni kokuba ivatisiwe ite yabiza izembe yaya kuteza inkuni. Ifikileke endle ayigaulanga zinkuni, kodwa isuke yalilahla izembe yazimela yaya kowayo.

Kute kwakuba ifikele kowayo udade wayo ubuzile ukuba ezingubo zinhle uzitatepina. Udade wayo uyixelele, yati ke " nam ndiyaya kulomzi."

Uteke udade wayo, " ngaupulapule ndikuxelele isimo salomzi." Kodwake udade wake ukupendula, " andifuni ukuba undixelele nto ngokuba nawe akuzange uyalwe mhla wemka."

Uhambile ke kwaoko waya kufika ngokuhlwa kulomzi ka Nyokalide.   Kuteke isahleli unina ka Nyokalide wayinika amazimba ukuba mayiwasile yenze isonka.   Site sakuvutwa wasisa endlwini ka Nyokalide.   Kute ngokuhlwa wafika umninimzi, yaza intombi leyo yamnika isonka namasi.   Kute bakugqiba ukudla baya kulala, kute kwakusa wemka u-Nyokalide.

Yaza intombi yaya kokwayo.   Unina ubuye wayivatisa lentombi kwanjengokuba ebeyivatisile enkulu.   Iteke yaboleka izembe yayakuteza inkuni.   Kantike yenza iqinga lokuzimela.

Kuteke namhla indoda yabaputuma abafazi bayo, yayakufika xa litshonayo ilanga ebukweni.

Bamkwelela indlu umyeni yokulala.   Kute xa adlayo abantu balomzi bafumbela izitungu zenca watshiswake nendlu umyeni. Wafake ngokunjalo.

STORY OF LONG SNAKE.

Once upon a time a certain girl left her father's place and went to the village of Long Snake. Having arrived at the village of Long Snake she remained there, but the owner of the place was absent. The only person present was the mother of the owner of the place.

Then in the evening the mother of Long Snake gave that girl some millet that she might grind it. After it was ground she made bread. When it was ready the mother of Long Snake said, "bring this bread into the house of Long Snake."

A short time after that girl went into the house the owner of the place arrived. Then she gave him bread and fermented milk,[*] and he ate. When they had finished the food they went to sleep. Then early in the morning Long Snake went away, because in the daytime he lived in the open country.

The girl went to the house of the parents of Long Snake. The mother of Long Snake clothed her with a very beautiful robe. After she was dressed she called for an axe and went to cut firewood. Having arrived in the open fields she did not cut the firewood, but she threw away the axe and ran to her father's place.

After she arrived at her father's place her sister enquired where she had got that beautiful robe. Her sister told her, and she said "I am also going to that village."

* It is not in accordance with Bantu custom for a girl to serve out amasi or fermented milk to a man, but in this case the circumstances were exceptional.

Her sister said, " just listen to what I tell you of the custom of that village." But her sister said in reply, " I do not want you to tell me anything because you yourself were not warned before you went."

Then at once she journeyed and went until she arrived in the evening at the village of Long Snake. When she sat down the mother of Long Snake gave her millet that she might grind it and make bread. When it was ready she took it into the house of Long Snake. Then in the evening the owner of the place arrived, and the girl gave him bread and fermented milk. When they had finished eating they went to sleep, and early in the morning Long Snake went away.

Then the girl went to the house of Long Snake's parents. His mother also clothed that girl in the same manner as she had dressed the elder one. Then she borrowed an axe and went to cut fuel. In doing so she made an excuse to run away.

On this day however the man went after his wives, and arrived at his father-in-law's place as the sun was setting.

They went out of the house that the bridegroom might sleep in it. While he was eating, the people of the village piled up bundles of grass, and the bridegroom was burned in the house. In this manner he died.*

STORY OF LITTLE RED STOMACH.

There was, in times of old, a certain boy by the name of Little Red Stomach. On a certain day that boy went to till the ground. While he was hoeing he became thirsty, and accordingly he went to drink water out of a pool.

Then suddenly his mother came, and said, " do not drink that water, because you do not know the owner." He said, " I will drink." Then his mother answered and said, " you will be killed by the owner of the water." " I do not care, because I will die alone," he replied. Then his mother said, " I will go away when you drink this water."

Accordingly his mother went away. Little Red Stomach then drank. " Why is it that you have drunk my water ? Did

* This story is one of a class very common among the Bantu, in which a man assumes the outward form of an inferior animal, and while partaking partly of the nature of the beast, still retains the faculties of a human being. Usually the man has been bewitched by an enemy, and is ultimately restored to his human form by a kiss from a devoted maiden.

not your mother tell you not to drink of this water ? " said the owner of the water. " I will kill you, because your mother told you that you were not to drink this water," said the owner of the water often.

After this, Little Red Stomach closed his eyes, and was swallowed by this beast. The beast then went away to the place where it lived, in a large pool of water. When the beast reached that pool of water, he remained outside of it, on account of the weight of his stomach.

When this beast had thus remained a while, a large frog came up out of the pool, and said, " did I not tell you that you must not swallow that person who drinks your water, because you will die and then we shall have no one to take charge of us ? " After this frog had so spoken, he sank down there, in the pool of water.

About sunset that animal said, " I have a stomach ache." As it was so, all the animals collected at that pool of water, and he said, " pay attention to the thing that I tell you." Then all the little animals that lived in that pool of water paid attention. He said, " all of you are left here without a friend." Then accordingly they all went away to their friends.

After they had all gone away, this animal died. But Little Red Stomach was still alive in the stomach of the animal. He pulled out his knife, and cut open the stomach of the animal, and came out. When he had come out, he went home.

Having arrived at his home, he said to his mother, " did I not tell you that I would not die ? " " I did not know, my child, that you had a plan of safety," said his mother. Then Little Red Stomach remained at the village of his parents.

Story of Five Heads.

Once upon a time two girls were going to dig wild carrots. One of them said, " I will not go." " Why is it that you are unwilling to go with me ? " asked the other girl. She answered, " I want to be married to Five Heads." " As you say so, tell father," said the other girl.

Then, after that, she went away to the village of Five Heads. When she arrived, the man in charge of that village inquired where she came from ? Accordingly she told where she came from, and what her business was at the village of Five Heads. Then a little old woman went away and told the mother of Five

Heads what was said by the strange girl. When the mother of Five Heads heard that, she went and brought the girl into his house. She took a mat and spread it on the ground. Then, in the evening, Five Heads arrived from hunting.

She asked that person, "where do you come from?" His mother said, "ask of her." Accordingly Five Heads asked her where she came from. The girl told him why she had come to his village. Then said Five Heads, "before I marry you, I will send a message to your father, that you may know you are allowed by him to be married to me." That girl agreed that the message should be sent. An answer was returned that they had no objection, if the girl loved that person.

Accordingly Five Heads said to the people of his village, "are you willing that I should marry this girl?" They were willing. He gave for her twenty head of cattle. The ikazi was sent to the father of the girl. The parents were very well satisfied. There came a message to the effect that they were very well satisfied. After a while that girl was made the great wife at the village of Five Heads.*

A MORE COMPLETE STORY OF FIVE HEADS.

There was once a man living in a certain place, who had two daughters big enough to be married. One day the man went over the river to another village, which was the residence of a great chief. The people asked him to tell them the news. He replied that there was no news in the place he came from. Then the man inquired about the news of their place. They said the news of their place was that the chief wanted a wife.

The man went home and said to his two daughters: "which of you wishes to be the wife of a chief?" The eldest replied: "I wish to be the wife of a chief, my father." The name of that girl was Mpunzikazi. The man said: "at that village which I visited, the chief wishes for a wife; you, my daughter, shall go."

The man called all his friends, and assembled a large company to go with his daughter to the village of the chief. But the girl

* Five Heads, literally Heads Five,—Makanda Mahlanu—appears frequently in stories told by the coast tribes. He was a chief who was bewitched and obliged to assume the form of a monstrous snake with five heads, but was restored to his proper appearance by the devotion of a girl.

would not consent that those people should go with her. She said : "I will go alone to be the wife of the chief." Her father replied : "how can you, my daughter, say such a thing ? Is it not so that when a girl goes to present herself to her husband she should be accompanied by others ? Be not foolish, my daughter." The girl still said : "I will go alone to be the wife of the chief." Then the man allowed his daughter to do as she chose.

She went alone, no bridal party accompanying her, to present herself at the village of the chief who wanted a wife. As Mpunzikazi was in the path, she met a mouse. The mouse said : "shall I show you the way ? " The girl replied : "just get away from before my eyes." The mouse answered : "if you do like this, you will not succeed." Then she met a frog. The frog said : "shall I show you the way ? " Mpunzikazi replied : "you are not worthy to speak to me, as I am to be the wife of a chief." The frog said : "go on then ; you will see afterwards what will happen." When the girl got tired, she sat down under a tree to rest. A boy who was herding goats in that place came to her, he being very hungry. The boy said : "where are you going to, my eldest sister ? " Mpunzikazi replied in an angry voice : "who are you that you should speak to me ? Just get away from before me." The boy said : "I am very hungry ; will you not give me of your food ? " She answered : "get away quickly." The boy said : "you will not return if you do this."

She went on her way again, and met with an old woman sitting by a big stone. The old woman said : "I will give you advice. You will meet with trees that will laugh at you : you must not laugh in return. You will see a bag of thick milk : you must not eat of it. You will meet a man whose head is under his arm : you must not take water from him." Mpunzikazi answered : "you ugly thing ! who are you that you should advise me ? " The old woman continued in saying those words.

The girl went on. She came to a place where were many trees. The trees laughed at her, and she laughed at them in return. She saw a bag of thick milk, and she ate of it. She met a man carrying his head under his arm, and she took water to drink from him.

She came to the river of the village of the chief. She saw a girl there dipping water from the river. The girl said : "where are you going to, my sister ? " Mpunzikazi replied : " who are you that you should call me sister ? I am going to be the wife of a chief." The girl drawing water was the sister of the chief. She said : " wait, I will give you advice. Do not enter the village by this side." Mpunzikazi did not stand to listen, but just went on.

She reached the village of the chief. The people asked her where she came from and what she wanted. She answered : " I have come to be the wife of the chief." They said : " who ever saw a girl go without a retinue to be a bride ? " They said also : " the chief is not at home ; you must prepare food for him, that when he comes in the evening he may eat." They gave her millet to grind. She ground it very coarse, and made bread that was not nice to eat.

In the evening she heard the sound of a great wind. That wind was the coming of the chief. He was a big snake with five heads and large eyes. Mpunzikazi was very much frightened when she saw him. He sat down before the door and told her to bring his food. She brought the bread which she had made. Makanda Mahlanu (Five Heads) was not satisfied with that bread. He said : " you shall not be my wife," and he struck her with his tail and killed her.

Afterwards the sister of Mpunzikazi said to her father : " I also wish to be the wife of a chief." Her father replied : " it is well, my daughter ; it is right that you should wish to be a bride." The man called all his friends, and a great retinue prepared to accompany the bride. The name of the girl was Mpunzanyana.

In the way they met a mouse. The mouse said : " shall I show you the road ? " Mpunzanyana replied : " if you will show me the way I shall be glad." Then the mouse pointed out the way. She came into a valley, where she saw an old woman standing by a tree. The old woman said to her : " you will come to a place where two paths branch off. You must take the little one, because if you take the big one you will not be fortunate." Mpunzanyana replied : " I will take the little path, my mother." She went on. Afterwards she met a coney. The coney said : " the village of the chief is close by. You will meet a girl by the river : you must speak nicely to her. They will give you millet to grind : you must grind it well. When you see your husband, you must not be afraid." She said : " I will do as you say, coney."

In the river she met the chief's sister carrying water. The chief's sister said : "where are you going to ?" Mpunzanyana replied : "this is the end of my journey." The chief's sister said : "what is the object of your coming to this place ?" Mpunzanyana replied : "I am with a bridal party." The chief's sister said : "that is right, but will you not be afraid when you see your husband ?" Mpunzanyana answered : "I will not be afraid."

The chief's sister pointed out the hut in which she should stay. Food was given to the bridal party. The mother of the chief took millet and gave to the bride, saying : "you must prepare food for your husband. He is not here now, but he will come in the evening."

In the evening she heard a very strong wind, which made the hut shake. The poles fell, but she did not run out. Then she saw the chief Makanda Mahlanu coming. He asked for food. Mpunzanyana took the bread which she had made, and gave it to him. He was very much pleased with that food, and said : "you shall be my wife." He gave her very many ornaments.

Afterwards Makanda Mahlanu became a man, and Mpunzanyana continued to be the wife he loved best.

STORY OF THE BIRD THAT MADE MILK.

There was once upon a time a poor man living with his wife in a certain village. They had three children, two boys and a girl. They used to get milk from a tree. That milk of the tree was got by squeezing. It was not nice as that of a cow, and the people that drank it were always thin. For this reason those people were never glossy like those who are fat.

One day the woman went to make a garden. She began by cutting the grass with a pick,* and then putting it in a big heap. That was the work of the first day, and when the sun was just

---

* *Ikuba*, a pick or hoe. Before the advent of Europeans, the largest implement that was made was this instrument for breaking up the ground. It was of nearly the same shape as a European hoe ; but in place of having an eye, into which a handle could be fastened, it was made with a top like a spike, which was driven into the large knob of a long and heavy club. It was at best a clumsy tool. Among the Bantu of the coast the work of cultivating the ground fell entirely upon the women in olden times. The introduction of the plough has caused a change in this respect, but to the present day the planting and weeding are performed by females.

about to set she went home. When she left, there came a bird to that place, and sang this song :

> " Weeds of this garden,
> Weeds of this garden,
> Spring up, spring up.
> Work of this garden,
> Work of this garden,
> Disappear, disappear."

It was so. The next morning, when she returned and saw that, she wondered greatly. She again put it in order on that day, and put some sticks in the ground to mark the place. In the evening she went home and told that she had found the grass which she had cut growing just as it was before. Her husband said : " how can such a thing be ? You were lazy and didn't work, and now tell me this falsehood. Just get out of my sight, or I'll beat you."

On the third day she went to her work with a sorrowful heart, remembering the words spoken by her husband. She reached the place, and found the grass growing as before. The sticks that she stuck in the ground were there still, but she saw nothing else of her labour. She wondered greatly. She said in her heart, " I will not cut the grass off again, I will just hoe the ground as it is." She commenced. Then the bird came and perched on one of the sticks. It sang :

> " Citi, citi,
> Who is this cultivating the ground of my father ?
> Pick, come off,
> Pick handle, break,
> Sods, go back to your places."

All these things happened. The woman went home and told her husband what the bird had done. Then they made a plan. They dug a deep hole in the ground, and covered it with sticks and grass. The man hid himself in the hole, and put up one of his hands. The woman commenced to hoe the ground again. Then the bird came and perched on the hand of the man, and sang :

> " This is the ground of my father.
> Who are you, digging my father's ground ?
> Pick, break into small pieces ;
> Sods, return to your places."

It was so. Then the man tightened his fingers and caught the bird. He came up out of the place of concealment. He said to the bird : " as for you who spoil the work of this garden, you will not see the sun any more. With this sharp stone I will cut off your head."

Then the bird said to him : " I am not a bird that should be killed. I am a bird that can make milk." The man said : " make some then." The bird made some milk in his hand. The man tasted it. It was very nice milk. The man said : " make some more milk, my bird." The bird did so. The man sent his wife for a milk basket.* When she brought it, the bird filled it with milk. The man was very much pleased. He said : " this pretty bird of mine is better than a cow."

He took it home and put it in a jar. After that he used to rise even in the night and tell the bird to make milk for him. Only he and his wife drank of it. The children continued to drink of the milk of the tree. The names of the children were Gingci, the first-born son ; Lonci, his brother ; and Dumangashe, his sister. That man then got very fat indeed, so that his skin became shining.

The girl said to her brother Gingci : " why does father get fat and we remain so thin ? " He replied : " I do not know, perhaps he eats in the night." They made a plan to watch. They saw him rise in the middle of the night. He went to the big jar and took an eating mat off it. He said : " make milk, my bird." He drank much. Again he said : " make milk, my bird," and again he drank till he was very full. Then he lay down and went to sleep.

The next day the woman went to work in her garden, and the man went to visit his friend. The children remained at home, but not in the house. Their father fastened the door of the house and told them not to enter it on any account till his return. Gingci said : " to-day we will drink of the milk that makes father fat and shining ; we will not drink of the milk of the euphorbia to-day." The girl said : " as for me, I also say let us drink of father's milk to-day."

They entered the house. Gingci removed the eating mat from the jar, and said to the bird : " my father's bird, make milk for me." The bird said : " if I am your father's bird, put me by

---

* *Itunga,* a basket used to milk the cows in. It is woven so nicely as to be watertight.

the fireplace, and I will make milk." The boy did so. The bird made just a little milk. The boy drank, and said: "my father's bird, make more milk." The bird said: "if I am your father's bird, put me by the door, then I will make milk." The boy did this. Then the bird made just a little milk, which the boy drank. The girl said: "my father's bird, make milk for me." The bird said: "if I am your father's bird, just put me in the sunlight, and I will make milk." The girl did so. Then the bird made a jar full of milk. After that the bird sang:

> " The father of Dumangashe came, he came,
> He came unnoticed by me.
> He found great fault with me.
> The little fellows have met together,
> Gingci, the brother of Lonci.
> The Umkomanzi cannot be crossed,
> It is crossed by swallows
> Whose wings are long."

When it finished its song it lifted up its wings and flew away. But the girl was still drinking milk. The children called it, and said: "return, bird of our father," but it did not come back. They said: "we shall be killed to-day." They followed the bird. They came to a tree where there were many birds. The boy caught one, and said to it: "my father's bird, make milk." It bled. They cried: "this is not our father's bird." This bird bled very much; the blood ran like a river. Then the boy released it, and it flew away. The children were seized with fear. They said to themselves: "if our father finds us, he will kill us to-day."

In the evening the man came home. When he was yet far off, he saw that the door had been opened. He said: "I did not shut the door that way." He called his children, but only Lonci replied. He asked for the others. Lonci said: "I went to the river to drink; when I returned they were gone." He searched for them, and found the girl under the ashes and the boy behind a stone. He inquired at once about his bird. They were compelled to tell the truth concerning it.

Then the man took a riem and hung those two children on a tree that projected over the river. He went away, leaving them there. Their mother besought their father, saying that they should be released, but the man refused. After he was gone, the boy tried to escape. He climbed up the riem and held on to the tree; then he went up and loosened the riem that was tied to his sister. After that they climbed up the tree, and then went away from their home. They slept three times on the road.*

They came to a big rock. The boy said : " we have no father and no mother ; rock, be our house." The rock opened, and they went inside. After that they lived there in that place. They obtained food by hunting animals,—they were hunted by the boy.

When they were already in that place a long time, the girl grew to be big. There were no people in that place. A bird came one day with a child, and left it there by their house. The bird said : " so have I done to all the people."

After that a crocodile † came to that place. The boy was just going to kill it, but it said : " I am a crocodile, I am not to be killed, I am your friend." Then the boy went with the crocodile to the house of the crocodile, in a deep hole under the water. The crocodile had many cattle and much millet. He gave the boy ten cows and ten baskets of millet. The crocodile said to the boy " you must send your sister for the purpose of being married to me."

The boy made a fold to keep his cattle in ; his sister made a garden and planted millet. The crocodile sent more cattle. The boy made a very big fold, and it was full of cattle. At this time there came a bird. The bird said : " your sister has performed the custom, and as for you, you should enter manhood (*i.e.* be circumcised)." The crocodile gave one of his daughters to be the wife of the young man.

The young woman went to the village of the crocodile, she went to be a bride. They said to her : " whom do you choose to be your husband ? " The girl replied : " I choose crocodile." Her husband said to her : " lick my face." She did so. The crocodile cast off its skin, and arose a man of great strength and fine appearance. He said : " the enemies of my father's house did that ; you, my wife, are stronger than they."

* This is equivalent to saying that they travelled for three days.

† There are no crocodiles in the rivers south of Natal, but the reptile and its habits are well known to the people from traditions. It is not unlikely that their belief in a water-spirit which has power to charm people and entice them into rivers to their destruction may have originated in the fact of their having migrated from a country where these destructive animals were common, as the spirit and the reptile have the same name. In this story it is seemingly a crocodile that appears, but very shortly we learn that it is really a man who has been bewitched and forced to assume that form.

After this there was a great famine, and the mother of those people came to their village. She did not recognize her children, but they knew her and gave her food. She went away, and then their father came. He did not recognize them either, but they knew him. They asked him what he wanted. He told them that his village was devoured by famine. They gave him food, and he went away. He returned again. The young man said : " you thought we would die when you hung us in the tree." He was astonished, and said : " are you indeed my child ? "

Crocodile then gave them (the parents) three baskets of corn, and told them to go and build on the mountains. He (the man) did so and died there on the mountains.

SEROLONG VERSION OF THE STORY OF THE BIRD THAT MADE MILK.*

It is said that there was once a great town in a certain place, which had many people living in it. They lived upon grain only. One year there was a great famine. There was in that town a poor man, by name Masilo, and his wife. One day they went to dig in their garden, and they continued digging the whole day long.† In the evening, when the digging companies returned home, they returned also. Then there came a bird and stood upon the house which was beside the garden, and began to whistle, and said : " Masilo's cultivated ground, mix together." The ground did as the bird said. After that was done the bird went away.

In the morning, when Masilo and his wife went to the garden, they were in doubt, and said : " is it really the place we were digging yesterday ? " They saw it was the place by the people working on each side. The people began to laugh at them, and mocked them, and said : " it is because you are very lazy."

* This story was written down for me in English by an educated grandson of the late chief Moroko of the Baseleka branch of the Barolong tribe. He informed me that he had often heard it told when he was a little boy, and that he believed every Morolong woman knew it by heart. Here then is a story current among people of the interior, almost identical in its principal features with one current among the coast tribes, though these two branches of the Bantu family cannot understand each other, and migrated from different parts of the continent. It must therefore be of great age.

† Among the interior tribes poor men frequently assist their wives to break up rough ground for gardens.

They continued to dig again that day, and in the evening they went home with the others. Then the bird came and did the same thing. When they went back next morning, they found their ground altogether undug. Then they believed that they were bewitched by some others.

They continued digging that day again. But in the evening when the companies returned, Masilo said to his wife : " go home ; I will stay behind to watch and find the thing which eats our work." Then he went and laid himself down by the head of the garden, under the same house which the bird used always to stand upon. While he was thinking, the bird came. It was a very beautiful bird. He was looking at it and admiring it, when it began to speak.

It said : "Masilo's cultivated ground, mix together." Then he caught it, and said : " ah ! is it you who eat the work of our hands ? " He took out his knife from the sheath, and was going to cut the head of the bird off. Then the bird said : " please don't kill me, and I will make some milk for you to eat." Masilo answered : " you must bring back the work of my hands first." The bird said : " Masilo's cultivated ground appear," and it appeared. Then Masilo said : " make the milk now," and, behold, it immediately made thick milk, which Masilo began to eat. When he was satisfied, he took the bird home. As he approached his house, he put the bird in his bag.

When he entered his house, he said to his wife : " wash all the largest beer-pots which are in the house," but his wife was angry on account of her hunger, and she answered : " what have you to put in such large pots ? " Masilo said to her : " just hear me, and do as I command you, then you will see," When she was ready with the pots, Masilo took his bird out of his bag, and said : " make milk for my children to eat." Then the bird filled all the beer-pots with milk. They commenced to eat, and when they were finished, Masilo charged his children, saying : " beware that you do not tell anybody of this, not one of your companions." They swore by him that they would not tell anybody.

Masilo and his family then lived upon this bird. The people were surprised when they saw him and his family. They said : " why are the people at Masilo's house so fat ? He is so poor, but now since his garden has appeared he and his children are so fat ! '' They tried to watch and to see what he was eating. but they never could find out at all.

One morning Masilo and his wife went to work in their garden, and about the middle of the same day the children of that town met together to play. They met just before Masilo's house. While they were playing, the others said to Masilo's children : '' why are you so fat while we remain so thin ? '' They answered : '' are we then fat ? We thought we were thin, just as you are.'' They would not tell them the cause. The others continued to press them, and said : '' we won't tell anybody.'' Then the children of Masilo said : '' there is a bird in our father's house which makes milk.'' The others said : '' please show us the bird.''

They went into the house and took it out of the secret place where their father had placed it. They ordered it as their father used to order it, and it made milk, which their companions drank, for they were very hungry. After drinking they said : '' let it dance for us,'' and they loosened it from the place where it was tied. The bird began to dance in the house, but one said : '' this place is too confined,'' so they took it outside of the house. While they were enjoying themselves and laughing, the bird flew away, leaving them in great dismay.

Masilo's children said : '' our father will this day kill us, therefore we must go after the bird.'' So they followed it, and continued going after it the whole day long, for when they were at a distance it would sit still for a little while, and when they approached it would fly away. When the digging companies returned from digging the people of that town cried for their children, for they did not know what had become of them. But when Masilo went into the house and could not find his bird, he knew where the children were, but he did not tell any of their parents. He was very sorry for his bird, for he knew that he had lost his food.

When evening set in, the children determined to return to their homes, but there came a storm of rain with heavy thunder, and they were very much afraid. Among them was a brave boy, named Mosemanyanamatong, who encouraged them, and said : '' do not be afraid ; I can command a house to build itself.'' They said : '' please command it.'' He said : '' house, appear,'' and it appeared, and also wood for fire. Then the children entered the house and made a large fire, and began to roast some wild roots which they dug out of the ground.

While they were roasting the roots and were merry, there came
a big cannibal, and they heard his voice saying : "Mosemanyanamatong, give me some of the wild roots you have." They were
afraid, and the brave boy said to the girls and to the other boys :
"give me some of yours." They gave to him, and he threw the
roots outside. While the cannibal was still eating, they went out
and fled. He finished eating the roots, and then pursued them.
When he approached they scattered some more roots upon the
ground, and while he was picking them up and eating, they
fled.

At length they came among mountains, where trees were
growing. The girls were already very tired, so they all climbed
up a tall tree. The cannibal came there, and tried to cut the tree
down with his sharp and long nail. Then the brave boy said to
the girls : "while I am singing you must continue saying : tree
be strong, tree be strong." He sang this song :

> "It is foolish,
> It is foolish to be a traveller,
> And to go on a journey
> With the blood of girls upon one !
> While we were roasting wild roots
> A great darkness fell upon us.
> It was not darkness,
> It was awful gloom ! "

While he was singing, there came a great bird and hovered over
them, and said : "hold fast to me." The children held fast to
the bird, and it flew away with them and took them to their own
town. It was midnight when it arrived there, and it sat down
at the gate of Mosemanyanamatong's mother's house. In the
morning, when that woman came out of her house, she took ashes
and cast upon the bird, for she said : "this bird knows where
our children are." At midday the bird sent word to the chief,
saying : "command all your people to spread mats in all the
paths." The chief commanded them to do so. Then the bird
brought all the children out, and the people were greatly delighted.

STORY OF THE GIRL WHO DISREGARDED THE CUSTOM OF NTONJANE.

There was once a chief's daughter who had reached the age
when it was necessary for her to observe the *ntonjane*. She was

therefore placed in a hut, in which she was to remain during the period of the ceremony. One day her companions persuaded her to go and bathe in a stream near at hand, though this was against the custom of the ntonjane. When they came out of the water, they saw a snake with black blotches, called the Isinyobo-lokondwana, near their clothes. They were very much afraid and did not know what to do at first. But by-and-by one of them commenced to sing these words :

> " Sinyobolokondwana,
> Sinyobolokondwana,
> Bring my mantle ! "

The snake replied :

> " Take it,
> And pass on."

The companions of the chief's daughter, one after the other, asked the snake for their mantles in this manner, and obtained permission to take them. Last of all was the chief's daughter. But instead of speaking to the snake respectfully as the others had done, she said mockingly, " Ngcingcingci, ngcingcingci." * So the snake became very angry, and bit her, when she immediately became of the same hideous colour as it was. Her companions were so frightened that they left her and ran away home. They put another girl in the hut, and pretended that she was the chief's daughter. The girl, thus left alone, went to a forest close by, and climbed up a tree to hide herself.

About this time the chief was killing an ox on account of his daughter, and so he sent a young man to the forest to get pieces of wood to peg out the skin. The young man was cutting sticks, when he heard some one crying : " Man cutting sticks, tell my father and my mother that the sinyobolokondwana bit me." He heard this repeated twice, and, without looking to see what was crying, he ran home and told the chief. Two young men were then sent back with him to see what it was, one of these happening to be the girl's brother. These two were told to hide themselves and listen while the other cut the sticks. They did so, and heard the voice crying as before. Then the brother of the girl knew the voice of his sister, and they all went to the tree where she was, and took her home with them.

* Words without meaning, but used to express contempt, being merely a repetition of the sound ngci.

The chief was very much surprised to see his daughter in that state, and was so angry with her companions for taking her to the river, and then for substituting another girl so as to deceive him, that he caused them all to be killed.

Then he sent some of his men with forty cattle to take his daughter to a distant country, where she was to remain far away from him. They did as they were told, and built huts in that place to live in. After they had been there a long time, they found that the cows which the chief sent with them were giving more milk than they could consume, so they poured what was left in a hole in the ground. To their amazement the milk rose, and rose, and rose, higher and still higher, till at last it stood up out of the ground like a great overhanging rock. They called the girl to see this wonderful thing that was happening. In her curiosity she went close to the precipice, when it fell down on her, and, as the milk ran over her, all her ugly blotched skin disappeared, and she was again beautiful as at first.

Soon afterwards a young chief who was passing by saw the girl, and fell in love with her. He thought she was the daughter of one of the men who were there to protect her, but when he made inquiries they told him she was the daughter of their chief. Then he went to her father, and some of the men went also to tell how the milk had cured the girl. The young chief had very many cattle, which he offered to her father. So the old chief agreed to let him marry the girl, and she became his great wife, and was loved by him very dearly.*

STORY OF SIMBUKUMBUKWANA.

There was a man whose wife had no children, so that he was much dissatisfied. At last he went to a wise woman (igqirakazi) and asked her to help him in this matter. She said : " you must bring me a fat calf that I may get its tallow to use with my medicine " (or charms—the Xosa word is imifizi).† The man

---

* A large proportion of Bantu tales have a similar termination with many English ones : the heroine gets married to a prince. These show that a desire for worldly rank is as great in the one people as in the other. Most Bantu tales are destitute of moral teaching from our point of view. What recommendation, for instance, has the girl in this story to the favour of the young chief ?

† Charms and medicines for the cure of diseases are classed together by the Bantu. Some of the women as well as of the men have really a wonderful

went home and selected a calf without horns or tail, which he took to the wise woman. She said : " your wife will have a son who will have no arms and no legs, as this calf has no horns and no tail." She told him further that he was not to inform any one of this.

The man returned to his home and told his friends what was to happen. Not long after this his wife bore a child, but it was a daughter and had arms and legs. The man would not own that child, he said it was not his. He beat his wife, and commanded her to take the child away and leave it to perish. Then he went to the wise woman and told her what had taken place. The wise woman said : " it was because you did not obey my command about keeping this matter to yourself, but your wife will yet have a son without arms and without legs." It was so. His wife bore another child, which was a boy without arms and without legs, therefore he was called Simbukumbukwana. He began to speak on the day of his birth. During this time the girl that was first born was growing up in the valley where her mother left her ; she lived in a hole in an antheap, and ate honey, and nongwes, and gum.

One day the mother of Simbukumbukwana went to work in her garden, and left the boy at home with the door fastened. While she was away the girl came ; she stood at a distance, and said : " where are the people ? " There came a voice from inside which said : " here am I." She said : " who are you ? " The voice replied : " I am Simbukumbukwana." She said : " open for me." He answered : " how can I open ? I have no legs and no arms." She said : " my mother's Simbukumbukwana, have legs and arms." (Simbukumbukwana sikama, yiba nemilenze nemikono).

Then legs and arms came on the boy, and he arose and opened for his sister. She went in and swept the floor ; then she took millet and ground it and made bread. She told her brother when his parents asked him who did these things to say that he did them himself, and if they should ask him to do them again to reply : " I have done it already." Then she said : " my mother's

knowledge of the properties of herbs and roots. They are acquainted with various vegetable poisons and with their antidotes, and not unfrequently make use of them. The Bantu are perfect slaves to charms, and hardly ever undertake any matter of importance without using them.

Simbukumbukwana, sink legs and sink arms." (Simbukumbukwana sikama, tshona milenze, tshona mikono). Then his legs
and arms shrank up, and his sister went away.

After a time his father and his mother came home; they went
in and saw the clean floor and bread ready for eating. They were
surprised, and said to Simbukumbukwana: "who did this?"
He replied: "I did." They said: "do so again that we may
see you." He answered: "I have done it already."

The next day the woman went again to work in her garden,
but the man hid himself to watch what would happen. After a
time the sister of Simbukumbukwana came and said: "where
are the people?" (Exactly the same conversation as before).
She went in and began to smear the floor; water was wanting,
so she sent Simbukumbukwana to the river for some. His joy
in walking was great, so that he did not stop at the river, but put
the pot down there and continued to go forward. The girl thought
he ought not to be so long absent, for the river was close by, so she
went to look for him. She saw him walking up a hill far away,
and she called to him to return. He would not. Then she sang:
"Simbukumbukwana sikama, tshona milenze, tshona mikono,"
and immediately his legs and arms shrank up. Then she was
going away, but her father came out and caught her; he kissed
her, and said she must remain with him.

Her mother was coming home, when she saw something moving
on the hillside. She went to see what it was, and found her son.
She said: "how did you come here?" He replied: "I came
by myself." She said: "let me see you go farther." He
answered: "I have done it already." Then she put him on her
back and went home. She found her daughter there, and her
husband much pleased. The girl said: Simbukumbukwana
sikama, yiba nemilenze nemikono, and legs and arms came on
him.

One day his sister and some other girls went to get red clay,
and he followed them. When they looked behind they saw him,
and his sister got angry. She said to him: "what do you want
here?" He replied: "I am going for red clay for my mother."
His sister compelled him to sit down; but as soon as they went
on, he followed; then his sister beat him, and left him in the path.

After that there was a heavy storm of rain, but none fell where
the little boy was. When the rain was over, the other girls said

to the one who had beaten her brother : " let us go and look after the little boy." They went and saw he was quite dry. He called to his sister : " you have beaten me," but she asked him to forgive her. Then he said : " I want my father's house to be here," and immediately it came. He said : " I want the fire of my father to be here," and there was a fire. He said to them : " now go in ; although you have beaten me, there is a house and fire for you." He said afterwards : " I want the cattle of my father to be here," and at once they were all there. That was a nice place, so they remained there ever after.

Story of Sikulume.

There was once in a certain village an old man who was very poor. He had no children, and only a few cattle. One day, when the sky was clear and the sun was bright, he sat down by the cattle-fold. While he was sitting there, he noticed some birds close by which were singing very joyfully. He listened for a while, and then he stood up to observe them better. They were very beautiful to look upon, and they sang differently from other birds. They had all long tails and topknots on their heads. Then the old man went to the chief and told him what he had seen. The chief said : " how many were they ? " The old man replied : " there were seven."

The chief said : " you have acted wisely in coming to tell me ; you shall have seven of the fattest of my cows. I have lost seven sons in battle, and these beautiful birds shall be in the place of my seven sons. You must not sleep to-night, you must watch them, and to-morrow I will choose seven boys to catch them. Do not let them out of your sight by any means." In the morning the chief ordered all the boys of the village to be assembled at the cattle-fold, when he spoke to them of the birds. He said : " I will choose six of you, and set my son who is dumb over you, that will make seven in all. You must catch those birds. Wherever they go you must follow, and you must not see my face again without them." He gave them weapons, and instructed them that if any one opposed them they were to fight till the last of them died.

The boys set off to follow those beautiful birds. They chased them for several days, till at last the birds were exhausted, when each of the boys caught one. At the place where they caught the birds they remained that night. On the morning of the next day they set out on their return home. That evening they came to a hut in which they saw a fire burning, but no one was there. They went in, and lay down to sleep. In the middle of the night one of those boys was awake. He heard some one saying : "there is nice meat here ; I will begin with this one, and take this one next, and that one after, and the one with small feet the last." The one with the small feet was the son of the chief. His name was Sikulume, for he had never been able to speak till he caught the bird. Then he began to talk at once.

After saying those words the voice was still. Then the boy awakened his companions, and told them what he had heard. They said : "you have been dreaming ; there is no one here ; how can such a thing be ? " He replied : " I did not dream ; I spoke the truth." Then they made a plan that one should remain awake, and if anything happened, he should pinch the one next him, and that one should pinch the next, till all were awake.

After a while the boy who was listening heard some one come in quietly. That was a cannibal. He said the same words again, and then went out for the purpose of calling his friends to come to the feast. The boy awakened his companions according to the plan agreed upon, so that they all heard what was said. Therefore, as soon as the cannibal went out, they arose and fled from that place. The cannibal came back with his friends, and when the others saw there was no one in the hut, they killed and ate him.

As they were going on, Sikulume saw that he had left his bird behind. He stood, and said : " I must return for my bird, my beautiful bird with the long tail and topknot on its head. My father commanded that I must not see his face again unless I bring the bird." The boys said : "take one of ours. Why should you go where cannibals are ? " He replied : " I must have the one that is my own." He stuck his assagai in the ground, and told them to look at it. He said : " if it stands still, you will know I am safe ; if it shakes, you will know I am running ; if it falls down, you will know I am dead." Then he left them to return to the hut of the cannibals.

On the way he saw an old woman sitting by a big stone. She said : " where are you going to ? " He told her he was going for his bird. The old woman gave him some fat, and said : " if the cannibals pursue you, put some of this on a stone." He came to the hut and got his bird. The cannibals were sitting outside, a little way back. They had just finished eating the owner of the hut. When Sikulume came out with his bird they saw him and ran after him. They were close to him, when he took some of the fat and threw it on a stone. The cannibals came to the stone, and began to fight with each other. One said : " the stone is mine." Another said : " it is mine." One of them swallowed the stone. When the others saw that, they killed him and ate him.

Then they pursued again after Sikulume. They came close to him again, when he threw the remainder of the fat on another stone. The cannibals fought for this also. One swallowed it, and was killed by the others. They followed still, and Sikulume was almost in their hands, when he threw off his mantle. The mantle commenced to run another way, and the cannibals ran after it. It was so long before they caught it that the young chief had time to reach his companions.

They all went on their way, but very soon they saw the cannibals coming after them. Then they observed a little man sitting by a big stone. He said to them : " I can turn this stone into a hut." They replied : " do so." He turned the stone into a hut, and they all went inside, the little man with them. They played the iceya there. The cannibals came to the place and smelt. They thought the hut was still a stone, for it looked like a stone to them. They began to bite it, and bit till all their teeth were broken, when they returned to their own village.

After this, the boys and the little man came out. The boys went on. When they reached their own home they saw no people, till at length an old woman crept out of a heap of ashes. She was very much frightened, and said to them : " I thought there were no people left." Sikulume said : " where is my father ? " She replied : " all the people have been swallowed by the inabulele " (a fabulous monster). He said : " where did it go to ? " The old woman replied : " it went to the river."

So those boys went to the river, and Sikulume said to them : " I will go into the water, and take an assagai with me. If the water moves much, you will know I am in the stomach of the inabulele ; if the water is red, you will know I have killed it."

Then he threw himself into the water and went down. The inabulele swallowed him without tearing him or hurting him. He saw his father and his mother and many people and cattle. Then he took his assagai and pierced the inabulele from inside. The water moved till the inabulele was dead, then it became red. When the young men saw that, they cut a big hole in the side of the inabulele, and all the people and the cattle were delivered.

One day Sikulume said to another boy : " I am going to the doctor's ; tell my sister to cook food for me, nice food that I may eat." This was done. He said to his sister : " bring me of the skin of the inabulele which I killed, to make a mantle." She called her companions, and they went to the side of the river. She sang this song :

> " Inabulele,
> Inabulele,
> I am sent for you,
> By Sikulume,
> Inabulele."

The body of the inabulele then came out. She cut two little pieces of the skin for sandals, and a large piece to make a mantle for her brother.

When he was a young man, Sikulume said to his friends : " I am going to marry the daughter of Mangangezulu." They replied : " you must not go there, for at Mangangezulu's you will be killed." He said : " I will go." Then he called those young men who were his chosen friends to accompany him. On the way they came to a place where the grass was long. A mouse came out of the grass, and asked Sikulume where he was going to. He replied : " I am going to the place of Mangangezulu." The mouse sang this song :

> " Turn back, turn back, Sikulume,
> No one ever leaves the place of Mangangezulu.
> Turn back, turn back, O chief."

Sikulume replied : " I shall not turn back." The mouse then said : " As it is so, you must kill me and throw my skin up in the air." He did so. The skin said : " you must not enter by the front of the village ; you must not eat off a new mat ; you must not sleep in a hut which has nothing in it." They arrived at the village of Mangangezulu. They entered it from the wrong side,

,so that all the people said : " why is this ? " They replied : " it is our custom." Food was brought to them on a new mat, but they said : " it is our custom to eat off old mats only." An empty hut was given to them to sleep in, but they said : " it is our custom only to sleep in a hut that has things in it."

The next day the chief said to Sikulume and his companions : " you must go and tend the cattle." They went. A storm of rain fell, when Sikulume spread out his mantle and it became a hut as hard as stone, into which they all went. In the evening they returned with the cattle. The daughter of Mangangezulu came to them. Her mother pressed her foot in the footprint of Sikulume, and he became an eland. The girl loved the young chief very much. When she saw he was turned into an eland, she made a great fire and drove him into it. Then he was burned, and became a little coal. She took the coal out and put it in a pot of water, when it became a young man again.

Afterwards they left that place. The girl took with her an egg, a milksack, a pot, and a smooth stone. The father of the girl pursued them. The girl threw down the egg, and it became a mist. Her father wandered about in the mist a long time, till at length it cleared away. Then he pursued again. She threw down the milksack, and it became a sheet of water. Her father tried to get rid of the water by dipping it up with a calabash, but he could not succeed, so he was compelled to wait till it dried up. He followed still. The girl threw down the pot, and it became thick darkness. He waited a long time till light came again, when he followed them. He could travel very quickly. He came close to them, and then the girl threw down the smooth stone. It became a rock, a big rock with one side steep like a wall. He could not climb up that rock, and so he returned to his own village.

Then Sikulume went home with his wife. He said to the people : " this is the daughter of Mangangezulu. You advised me not to go there, lest I should be killed. Here is my wife." After that he became a great chief. All the people said : " There is no chief that can do such things as Sikulume."

STORY OF THE CANNIBAL'S WONDERFUL BIRD.

A number of girls once went away from their homes early in the morning for the purpose of getting red clay. Among them was the daughter of a chief, a very pretty girl. After they had collected the red clay, they were about to return home, when one of them proposed that they should bathe in a large pool of water that was there. To this they all agreed, and so they went into the water and played about in it for a long time. At last they dressed themselves again, and set out for home ; but when they had gone some distance, the chief's daughter noticed that she had forgotten one of her ornaments, which she had taken off when they went to bathe. So she asked one of the girls to return with her to get it. The girl refused. Then she asked another girl, and another, but one and all refused to go back. She was thus obliged to return to the water alone, while the other girls went home.

On arriving at the pool, a big ugly cannibal with only one leg came up to her, caught her, and put her in his bag. She was so frightened that she lay quite still. The cannibal then took her round to the different villages and made her sing for him. He called her his bird. When he came to a village he asked for meat, and when it was given to him he said : "Sing, my bird." But he would never open the bag so that any one could see what sort of a bird he had.

When the girls reached home, they told the chief that his daughter had reached the age of ntonjane, and they selected one of themselves and shut her up in a hut. The chief believed that story, and so he killed a large ox and said the people must eat. That day they ate fat beef, and were very merry. The boys took meat, and went away from the village to eat it. The cannibal, who did not know that the girl's father was chief at this place, came there just at this time. He said to the boys if they would give him meat he would make his bird sing for them. So they gave him meat, and he said : "Sing, my bird." The girl's brother was among those boys, and he thought the bird sang like his sister, but he was afraid to ask the cannibal to let him see. He advised the cannibal to go to the village where the men were, and told him there was plenty of meat that day.

The cannibal went to the village and made his bird sing. The chief wanted very much to see the bird, but the cannibal would not open the bag. The chief offered him an ox for the bird, but the cannibal declined the offer. Then the chief made a plan. He asked the cannibal to go for some water, and said he would give him plenty of beef when he returned. The cannibal said he would go if they would promise not to open his bag while he was away. They all promised not to touch the bag. They gave the cannibal a leaky pot to carry the water in, so that he was gone a long time. As soon as he was out of sight the chief opened the bag and took his daughter out. At first he could not believe it was his daughter, for he thought she was observing ntonjane. But when he knew how those other girls had deceived him he said they must all die, and so they were killed. Then he put snakes and toads in the bag, and tied it up again.

When the cannibal came back he complained of the leaky pot, but they gave him plenty of meat to satisfy him, so he picked up his bag and went away. He did not know what had happened while he was absent. When he came near his own house he called to his wife : " Make ready to cook." He sent and called all the other cannibals to come to a feast, and they came expecting to get something nice. He let them wait a little to get very hungry. Then he opened his bag and thought to take the girl out, but found only snakes and toads in it. The other cannibals were so angry when they saw this, that they killed him and made their feast of him.

Story of the Cannibal Mother and her Children.

There was once a man and a woman who had two children, a son and a daughter. These children lived with their grandfather. Their mother was a cannibal, but not their father. One day they said to their grandfather : " We have been long with you, we should like very much to go and see our parents." Their grandfather said : " Ho ! will you be able to come back ? Don't you know your mother is a cannibal ? " After a time he consented. He said : " You must leave at such a time that you may arrive there in the evening, so that your mother may not see you, only your father." The boy's name was Hinazinci. He said : " Let us go now, my sister."

They started when the sun was set. When they arrived at their father's house, they listened outside to find out if their mother was there. They heard the voice of their father only, so they called to him. He came out, and when he saw them he was sorry, and said : " Why did you come here, my dear children ? Don't you know your mother is a cannibal ? " Just then they heard a noise like thunder. It was the coming of their mother. Their father took them inside and put them in a dark place, where he covered them with skins.

Their mother came in with an animal and the body of a man. She stood and said: "There's something here. What a nice smell it has!" She said to her husband: "Sohinazinci, what have you to tell me about this nice smell that is in my house? You must tell me whether my children are here." Her husband answered: "What are you dreaming about? They are not here." She went to the place where they were, and took the skins away. When she saw them, she said: "My children, I am very sorry that you are here, because I must eat people." She cooked for them and their father the animal she had brought home, and the dead man for herself. After they had eaten, she went out.

Then their father said to them: "When we lie down to sleep, you must be watchful. You will hear a dancing of people, a roaring of wild beasts, and a barking of dogs in your mother's stomach. You will know by that she is sleeping, and you must then rise at once and get away." They lay down, but the man and the children only pretended to go to sleep. They were listening for those sounds. After a while they heard a dancing of people, a roaring of wild beasts, and a barking of dogs. Then their father shook them, and said they must go while their mother was sleeping. They bade their father farewell, and crept out quietly, that their mother might not hear them.

At midnight the woman woke up, and when she found the children were gone, she took her axe and went after them. They were already a long way on their journey, when they saw her following them. They were so tired that they could not run. When she was near them, the boy said to the girl: "My sister, sing your melodious song, perhaps when she hears it she will be sorry and go home without hurting us." The girl replied: "She will not listen to anything now, because she is in want of meat." Hinazinci said: "Try, my sister, it may not be in vain." So she sang her song, and when the cannibal heard it, she ran backwards to her own house.

There she fell upon her husband, and wanted to cut him with the axe. Her husband caught hold of her arm, and said: "Ho! if you put me to death, who will be your husband?" Then she left him and ran after the children again. They were near their grandfather's village, and were very weak when their mother overtook them. The girl fell down, and the cannibal caught her and swallowed her. She then ran after the boy. He fell just at the entrance of his grandfather's house, and she picked him up and swallowed him also. She found only the old people and the children of the village at home, all the others being at work in the gardens. She ate all the people that were at home and also all the cattle that were there.

Towards evening she left to go to her own home. There was a deep valley in the way, and when she came to it she saw a very beautiful bird. As she approached it the bird got bigger and bigger, until at last when she was very near it, it was as big as a hut. Then the bird began to sing its song. The woman looked at it, and said to herself: "I shall take this bird home to my husband." The bird continued its song, and sang:

> "I am a pretty bird of the valley,
> You come to make a disturbance at my place."

The bird came slowly towards her, still singing its song. When they met, the bird took the axe from the woman, and still sang the same song. The cannibal began to be afraid. She said to the bird: "Give me my axe, I do not wish for your flesh now." The bird tore one of her arms off. She said: "I am going away now, give me what is mine." The bird would not listen to her, but continued its song.

She said again: "Give me my axe and let me go. My husband at home is very hungry, I want to go and cook food for him." The bird sang more loudly than before, and tore one of her legs off. She fell down and cried out: "My master, I am in a hurry to go home. I do not want anything that is yours." She saw that she was in danger. She said to the bird again: "You don't know how to sing your song nicely, let me go, and I will sing it for you." The bird opened its wings wide, and tore open her stomach. Many people came forth, most of them alive, but some were dead. As they came forth she caught them and swallowed them again. The two children were alive, and they ran away. At last the woman died.

There was great rejoicing in that country. The children returned to their grandfather, and the people came there and made them rulers of the country, because it was through them the cannibal was brought to death. The girl was afterwards married to a son of the great chief, and Hinazinci had for his wife the daughter of that great one.

Story of Mbulukazi.

There was once a man who had two wives, one of whom had no children, and for that reason she was not loved by her husband. Her name was Numbakatali. The other wife had one daughter who was very black, and several children besides, but they were all crows. The one who had no offspring was very downcast on that account, and used to go about weeping all day. Once when she was working in her garden, and crying as usual, two doves came and perched near her. One of them said to the other: "Dove, ask the woman why she is crying." So the dove questioned her. She replied: "It is because I have no children, and my husband does not love me. His other wife's children are crows, which come and eat my corn, and she laughs at me." The dove said: "Go home, and get two earthen jars, and bring them here."

Numbakatali went and got them. Then the doves scratched her knees till the blood flowed, and put the blood in the jars. The woman gave the doves some corn to eat, after which she took the jars home to her hut, and set them carefully down in a corner. Every day the two doves came to be fed, and always told the woman to look at what was in the jars. At last, when she looked one day, she saw two children, one a boy, the other a girl, and both very handsome. She was very much delighted at the sight, but she did not tell any one.

When the children grew a little she made a snug place for them in the hut, where they were to sit all day, because she did not wish them to be seen. Always before she went to her work she charged them not to go out, and as her husband never came to see her, no one knew of the existence of these children except herself and a servant girl. But one day, when they were big, she went out, and after she was away some time, the boy said to his sister: "Come, let us help our mother by bringing water from the river."

So they went for water, but they had not reached the river when they met a company of young men with a chief's son, who was looking for a pretty girl to be his wife. The young chief was called Broad Breast, because his chest was very wide, and it was also made of a glittering metal that shone in the sun. These men asked for water to drink. The boy gave them all some water, but the young chief would only take it from the girl. He was very much smitten with her beauty, and watched her when she left, so as to find out where she lived. As soon as the young chief saw the hut that the girl went to, he returned home with his party and asked his father for cattle with which to marry her. The chief, who was very rich, gave his son many fine cattle, with which the young man went to the girl's mother's husband, and said : " I want to marry your daughter."

So the girl who was very black was told to come, but the young chief said : " That is not the one I want, the one I saw was lighter in colour and much prettier." The father replied : " I have no other children but crows." But Broad Breast persisted, so the man called his wives, both of whom denied that there was such a girl. However, the servant girl went to the man and privately told him the truth. In the evening he went to his wife's hut, and to his great joy saw the boy and his sister. He was so delighted that he remained there that night, and after talking it over with his wife, he agreed to let Broad Breast marry the girl.

In the morning a mat was spread in the yard, and the young chief was asked to sit down. The two children and the servant girl who told their father about them were also called, and they all sat down on the mat. The young chief, as soon as he saw her, said : " This is the girl I meant." He stayed part of the day, and then with his attendants went to his father for more cattle, which, having obtained, he brought them to the father of the girl.

The mother of the very black girl and the crows was very jealous when she saw such a fine young chief coming with so many cattle. She wanted her daughter to be the one that was to be married, so she dressed her as finely as she could, but she had no such pretty clothes as the other girl had. Her name was Mahlunguluza, for she was called after the crows, who were the other children of her mother. The pretty girl's name was Mbulukazi, which name was given to her because her handsome dress was made of the skin of a mbulu.

The mother of Mahlunguluza spoke to the young chief about her daughter, and so he married both the girls. Their father gave to each an ox, with which they went to their new home. Mbulukazi's ox was a pretty young one, and Mahlunguluza's ox was an old and poor one. When they arrived, Broad Breast gave to Mbulukazi a very nice new hut to live in, but to Mahlunguluza was given an old one quite in ruins. Then the very black one saw she was not loved, so she made a plan to kill her sister. One day she told her she heard their father was sick, and proposed that they should go to see him.

Mbulukazi consented, and as soon as they obtained leave from their husband they left. Their road led them along the edge of a cliff, below which was a deep pool of water. Mahlunguluza lay down on the rock, and said : " Come, see what is here in the water." Her sister lay down with her head over the edge of the rock, when Mahlunguluza jumped up quickly and pushed her over. Mbulukazi sank in the water and was drowned. Then the very black one returned home, and when her husband asked where Mbulukazi was, she said that she was still with their father.

The next day the ox of the drowned one came running to the village and walked about lowing for a while, after which it tore down the old ruined hut of Mahlunguluza with its horns. Its actions attracted the notice of the men, and they said : " Surely this ox means something, why is it doing this ? " Then it went to the deep pool of water, the men following it ; it smelt all over the rock, and then jumped into the water and brought out the body of Mbulukazi. The ox licked her till her life came back, and as soon as she was strong once more, she told what had happened.

They all went home rejoicing greatly, and informed Broad Breast. When the young chief heard the story he was angry with Mahlunguluza, and said to her : " Go home to your father, I never wanted you at all, it was your mother who brought you to me." So she had to go away in sorrow, and Mbulukazi remained the great wife of the chief.

CHAPTER XIII.

Specimens of Bantu Folklore (*continued*).

Story of Hlakanyana.*

Once upon a time there was a village with many women in it. All the women had children at the same time except the wife of the chief. The children grew, and again all the women gave birth to others. Only the wife of the chief had no child. Then the people said : " Let us kill an ox, perhaps the wife of the chief will then bear a child." While they were killing the ox, the woman heard a voice saying : " Bear me, mother, before the meat of my father is all finished." The woman did not pay any attention to that, thinking it was a ringing in her ears. The voice said again : " Bear me, mother, before the meat of my father is all finished."

The woman took a small piece of wood and cleaned her ears. She heard that voice again. Then she became excited. She said : " There is something in my ears ; I would like to know what it is. I have just now cleaned my ears." The voice said again : " Make haste and bear me, mother, before the meat of my father is all finished." The woman said : " What is this ? there was never a child that could speak before it was born." The voice said again : " Bear me, mother, as all my father's cattle are being finished, and I have not yet eaten anything of them." Then the woman gave birth to that child.

When she saw that to which she had given birth, she was very much astonished. It was a boy, but in size very little, and with a face that looked like that of an old person. He said to his mother : " Mother, give me a skin robe." His mother gave him a robe.

---

* I have greatly reduced this story in bulk by leaving out endless repetitions of exactly the same trick, but performed upon different individuals or animals. In all other respects it is complete. The word Hlakanyana means the little deceiver.

Then he went at once to the kraal where the ox was being killed. He asked for some meat, saying : " Father, father, give me a piece of meat."

The chief was astonished to hear this child calling him father. He said : " Oh, men, what thing is this that calls me father ? " So he continued with the skinning of the ox. But Hlakanyana continued also in asking meat from him. The chief became very angry, and pushed him, and said : " Get away from this place." Hlakanyana answered : " I am your child, give me meat." The chief took a little stick, and said : " If you trouble me again, I will strike you with this." Hlakanyana replied : " Give me meat first, and I will go away ; " but the chief would not answer, because he was very angry.

Hlakanyana continued asking. Then the chief threw him outside the kraal, and went on with his work. After a little time the child returned, still asking. So the chief said to the men that were with him : " What strange thing is this ? " The men replied : " We don't know him at all." The chief asked of them also advice, saying : " What shall I do ? " The men replied : " Give him a piece of meat." So the chief cut off a piece of meat and gave it to him. Hlakanyana ran to his mother and gave the meat to her to be cooked.

Then he returned to his father, and said again : " Father, give me some meat." The chief just took him and trampled upon him, and threw him outside of the kraal, thinking that he was dead. But he rose again and returned to his father, still saying : " Father, give me some meat." Then the chief thought to get rid of him by giving him meat again. The chief gave him a piece of liver. Hlakanyana threw it away. Fat was then given to him. He put it down on one side. Flesh was then given to him, and a bone with much marrow in it. Hlakanyana said : " I am a man to-day." He said : " This is the beginning of my father's cattle."

At this time the men were saying to each other : " Who will carry the meat to our huts ? " Hlakanyana answered :   I will do it." They said : " How can such a thing as you are carry meat ? " Hlakanyana replied : " I am stronger than you ; just see if you can lift this piece of meat." The men tried, but could not lift it. Then Hlakanyana took the piece of meat and carried it out of the kraal. The men said : " That will do now, carry our meat for us." Hlakanyana took the meat and carried it to the house of his mother. He took blood and put it on the eating mats at the houses of the men.

The men went to their houses, and said : " Where is our meat ? " They called Hlakanyana, and asked him what he had done with the meat. He replied : " Surely I put it here where the blood is. It must have been taken by the dogs. Surely the dogs have eaten it." Then those men beat the women and children because they did not watch that the dogs did not take the meat. As for Hlakanyana, he only delighted in this trick of his. He was more cunning than any of the old men.

Hlakanyana said to his mother that she must put the meat in the pot to cook, but that it must not be eaten before the next morning. It was done. In the night this cunning little fellow rose and went to the pot. His mother heard something at the pot, and struck with a stick. Hlakanyana cried like a dog. His mother said : " Surely a dog is eating the meat." Hlakanyana returned afterwards, and left nothing but bones in the pot. In the morning he asked his mother for meat. His mother went to the pot, and found nothing but bones. The cunning little fellow pretended to be astonished. He said : " Where is the meat, mother ? " His mother replied : " It has been eaten by a dog." Hlakanyana said : " As that is so, give me the bones, for you who are the wife of the chief will not eat from the same pot with a dog." His mother gave him the bones.

Hlakanyana went to sleep in the same house with the boys. The boys were unwilling to let him sleep with them. They laughed at him. They said : " Who are you ? You are just a child of a few days." Hlakanyana answered : " I am older than you." He slept there that night. When the boys were asleep, he got up and went to the cattle kraal. He killed two cows and ate all their insides. He took blood and smeared it on one of the boys who was sleeping. In the morning the men found those two dead cows. They said : " Who has done this thing ? " They found the boy with blood upon him, and killed him, because they thought he was the robber. Hlakanyana said within himself : " I told them that I was older than they are ; to-day it is seen who is a child and who is a man."

Another day the father of Hlakanyana killed an ox. The head was put in a pot to be cooked. Then Hlakanyana considered in his mind how he could get that meat. So he drove all the cattle of the village into a forest, a very thick forest, and tied them by their tails to the trees. After that he cut his arms and legs and breast with a sharp stone, and stood on a hill and cried out with a loud voice: "The enemy has taken our cattle; the cattle are being driven away. Come up, come up; there is an army going away with the cattle." The men ran quickly to him. He said to them: "Why are you eating meat while the enemy is going away with the cattle? I was fighting with them; just look at my body."

They saw he was covered with blood, and they believed it was as he said. So the men took their assagais and ran after the cattle, but they took the wrong way. Only one old man and Hlakanyana were left behind. Then Hlakanyana said to the old man: "I am very tired with fighting; just go to the river, grandfather, and get some water." The old man went, and as soon as he was alone Hlakanyana ate the meat which was in the pot. When the old man returned with the water he was very tired, for the river was far for an old man to go to, therefore he fell asleep. When he was sleeping, Hlakanyana took a bone and put it beside the old man. He also took some fat and put it on the mouth of the old man. Then he ran to the forest and loosened the cattle that were tied by the tails.

At this time the men were returning from seeking the enemy. Hlakanyana was coming also from the other side with the cattle. He shouted: "I have conquered the enemy." He also said: "The meat must be eaten now." When they opened the pot they found no meat. They found only dung, for Hlakanyana had filled the pot with dung. Then the men said: "Who has done this?" Hlakanyana answered: "It must be the old man who is sleeping there." They looked, and saw the bone by the side of the old man and the fat on his mouth. Then they said: "This is the thief." They were intending to kill the old man because he had stolen the meat of the chief.

When the children saw that the old man was to be killed, they said that he did not eat the meat of the chief. The men said: "We saw fat on his mouth and a bone beside him." The children replied: "He did not do it." The men said: "Tell us who did it." The children answered: "Hlakanyana ate the meat and put dung in the pot. We were concealed, and we saw him do it." Hlakanyana denied. He said : "Let me go and ask the women ; perhaps they saw who ate the meat of the chief." The men sent a young man with him to the women ; but when they were a short distance away, Hlakanyana escaped.

The chief sent an army after him. The army pursued, and saw Hlakanyana sitting by a bush. They ran to catch him. When they came to the bush, only an old woman was sitting there. They said to her : "Where is Hlakanyana ? " The old woman replied : "He just went across that river. See, you must make haste to follow him, for the river is rising." The army passed over the river quickly. Then that old woman turned into Hlakanyana again. He said in himself : "I will now go on a journey, for I am wiser than the counsellors of my father, I being older than they."

The little cunning fellow went to a village, where he saw an old woman sitting beside her house. He said to her : "Would you like to be made young, grandmother ? " The old woman replied : "Yes, my grandchild ; if you could make me young, I would be very glad." Hlakanyana said : "Take that pot, grandmother, and go for some water." The old woman replied : "I cannot walk." Hlakanyana said : "Just try, grandmother ; the river is close by, and perhaps you will be able to reach it " The old woman limped along and got the water.

Then Hlakanyana took a large pot and set it on the fire, and poured the water into it. He said to the old woman : "You must cook me a little first, and then I will cook you a little." The old woman agreed to that. Hlakanyana was the first to be put in the pot. When the water began to get hot, he said : "Take me out, grandmother ; I am in long enough." The old woman took him out, and went in the pot for her turn. Soon she said : "Take me out now, my grandchild ; I am in long enough." Hlakanyana replied : "Not yet, grandmother, it is not yet time." So the old woman died in the pot. Hlakanyana took all the bones of the old woman and threw them away. He left only the toes and the fingers. Then he took the clothing of the old woman and put it on.

The two sons of this old woman came from hunting. They went into the hut, and said : "Whose meat is this in the pot ? " Hlakanyana was lying down. He said in a voice like that of their mother : "It is yours, my sons." While they were eating, the younger one said : " Look at this, it is like the toe of mother." The elder one said : " How can you say such a thing ? Did not mother give us this meat to eat ? " Again the younger one said : " Look at this, it is like the finger of mother." Hlakanyana said : " You are speaking evil of me, my son."

Hlakanyana said in himself : " I shall be discovered ; it is time for me to flee." So he slipped quietly out of the house and went on his way. When he got a little way off, he called out : " You are eating your mother. Did any one ever see people eating their mother before ? " The two young men took their assagais and ran after him with their dogs. They came to the river ; it was full. The cunning fellow changed himself into a little round stone. One of the young men picked up this stone, saying : " If I could see him, I would just throw this stone at him." The young man threw the stone over the river, and it turned into Hlakanyana again. He just laughed at those young men. Hlakanyana went on his way. He was singing this song :

Ndahlangana Nonothloya.	I met with Nonothloya.
Sapekapekana,	We cooked each other,
Ndagwanya,	I was half cooked,
Wapekwa wada wavutwa.	She was well cooked.

Hlakanyana met a boy tending some goats. The boy had a digging-stick * with him. Hlakanyana proposed that they should pursue after birds, and the boy agreed. They pursued birds the whole day. In the evening, when the sun set, Hlakanyana said : " It is time now to roast our birds." The place was on the bank of a river.

Hlakanyana said : " We must go under the water and see who will come out last." They went under the water, and

* This and another part of the story of Hlakanyana show Hottentot influence upon a Xosa tale. I have been informed that Arab influence is even more perceptible in many of the tales common to the Bantu in the lake regions, though the groundwork of them all is unquestionably Bantu. William Koyi, a Christian Xosa who went with the first mission party from Lovedale to Lake Nyassa, and remained there with one short interval until his death, when on a visit to his early home informed me that after he had learned the language of the people there he was surprised to hear the stories given in this volume told nearly as he had heard them related by women of his family when he was a boy. He also found the imfumba the commonest game of the children in that part of Africa.

Hlakanyana came out last. The cunning fellow said : "Let us try again." The boy agreed to that. They went under the water. Hlakanyana came out quickly and ate all the birds. He left the heads only. Then he went under the water again. The boy came out while he was still under the water. When Hlakanyana came out he said : "Let us go now and eat our birds." They found all the birds eaten. Hlakanyana said : "You have eaten them, because you came out of the water first, and you have left me the heads only." The boy denied having done so, but Hlakanyana said : "You must pay for my birds with that digging-stick." The boy gave the digging-stick, and Hlakanyana went on his way.

He saw some people making pots of clay. He said to them : "Why do you not ask me to lend you this digging-stick, instead of digging with your hands ? " They said : "Lend it to us." Hlakanyana lent them the digging-stick. Just the first time they stuck it in the clay it broke. He said : "You have broken my digging-stick, the digging-stick that I received from my companion who ate my birds and left me with the heads." They gave him a pot.

Hlakanyana carried the pot till he came to some boys who were herding goats. He said to them : "You foolish boys, you only suck the goats, you don't milk them in any vessel ; why don't you ask me to lend you this pot ? " The boys said : "Lend it to us." Hlakanyana lent them the pot. While the boys were milking the pot broke. Hlakanyana said : "You have broken my pot, the pot that I received from the people who make pots, the people who broke my digging-stick, the digging-stick that I received from my companion, my companion who ate my birds and left me with the heads." The boys gave him a goat.

Hlakanyana came to the keepers of calves. He said to them "You foolish fellows, you only sit here and eat nothing. Why don't you ask me to let you suck this goat ? " The keepers of calves said : "Allow us to suck this goat." Hlakanyana gave the goat into their hands. While they were sucking, the goat died. Hlakanyana said : "You have killed my goat, the goat that I received from the boys that were tending goats, the boys that broke my pot, the pot that I received from the people who make pots, the people who broke my digging-stick, the digging-stick that I received from my companion, my companion who ate my birds and left me with the heads." They gave him a calf.

Hlakanyana came to the keepers of cows. He said to them : "You only suck the cows without letting the calf suck first. Why don't you ask me to lend you this calf, that the cows may be induced to give their milk freely ? " They said : "Lend us the calf." Hlakanyana permitted them to take the calf. While the calf was in their hands it died. Hlakanyana said : "You have killed my calf, the calf that I received from the keepers of calves, the keepers of calves that killed my goat, the goat that I received from the boys that were tending goats, the boys that broke my pot, the pot that I received from the people who make pots, the people who broke my digging-stick, the digging-stick that I received from my companion, my companion who ate my birds and left me with the heads." They gave him a cow.

Hlakanyana continued on his journey. He saw a young man going the same way. He said : "Let us be companions and travel together." The young man agreed to that. They came to a forest. Hlakanyana said : "This is the place for picking up keries." They picked up keries there. Then they reached another place, and Hlakanyana said : "This is the place for throwing away keries." They threw the keries away. Again they came to another place, and Hlakanyana said : "This is the place for throwing away spoons." The companion of Hlakanyana threw his spoon away, but the cunning little fellow only pretended to throw his away. In fact, he concealed his spoon. They went on.

They came to another place, and Hlakanyana said : "This is the place for throwing knives away." It happened again as with the spoons. Hlakanyana concealed his knife, when his companion threw his away. They came to a certain place, and Hlakanyana said : "This is the place for throwing away izilanda " (awls used to make holes in skins when they are sewed together, and also for taking thorns out of the bare feet and legs of pedestrians). His companion threw his isilanda away, but Hlakanyana kept his.

They went on and reached a place where they had to walk on thorns. Afterwards they looked at their feet, and saw many thorns in them. Hlakanyana said : "Let us sit down and take out the thorns." His companion replied : "I cannot do so, because I have no isilanda." Then Hlakanyana took the thorns out of his feet, and the other was obliged to walk lame.

They came to a village. The people said to them : "Tell us the news." Hlakanyana replied : "Just give us something to eat first, look at our stomachs and behold the pinchings of hunger." The people of that village brought meat. Hlakanyana said to his companion : "Now let us eat." The companion of Hlakanyana answered : "I have no knife." Hlakanyana said : "You are just a child ; I shall not lend you my knife." The people of that village brought millet and put it before them. Hlakanyana said to his companion : "Why do you not eat ? " He answered, "I have no spoon." Hlakanyana said : "You are just a child ; I shall not lend you my spoon." So Hlakanyana had all the meat and the millet to himself.

Hlakanyana met a girl herding some goats. He said : "Where are the boys of your village, that the goats are herded by a girl ? " The girl answered : "There are no boys in the village." He went to the father of the girl and said : "You must give me your daughter to be my concubine, and I will herd the goats." The father of the girl agreed to that. Then Hlakanyana went with the goats, and every day he killed one and ate it till all were done. He scratched his body with thorns. The father of the girl said : "Where are all the goats ? " Hlakanyana replied : "Can you not see how I have been fighting with the wild dogs ? The wild dogs have eaten the goats. As for me, I will stay here no longer." So he went on his way.

As he was going on, he saw a trap for catching birds. There were some birds in it. Hlakanyana took the birds out and ate them. The owners of the trap were cannibals. They saw the footprints of Hlakanyana, and said : "This is a little boy that is stealing our birds." They watched for him. Hlakanyana came again to the trap and saw a bird caught in it. He was just going to take the bird out when the cannibals caught him. They made a big fire and put a pot on for the purpose of cooking him. Hlakanyana saw two oxen. One was white, the other was red. He said to the cannibals : "You can take which one of these oxen you like instead of me." The cannibals said : "We will take the white one, because it is white (*i.e.* fat) inside also." Then Hlakanyana went away with the red ox. The cannibals ate the white ox, and then pursued after Hlakanyana. They came up to him by a big stone. He jumped on the stone, and sang this song :

Ndahamba ndayakuva indaba   I went to hear the news
Zemvula ku mankazana.   About rain from the girls.

The cannibals began to dance when they heard him sing. Then he ran away, and the stone continued to sing that song.

As he was journeying, Hlakanyana came to a place where some baboons were feasting. He asked them for some food. The baboons replied : " If you will go for some water for us, we will give you food." He agreed to that. When he returned with the water, the baboons refused to give him food. Then Hlakanyana shouted loudly and said : " At my village there is a marriage of baboons to-day." When the baboons heard that they fled, old and young. So Hlakanyana remained there, and ate all the food.

As he was going along, he saw a hyena building a house, having cooked some meat. Hlakanyana asked the hyena to give him some. The hyena said : " No, I will not give you any ; it is too little even for me." Hlakanyana said : " Will you not have me to assist in building ? " The hyena replied : " I would have you without delay if you are intending to help me." While they were fastening the thatch, Hlakanyana sewed the hair of the tail of the hyena fast. Then he took the pot and sat down. The hyena said : " Let that pot alone, Hlakanyana." He replied : " I am going to eat now." The hyena wanted to come down, but he found his tail was fast. Hlakanyana ate all the meat, and threw the bones at the hyena. The hyena tried to frighten him by saying there were many hyenas coming quickly to devour him. He just answered : " That is false ; " and continued eating till the meat was finished. Then he went on his way.

Hlakanyana came to a river. He saw an iguana that was playing on an ugwali (a simple musical instrument). Hlakanyana said to the iguana : " Lend me your ugwali for a little, please." The iguana said : " No, you will run away with my ugwali." Hlakanyana replied : " How can I run away with a thing that is not mine ? " So the iguana lent him the ugwali. When Hlakanyana saw that he could play upon the instrument nicely, he ran away with it. The iguana pursued him. Then Hlakanyana changed himself into a rush. The iguana took that rush and threw it across the river, saying : "If I could see him, I would throw him like this." Then the rush turned to be Hlakanyana again, and he went on his way playing on the ugwali of the iguana.

Hlakanyana came to the house of a leopardess. He proposed to take care of her children while the leopardess went to hunt animals. The leopardess agreed to that. There were four cubs. After the leopardess had gone to hunt, Hlakanyana took one of the cubs and ate it. At the time for giving food, the leopardess came back and said : "Give me my children that I may suckle them." Hlakanyana gave one. The mother said : "Give all at once." Hlakanyana replied : "It is better that one should drink and then another." The leopardess agreed to that. After three had drunk he gave the first one back the second time. Then the leopardess went to hunt again.

Hlakanyana took another of the cubs and ate it. He also made the door of the house very small so that the mother of the cubs could not come in, and then he made a little hole in the ground at the back so that he could go out. The next day the leopardess came to give her children suck. There were only two left now. Hlakanyana gave them both back the second time. After that the leopardess went away as before.

Hlakanyana ate another of the cubs, so that only one was left. When the mother came, he gave this one four times. When he gave it the last time the leopardess said : "Why does my child not drink to-day ? " It was already full, and did not want to drink more. Hlakanyana replied : "I think this one is sick." The mother said : "You must take good care of it." Hlakanyana promised to do so, but when the leopardess was gone he ate that one also.

The next day when the leopardess came there was no cub left to give her. She tried to get in the house, but the door was too small. She sat down in front to watch. Then Hlakanyana went out through the hole he had made in the ground behind. The leopardess saw him and ran after him. He went under a big rock, and cried out loudly for help, saying the rock was falling. The leopardess said : "What is that you are saying ? " Hlakanyana replied : "Do you not see that the rock is falling ? Just hold it up while I get a prop and put under it." The leopardess went to hold the rock up, and Hlakanyana did not return. He just ran away from that place.

Hlakanyana came to the village of the animals. The animals had trees that bore fruit. There was one tree that belonged to the chief of the animals only. This tree was a very good one, bearing much fruit on it. One day when all the animals were assembled, Hlakanyana asked them the name of the tree of the chief. They did not know the name of that tree. Then Hlakanyana sent a monkey to the chief to ask the name of the tree. The chief told the monkey. As the monkey was returning, he struck his foot against a stone and fell down, which caused him to forget the name of the tree.

In the night when all were sleeping, Hlakanyana went up the tree of the chief and ate all the fruit of it. He took a branch of the tree and fastened it to one of the monkeys. In the morning when the animals awoke and found that the tree of the chief was finished in the night, they asked each other : " What became of the fruit of the chief's tree ? What became of the fruit of the tree of the chief ? " Hlakanyana looked at the monkey with the branch on him, and said : " It is eaten by the monkey ; it is eaten by the monkey ; look at the branch on him." The monkey denied, and said : " I don't know anything about it. I never ate the fruit of the tree of the chief."

Hlakanyana said : " Let us make a plan to find out who ate the fruit of the tree of the chief." All the animals agreed to this. Hlakanyana said : " Let us put a rope from one rock to another, and let all go over it. He that has eaten the fruit of the tree will fall down from that rope." One of the monkeys went over first. The next was Hlakanyana himself. He went over carefully and avoided falling. It came to the turn of that monkey with the branch on. He tried to go, but when he was in the middle he fell down. Hlakanyana said therefore : " I have told you that it is this monkey." After that he went on his way.

Hlakanyana came to the house of a jackal. He asked for food, but the jackal said there was none. Then he made a plan. He said to the jackal : " You must climb up on the house and cry out with a loud voice, ' We are going to be fat to-day because Hlakanyana is dead.' " The jackal did so. All the animals came running to hear that news. They went inside the house, because the door was open. Then Hlakanyana shut the door, and the animals were caught. After that Hlakanyana killed the animals and ate.

Hlakanyana returned to the home of his father again. He was told that his sister had gone away for some red clay. When she was returning he shouted : "Let all the black cattle which have white teeth be killed. The daughter of my father is coming who has white teeth." The chief said : "What is the matter with you, Hlakanyana ?" He just repeated the same thing. The chief said : "Let a black ox be killed, but you must not break any of its bones, because it belongs to the daughter of a chief." So Hlakanyana got fat meat to eat that day.

Hlakanyana went out one day to tend the calves of his father. He met a tortoise. He said : "Where are you going to, tortoise ?" The tortoise answered : "To that big stone." Hlakanyana said : "Are you not tired ?" The tortoise replied : "No, I am not tired." Hlakanyana took it and put it on his back. Then he went to the house of his mother. His mother said : "What have you got there, my son ?" Hlakanyana answered : "Just take it off my back, mother." The tortoise held fast to Hlakanyana, and would not be pulled off. His mother then heated some fat and poured on the tortoise. The tortoise let go quickly, and the fat fell on Hlakanyana and burnt him, so that he died. That is the end of this cunning little fellow.

Story of Ironside and his Sister.

A long time ago a woman who went to cultivate her garden took her little daughter with her, and before she began to hoe the ground she laid the child down in the shade of a tree. About midday there came two birds and flew away with the girl. They carried her across a great river, and laid her gently down in a pumpkin field on a plain. As the birds were carrying her away, she called to her mother, who took no notice of her cries, because she could not imagine her child was being carried away. In the afternoon the girl was missing, and her mother searched for her without success. She made inquiries of the neighbours, and some of them told her they had heard the child crying : "I am going away with the birds."

The plain on which the little girl was put down was near a town in which lived a nation of cannibals who had one leg much longer than the other. There she remained alone till the next day. That night the chief of the cannibals dreamed that he saw a very pretty girl in that place, so in the morning he sent a party of men to look for her. When the girl saw them coming she was afraid, and hid herself among the pumpkins. But the men had already noticed where she was, so they easily found her, and took her home with them. The chief was very much pleased with her appearance. He gave her to his mother to take care of, and when she grew up he took her to be his wife.

Afterwards she had two children, one very pretty, and with two legs like her own ; the other ugly, and like its father, with one leg longer than the other. The cannibals saw the advantage of having two legs of equal length, and they became jealous of the woman and her child. They told the chief it would be dangerous to allow the child to grow up, because then a nation stronger than themselves might arise. They persuaded him to consent to her being put to death, and then they rejoiced greatly, because she was very fat, and they intended to eat her ; but one of them, who had more compassion than the others, told the woman what they were about to do.

After the little girl had been taken away by the birds, her mother had a son, one of whose sides was flesh like other people's, and the other side was iron. His mother told him of his sister who was lost, and when he became a man he determined to go in search of her. In his journey he came to a great river full of water. He had an iron rod in his hand, with which he struck the water, and at the same time he called out with a loud voice : " River, I have no sister. Be empty." Then the river dried up, and he went safely across.

After this he came to the stream where the cannibals drew their water, and concealed himself among the reeds which grew on its banks. While he was there his sister came to get water, and he at once knew who she was. She, of course, did not know him, but he told her he was her brother. Then she said the cannibals would eat him if he went to their town without an introduction. So they arranged that he should smear himself with mud and go to the top of a high hill, and when he was coming down she would tell the cannibals who he was.

Ironside went on the hill, and as soon as he came in sight of the town his sister said : "There is the servant of the wife of the chief of the cannibals." These words she repeated twice. When Ironside reached the town, a mat was brought to him and spread in front of his sister's house; but after a time he was allowed to go inside, still covered with mud.

The next day they all went to hunt, and Ironside killed more game than the others, upon which they became envious of him. This was shortly before the cannibals agreed to kill and eat the daughter of their chief. When the one who had compassion made known what was about to be done, Ironside was present and heard what was arranged. He said to his sister that she must pluck the hair from her head and scatter it about in different directions. This she did, after which Ironside and his sister and her child left the town in haste. The cannibals came, and when they could not find the child they called her loudly by name. Then the tufts of hair all answered in her voice, and the seekers became confused.

Ironside and his companions, having two legs, could walk much quicker than the cannibals, and soon they were on the other side of the large river. The child trembled, and was very much frightened; but Ironside told her not to fear at all. After they had crossed Ironside struck the river with his iron rod, and said: " River, I have found my sister. Be full." Then the water rose very high, quite to the top of the banks.

A party of cannibals who were in pursuit came to the river after it was full, and Ironside made a long rope, and threw the end over to them. They caught hold of it, thinking that he would pull them across; but when they were in the middle of the river he let go the rope, and they were all drowned. Another party then came and asked where their companions were. Ironside said they had gone to a ford farther down; but they knew that was not true, so they returned home. Afterwards they discovered who it was that gave warning of their intentions, and they killed and ate that one.

Ironside took his sister home to her mother, who received her with the greatest joy, never having forgotten her during that long time.

Story of the Glutton.

There was once a man who quarrelled with his wife, so that she left him, and went home to her father's place. When she got home she found nobody, for all the people had been swallowed by a monster. She went into the house that used to be her father's, and noticed that there were footprints of animals and spots of blood all over the floor. She then got into the top of the hut and hid herself. She heard the monster coming, saying :

> " Oh man, Oh man,
> I have eaten,
> And am still living."

She kept awake. Shortly the house was filled with all kinds of animals, which made a fire, cooked their food, ate it, and slept. Next morning they awoke, and all went out to search for something to eat. The woman had two children born while the animals were away. She came down from her hiding-place, and took up a stone used for raising pots above the fire (called isoko), and went again into her hiding-place.

The animals returned in the evening, and while their pots were on the fire, she threw down the stone into one of them. The animals all rushed out of the house. Outside they held a consultation, and their chief decided that those living in holes should go to the holes, that those living in forests should go to the forests, and that those living in rivers should go to the rivers. After this the woman set a trap, and succeeded in catching a buffalo, but she could not skin it. She saw a glutton (called an igongqongqo, a fabulous monster, like a man, but capable of devouring enormous quantities of food) coming, and asked him to help her. He consented. He pulled out his knife and skinned the buffalo. She gathered some wood, and kindled a fire for the purpose of roasting the liver. The glutton roasted it. She went away and picked up an empty calabash, and when she returned she found the glutton roasting the legs, having already eaten the liver. She then said : " I am going for water."

She got behind a bush, and blew the empty calabash. The glutton wondered what this was, and called her. She continued blowing, until the glutton was so frightened that he took his bag and put the remainder of the meat into it, and ran away. She followed him, still blowing, until he threw away the bag containing the meat. She still followed, blowing. The glutton stumbled, and fell into a thorny bush, where he was held fast. The woman then ceased blowing, and heard him blubbering out :

> " Let me alone, lu bo bo,
> Let me alone, lu bo bo."

She blew again, and he struggled and got free. He ran away with all his might. She then took the bag home with her, made a fire, and cooked the meat. When it was ready she took it to her hiding-place, and lived on it till her children were able to run about outside.

One day these twins asked their mother to make bows and arrows for them. Their mother advised them not to wander away from the hut, saying to them : "The glutton will swallow you." But at a certain time they left home, and went in the direction where the monster lived. They found it asleep, and shot it with their arrows in both eyes. The boys returned home, and told their mother. Next day they went to the place, and found the glutton dead. The boys heard people talking inside the glutton. Having told their mother, she took a knife and cut it open, when people came out, and cattle, and dogs. The people asked : "Who killed the glutton ? " The mother of the twins told them, and they rewarded the boys with a large number of cattle.

STORY OF TANGALIMLIBO.

There was once a man who had two wives, one of whom had no children. She grieved much about that, till one day a bird came to her and gave her some little pellets. The bird said she must eat of these always before she partook of food, and then she would bear a child. She was very glad, and offered the bird some millet. But the bird said : "No, I do not want millet." The woman then offered an *isidanga* (an ornamental breast-band which women wear), but the bird said it had no use for that. Then she got some very fine gravel and placed before the bird, which it received at her hands.

After this the woman had a daughter. Her husband knew nothing of what had happened, because he never went to her house. He did not love her at all, for the reason that she bore no children. So she said : " I will keep my daughter in the house till my husband comes ; he will surely love me when he sees that I have such a beautiful child." The name given to the girl was Tangalimlibo.

The man went always to the house of the other wife, and so it happened that Tangalimlibo was grown to be a young woman when her father first saw her. He was very much pleased, and said : " My dear wife, you should have told me of this before."

The girl had never been out of the house in the daytime.   Only in the night she had gone out, when people could not see her.

The man said to his wife : " You must make much beer, and invite many people to come and rejoice with me over this that has happened." The woman did so.   There was a big tree in front of the kraal, and the mats were spread under it.   It was a fine sunny day, and very many men came.   Among them was the son of a certain chief, who fell in love with Tangalimlibo as soon as he saw her.   When the young chief went home he sent a message to the father of the girl that he must send her to him to be married.   The man told all his friends about that.   He told them also to be ready at a certain time to conduct his daughter to the chief.   So they came and took her, and the marriage feast was very great.   The oxen were many which were killed that day.   Tangalimlibo had a large and beautiful ox given to her by her father.   It was called by her name.   She took off a piece of her clothing and gave it to the ox, which ate it.

After she had been married some time, this woman had a son. She was loved very much by her husband, because she was pretty and industrious ;   only this thing was observed of her, that she never went out in the daytime.   Therefore she received the name Sihamba Ngenyanga (the walker by moonlight).

One day her husband went to a distant place to hunt with other men.   There were left at his home with this woman only her father-in-law, her mother-in-law, and a girl who nursed the little child.   The father-in-law said : " Why does she not work during the day ? "   He pretended to become thirsty, and sent the girl to Tangalimlibo to ask for water, saying : " I die with thirst." The woman sent water to her father-in-law, but he threw it on the ground, saying : " It is water from the river I desire."   She said : " I never go to the river in the daytime."   He continued to ask, saying again : " I die with thirst."   Then she took a milk-basket and a calabash ladle, and went weeping to the river.   She dipped the ladle in the water, and it was drawn out of her hand. She dipped the milk-basket in the water, and it was drawn away from her.   Then she tried to take some water in her mantle, and she was drawn under the surface.

After a little time the girl was sent to look for her, but she came back, saying : " I found her not who is accustomed to draw water only in the night."

Her father-in-law drove oxen quickly to the river. He took the big ox that was called by her name and killed it. He put all the flesh and everything else that was of that ox into the river, saying : "Let this be instead of my child." A voice was heard saying : "Go to my father and my mother and say to them that I am taken by the river."

That evening the little child of Tangalimlibo was crying very bitterly. Its father was not yet home. Its grandmother tried by every means to keep it from crying, but in vain. Then she gave it to the nurse, who fastened it on her back. Still the child continued to cry. In the middle of the night the nurse went down to the river with the child, singing this song :

> "It is crying, it is crying,
> The child of Sihamba Ngenyanga ;
> It is crying, it will not be pacified."

Then the mother of the child came out of the river, and wailed this song :

"It is crying, it is crying, Sihamba Ngenyanga,
The child of the walker by moonlight. Sihamba Ngenyanga.
It was done intentionally by people whose names are unmentionable. Sihamba Ngenyanga.
They sent her for water during the day. Sihamba Ngenyanga.
She tried to dip with the milk-basket, and then it sank. Sihamba Ngenyanga.
Tried to dip with the ladle, and then it sank. Sihamba Ngenyanga.
Tried to dip with the mantle, and then it sank. Sihamba Ngenyanga."

Then she took her child and put it to her breast to suck. When the child had finished sucking, she gave it back to the nurse, telling her to take it home. She commanded the nurse never to say to any one that she came out of the water, and told her that when people asked where the child got food she must say she gave it berries to eat. This continued for some days. Every night the nurse took the child to the river, when its mother came out and suckled it. She always looked round to see that no one was present, and always put the same command on the girl.

After a time the father of the child returned from hunting. They told him of Tangalimlibo's going to the river and not returning. Then the nurse brought the child to him. He inquired what it ate, and was told that berries were given to it. He said : "That cannot be so ; go and get some berries, and let me see my child eat them." The girl went and brought some berries, but they were not eaten by the child. Then the father of the child beat the girl until she told him the truth. She said she went at night to the river, when the mother came out and caressed her child and gave it of her milk.

Then they made a plan that the husband of Tangalimlibo should hide himself in the reeds and try to catch his wife when she came out of the water. He took the skin of an ox and cut it into a long riem, one end of which he fastened round his waist. The other end he gave to the men of that place, telling them to hold it fast and to pull hard when they felt it being drawn from them. At night the man hid himself in the reeds. Tangalimlibo came out of the water and looked all round while she was singing her song. She asked the girl if any one was there, and when the girl replied that there was no one she took her child. Then her husband sprang upon her, clasping her very tight. She tried to pull back, but the men at the village drew upon the riem. She was drawn away, but the river followed her, and its water turned into blood. When it came close to the village, the men who were pulling at the riem saw it, and became frightened. They let the riem go, when the river at once went back, taking Tangalimlibo with it.

After that her husband was told of the voice which came from the water, saying: "Go to my father and my mother and tell them I am taken by the river." He called his racing ox, and said: "Will you, my ox, take this message to the father and mother of Tangalimlibo?" The ox only bellowed. He called his dog, and said: "Will you, my dog, take this message to the father and mother of Tangalimlibo?" The dog only barked.

Last of all he called the cock. He said: "Will you, my cock, take this message to the father and mother of Tangalimlibo?" The cock answered: "I will do so, my master." He said: "Let me hear what you will say." The cock answered: "I will sing

"I am a cock that ought not to be killed—Cock-a-doodle-doo!
 I have come to intimate about Tangalimlibo—Cock-a-doodle-doo!
 Tangalimlibo is dead—Cock-a-doodle-doo!
 She dipped water for a person that cannot be named—Cock-a-doodle-doo!
 It was tried to send an ox; it bellowed—Cock-a-doodle-doo!
 It was tried to send a dog; it barked—Cock-a-doodle-doo!"

The chief said: "That is good, my cock, go now." As the cock was going on his way, some boys who were tending calves saw him. One of them said to the others : "Come here, come here, boys ; there is a cock for us to kill." Then the cock stood up, and sang his song. The boys said : "Sing again, we did not hear you plainly." So he sang again : "I am a cock " &c. (as above). Then the boys let him go on his way.

He travelled far from that place, and came to a village where the men were sitting in the kraal. He flew up on the back of the kraal to rest himself, and the men saw him. They said : "Where does this cock come from ? We thought all the cocks here were killed. Make haste, boys, and kill him." The cock began to sing his song. Then the men said : "Wait, boys, we wish to hear what he says." They said to him : "Begin again, we did not hear you." The cock said : "Give me some food, for I am very hungry." The men sent a boy for some millet, and gave it to him. When he had eaten, he sang his song. The men said : "Let him go," and he went on his way.

Then he came to the village of the father of Tangalimlibo, to the house of those he was seeking. He told the message he was sent to carry. The mother of Tangalimlibo was a woman skilful in the use of medicines. She said to her husband : "Get a fat ox to go with us." They arrived at the river, and killed the ox. Then that woman worked with her medicines while they put the meat in the water. There was a great shaking and a rising up of the river, and Tangalimlibo came out. There was great joy among those people when they took her home to her husband.

The Runaway Children, or the Wonderful Feather.

Once in a time of famine a woman left her home and went to live in a distant village, where she became a cannibal. She had one son, whose name was Magoda. She ate all the people in that village, until only herself and Magoda remained. Then she was compelled to hunt animals, but she caught people still when she could. In hunting she learned to be very swift of foot, and could run so fast that nothing she pursued could escape from her.

Her brother, who remained at home when she left, had two daughters, whom he did not treat very kindly. One day he sent them to the river for water, which they were to carry in two pots. These pots were made of clay, and were the nicest and most valuable in the village. One of the girls fell down on a rock and broke the pot she was carrying. Then she did not know what to do, because she was afraid to go back to her father. She sat down and cried, but that did not help, the pot would not be whole again. Then she said to her sister : " Let us go away to another place, where our father will not be able to find us." She was the younger and the cleverer of the two, and so she persuaded her sister.

They walked away in the opposite direction from their home, and for two days had nothing but gum to eat. Then they saw a fire at a distance, and went to it, where they saw a house. It was the house of their aunt, but they did not know it. They were afraid to go in, but Magoda came out and talked to them. When he heard who they were, he was sorry for them, and told them their aunt was a cannibal, giving them advice not to stay there. But just then they heard her coming, so they went into Magoda's house and hid themselves, for he lived in one house and his mother in another.

The woman came and said : " I smell something nice ; what is it, my son ? " Magoda said there was nothing. She replied : " Surely I smell fat children." But as she did not go in, they remained concealed that night.

The next morning the mother of Magoda went out to hunt, but she did not go far, so the children could not get away. They went into her house, where they saw a person with only one arm, one side, and one leg. The person said to them : " See, the cannibal has eaten the rest of me ; take care of yourselves."

When it was nearly dark, the mother of Magoda came home again, bringing some animals which she had killed. She smelt that children had been in the house, so she went to her son's house and looked in. She said to Magoda : " Why do you not give me some ? Do I not catch animals for you ? "

Then she saw the children, and was very glad. She took them to her house, and told them to sleep. They laid down, but were too frightened to close their eyes. They heard their aunt say : " Axe, be sharp ; axe, be sharp ; " and to let her know that they were awake, they spoke of vermin biting them. After a while the cannibal went to sleep, when they crept out, first putting two blocks of wood in their places, and ran away as fast as they could. When the mother of Magoda awoke, she took the axe and went to kill them, but the axe fell on the blocks of wood.

As soon as it was day, the cannibal pursued the children. They looked behind, and saw clouds of dust which she made as she ran. There was a tall tree just in front of them, so they hastened to climb up it, and sat down among the branches. The mother of Magoda came to the tree and commenced to cut it down; but when a chip fell out, a bird (ntengu) sang :

> "Ntengu, ntengu,
> Chips, return to your places,
> Chips, return to your places,
> Chips, be fast."

The chip then went back to its place and was fast again. This happened three times; but the mother of Magoda, who was very angry, caught the bird and swallowed it. When she put it in her mouth, one of the feathers dropped to the ground. Then she began to chop at the tree again; but as soon as a chip was loose the feather sang :

> "Ntengu, ntengu,
> Chips, return to your places,
> Chips, return to your places,
> Chips, be fast."

The chip then stuck fast again. The cannibal chopped till she was tired, but the feather continued to keep the tree from receiving harm. Then she tried to catch the feather, but it flew about too quickly for her, until she sank down exhausted on the ground at the foot of the tree. The children up in the branches could see a long way off; and as they strained their eyes, they observed three dogs as big as calves, and they knew these dogs belonged to their father, who was seeking for them. So they called them by name, and the dogs came running to the tree and ate up the cannibal, who was too tired to make her escape. Thus the children were delivered, and their father was so glad to get them back again that he forgave them for breaking the pot and running away.*

* There are three or four versions of this story, but all agree in the main points. In one, it is the grandmother of the children who is the cannibal, in another, it is their mother, and in a third it is the husband of their aunt. One version makes Magoda escape with the children, and introduces a great deal of obscenity. The parts referring to the bird and the manner of the children's delivery are the same in all. So also is the episode of the broken pot, but the conversation between the two girls differs in some respects. The ntengu is rather larger than a swallow, and is of a bright bluish-black colour. It may often be seen on the backs of cattle, seeking for insects on which it feeds.

Story of Kenkebe.

There was once a great famine in a certain country, and the people were obliged to eat wild plants to keep themselves alive. Their principal food during this time was nongwes (*Hypoxis*), which they dug out of the ground. There was living at that place a man called Kenkebe, and one day his wife said to him: "My husband, go to my father and ask him to give us some corn." The man said: "Yes, I will go." So he rose up early in the morning, and went on till he arrived at his father-in-law's village, where he was received with every mark of kindness. A very large ox was killed for his entertainment. It was so large that it was six days before it was all eaten.

His father-in-law asked of him the news. He said: "There is no news to tell to friends. All the news is this, that at my home there is not a grain to be eaten. Famine is over our heads. Will you give us some corn, for we are dying?" His father-in-law gave him seven bags (*i.e.*, skins of animals dressed entire) full of millet, and his wife's sisters went with him to carry them. When they came to a valley close by his home, he told his sisters-in-law that they could now go back to their father. They said: "How will you manage to carry all those bags alone?" He replied: "I shall be able to carry them all now, because we are not far from my home." So those girls went back to their father.

Then he carried the bags one by one, and hid them in a cave under a great rock that was there. Afterwards he took some of the millet and ground it. When it was ground very fine he made it into cakes just like nongwes. Then he dug some real nongwes out of the ground, and went home to his wife. He said to her: "There is a great famine at your father's also. I found the people there eating themselves." He told his wife to make a fire. Then he pretended to cut a piece of meat out of his thigh, and said: "So they are doing at your father's village. Now, my wife, let us do the same." His wife cut a piece from her leg and roasted it. The piece that Kenkebe put on the fire was some that he brought home with him. Then Kenkebe's little boy said: "Why does my father's meat smell nice in roasting, and my mother's meat does not smell nice?" Kenkebe answered: "It is because it is taken from the leg of a man."

After this he gave his wife some nongwes to roast. He took for himself some of those he had made of millet. The little boy said : " Why do my father's nongwes smell nice in roasting, and my mother's do not smell nice ? " Kenkebe said : " It is because they were dug by a man." After eating, he went outside, but he had dropped one of his nongwes by the fire. When he went out the boy found that nongwe. He broke it in two and gave half to his mother. He said : " There is a difference between our nongwes and those of father." His mother said : " Yes, my child, this one is made of millet."

The next morning, just at the first beginning of dawn, Kenkebe got up and went away with a pot in his hand. The boy was awake, and saw his father go out. So he called to his mother, and said : " Mother, mother, wake, my father is going away with the pot in his hand." So she got up, and they followed after Kenkebe. They saw him go to the cave, where he took some corn out of one of the bags and began to grind it. Then they went on top of the rock, and rolled a big stone over.

When Kenkebe saw the stone coming he ran away, but it followed close behind him. He ran down the valley, the stone kept running too. He jumped into a deep hole in the river, down went the stone too. He ran up the hill, up went the stone also. He ran over the plain, but whenever he turned to look, the stone was there just behind him. So it continued all that day. At night he reached his own house, and then the stone stopped.

His wife had already come home, and had brought with her one of the bags of millet. Kenkebe came in crying. His wife said to him : " Why do you cry as if you were a child ? " He said : " Because I am very tired and very hungry." She said : " Where are your clothes and your bag ? " He replied : " I was crossing a river, and I fell down. The stream carried away my mantle, and my bag, and my keries, and everything that was mine." Then his wife gave him his mantle, which she had picked up when he was running away, and she said to him : " You are a very foolish man to do such things. There is no food for you to-night."

The next morning Kenkebe rose early and went out to hunt with his two dogs. The name of the one was Tumtumse, and the name of the other was Mbambozozele. He found an eland with a young calf, which he drove to his place. He cut an ear off the calf and roasted it in the fire. It was fat, and he liked it so much that he cut the other ear off and cooked it also. Then he wished to kill the calf, but he said to himself : "If I kill this calf I shall not be able to get milk from this eland." So he called his two dogs, and said to the one : "Tumtumse, my dog, if I kill this calf, will you imitate it and suck the eland for me ? " The dog said : "No, I will bark like a dog." Kenkebe said : "Get out of my sight and never come near me again, you ugly, useless animal." He said to the other : "Mbambozozele, my dog, if I kill this calf, will you imitate it and suck the eland for me ? " The dog said : "I will do so."

Then he killed the calf and ate it. He took the skin and put it upon Mbambozozele, so that the eland thought it was her calf that sucked before Kenkebe milked her. But one day the dog was sucking too long, and Kenkebe wanted him to leave off. He tried to drink just a few drops more, when his master got angry and struck him with a stick. Thereupon the dog began to howl, and the eland saw how she had been deceived. At once she ran after Kenkebe and tried to stick him with her horns. He ran one way and the eland ran after him, then he ran another way, and still the eland chased him. His wife came out and saw him running. She cried out to him : "Jump up quickly on the big stone." He did so, and the eland ran with such fury against that stone that it broke its head and fell down dead.

They then cut the eland up and wanted to cook it, but there was no fire. Kenkebe said to his son : "Go to the village of the cannibals that is on that hill over the valley, and ask for some fire ; but do not take any meat with you, lest they should smell it." The boy went, but he hid a piece of meat and took it with him. When he got to the first house he asked for fire, but they sent him to the next. At the next they sent him farther, and so he had to go to the house that was farthest away. An old woman lived there. The boy gave her a little piece of meat, and said : "Do not cook it till I am far away with the fire."

But as soon as the boy was gone, she put it on the coals. The smell came to the noses of the cannibals, and they ran to the place and swallowed the old woman, and the meat, and the fire, and even the ashes. Then they ran after the boy. When he came near his own house, he cried out : "Hide yourselves, you that are at home." His father said : "My son is saying we must gather wood that will make coals." His mother said: "No, he is saying we must hide ourselves." The boy cried again: "Hide yourselves." Then his mother hid herself in a bush; an old woman that was there covered herself with ashes, and Kenkebe climbed up into a tree, with the breast of the eland in his hand. The boy slipped into a hole that was by the side of the path.

The cannibals came to the place. First they ate the eland. Then one of them said: "Search under the ashes." There they found the old woman, and they ate her. Then they said: "Search in the tree." There they found Kenkebe. He cried very much, but they would not spare him. They ate him and the breast of the eland. Then the wise one said: "Look in the bush." They looked there and found the wife of Kenkebe. They said: "We will eat her another time," and so they took her home with them. They did not look for the boy.

The woman made a plan to escape. She made beer for the cannibals, and they all came to drink. They sat together in a big house, and drank very much beer. Then she said: "Can I go out?" They said: "You can go, but come back quickly." She said: "Shall I close the entrance?" They said: "Close it." Then she took fire and put it on the house, and all those cannibals were burnt to death. So the woman escaped, and afterwards lived happily with her son.*

ANOTHER STORY OF KENKEBE.

At a certain time Kenkebe went to get his wife at the place of her parents. When he was on the way, he met a crow. He borrowed its eyes. Then he arrived at his wife's parents' place with the eyes of the crow. When he arrived, his wife said: "Where are your own eyes?" He replied: "My eyes have been taken away by the crows." Then his wife said: "Let us go home." When they reached home, his wife said: "Take those eyes, you silly one, to their owner, and bring back your own." Accordingly Kenkebe went for his eyes and got them back.

* In the above story Kenkebe is represented as the personification of selfish greed. In this character his name has passed into a common proverb: Sibayeni sonke, Kenkebe, We are all bridegrooms, Kenkebe. This saying is used to any one who does not readily share food with others. It means, we are all entitled to a portion, you greedy one. A Xosa, when eating, commonly shares his food with any others who may be present at the time.

Then, as he was returning, he met an ant, and exchanged stomachs with it. When he arrived at his house, his wife gave him food. After he had finished eating, he went to milk a cow. When he was gone out, his little boy went to the place where he had been sitting. He said : "Mother, this food that is spilt here, whose is it ?" His mother replied : "Perhaps it has been spilt by your father. You must not eat it until your father comes." When Kenkebe came in, his wife said : "Where does this food come from ?" The man replied : "My stomach has been borrowed by an ant." His wife said : "You must go and take this stomach back to-morrow." He went to do so. When he arrived at the ant's place, he demanded his stomach. His stomach was given to him, and then he went home.

Story of the Great Chief of the Animals.

There was once a woman who had occasion to leave her home for a short time, and who left her children in charge of a hare. The place where they lived was close to a path, along which droves of wild animals were accustomed to pass. Soon after the woman left, the animals appeared, and the hare at sight of them became frightened. So she ran away to a distance, and stood to watch. Among the animals was one terrible monster, which called to the hare, and demanded to know what children these were. The hare told their names, upon which the animal swallowed them entire.

When the woman returned, the hare told her what had happened. Then the woman gathered some dry wood, and sharpened two pieces of iron, which she took with her and went along the path.

Now this was the chief of the animals; therefore when she came on a hill over against him, the woman began to call out that she was looking for her children. The animal replied : "Come nearer, I cannot hear you." When she went, he swallowed her also. The woman found her children alive, and also many other people, and oxen, and dogs. The children were hungry, so the woman with her pieces of iron cut some flesh from the animal's ribs. She then made a fire and cooked the meat, and the children ate. The other people said : "We also are hungry, give us to eat." Then she cut and cooked for them also.

The animal felt uncomfortable under this treatment, and called his counsellors together for advice, but they could suggest no remedy. He lay down and rolled in the mud, but that did not help him, and at last he went and put his head in the kraal fence, and died. His counsellors were standing at a distance, afraid to approach him, so they sent a monkey to see how he was. The monkey returned and said : " Those whose home is on the mountains must hasten to the mountains ; those whose home is on the plains must hasten to the plains ; as for me, I go to the rocks." Then all the animals dispersed.

By this time the woman had succeeded in cutting a hole through the chief's side, and came forth, followed by her children. Then an ox came out, and said : " Bo ! bo ! * who helped me ? " Then a dog, who said : " Ho ! ho ! * who helped me ? " Then a man, who said : " Zo ! zo ! * who helped me ? " Afterwards all the people and cattle came out. They agreed that the woman who helped them should be their chief.

When her children became men, they were out hunting one day, and saw a monstrous cannibal, who was sticking fast in a mud hole. They killed him, and then returned to tell the men of their village what they had done. The men went and skinned the cannibal, when a great number of people came out of him also. These joined their deliverers, and so that people became a great nation.

Story of Demane and Demazana.

Once upon a time a brother and sister, who were twins and orphans, were obliged on account of ill usage to run away from their relatives. The boy's name was Demane, the girl's Demazana. They went to live in a cave that had two holes to let in air and light, the entrance to which was protected by a very strong door, with a fastening inside. Demane went out hunting by day, and told his sister that she was not to roast any meat while he was absent, lest the cannibals should discover their retreat by the smell. The girl would have been quite safe if she had done as her brother commanded. But she was wayward, and one day she took some buffalo meat and put it on a fire to roast.

A cannibal smelt the flesh cooking, and went to the cave, but

---

* Imitating the voice of an ox, a dog, and a man coughing.

found the door fastened. So he tried to imitate Demane's voice and asked to be admitted, singing this song :

> " Demazana, Demazana,
> Child of my mother,
> Open this cave to me.
> The swallows can enter it.
> It has two apertures."

Demazana said : " No. You are not my brother ; your voice is not like his." The cannibal went away, but after a little time came back again, and spoke in another tone of voice : " Do let me in, my sister." The girl answered : " Go away, you cannibal ; your voice is hoarse, you are not my brother."

So he went away and consulted with another cannibal. He said : " What must I do to obtain my desire ? " He was afraid to tell what his desire was, lest the other cannibal should want a share of the girl. His friend said : " You must burn your throat with hot iron." He did so, and then no longer spoke hoarse. Again he presented himself before the door of the cave, and sang :

> " Demazana, Demazana,
> Child of my mother,
> Open this cave to me.
> The swallows can enter it.
> It has two apertures."

The girl was deceived. She believed him to be her brother come back from hunting, so she opened the door. The cannibal went in and seized her. As she was being carried away, she dropped some ashes here and there along the path. Soon after this, Demane, who had taken nothing that day but a swarm of bees, returned and found his sister gone. He guessed what had happened, and followed the path by means of the ashes until he came to Zim's dwelling. The cannibal's family were out gathering firewood, but he was at home, and had just put Demazana in a big bag, where he intended to keep her until the fire was made.

Demane said : " Give me water to drink, father." Zim replied : " I will, if you will promise not to touch my bag." Demane promised. Then Zim went to get some water ; and while he was away, Demane took his sister out of the bag, and put the bees in it, after which they both concealed themselves.

When Zim came with the water, his wife and son and daughter came also with firewood. He said to his daughter : " There is something nice in the bag ; go and bring it." She went, but the bees stung her hand, and she called out : " It is biting." He sent his son, and afterwards his wife, but the result was the same. Then he became angry, and drove them outside, and having put a block of wood in the doorway, he opened the bag himself. The bees swarmed out and stung his head, particularly his eyes, so that he could not see. There was a little hole in the thatch, and through this he forced his way. He jumped about, howling with pain. Then he ran and fell headlong into a pond, where his head stuck fast in the mud, and he became a block of wood like the stump of a tree. The bees made their home in the stump, but no one could get their honey, because when any one tried his hand stuck fast.

Demane and Demazana then took all Zim's possessions which were very great, and they became wealthy people.

Story of the Girl and the Mbulu.*

There was once a widow woman who had one son and two daughters. On a certain day she went to her garden, taking with her one of the girls. While she was away the boy quarrelled with his sister and killed her. In the course of the day the woman sent the girl who was with her to the hut, and when she came there a fly told her what had happened. She did not believe it. Then a mouse told her the same thing, but still she did not believe it was true. Afterwards the fly told her to look in a certain place, and there she saw the head and the bones of her sister.

When the woman came home and found out what had happened, she killed her son. Then she gave the girl a stick, and told her to go to her uncle's house, saying that when she got there she must strike the ground with the stick, and all the clothes and other things that belonged to her would then rise up out of the earth. The woman said she was now all alone, and therefore intended to kill herself.

The girl was very sorry, but she did as her mother told her. When she was a little way off she looked back and saw smoke coming out of the hut, from which she knew that her mother had

---

* The mbulu is a fabulous creature, firmly believed in by little folks. It can assume the human form, but cannot part with its tail. One of its peculiarities is that it never speaks the truth when it is possible to tell a falsehood.

burned herself and was no longer a person under the sun. After this she met an old woman, who called to her, but she took no heed and walked on. Next she met a mbulu at a place close by a river. The mbulu said that whoever wetted any part of the body in crossing the river must go in and bathe. The girl was standing on the bank, and the mbulu struck the water with its tail and splashed it in her face, so that she had to go in and bathe. Then the mbulu took her clothes and put them on. When the girl came out of the water she asked for her clothes, but the mbulu said : " I will give them when you are dry."

So they went on together. After a while the girl asked again, and the mbulu said : " I will give them when we get to the village." But when they arrived there the mbulu said : " You must tell the people here that you are my servant, and that I am the daughter of a chief." The poor girl was so afraid that she promised to do so. They were well received at the village, because the people believed that the mbulu was a great person. They wondered at her voice, but she told them she had been ill and her throat was not well yet.

After a time one of the men of that kraal married the mbulu, and the real girl was sent to the gardens to drive the birds away from the millet. While engaged in this occupation she used to sing about the mbulu taking her clothes and passing itself off for a person, until the women who worked in the gardens took notice of this song of hers. Then they made a plan to find out if what the girl was singing was the truth. They said : " The tail of a mbulu will want mice and fat," so they set snares to catch the mice. In the night the tail was pursuing mice, and itself got fast in a snare. The mbulu then asked the man who was married to her to go and get some medicine, as she was sick, and when the man went she took off the snare.

After this they made another plan. They said : " The tail of a mbulu will seek milk," so they dug a hole in the ground, put milk in it, and required every one in the village to jump over the hole. The mbulu was unwilling at first, but they urged her. She tried to jump quickly, but the tail could not pass the milk. When it went down the people saw that this was a mbulu, so they killed it and buried it in that hole.

After this the same man who had married the mbulu took the girl to be his wife. She had a child, and one day when it was playing a square gourd came out of the ground where the mbulu was buried, and tried to kill the infant. But the people chopped the gourd in pieces, and burned it. They afterwards threw the ashes into a river, so that nothing more could come of that mbulu.

CHAPTER XIV.

Rapid Increase of the Bantu in number.

In many other countries where Europeans have settled, as for instance in the United States of America, in Canada, in Australia, and in New Zealand, the earlier uncivilised inhabitants have dwindled away, and in one—Tasmania—have entirely died out. The chief cause of this has been the introduction of new diseases, which had spent their force upon Europeans long ago, and had consequently ceased to be very destructive to them, but which swept off the uncivilised people, who had not gone through the same hardening process, in an appalling manner. Chief among the diseases that operated in this way, and that opened vast territories to European occupation, was the small-pox. In former times, when no preventive for this scourge was known, its introduction into a new country was followed by the almost complete extermination of the barbarous inhabitants. In South Africa in the eighteenth century its ravages were terrible. Whole tribes of Hottentots utterly disappeared before it, and even the Bantu did not entirely escape, for the section of the Tembus living between the Kei and Bashee rivers perished almost to a man. The state of constant warfare in which these people lived, however, preserved the neighbouring tribes from the same fate. They were so isolated that others did not come in contact with them, especially when it was reported that they were bewitched and were dying like locusts in a storm of hail.

Then came the discovery that small-pox could be prevented by vaccination, and the Bantu were spared from the fate that had overtaken the Hottentots. The Europeans who introduced the disease into Capetown did all that was possible to prevent its spreading, and ultimately taught the dark coloured tribes how to ward off danger from it. Consumption, another fell disease that has worked havoc among many barbarous nations, was almost unknown in South Africa until recent years. Europeans suffering from pulmonary complaints came to this country to be cured, and if the disease was not too far advanced they were usually restored to perfect health in its warm dry air. For a long time they did not come in close contact with Bantu, and consequently did not communicate the disease to them. The dark-skinned people, sprung from robust parents, for all the weaklings were destroyed in infancy, living on plain but substantial food, using little clothing, but lubricating their persons, and passing their days in the open air of a mild climate, with a moderate amount of exercise, enjoyed much more perfect health than falls to the dwellers in civilised Europe or America.

Thus after the awful destruction of human life by the wars of Tshaka, when in the fourth decade of the nineteenth century European dominion was established northward as far as the Limpopo and the surviving Bantu could emerge from the mountains and deserts and cultivate the ground and breed cattle once more, there was a people possessing greater power of increasing their number rapidly than any other on the face of the earth. The European governments removed all the checks to speedy growth that had existed in early years. They prevented the tribes from fighting with and slaughtering each other, and they would not permit the putting to death of individuals charged with dealing in witchcraft. They suppressed to some extent the arbitrary power of the chiefs over the lives of their people. In most localities, though not in all, they even prohibited the sale of intoxicating liquor to the barbarians. For some time the effect was hardly noticed, but at length it became so apparent that every one was forced to observe it. The locations assigned to the Bantu, more than ample in size when they were first set apart, became overcrowded, and the surplus population flowed out into places previously vacant. The crown lands were invaded, private farms were occupied by Bantu families on lease, a system which, when once commenced, had a tendency to spread, for the neighbouring farmers were forced to do the same, or remain to be plundered, and there was a constant application to the governments for land, always more land. The great uninhabited wastes that every traveller in the fourth decade of the nineteenth century described were half a century later teeming with human life.

A comparison of the number of children under fifteen with that of females over fifteen years of age in different parts of the world in 1881 shows the surprising rate of increase of the Bantu at that time. The census of England and Wales in that year showed the proportion to be 110·17 to 100, in Canada it was 124·73 to 100, in the European population of the United States it was (census of 1880) 130·76 to 100, in Australia 145·62 to 100, and in New Zealand 177·16 to 100. In the census returns of the Cape Colony in 1875 the proportion of Bantu children under fifteen to females over fifteen years of age is given as 169·98 to 100, but these include all the drunkards and all the degraded residents in the town locations, so the return must be taken as of the Bantu under the least favourable circumstances at that time for increasing their number. It is certain that a census taken almost anywhere else in South-Eastern Africa would have shown a larger proportion of children under fifteen to females over that age. On every occasion where large parties have been accurately numbered,—as in instances of their removal when they were provided with food by the government in different quantities for men, women, and children of both sexes under fifteen years of age,*—this was the case. In a considerable number of such cases the lowest proportion was 195 children to 100 females over fifteen.

In the negroes of the United States the proportion of children under fifteen to females over that age was 172·28 to 100. Bring-

---

* In the case of infants at the breast with the sanction of the government I allowed the mother a child's ration extra when the Gaikas of Ngonyama were removed by me from the frontier during the war of 1878. This was also the rule with regard to the women and children sent to Capetown during the war, and with regard to the people of Sandile and Anta who were removed to Kentani from the present district of Cathcart, so that the ration returns are safe guides.

ing these proportions together that they may be seen in one glance, the ratio was

England and Wales	110·17
Dominion of Canada	124·73
United States, European	130·76
Australia	145·62
Bantu of South Africa under the least favourable circumstances	169·98
United States, negro	172·28
New Zealand, where all the conditions were most favourable to the increase of the Europeans	177·16
Bantu of South Africa under ordinary circumstances, about	195·00

Early in 1885 a circular containing several questions having reference to this matter was issued at the request of the author of this volume by the native affairs department of the Cape government to the officers in the territories occupied by Bantu, and copies were also supplied to the missionaries and leading traders with a request that they would kindly assist in the investigation. The returns sent in were voluminous, but the substance of them all when condensed was as follows :

Question 1. To what cause or causes do you assign the great increase of the Bantu in number during recent years ?

To this question the replies were almost uniform in language, and entirely uniform in effect: To the controlling power of the civilised governments.

While, except in that very small section of the people that had embraced Christianity, there was nothing to affect sensibly any of the causes that in former times tended to a rapid increase of population,—such as early marriages, polygamy which secured that no woman capable of childbearing should remain single, constitutional vigour, freedom from heritable diseases, and absence of care and anxiety as to provision for children,—the ancient checks upon overgrowth had been removed.

(*a*) Tribal wars and feuds between clans, by which great numbers of people were formerly destroyed, had been prevented.

(*b*) The execution of people on charges of dealing in witchcraft had been suppressed.

(*c*) A better and surer supply of food than in ancient days was secured. The introduction of the plough had enabled the people to grow much more corn, and in seasons of drought they could procure food in return for labour or in exchange for property of any kind. The improved means of intercourse admitted of food supplies being sent to any part of the country where there was a demand for them.

Question 2. Which people attain the greatest average age, the Bantu or the European ? On what calculations do you base your reply ?

To this question the answers from nearly all the old and experienced magistrates, missionaries, and traders were to the effect that the average life of the black man is longer than that of the European. This opinion was based upon

(*a*) The very large number of blacks then living who remembered and took part in the battle of Amalinde in 1818, the flight of the Fingos from Natal in 1821 and 1822, the wars of Moselekatse and the depopulation of the territory between the Orange and Limpopo rivers, 1821 to 1830, the defeat of the Amangwane in 1828, and other notable events of more than fifty years before 1885.

(*b*) A comparison of Bantu and Europeans known to be of the same age, when the former invariably have the appearance of being the younger of the two. A black man of fifty does not look older than a European of forty.

(*c*) The general good health of the Bantu, in which prolonged observation shows that they greatly surpass Europeans.

Question 3. Are there any causes in operation tending to affect the future increase of the Bantu population ? In the reply to this question, please state the effects of embracing Christianity, of drunkenness, of syphilis, &c., upon the birth rate of the people under your observation.

The answers were varied, and all given merely as expressions of opinion.

Most of the writers considered that the rate of increase of that time would not long be maintained, because the struggle for existence must become more intense with the pressure of population. The limit of food supply, both in flesh and in grain, which the country was capable of producing without such artificial aids as manuring and irrigating, must soon be reached. Then would come care and necessity for forethought, which would prevent early marriages. Already in some localities there was a tendency to postpone the marriage of girls to a later age than formerly. Fingo girls especially, when in service with Europeans and earning wages for their fathers, were frequently allowed to remain unmarried until the age of twenty.

The effects of embracing Christianity were viewed in very different lights. Some of the missionaries were of opinion that the birth rate would be increased if the deplorable immorality of the uncivilised blacks should give place to purity of life. Others thought that enforced monogamy coupled with virtuous habits would greatly decrease the number of children born. Many of the magistrates and traders referred to the increase of disease among the semi civilised natives as an indication that the birth rate would probably be less if Christianity were generally adopted. This increase of disease was attributed to

(*a*) Less cleanly habits. The uncivilised black bathed frequently and then rubbed grease and red clay over his body. His semi civilised brother obtained a suit of European clothing, which he seldom washed. His shirt was not once removed from his body till it was worn out. Of course there were exceptions, but this was commonly the case.

(*b*) Exposure to wet. The greased black man took no harm from being out in rain. His kaross was kept dry. The black man in European clothing, owing to his improvidence, seldom had a change of garments, and when he had been drenched with rain usually sat by a fire to dry himself.

(*c*) The cares and anxieties which even semi civilisation increased.

(*d*) Less bodily exercise.

All the returns agreed in the view that the unrestrained use of intoxicating liquors would not only diminish the birth rate, but speedily destroy the people. Barbarians are incapable of resisting the temptation to use spirituous liquor to excess when it is within easy reach. But as yet drunkenness had no perceptible effect upon the birth rate among the people of the purely Bantu territories, because the sale of spirits had not been permitted by law, and the contraband trade had not been very great. It was in the colony proper that the destructive effects of drunkenness could be seen.

As to syphilis, different opinions were expressed. In the purely Bantu districts it was then prevalent only among those persons who had come into close contact with vagrant Europeans. One missionary stated that it appeared from observations he had made to be more easily eradicated from blacks than from Europeans. Two magistrates reported that some of the Bantu herbalists appeared to have remedies of their own and cured it easily. On the other hand, several missionaries regarded it as a coming evil, the deleterious consequences of which must be widely felt, owing to the immoral habits of the uncivilised Bantu.

Question 4. What is the average age at which Bantu women are married ?

The replies to this question were as varied as the tribes with which the writers were residing.

There was a general agreement that marriage might take place immediately after the ceremony which girls go through upon attaining the age of puberty, usually about thirteen, and that in all the tribes it did sometimes take place shortly after. But while with some tribes such early marriages were very frequent, with others they were very rare. The Betshuana and Basuto tribes were those in which early marriages were common. With some of these the average would be as low as fourteen, with others it would be fifteen. Bantu girls along the coast as a rule were not married so early. In some of the tribes sixteen was the average age while in others it would probably be as high as seventeen. There were mission stations on which it was as high as eighteen and even nineteen.

For the whole of the Bantu tribes south of the Limpopo the average would probably be between fifteen and sixteen; but this estimate could only be regarded as conjecture formed from such information as was available. The object which the father or guardian had in view in bringing about the marriage of girls before they were fully developed was variously stated to be

(*a*) To settle them respectably in life, for which purpose alliances were sought with influential families, the proposals being frequently made by the guardians of the females.

(*b*) To preserve the girls from loss of reputation, which delay in marriage would probably cause.

(*c*) To prevent capital from lying waste. A girl represented a certain number of cattle, the increase and milk of which took the place of interest on money invested.

(*d*) To perpetuate the customs of his forefathers, or in other words to do as every one else in the circle of his acquaintance was doing and as his people had done as long as memory or tradition went back.

(*e*) That his posterity might be numerous in the land.

Question 5. Can you give any information upon the relative number of births and deaths in places not affected by emigration or immigration?

The almost invariable replies to this query were either that owing to no records of births and deaths having been kept, or that owing to the roving habits and frequent change of residence of the Bantu, no reliable information could be given. Only five returns in all were sent in, representing five mission stations and small kraals, at which during certain stated periods the total number of births was 379 and the total number of deaths 125.

Question 6. What is the average number of children of women married (*a*) to monogamists, (*b*) to polygamists? In the reply to this query, please state the number of women from whom the calculations are made. The greater the number the better, but care must of course be taken not to include women who are still capable of childbearing. The only reliable plan will be to question the old women, and ascertain from each one exactly how many children she has given birth to and how many wives her husband has had. If the husband was a monogamist, note whether Christianity had been embraced. The greatest possible accuracy is requisite to make the reply to this query of value.

To this question a good many carefully drawn up tables were sent in, particularly from some of the older magistrates and from several missionaries. One from Donald Strachan, Esq., merchant, of Umzimkulu, was especially valuable, from the great pains that had evidently been taken to obtain reliable information. Altogether these returns embraced 393 women, the wives or widows of monogamists, mostly professing Christians, and 591 women, the wives or widows of polygamists. In a few instances it was noted that the women might not yet have passed the age of childbearing. The 393 women, wives of monogamists, had borne 2223 children, that is on an average 5·65 children to each woman. The 591 women, wives of polygamists, had borne 3298 children, that is on an average 5·58 children to each woman. Thus monogamy in this respect made hardly any appreciable difference in the birth rate. Christianised Bantu girls did not marry at as early an age as the others, but the interval between the births of children in families who had embraced Christianity was usually shorter than with women in an uncivilised state, owing to a superstitious feeling of the latter which required them to live in strict seclusion from intercourse with their husbands and lovers during the period of giving suck to their children, usually from two to three years.

But the death rate of the Christian Bantu was so much higher than that of the others that the balance was more than equalised. Some of the returns merely gave the total number of children each woman named had given birth to, but others had been so carefully arranged as to give the sexes of the children born—showing that more boys than girls were brought into the world—and gave the numbers living when the information was obtained and the numbers that had died. Of the children of polygamists 73 per cent were still living, while of the children of monogamists only 67 per cent were alive. The larger death rate among monogamists was explained by the facts that chest diseases had become not uncommon on mission stations, and that the children were perceptibly less robust, owing to their changed conditions of living.

The widows of polygamists continued to bear children as if their husbands were still living. In some instances a widow returned to her father or nearest male relative, and was remarried, when her children after the second marriage belonged by law to her second husband. But in most instances she remained with her dead husband's relatives, because she could not take his children away with her. In such cases either a brother of her dead husband had taken her, or she had a male companion formally allotted to her, and she had her lover. All the children she gave birth to were under any of these circumstances considered as her dead husband's.

The number of women who had never borne children was less than three per cent of the whole; a few had borne ten and eleven each; but the great majority ranged from four to eight.

The numbers in these tables are too small for the averages here given to be considered more than approximately correct. To arrive at anything like accuracy, similar statistics must be collected for many years and by competent persons in all parts of the Bantu territories.

Question 7. Can you explain why decrepid, infirm, and half breed children are not found among the Bantu?

The answers were to the effect that owing to the robust constitutions of the people very few decrepid children were born. In olden times such children were destroyed by filling their mouths with earth. At the time these queries were replied to they were commonly neglected, or it was given out that they were lost or that some accident had happened to them. In one way or other they generally disappeared at a very early age. Still, a few were to be found, but always on mission stations or in places where European influence was prevalent. Albinos were met with occasionally, and they were suffered to live. As for half-breed children, they were seldom found except in places where the people had become semi-civilised, or where ship-wrecked or renegade white men had been living as adopted members of a clan. There was no disgrace to which a Bantu female was subject equal in the opinion of her people to that of giving birth to a half-breed child. Abortion or infanticide would be resorted to, if the customs of the tribe had not previously been partly abandoned and those of Europeans adopted. In this respect the Bantu were the very opposite of the Hottentots, whose females had no repugnance to intercourse with white men. Owing probably to inter-marriages with near relatives, many idiotic children were born among the branches of the Basuto.

Question 8. Have you observed what effect great difference of age between man and wife has upon the number of children among the Bantu ?

The replies were uniform that it had no effect whatever. Men did not marry women older than themselves. Old men very frequently married girls, but nearly every uncivilised black woman had a lover as well as a husband. This fact could not be left out of consideration when studying the effects of poly-gamous marriages. It was taken as a matter of course that a woman married to a polygamist, unless he was a chief of very high rank, would form a connection with some other man. She did not sink in the slightest degree in the estimation of other women by so doing. The offence was punishable by Bantu law, the lover being subject to a fine and the woman to chastise-ment by her husband, but in most instances it passed unnoticed as an ancient custom of the people.

A quarter of a century has passed away since the returns here given were sent in, and in 1910, though it is impossible from any statistics in existence to give accurately the rate of increase of all the Bantu south of the Zambesi at the present time, it can be stated that it is certainly less than it was at the commencement of this period, though it is possibly even now as high as that of Europeans in any part of the world. Poly-gamy has decreased in this sense, that fewer men in proportion to the whole number have more than one wife, but there are as yet no old maids among the Bantu, for a few wealthy men secure the surplus females.

Disease, however, is far more rife among them than in former times. Syphilis has spread among the Betshuana to an alarming extent, and is seriously affecting the rate of increase of that branch of the Bantu family. Consumption seems to have taken a firm hold of the coast tribes, and is producing a similar effect. What can be done to prevent the ravages of these diseases is being done by the European authorities, but the habits of the people are such that it is much more difficult to deal with them thoroughly in sanitary matters than it would be to deal with white colonists in similar circumstances.

Then the struggle for existence is very much greater now than it was when the men lived an idle and contented life, and the women cultivated their gardens. In many localities the people have become too numerous for the ground, and consequently some have no gardens to work in. Tens of thousands of the men find it necessary to labour for wages in the mines, and return to their homes in many instances with their constitutions debilitated, though all possible care is taken of them. Anxieties and worries, to which in olden times they were absolute strangers, are now their lot in common with Europeans, and they find it hard to bear up against them. Youths who realise that the support of children will fall upon them do not marry at as early an age as they did when it was so easy to provide for all their simple needs.

More than all these causes together, the decrease in the rate of productiveness of the Bantu south of the Zambesi must be attributed to the loss of nearly all their horned cattle by the ravages of runderpest and other diseases since 1896. Cattle constituted their wealth, and upon fermented milk they depended for subsistence quite as much as upon the produce of their gardens. The loss of this to them was what the loss of wheaten bread would be to the people of England. They are getting cows together again, but it will be a very long time, if it ever comes, before the great herds that formerly fed on their pastures are seen there once more. Meanwhile the substitution of new kinds of food is detrimental to their health, and children especially suffer from it. The rate of mortality among infants has become much higher than it was in earlier days, and the stamina of the adults is less. In a word, they are undergoing a great change in their diet as well as in their mode of living, and until they become habituated to the new environment in which circumstances beyond their control have placed them, they cannot increase at such an amazing rate as they did when everything was in their favour.

CHAPTER XV.

The Mystery of South Africa.

At some unknown period in the past the territory between the lower Zambesi river and the twenty-fifth parallel of south latitude was occupied by a people well advanced in civilisation. Their nationality is uncertain, and nearly everything connected with them is involved in mystery. They were miners, and were skilled in looking for gold-bearing reefs and working them when found. It is not impossible, though it is only a conjecture of some writers, that traders from the great commercial city of Tyre on the eastern shore of the Mediterranean sea visited this part of the African continent, and that in holy scripture an account of their visits is given. The conditions mentioned of the fleets that went down the Red sea to Ophir in the time of Solomon are not inapplicable to voyages to the mouths of the Zambesi or the Sabi, or to Sofala, and the articles—gold, silver, precious stones, almug trees, ivory, apes, and peacocks—with which they returned are all found in South-Eastern Africa, if by almug trees ebony or some other very hard wood is meant, by precious stones pearls, and by peacocks the bustards that to-day are called wilde pauwen (wild peacocks) by the Dutch colonists. The name of the bird given in the bible is said, however, to be of Tamil origin, and to be used for the peacock (*pavo cristatus*) at the present day in Ceylon. This appears to be the greatest impediment to the supposition that the Ophir of scripture is the Rhodesia of to-day, but as almost to a certainty there was intercourse between Eastern Africa and Southern India in those times, an African bird might have received from strangers a Dravidian name.

The object that brought the first civilised explorers to South Africa can only be conjectured. They may have come in search of ivory, which from very early times was a valuable article of commerce, and the fact that elephants were plentiful in the country may have been ascertained either by the crews of vessels driven to the coast or by hunters pushing their way down from the north. The elephant hunters may have found gold, and then mining would have commenced. This, however, is mere surmise, and there are obstacles in the way of accepting it or any other supposition that has yet been made. For instance, it is not likely that either hunters or ivory traders would recognise the presence of the precious metal in quartz reefs in a country where alluvial gold is found only in a few localities and in small quantities. Thus it is not possible to say how, when, or by whom gold was first discovered in the Rhodesia of our day, any more than it is to say how, when, or by whom tin was first discovered in Cornwall.

What is certain is that at some time in the remote past, of which there is neither written record nor tradition now, mining operations were carried on over an immense tract of country south of the lower Zambesi. The miners were sufficiently skilful to be able to sink pits and run underground galleries along reefs, but they were obliged to cease operations when water began to flow in, as they had no means except buckets and human labour for keeping the excavations dry. The quantity of a reef that could be removed depended thus entirely upon its position, and where drainage was good, depths of over one hundred and fifty feet or 45·72 metres were reached.

With the appliances at the disposal of the most advanced people of that time there was only one way apparently in which this kind of mining could be carried on successfully, for a vast amount of labour was needed in excavating the gold-bearing rock, bringing it to the surface of the ground, there crushing it to powder, and then washing the dust to obtain perhaps a thirty or forty thousandth part of gold from it, though the value of that metal relatively to other articles must then have been very much greater than it is now. With a large number of slaves or Indian labourers compelled to work for next to nothing, some employed in extracting and crushing rock and others in raising food, it was possible to make gold-mining profitable, and it may be taken for certain that this was the condition of things at that time in the territory called Rhodesia to-day.

Among various articles manufactured by these people that have been found where they were left or lost are an ingot mould, crucibles, and beads, tacks, and thin plates of beaten gold. The thin plates in little squares of uniform size were intended to overlay wood, perhaps the ceilings and columns of grand buildings in other parts of the world, and the wedge-shaped tacks were for fastening them on. Many of these plates and tacks have been found.

Over the whole country where mining was carried on, ruins of stone buildings and walls are scattered, implying a prodigious amount of labour exerted over a long period of time. The oldest of the ruins may be of much later origin than the commencement of the mining operations, but the articles found in the debris beside them prove that some of them were strongholds and factories of miners and workers in gold. Others, however, seem to have had no connection with mining industry, but to have been fortifications constructed for purposes of defence by people subject to attack by enemies.

Here another mystery is opened up. Who could the enemies of the gold miners have been, that necessitated the erection of strongholds in the interior and a line of forts along the Sabi river down to the place of entrance on the coast of the Indian sea? Invasion must have been feared, which implies that there was more than one great seafaring power in existence at the time, and that the knowledge of the wealth of South Africa was widely spread. Little, or rather nothing at all, do we know indeed of what was transpiring when, as modern mining engineers inform us, gold to the value of over a hundred million pounds sterling of our day must have been taken out of the rocks of Rhodesia.

In the ancient structures the workmanship, though solid, was not of a graceful order. The arch was unknown, the outer walls, though circular or elliptical, were not perfectly regular in form, nor were they either absolutely perpendicular or of the same slope along their whole length or of equal thickness throughout. The men who planned and built them were not sufficiently refined to appreciate mathematical correctness of shape or finish. The stones used in them, taken from strata or layers of granite which could be broken off like slabs and which were consequently flat on two surfaces and of equal thickness, were trimmed at the sides, so that the courses are perfectly regular. They were laid as close to each other as it was possible to get them, and no cement or plaster was used to bind them, though excellent cement was employed in making floors and drains.

The most imposing of the ruins is that known as Great Zimbabwe (more correctly Zimbabgi), in latitude 20° 16′ 30″ south, longitude 31° 10′ 10″ east of Greenwich, 22·4 kilometres or fourteen miles from the present township of Victoria. The building there that has attracted most attention is elliptical in form, two hundred and ninety-two feet or eighty-nine metres in its greatest length by sixty-seven metres in greatest breadth, and was built of blocks of stone flat above and below when taken from the rock and trimmed to about double the width of ordinary bricks, but of varying lengths. The greatest height of the wall still standing is thirty-five feet or 10·68 metres, and its thickness varies from sixteen feet two inches or 4·9 metres to five feet or a metre and a half. The only ornamentation consists of two courses of stone laid in oblique positions in contrary directions along a fourth part of the wall near the top. A solid conical stone tower, seventeen metres in circumference at the base and still about nine metres high, stands within the wall of this building, and is of very superior workmanship, the stones having been accurately trimmed to meet the requirements of the different parts of the cone. Under the debris covering the cement floor of this great building numerous stone phalli have been found, indicating that the religion of the builders was a form of nature worship.

The labour required for the erection of such a building, or of another of great size on a hill close by, would be enormous in amount at the present day; what then must it have been when mechanical appliances such as are now in common use were unknown?

It is generally believed that the mines and ruins here referred to indicate a remote period of occupation, of great but unknown length, which can be distinguished by skilful underground excavations and by structures in which the stones are laid in regular courses like bricks and the walls are built solidly from side to side, not faced and filled in between with rubbish. In connection with these buildings carved birds of soapstone, stone phalli, and gold ornaments are found. Mr. Richard N. Hall, the gentleman who can speak with the greatest authority on this subject, is of opinion that the mouth of the Sabi river was the port used by the people who left these memorials of their skill and enterprise behind them.

This period came suddenly to an end, but neither the cause nor the time has yet been ascertained. One might form a conjecture that some great revolution in the affairs of Asia, such as the wide conquests of Alexander the Great of Macedon, or the wresting of the commerce of the Indian sea from the Arabs and Indians by the Greeks of Egypt under Roman dominion, was the cause, but there are difficulties in the way of adopting such a view, particularly as it gives no explanation of the removal of the entire body of the inhabitants then residing on the mining area. Even supposing the mines to have been worked and the buildings to have been erected by male slave labour sent from some distant country, it is difficult to believe that during the long period of occupation the higher classes were entirely unaccompanied by females, or that there were no families at all in South Africa when the abandonment took place. But if there were what became of them? The abandonment was not only complete, but sudden, for heaps of uncrushed quartz were left behind near the mouths of the pits, and the floor of the great temple Zimbabwe was thickly strewn with gold ornaments, thrown away in haste by the last of those who worshipped there. Some day light may be thrown on this subject by discoveries in Africa or in Southern Asia, and therefore it is wisest to make no conjectures at present, but to wait until time or accident solves the mystery.

The aborigines must have disappeared entirely from the locality occupied by the miners, for there was no way by which two classes of people, so dissimilar in everything, could live together on the same soil. They may have been exterminated, or they may have retired to other parts of the country, there is no way of ascertaining what became of them. One thing only is certain, that those living outside of the mining area, and who must have known something of what was going on there, learnt absolutely nothing from the strangers, but remained as wild and as savage as they were before.

The first mining period had passed away, and then, after an interval of unknown duration, but long enough for dust and mould to accumulate on the floor of the Zimbabwe temple and conceal the stone phalli and gold trinkets and other articles lying there, came another body of strangers and settled in the country. No one knows where they came from, or even the approximate date of their arrival, but they also have left almost imperishable memorials of their existence in the land. They were not such expert miners as their predecessors, for they did not venture underground, but worked only on the outcrops of reefs and washed the soil for alluvial gold. The ancient pits may even then have been filled with silted soil, as they were at the close of the nineteenth century when great trees were growing in some of them, and so no traces of the mines may have been left to catch the eye. Nor were they such skilful builders in stone, though the ruins of their structures are almost incredible in extent. The walls that they built were of undressed though selected stone, and thickness was gained by filling up the centre with rubbish, the ends were square, not beautifully rounded as in the more ancient buildings, and no provision was made for drainage. Sometimes, as in the Zimbabwe temple itself, they added walls to the old buildings, when the inferiority of their work is at once apparent by contrasting it with the other. They did not even clear away the soil that had accumulated on the floor, but built upon it, so that the treasures it concealed were left undisturbed for Europeans at the close of the nineteenth century to gather.

But in one respect they surpassed the earlier occupants. Along the Inyanga range they terraced the slopes in order to cultivate them, and irrigated the ground by means of watercourses and dams as skilfully constructed as they would be by modern engineers. At first sight it might seem that to conserve water nothing more was necessary than to construct dams across the courses of streams, but so violent were the floods in the rainy season that unless the dams were immensely strong they would certainly be swept away. Under such circumstances artificial reservoirs were requisite, into which water could be led when the streams were full, and from which it could be drawn into furrows for irrigating purposes when dry weather set in. Such reservoirs required skill and much labour to construct and afterwards to preserve in order. This part of South Africa must, therefore, have presented a scene of industry that is not easy to realise by those who know it at the beginning of the twentieth century of the Christian era.

In none of the ruins of these people have gold ornaments, or stone phalli, or carved birds been found, everything connected with them is of an inferior order. But so little has yet been done by competent persons in the way of thoroughly examining any of the ruins of buildings in the vast area of Rhodesia, that next to nothing can be stated with absolute certainty regarding them. Blocked up to the depth of many feet with the kitchen middens of recent Bantu occupants and with mould in which trees and bushes are growing, it needs time and much labour to explore them and to sift the soil taken from and around them. But so far the only man who has spent years in this occupation —the greater portion of the time at Great Zimbabwe—is Mr. Richard N. Hall, whose conclusions are those given in this chapter. The visits of Mr. Theodore J. Bent and Dr. D. Randall MacIver, both of whom have issued most interesting volumes on this subject, were too fleeting to enable them to make thorough investigations even of the limited number of ruins which they inspected.

It is conjectured by some that the people who erected the structures of the second period disappeared also in some mysterious way, while others suppose that they remained until the arrival of the first Bantu immigrants, by whom the greater number were destroyed and the remainder incorporated. The last alternative seems most unlikely, however, for there is very strong proof that the country was inhabited by Bushmen when Bantu first entered it. The Bushman occupation is recorded in rock pictures, many of which remain to this day. Still another supposition is that the structures of the second period were erected after the Bantu immigration, and by the hands of Bantu under the guidance of Asiatics. But there are difficulties in the way of accepting this theory. It cannot be imagined that the Inyanga terraces and irrigation works were constructed by Bantu even under compulsion, and the absence in the sixteenth century of all traditions and knowledge concerning the erection of the buildings, with the prevalent belief of that time that they were the result of supernatural agency, would seem to overthrow it. The disappearance of the builders of the second period, as well as that of the miners and builders of the first, like their arrival, is as yet an unsolved mystery, and we can only trust to time for enlightenment.

There being nothing accessible to work with beyond what is stated here, all that is absolutely certain regarding this subject is that at some unknown periods in the past two distinct types of men, differing in culture and in creed, occupied the country between the lower Zambesi and the twenty-fifth parallel of south latitude, though probably only a portion of it at any time, and that each in turn disappeared, leaving an enormous number of structures of stone, which the Bantu who at a later date took possession of the same territory, and who can imitate, though they cannot initiate, used to some extent as models for the rough walls or rather piled up lines of stones that they still make for various purposes.

The reader who wishes to know the views and reasonings of archæologists on this subject may consult Mr. Richard N. Hall's *Pre-Historic Rhodesia,* an octavo volume of 516 pages, published in London in 1909. This is the latest volume relating to the ruins issued from the press, and was written to refute Professor David Randall MacIver's theory that the stone structures were the work of Bantu, as enunciated in his beautifully illustrated *Mediæval Rhodesia*, a quarto volume of 106 pages, published in London in 1906. Other works that may be consulted on the subject are Mr. Theodore J. Bent's *The Ruined Cities of Mashonaland*, a crown octavo volume of 427 pages, published in London in 1896, Messrs. R. N. Hall and W. G. Neal's *The Ancient Ruins of Rhodesia*, a demi octavo volume of 452 pages, published in London in 1904, and Mr. R. N. Hall's *Great Zimbabwe*, a demi octavo volume of 503 pages, published in London in 1905.

The question remains, what effect had the occupation of a part of Africa south of the Zambesi by men advanced in culture upon any of the people with whom this volume deals? As for the Bushmen, the answer is that upon them it had no effect whatever. Those savages must have abandoned the area inhabited by the strangers, but only to return, probably many centuries later, when those strangers were there no more. What were gold mines or great stone structures to them? No more than to the jackals or the baboons that lived on the same soil. They learned nothing from them, nor did they make any use of them, but when the miners and the builders had gone away and the game entered the vacant space once more, they followed and hunted and danced and feasted where their remote ancestors had done the same long before. Perhaps they gazed with something akin to wonder upon a vast building like Great Zimbabwe, or conjured up evil spirits in the picturesque gorges between the cliffs where the Khami ruins lie, but they took no more thought of the work of human hands than of the rocks that nature had formed. They had no eye for anything but game and edible plants, and so the foreign occupation did nothing to make them more intelligent or in any way wiser than their ancestors had been. There is no indication whatever of the slightest intermixture of blood having taken place.

Upon the Hottentots, who never came within many hundred kilometres of the area of the stone buildings, and who must have been in the far distant north when the mining operations were going on, if even they were in existence at that time, the presence in South Africa of strangers could of course have had no effect at all.

Neither could it have had any effect upon the Bantu of the coast, who also never came near the area of the stone buildings except when they passed through it in their devastating march from the north-west, but it may have had upon those of the interior, who if they were not south of the Zambesi during the later period mentioned, which is doubtful, certainly copied some of the work done, though imperfectly, and may have had their faculties sharpened, and their skill in mechanical arts increased by what they saw before them.

INDEX.